Causatives and Causation

LONGMAN LINGUISTICS LIBRARY

General editors:

R. H. ROBINS, *University of London*

MARTIN HARRIS, *University of Manchester*

GEOFFREY HORROCKS, *University of Cambridge*

For a complete list of books in the series see pages v and vi

Causatives and Causation:

A Universal-Typological Perspective

JAE JUNG SONG

Routledge
Taylor & Francis Group

LONDON AND NEW YORK

First published 1996 by Addison Wesley Longman Limited

Published 2013 by Routledge
2 Park Square, Milton Park, Abingdon, Oxon OX14 4RN
711 Third Avenue, New York, NY 10017, USA

Routledge is an imprint of the Taylor & Francis Group, an informa business

ISBN 13: 978-0-582-28918-5 (pbk)

British Library Cataloguing-in-Publication Data
A catalogue record for this book is available from the British Library

Library of Congress Cataloging-in-Publication Data
Song, Jae Jung, 1958–
    Causatives and causation: a universal-typological perspective / Jae Jung Song.
      p. cm. – (Longman linguistics library)
    Includes bibliographical references (p.) and index.
    ISBN 0-582-28918-1 (ppt). – ISBN 0-582-28919-X (csd)
     1. Causative (Linguistics) 2. Grammar, Comparative and general-
Syntax. I. Title. II. Series.
P292.S6 1996
    415–dc20
                                               95-53737
                                                CIP

Set by 33 in 10/12 Times

General editors:
R. H. ROBINS,
University of London

MARTIN HARRIS,
University of Manchester

GEOFFREY HORROCKS,
University of Cambridge

A Short History of Linguistics
Third Edition
R. H. ROBINS

Text and Context
Explorations in the Semantics and
Pragmatics of Discourse
TEUN A. VAN DIJK

Introduction to Text Linguistics
ROBERT DE BEAUGRANDE and
WOLFGANG ULRICH DRESSLER

Psycholinguistics
Language, Mind, and World
DANNY D. STEINBERG

Principles of Pragmatics
GEOFFREY LEECH

Generative Grammar
GEOFFREY HORROCKS

The English Verb
Second Edition
F. R. PALMER

A History of American English
J. L. DILLARD

English Historical Syntax
Verbal Constructions
DAVID DENISON

Pidgin and Creole Languages
SUZANNE ROMAINE

A History of English Phonology
CHARLES JONES

Generative and Non-linear
Phonology
JACQUES DURAND

Modality and the English Modals
Second Edition
F. R. PALMER

Semiotics and Linguistics
YISHAI TOBIN

Multilingualism in the British Isles
I: The Older Mother Tongues and
Europe
Edited by SAFDER ALLADINA and VIV
EDWARDS

Multilingualism in the British Isles
II: Africa, The Middle East and Asia
Edited by SAFDER ALLADINA and VIV
EDWARDS

Dialects of English
Studies in Grammatical Variation
Edited by PETER TRUDGILL and
J. K. CHAMBERS

Introduction to Bilingualism
CHARLOTTE HOFFMANN

Verb and Noun Number in English:
A Functional Explanation
WALLIS REID

English in Africa
JOSEF SCHMIED

Linguistic Theory
The Discourse of Fundamental Works
ROBERT DE BEAUGRANDE

Contents

Preface

It was when I was a third-year undergraduate student in linguistics that I first came across Bernard Comrie's paper 'Causatives and universal grammar', which was published in *Transactions of the Philological Society* (1975). I cannot say that it really grabbed me at that time, probably because I could not fathom its conceptual content fully. But I remember vividly that I was impressed by the number of the languages that were surveyed in the study. In hindsight, however, his work must have made a considerable impact on me as a budding linguist, since as I much later came to grips with his theory, I realized that I wished to carry out research on causatives more than anything else (or, to succumb to the spirit of this book, Comrie's paper **caused** me to think about working on causatives). At the same time, I felt that any future typological research on causatives would desperately need improvement in four main areas. First, it needed to rely on a much larger data base (comparable in size to those used in current studies of word order). Secondly, it needed to examine and recognize the full richness and variety of causative types, not just the morphological one, which all theories of causatives were 'besotted' with. Thirdly, it needed to say something about the way in which the human mind cognizes causation – no matter how tentative and speculative it might initially strike us all as – particularly because linguistic theories of causation all seemed to discuss various matters relating to causation, but not causation *per se*. Finally, notwithstanding their main focus on the morphological causative type (i.e. causative verbs built on basic verbs by means of affixes), theories of causatives all seemed to have little to say about origins of causative affixes. My thoughts had not changed much; as readers will find out, these are indeed the very issues that have directed me in the writing of the present book. There is also another, perhaps trivial in the eyes of some people, reason why I decided to write a book on causatives and causation. Being a linguist trained in a functional-typological tradition, I had found it unfortunate and even alarming to witness a more or less complete lack of research into causatives within the functional-typological framework (apart from Comrie's work), in stark contrast to the numerous contributions to the study of causatives within the generative framework. I hope that this book will help redress the balance, as it were.

Many people have contributed in one way or another to the completion of the present book. I am greatly indebted to those who kindly offered numerous suggestions and insightful comments on earlier versions of the book for improvement: Keith Allan, Barry Blake, R.M.W. Dixon, Johanna Nichols, Graham Mallinson, Kenichi Seto, and Anna Siewierska. I would also like to name and thank the following for providing me with support by reading part of the manuscript or by coming to my conference/seminar presentations at various places, and by offering helpful comments and suggestions: Edith Bavin, Geoffrey Benjamins, Hilary Chappell, Michael Clyne, Nick Evans, Connor Ferris, Bill Foley, Andrew Goatly, M.A.K. Halliday, Ruqaiya Hasan, K.P. Mohanan, Tara Mohanan, John Newman, and Peter Paul. None of these scholars shall answer for any remaining errors of fact or judgement, for which I alone bear full responsibilities.

Part of this book was published in somewhat different form in *Language Research, Lingua,* and *Transactions of the Philological Society.*

I have been fortunate in being able to write this book while associated with three different universities. Most of the research reported here would not have been possible without the generous financial assistance from Monash University, which is hereby thankfully acknowledged. I am grateful to the Department of English Language and Literature at the National University of Singapore, where I taught from 1990 to 1992, for providing an unusually conducive environment for discussing some of the ideas embodied in this book, and to the University of Otago, with which I am now affiliated, for allowing me sufficient time to turn my research into a book.

I would also like to thank Brodwyn Boock, Rita Falk, Fatimah, Lona Gottschalk, Jian Lin, Andrew Lonie, June Roder, Leonie Rousselot, and Siti for their secretarial and logistical assistance.

I also take this opportunity to thank the Longman series editors, Professor Martin Harris, Professor R.H. Robins, and Dr Geoffrey Horrocks, for their encouragement and suggestions, and the staff at Longman Higher Education, for being most helpful and thoughtful at all stages of the preparation of the book.

Last but not least, my heartfelt thanks go to my family for their forbearance and understanding of my erratic behaviour on weekdays and frequent absence on weekends during the writing of this book. But for their encouragement, what you hold in your hands would never have become a concrete reality.

Jae Jung Song
Dunedin, NZ
November 1995

Acknowledgements

A special debt of gratitude is expressed here to the authors of the descriptive grammars that have been consulted for the purposes of the present study. But for their work, a book like the present one would never be possible.

Abbreviations

A(BS)	absolutive	DUR	durative
ACC	accusative	DYN	dynamic
ACT	actor	E(RG)	ergative
AG	agent	EMP(H)	emphatic
ALL	allative	EXCL	exclusive
AM	accusative marker	FEM	feminine
AOR	aorist	FIN	finite
APPL	applicative	FUT	future
ART	article	GEN	genitive
ASP	aspect	GL	goal
AUX	auxiliary	HAB	habitual
BEN	benefactive	IMPERF	imperfective
CL	classifier	INCOMPL	incompletive
CLIT	clitic	IND	indicative
CM	construction marker	INF	infinitive
COM	comitative	INST	instrumental
COMP	complementizer	IO	indirect object
COMPL	complement	JUSS	jussive
CONJ	conjunction	LK	linker
CP	causative prefix	LOC	locative
CS	causative suffix	NEG	negative
DA	different actor	NF(IN)	non-finite
D(AT)	dative marker	NFUT	non-future
DEC(L)	declarative	NM	nominative marker
DEF	definite	NOM	nominative
DEP	dependent	NPRES	non-present
DET	determiner	NU	number
DIM	diminutive	O(BJ)	object
DIR	directional	OBL	oblique
DO	direct object	OP	object prefix
DPST	distant past	PASS	passive
DTR	ditransitivizer	PERF	perfective

PF	phonological filler	SEQ	sequential
PL	plural	SG	singular
POSS	possessive	SHT	subject high tone
POT	potential	SP	subject prefix
PRES	present	SR	switch reference
PROG	progressive	STA	status
PRT	particle	STAT	stative
PST	past	S(UB)	subject
PU(NT)	punctual	SUBJ	subjunctive
PURP	purposive	T/A	tense/aspect
P(RE)V	preverb	TOP	topic marker
Q	question	TPST	today's past
REAL	realis	TR	transitive
REFL	reflexive	UND	undergoer
REL	relativizer	V	verb
REPRES	realis present	1	first person
REPST	realis past	2	second person
RPST	remote past	3	third person
SA	same actor		

Dedicated to
All Field Linguists: Past, Present, Future.

Chapter 1

Preamble

1.1 Setting the scene

For the past three decades or so, the causative construction has truly been one of the most recurrent research topics studied by linguists of diverse theoretical persuasions. This is not entirely surprising in light of the fact that analysis of the causative construction calls for a careful synthesis of morphology, syntax, semantics, and even pragmatics. In fact, the causative is a kind of 'testing ground' where grammatical theories are pushed to their limits or even brought to their logical conclusions. For instance, the sixties and seventies witnessed the rise and fall of Generative Semantics. It was indeed an analysis of the causative that initially provided the theoretical basis for (highly transformational) Generative Semantics. Ironically, it was none other than the analysis of the causative that precipitated the demise of Generative Semantics as a viable grammatical theory, and subsequently called the whole framework of Transformational Grammar into question. As a result, a number of nontransformational or minimally transformational generative theories have now sprung to prominence (cf. Newmeyer 1980 [1986]).

The state of affairs is not so different in the eighties and nineties. The causative construction still remains as one of the main research topics which many linguists of both formal and functional orientations engage in.[1] For instance, the causative raises intriguing questions of theoretical significance in Government and Binding (GB) theory (e.g. Marantz 1984, Baker 1988). In Relational Grammar (RG), the causative is discussed with a view to developing universal grammatical relation changing laws or principles (e.g. Gibson and Raposo 1986, Davies and Rosen 1988). It is also one of the favourite research topics in Lexical-Functional Grammar (LFG) in that it is claimed to provide support for the lexical approach to what are regarded as syntactic problems in other generative theories (e.g. Mohanan 1983) or in that it poses interesting theoretical

1

questions concerning the mapping between argument structure and syntactic structure (e.g. Alsina 1992). The scene does not change much within the 'functional' school either. In fact, Comrie (1975, 1976b, 1981a [1989]), one of the pioneers in the functional-typological framework, deals with causatives and claims that the hierarchy of grammatical relations found crosslinguistically to be operative in relative clause formation can also be used to predict the grammatico-relational fate of the causee NP. Undoubtedly, the causative will continue to fascinate and preoccupy linguists of diverse theoretical backgrounds for years to come.

Naturally, the corollary of such a magnitude of research on the causative is a vast amount of literature on it. Therefore, it behooves the investigator to justify his reason(s) for undertaking further large-scale work on this intensively studied area.

All previous theories of causative constructions address one or more of the following issues:

(a) the formal (or morphological) classification of causatives, i.e. lexical, morphological, and syntactic causative types (Nedyalkov and Silnitsky 1973, Shibatani 1975, 1976c);
(b) grammatical and semantic correlates of (a), e.g. productivity, lexical decomposition, etc. (Dowty 1972, 1979, Shibatani 1975, 1976c, Foley and Van Valin 1984);
(c) the grammatico-relational fate of the causee NP or the subject NP of the (underlying) embedded clause, i.e. the hierarchy of grammatical relations (Aissen 1974a, Comrie 1975, 1976b, 1981a [1989], Gibson and Raposo 1986, Baker 1988);
(d) semantic types of causative, e.g. direct, indirect, manipulative, directive, etc. (Shibatani 1975, 1976c, Talmy 1976);
(e) semantic characterizations of the causee NP (*vis-à-vis* the causer NP), e.g. animacy, volition, control, etc. (Shibatani 1975, 1976c, Givón 1976b, 1980, Comrie 1981a [1989], Cole 1983);
(f) diagrammatic iconicity in lexical, morphological, and syntactic causatives (Givón 1980, Foley and Van Valin 1984, Haiman 1985a);
(g) amalgamation of the higher and lower clauses, or the higher and lower predicates, i.e. predicate raising, clause union, incorporation, etc. (Aissen 1974a, Gibson and Raposo 1986, Baker 1988); and
(h) (theory-specific) issues arising from (g) (Gibson and Raposo 1986, Baker 1988, Alsina 1992).

Although it is not meant to be exhaustive, the preceding list represents most of the major current issues concerning the causative. As can be seen from the list, these theories are all concerned with grammatical aspects of the causative (i.e. (a), (b), (c), and (g)), semantic aspects of the causee and its status *vis-à-vis* the causer (i.e. (b), (d), (e), and (f)), or theory-internal problems arising from the construction (i.e. (g) and (h)). For instance, three prototypical types – lexical, morphological, and syntactic – are recognized in the morphological classification of causatives, which in fact forms the basis of the traditional typology of causatives. The lexical causative type involves suppletion. In English, for example, there is no formal similarity between the basic verb *die* and the causative one *kill*, as in:

(1) ENGLISH
a. The terrorist died.
b. The policewoman killed the terrorist.

The morphological causative involves a more or less productive process in which causatives are derived from noncausative ones by adding a causative affix. Turkish provides a classic example of this type of causative, as in:

(2) TURKISH
a. Hasan öl-dü
   Hasan die-PST
   'Hasan died.'
b. Ali Hasan-ı   öl-dür-dü
   Ali Hasan-DO die-CS-PST
   'Ali killed Hasan.'

In (2.b), the causative suffix *-dür* is attached to the basic verb *öl-*, whereby the causative verb *öl-dür* is created. In the syntactic type of causative, there are separate predicates expressing the notion of cause and that of effect. Korean provides an example of this last causative type, as in:

(3) KOREAN
a. cini-ka   wus-əss-ta
   Jinee-NOM smile-PST-IND
   'Jinee smiled.'
b. kiho-ka   cini-ka   wus-ke   ha-əss-ta
   Keeho-NOM Jinee-NOM smile-COMP cause-PST-IND
   'Keeho caused Jinee to smile.'

The boundary between the two predicates (hence between the two clauses) is clearly indicated by the element *-ke* in (3.b). The lexical causative represents the nil distance between the expressions of cause and effect. The syntactic causative represents the maximum distance between the two expressions. The morphological causative occupies the middle point between the lexical and syntactic causative types, as it were. Languages may not, of course, 'fit neatly into one or other of these three types, rather a number of intermediate types are found' (Comrie 1981a [1989]: 159–160). Thus, these causative types are understood to represent three 'focal' points on the continuum of the physical or formal fusion of the expression of cause and that of effect (e.g. Bybee 1985a, Haiman 1985a).

However, what can be learned about causation from this morphological parameter? Not much, since, for one thing, it is not unique to the causative construction. Haiman (1985a: 102–147) demonstrates that the same kind of formal fusion is found crosslinguistically in the expressions of inalienable and alienable possession, coordination, complementation, etc. Givón (1980, 1990: 826–891) identifies a similar kind of formal fusion in what he refers to as interclausal coherence (i.e. degrees of bonding between clauses). In a similar vein, Foley and Van Valin (1984: 264–268) capture the formal fusion found in various clause linkage types by means of what they call the Syntactic Bondedness Hierarchy (ranging from the most tightly knit clause linkage to the most loosely knit). Bybee (1985a: 12) also proposes the continuum of fusion ranging from lexical to syntactic in order to explain the crosslinguistic distribution of verbal categories, such as tense, aspect, etc. The three causative types can, in fact, easily be mapped onto, for instance, Bybee's continuum of fusion. Thus, it is very unlikely that the morphological typology will be able to provide much insight into causation *per se* (cf. 5.2).

Indeed, why that is so can be better understood by examining various attempts that have been made over the years to correlate the morphological typology directly with various semantic causation types (e.g. Shibatani 1975, Talmy 1976). One such semantic parameter is the distinction between 'direct' causation and 'indirect' causation. The distinction is based on 'the mediacy of the relationship between cause and effect'. The temporal distance between cause and effect may be so close that it becomes difficult to clearly divide the whole causative situation into cause and effect (Comrie 1981a [1989]: 165). For example, if X pushes the vase over, and it falls, the relation between cause (i.e. X's pushing the vase over) and effect (i.e.

the vase's falling) is very direct. On the other hand, the temporal relation between cause and effect may also be more distant, in fact so distant that it is not easy to clearly divide the whole causative situation into the two parts, i.e. cause and effect. For example, X, an amateur motor mechanic, fiddles with Y's car so that unfortunately the brake begins to work ineffectively, and a few weeks later, Y is injured in an accident due to the failure of the brake. In this case, the relation between cause (i.e. X's fiddling with the car) and effect (i.e. Y's injury) will be very indirect. Languages are generally known to formally distinguish direct causation from indirect causation (Haiman 1985a: 108–111, 140–142). In order to express direct causation, languages tend to use the causative which exhibits a higher degree of fusion of the expression of cause and that of effect, whereas in order to express indirect causation, languages tend to use the causative in which there is a lower degree of fusion of the expression of cause and that of effect. In Nivkh, for instance, lexical causatives are used to encode direct causation, and morphological causatives, indirect causation (Comrie 1981a [1989]: 165–166). To put it differently, there is an iconic relation between the morphological typology and the semantic causative types in question (Haiman 1985a: 108–111). However, this kind of investigation does not directly concern causation *per se*, but rather only the temporal distance between cause and effect. Although it may have enriched our overall understanding of causation, the temporal distance between cause and effect does not explain the nature of causation itself.

Another semantic parameter that is often discussed with regard to causatives is the degree of control exercised by the causee in a causative situation. This is reflected grammatically in the signalling of the causee or the case marking of the causee NP in some languages. So, in Japanese, the accusative case *o* is used to mark the causee when it exercises a lower degree of control; when it exercises a higher degree of control, the causee is marked by the dative case *ni*, as in:

(4) JAPANESE
a. Hanako ga   Ziroo o   ik-ase-ta
   Hanako NOM Ziroo ACC go-CS-PST
   'Hanako made Ziroo go.'
b. Hanako ga   Ziroo ni   ik-ase-ta
   Hanako NOM Ziroo DAT go-CS-PST
   'Hanako got Ziroo to go.'

In (4.a), the causer may not rely on the causee's intention to realize the event of effect (i.e. Ziroo's going), whereas in (4.b) the causee retains a certain amount of control over the event of effect so that the causer may have to appeal to the causee's intention, as it were. So, the *o*-version in (4.a) may 'imply more coercive causation as opposed to less coercive causation of direction-giving represented by the *ni*-version' in (4.b) (Shibatani 1990: 309). Interesting as that may be, what can be discovered about causation *per se* when the relationship between the causer and the causee is described in terms of control (and animacy or volition for that matter)? Not much, since, clearly, causation is not equivalent to the (interpersonal) relationship between the causer and the causee, which only constitutes part of a causative situation. Indeed, semantic parameters such as control, animacy, or volition are found to be equally, if not more, relevant to grammatical phenomena other than the causative (e.g. case marking, grammatical voice, etc., as in Silverstein 1976a, Comrie 1981a [1989], Klaiman 1991, *inter alia*).

What about formal approaches to causatives? In a recent version of GB, Baker (1988: 147–154) argues that morphological causatives are verb incorporation. That is to say, the morphological causative has a biclausal d-structure and the lower verb (e.g. *öl-* in (2.b)) undergoes syntactic (or head-to-head) movement to combine with the higher verb or the matrix affixal verb (e.g. *-dür* in (2.b)). In contrast, LFG appeals to a lexical rule to account for the syntax of morphological causatives. When applied to a basic verb, the lexical rule adds one additional argument (i.e. the causer). Further, a new predicate (or PRED), CAUSE, is introduced, whereby the old PRED is converted to the PRED of an open complement (or XCOMP). What can, however, be understood about causation when what a movement rule does in one theory can instead be handled by a lexical or mapping rule in another theory or *vice versa*?[2] Nothing at all (at least in the present state of our knowledge), as can easily be imagined why.[3]

Previous theories of the causative all fail to address one issue, probably the most important one: What is it that the human mind cognizes as a causative situation? Do the languages of the world in turn reflect this? If so, how? To put it differently, what is it that relates the causative construction to causation? What causation really is, therefore, remains unclear, previous studies notwithstanding. No answer to this question has yet been offered, it seems, precisely because no 'factually adequate' typology of causative constructions has yet been made available (see Sanders 1976 on factually adequate typology). Indeed, previous theories are all concerned mainly with one causative type, i.e. the morphological causative type, while paying lip service to the other types, in particular to the syntactic type.[4] However, if, paraphrasing Langacker (1987: 47), cross-linguistic variation itself embodies the conventional means languages employ for the structuring and symbolization of semantic content, it is of utmost importance to first come up with an adequate typology of causative constructions, one that is 'sufficiently flexible enough to accommodate all different [causative] types' (Comrie 1981a [1989]: 219). Indeed, the major aim of the present book is to fill this empirical lacuna and to demonstrate that only by examining such an 'adequate' typology can one begin to understand how the human mind cognizes causation.

1.2 The present work

The work to be presented in this book has both less and more ambitious goals in mind. It is less ambitious in that it does not deal with the issues in (a) to (h) listed above, except for (c). It will, in fact, make a clean departure from them, at least in the main. Since the research to be reported here is both typologically and functionally oriented, a deliberate decision has thus been taken to provide a critical assessment of only what has so far been done within the functional-typological framework, namely Comrie (1975, 1976b, 1981a [1989]). This is not a place to discuss, let alone evaluate, achievements or breakthroughs made in the study of the causative within the generative framework. Since there are now quite a few diverse generative (or formal) theories in competition, it is simply impractical, if not impossible, to review even some of the advancements that have been made by these theories over the last three decades. That will indeed demand a separate treatment. More importantly, since the formalist and functionalist have very different theoretical perspectives (hence different research agendas), there really is not much point in discussing one's research in the other's frame of reference (cf. Langacker 1987: 34–40). Although this remark is never intended to thwart any attempt at seeking or promoting convergence between the two schools of thought, it seems futile to review or criticize the research done in one framework on the basis of the methodological and theoretical premises of the other. In this connection, Hawkins's (1983: 9) unequivocal comment bears mention *in toto*:

> ... Comrie's [1981a/1989] critique [of generativists' preoccupation of innateness] is beside the point, as he (along with most other typologists) is typically not addressing the kinds of theoretical questions that generative grammarians address, questions involving formal properties of grammars, rule complexity or markedness, the role of performance in relation to a theory of competence, the interaction between rules and between components, etc.

Thus, this book will deliberately avoid discussing any formal analysis of the causative construction, simply because the kinds of theoretical question that generative grammarians ask are radically or even asymmetrically different in nature from what it sets out to address.

The present work is less ambitious in one more respect. No attempt will be made to determine whether there are any correlations between the types of causative construction identified here and typological parameters such as (basic) word order, the ordering of affixes, etc., or areal and/or genetic distribution (Hawkins and Gilligan 1988, Bybee, Pagliuca, and Perkins 1990, Nichols 1992, Siewierska 1994, Siewierska and Bakker in press, *inter alia*). Certainly, to find such correlations is also a very important task that deserves the investigator's serious attention. To carry out such a task, however, one must first have a sound understanding of the distribution of the causative types. In other words, a factually adequate typology is an absolute prerequisite to the defining of the relationships between different typological parameters. There are also other equally important issues that the present book is devoted to addressing, namely the diachrony of causative affixes, and the functional basis of the typology. Suffice it here, therefore, to recognize the task of determining correlations between the causative types and other typological parameters as an empirical one that lies ahead in the study of causatives.

However, the present study is more ambitious in that it involves a language sample comparable in size to those used in current typological studies of (basic) word order, e.g. Hawkins (1983), Tomlin (1986), and Dryer (1992). The best known typological research on the causative is Comrie (1975, 1976b), in which only about 25 languages are surveyed. The sample used for purposes of the present research, on the other hand, consists of 408 languages. It is, of course, not just the size of the sample at issue, but there is also, unfortunately, a dearth of research done on the causative within the functional-typological framework. In fact, it may not be unfair to say that Comrie (1975, 1976b) represents the only piece of research carried out on causatives within this framework. In contrast, there are numerous, in fact too numerous to mention, contributions to the study of causatives made by generative grammarians (especially GB, RG, and LFG specialists). The present work is intended to redress the balance, as it were.

This book has another more ambitious goal to achieve: It attempts to provide a far richer typology of causative constructions than hitherto possible, by highlighting the crosslinguistic variation of the causative construction and also by assigning equal theoretical weight to all types of causative construction. There are three types of causative construction, the *COMPACT*, *AND*, and *PURP* types (the names are selected purely for mnemonic purposes, as will be clarified in Chapter 2). The *COMPACT* type includes the traditional lexical and morphological causative types, as exemplified in (1.b), (2.b), and (4). This type of causative construction is characterized by the physical contiguity of the expression of cause and that of effect. The extreme case of the contiguity in question is illustrated by the English causative verb *kill* in (1.b), which is not susceptible to a straightforward morpheme-by-morpheme analysis.

(1) ENGLISH
b.   The policewoman killed the terrorist.

In (2.b) or (4), on the other hand, the expression of cause (i.e. *-dür* or *-ase*) and that of effect (i.e. *öl-* or *ik-*) are identified as separate morphemes. There is still a certain degree of contiguity between the two expressions, because no other elements can intervene between them.

(2) TURKISH
b.   Ali Hasan-ı   öl-dür-dü
     Ali Hasan-DO die-CS-PST
     'Ali killed Hasan.'

(4) JAPANESE
a.   Hanako ga   Ziroo o   ik-ase-ta
     Hanako NOM Ziroo ACC go-CS-PST
     'Hanako made Ziroo go.'

b. Hanako ga   Ziroo ni   ik-ase-ta
   Hanako NOM Ziroo DAT go-CS-PST
   'Hanako got Ziroo to go.'

The following sentence in Vata is representative of the *AND* type of causative construction in that the clause of cause and that of effect are coordinated by means of the element *le*.

(5) VATA
    ǹ gbā le   yÒ-Ò   lī
    I speak CONJ child-DEF eat
    'I make the child eat.'

Finally, the *PURP* type of causative construction consists of two clauses, one denoting event$_x$ carried out for the purpose of realizing event$_y$ denoted by the other, as in:

(3) KOREAN
b. kiho-ka   cini-ka   wus-ke   ha-əss-ta
   Keeho-NOM Jinee-NOM smile-COMP cause-PST-IND
   'Keeho caused Jinee to smile.'

Traditionally, the form *-ke* in (3.b) is analysed as a complementizer or a subordinate marker, with the effect that the causative sentence in (3.b) is simply regarded as an instance of the syntactic causative type. In other words, the *PURP* type as in (3.b) and the *AND* type as in (5) are lumped together as the syntactic type in the traditional typology. In the new typology presented here, however, the exact semantic nature of the element *-ke* is identified as purposive, thereby raising the question as to why the purposive marker is used in the causative construction in the first place. What has not yet been recognized as a causative by both formal and functional linguists alike, i.e. the *PURP* type, is thus treated rightly as a causative construction *par excellence*. This is an extremely important 'discovery', especially because, as pointed out earlier, previous theories of the causative construction all seem to be lopsided by focusing mainly on the so-called 'morphological causative type' to the extent that the rich variety of the so-called 'syntactic causative type' in particular has been severely understated or even ignored to the detriment of a proper understanding of the causative construction and, consequently, of causation. Accordingly, the scope of research is widened, whereby a totally new perspective on the causative is brought to the fore. The widening of the research scope is, in fact, claimed to be one of the major contributions that this book makes to the study of causative constructions.

The present study is also more ambitious in that it attempts to delimit potential sources of causative affixes on the basis of the typology of causative constructions. The basic argument for this 'extension' is that since the typology of causatives sanctions only the three different types, the possible sources of causative affixes are limited likewise: the verb of cause, various instantiations of the term *PURP* and possibly of the term *AND*. It is thus made possible to trace the hitherto unknown origins of causative affixes in the languages of the world. In light of the diachronic scenario, the 'mysterious' co-occurrence of causative affixes and purposive elements found in some languages is also explained. Previously, this kind of attempt has been more or less confined to word order typology, albeit without much success (e.g. Vennemann 1973, 1975, Lehmann 1974, Hawkins 1983, *inter alia*). The book thus presents a *prima facie* case in support of the interface between synchrony and diachrony by means of typology (cf. Greenberg 1978b and Bybee 1988). It is hoped that it will be a useful contribution to the newly emerging research programme of 'diachronic typology' (Croft 1990: 203–245).

Finally, the present work makes an ambitious attempt to identify and delineate the extralinguistic basis of the new typology of causative constructions, albeit in an exploratory form. A temporally based cognitive structure of causation is proposed, whereby both the *AND* and *PURP* types of causative construction are sanctioned (as will be seen, the remaining *COMPACT* type is, however, regarded as a 'diachronic residue' of the two major types). The cognitive structure of causation can thus explain why the distribution of the causative types is the way it is. Although no strong psychological claim is made for it, the proposed cognitive structure of causation presents itself as a substantive hypothesis that can be tested against known facts of human cognition (cf. Langacker 1987: 56). Further, it is explicated how the originally noncausative constructions – coordinate and purposive – actually are pressed into service to express causation. The causative provides a fine example of the 'free ride policy' in language, whereby existing (or old) grammatical structures are recruited for new functions, and they further become grammaticalized or 'idiomatized' through frequent use (Hopper and Traugott 1993: 64). It is demonstrated that pragmatic inferencing is ultimately responsible for facilitating such a 'grammatical recruit-ment'. Discussion is also provided as to how pragmatic assumptions about human behaviour may be taken advantage of in the deductive inference which plays a vital role, for instance, in the *PURP* type of causative construction.

Consequently, the new perspective on the causative – the existence of the *PURP* type in particular – has implications for the study of causatives and causation. For instance, consider Shibatani's (1976c: 1–2) rigorous definition of a causative situation or causation:

> Two events qualify as a causative situation if
> (a) the relation between the two events is such that the speaker believes that the occurrence of one event, the 'caused event', has been realized at t_2, which is after t_1, the time of the 'causing event'; and if
> (b) the relation between the causing and the caused event is such that the speaker believes that the occurrence of the caused event is wholly dependent on the occurrence of the causing event; the dependency of the two events here must be to the extent that it allows the speaker to entertain a counterfactual inference that the caused event would not have taken place at that particular time if the causing event had not taken place, provided that all else had remained the same.

In particular, the condition in (b) requires that there should be a semantic entailment relation between the causing event and the caused event. This is why the following sentence is completely ungrammatical:

(6) ENGLISH
*The policewoman killed the terrorist, but he didn't die.

The causative verb *kill* in English is said to be implicative in that the truth of the caused event (i.e. the terrorist's death) holds, whenever that of the causing event (i.e. the policewoman's causing action) holds (cf. Kartunnen 1971a). The very existence of the *PURP* type of causative, however, rather flies in the face of the above definition of causation, because, as has already been pointed out, the *PURP* type of causative consists of two clauses, one denoting $event_x$ carried out for the purpose of realizing $event_y$ denoted by the other, and because $event_y$ has not yet occurred. To put it differently, the *PURP* type of causative (at least in its prototypical form) is nonimplicative; the truth of $event_y$ does not necessarily hold, even if that of $event_x$ holds. So, the following Korean causative sentence is fully grammatical (note that the element *-ke* is now correctly glossed as *PURP*; cf. (3.b)):

(7) KOREAN

kiho-ka	cini-ka	wus-ke	ha-əss-ina
Keeho-NOM	Jinee-NOM	smile-PURP	cause-PST-but

cini-ka   wus-ci=an-əss-ta
Jinee-NOM   smile-NEG-PST-IND
'Keeho caused Jinee to smile, but she didn't smile.'

Again, one is led right back to the question as to why the nonimplicative *PURP* type is used in the first place to express causation, which has been characterized as implicative, as in Shibatani's definition. This book indeed makes a serious attempt to explain this intriguing phenomenon by providing both the cognitive and pragmatic explanations of the typology of causative constructions.

1.3   Organization of the book

In Chapter 2, various decisions that are taken in setting up the language sample of 408 languages are first discussed. On the basis of that sample, then, a survey of causative constructions is carried out. The threefold universal typology of causative constructions is presented by illustrating each of the types with ample crosslinguistic data.

In Chapter 3, a diachronic model of causative affixes is constructed on the basis of the universal typology of causative constructions put forth in Chapter 2. The model is also exemplified, especially with respect to the *PURP* type of causative, by making reference to languages which actually display each stage of the diachronic evolution.

In Chapter 4, a case study of the hitherto unrecognized *PURP* type of causative construction is presented. Drawing on the theoretical insight of Role and Reference Grammar (Foley and Van Valin 1984, Van Valin 1993b), Korean, a language which possesses the *PURP* type of causative, is examined in great detail. It is shown there how the ordinary purposive construction is in the process of changing into a causative construction. Such an examination is deemed absolutely necessary, since it provides further support not only for the existence of the *PURP* type *per se*, but also for the diachronic model of causative affixes developed in Chapter 3.

In Chapter 5, an exploratory attempt is made to seek the functional explanations of the universal typology. The evidential system in Lhasa Tibetan (DeLancey 1984b, 1985a, 1986) is also discussed as independent evidence in support of the cognitive structure of causation.

In Chapter 6, the contribution made by Comrie (1975, 1976b, 1981a [1989]) to the study of causative constructions is critically evaluated. As has already been noted, his work in this area is, deservedly, one of the milestones in the functional-typological framework. Thus, a separate chapter is set aside for a close examination of his theory in its own right. It is, however, shown to be flawed in that there are only few languages that actually behave in the way that it predicts (but cf. Palmer 1994: 219). An alternative interpretation of what it intends to capture is proposed: languages rely on various grammatical measures to limit the number of core NPs per causative verb. What Comrie calls 'deviations from the paradigm case' are in fact some of the grammatical devices utilized for controlling the number of core NPs per causative verb.

In Chapter 7, the book comes to a close, recapitulating its main contributions to the study of causatives and causation.

1.4   Meeting the challenge

It has already been made clear that this book is not concerned with any 'formal' issues arising from, or any generative theories of, the causative. However, one challenge that (functional) typologists frequently face from formalists (e.g. Lightfoot 1979, Smith 1982, Coopmans 1983, 1984) concerns the former's emphasis on breadth (i.e. data from a wide range of languages) as opposed to the latter's depth in analysis (i.e. data, often very subtle in grammaticality, from a single language or a handful of languages) (but see Comrie 1983b, 1984b, and Hawkins 1985, for their own eloquent replies to this challenge). This could not be put more succinctly by Lightfoot (1979: 48):

> Principles of Universal Grammar or a theory of grammar will not be determined by **a superficial view of all the world's languages** [emphasis added].

Before briefly responding to this bold claim, it has to be clarified what is meant by 'a superficial view' in the context of generative grammar, in which Lightfoot operates. The following position taken by Langacker (1987: 81) would be branded as superficial in Lightfoot's opinion:

> The only way to demonstrate [the status of grammatical morphemes as symbolic units] is by analyzing a substantial and representative class of examples, including cases generally agreed to be void of semantic content, and showing that a coherent and revealing account of linguistic phenomena emerges just in case they are attributed specific meanings.

Because of their assumption about 'a sharp and valid distinction between lexical and grammatical morphemes' among others (see Langacker 1987: 11–55 for an absorbing discussion of such gratuitous assumptions in linguistic theory), generative practitioners are in general not at all concerned with such low-level grammatical elements (Langacker 1987: 27). For instance, they are not predisposed to recognize 'the possible semantic contribution of *be*, *by*, or the past-participial inflection on the verb' of a passive sentence, since they 'believe that the meanings of grammatical morphemes – if they are meaningful at all – can safely be ignored for purposes of grammatical analysis' (Langacker 1987: 27–28; also Givón 1979a: 22–41 on 'the gutting of the data base' in generative grammar). In fact, generative grammarians are known to be interested to discover 'high-level' abstract structural properties of universal grammar, because 'it is **only** by studying the properties of grammars that achieve higher levels of adequacy [e.g. descriptive and explanatory adequacies] ... that [they] can hope to sharpen and extend [the] understanding of the nature of linguistic structure [emphasis added]' (Chomsky 1970: 53).

Langacker's position will, however, be the *modus operandi* of the present book. Readers will notice that due attention is paid to the so-called 'low-level grammatical elements' 'generally agreed to be void of semantic content' in the constructing of a universal typology of causative constructions. What has already been alluded to in connection with the element *-ke* in the Korean *PURP*-type causative in (3.b) is a case in point. Along with works by other typologists (e.g. Comrie 1981a [1989], Givón 1984, 1990, Stassen 1985, Tomlin 1986, Nichols 1992, Siewierska and Bakker in press), the investigation to be presented in this book will demonstrate clearly that what Lightfoot calls a 'superficial view' of the languages of the world indeed leads to much more insight into, and thus far more exciting questions about, the causative construction and ultimately causation than hitherto possible. Readers are now invited to judge the matter for themselves on the basis of what follows.

Notes

1. Needless to say, the labels are used only very loosely. Within both formal and functional schools, there are diverse groups. There do not seem to be any appropriate terms available that can capture such theoretical diversity evident in the current formal and functional schools (cf. Nichols 1984).
2. In a recent development of LFG called the lexical mapping theory, syntactic functions are assigned to arguments by a set of mapping principles that are sensitive to both the thematic hierarchy and syntactic primitive features (Alsina 1992).
3. Readers should not be under the impression that all previous theories of the causative are being discounted here; all that is pointed out here is that the focus of these theories is not on causation *per se*, but on other matters relating to it.
4. Perhaps this is not surprising, since this particular type poses a host of theoretical questions for grammatical theories. Causation at least conceptually consists of two separate propositions, one for the cause event and the other for the effect event. The morphological causative, however, contains only a single verb, at least on the surface, from which a monoclausal structure must be projected. Thus, the mismatch between semantic biclausal structure and syntactic monoclausal structure must be resolved within the limits of the theoretical premises that these grammatical theories adhere to. Further, the lexical causative type does not feature in the discussion so much as the morphological causative type, because the former can be listed as a 'lexical oddity', since it is nonproductive. In contrast, the latter must be handled by syntax, since it is productive. In modern linguistic theories, a productive phenomenon must be handled by way of general rules or principles (Langacker 1987: 40–42 for further discussion).

Chapter 2

A typology of causative constructions

2.1 Language sample

A few words are in order as to the setting up of the sample which the new typology of causative constructions is based on. It consists of 408 languages selected from a data base of 613 languages (see Appendix). For lack of necessary information in their grammatical descriptions, 205 languages are excluded from the data base. Further, of the remaining 408 languages in the sample, 267 languages are minimally used, because the primary sources for these languages discuss only morphological means of expressing causation without indicating whether or not other types of causative construction are in use as well. It is, however, well known that languages do not rely on morphological means alone to express causation, since morphological causatives are lexically restricted to a great extent (e.g. Bybee 1985a: 17–19), syntactically constrained in terms of NP density control (as will be argued in Chapter 6), and semantically restricted (e.g. Shibatani 1975).

A convenience sample is opted for deliberately, since the primary aim of the present investigation is to characterize the formal variation of causative constructions, not to find correlations among different parameters (e.g. Greenbergian word order correlations). The sample used here is thus far from statistically unbiased in genetic and geographical terms (cf. Bell 1978, Perkins 1980, 1992, Tomlin 1986, Dryer 1989, and Rijkhoff, Bakker, Hengeveld, and Kahrel 1993). This procedural decision may strike readers as quite surprising in light of the fact that, nowadays, it has become almost a standard procedure for typologists to use a language sample statistically free from genetic and geographical biases. For instance, Tomlin is very adamant on this point when he (1986: 17–18) declares that the validity and reliability of any work in (syntactic) typology can be enhanced only when its language sample is statistically unbiased in genetic and geographical terms. One must not, however, be under the impression that recent developments in language sampling techniques, and the need to adhere to strict statistical requirements in constructing a language sample, are being ignored without any justification in this book.

In fact, there are a few reasons why a convenience sample is chosen instead of a statistical one for the present investigation. First, problems with the sampling techniques aside (e.g. Dryer 1989, Bybee 1985a: 25, and Croft 1990: 20–25), it must be realized that, given the current state of our knowledge of the world's languages, there is definitely a certain limit on the number of languages from which one can obtain reasonably reliable data. Although the actual number may vary depending on the object of inquiry (Stassen 1985: 13), the number may range from 400 to 600.[1] If this is indeed the case (and also if economically feasible), why not study all of them, rather than a small portion of them in the form (or name) of a statistically unbiased sample?

Secondly, there is no other way of enhancing the possibility of capturing the formal variation of a given function than by ever increasing the number of languages to be examined. The more languages, the better typology, if the typologist's primary goal is to establish the crosslinguistic formal variation, as Hawkins (1983: 10) points out: 'Once again, the larger the sample, the less skewed and more representative it will be of the ± 5000 currently spoken languages.' In a nutshell, statistical soundness can never take the place of empirical soundness. To further strengthen this point, one potential problem can be mentioned which must be thought out carefully. Suppose that one is interested in finding out what grammatical forms languages use to carry out a certain function. The size of the investigator's sample is, however, so small that some families are not even represented at all in the final sample (which is increasingly probable in smaller samples). Further, suppose that the languages in these unrepresented families make use of a particular type of construction which is not found in any of the families represented or selected in the sample. The validity of the final sample and of the resulting typology is obvious enough. Hypothetical as it may be, this particular scenario is demonstrative of the fallacy of so-called 'statistically sound' samples in certain cases (cf. Bybee 1985a: 25 for a similar warning).

Thirdly, since even genetically related or geographically contiguous languages are, more often than not, known to use quite diverse grammatical devices for the same function, one cannot always concur with Tomlin's insistence on statistical samples. Instructive in this context is Kenneth Pike's (1970: 11) candid astonishment at how differently the languages within the same Gur group in the Niger-Congo family express causation:

> This material from Bariba in Dahomey seems so different from Dagaari, Vagala, and Kasem of Ghana and from the Mbembe and Degema of the lower part of Nigeria, that I re-checked.... Somehow, the cultural universals of causation ... would have to be expressed in them also. Had the Bariba type of data been overlooked in these other languages, or did it in fact not exist?

If it is the case that the members of the same genetic or geographical group may be radically different or heterogeneous in terms of the grammatical means that they put to use for the same function, how can the language(s) selected from a given genetic or geographical group be regarded safely as representative of that group? This, however, does not seem to perturb typologists very much, since they believe that 'languages within genera are **generally fairly similar** typologically [emphasis added]' (Dryer 1989: 267). This is a methodological assumption which one must really be wary of, especially when working with small samples.

Finally, even crosslinguistic generalizations formulated on the basis of genetically and geographically unbiased samples are to be tested against more and more languages after all. Witness the recent 'discovery' of object-initial languages and its subsequent effect on linguistic theory (e.g. Derbyshire and Pullum 1981). Even if the typology were based on a statistically sound sample of, say, 50 to 100 languages, it would subsequently have to be tested or revised in light of far more languages, the grammatical descriptions of which may **already** be available! Therefore, the decision has been taken here to construct a typology of causative constructions on the basis of as many languages as the present writer's bibliographical and economic resources allow.

2.2 Some operating terms

Before the new typology of causative constructions is presented in full, some operating terms need to be introduced to facilitate discussion. They are S, V, cause and effect, and four combinations of these terms. S stands for a sentence or a clause. S_1 stands for the higher clause level, while S_2 stands for the lower clause level. V represents a verbal or predicate element. Cause and effect require no explanation. [Scause] means the clause which denotes a causing event (or the clause that contains the verb of cause), while [Seffect] is the clause that denotes the caused event (or the clause that contains the verb of effect). [Vcause] stands for verbal elements of cause, that is, those which denote the causer's causing action. [Veffect] stands for verbal elements of effect, that is, those which denote the caused action or the state of the causee brought about by the causer. In the following English sentence, [Scause] is *Mary brought (it) about*, whereas [Seffect] is *(that) John laughed*; *brought (... about)* is [Vcause], whereas *laughed* is [Veffect]. Further, *Mary* is the causer, whereas *John* is the causee.[2]

(1) ENGLISH
Mary brought it about that John laughed.

Similarly, in the Japanese example in (2) the causative suffix *-ase* is [Vcause], since it carries out the same function that the English causative lexical verb *brought (... about)* does in (1), while the basic verb *tomar-* is [Veffect].

(2) JAPANESE
Taroo-ga   Ziroo-o   tomar-ase-ta
Taro-NOM Ziro-ACC stop-CS-PST
'Taro made Ziro stop.'

Despite the actual surface differences, both the independent lexical causative verb *brought (... about)* and the causative suffix *-ase* are instantiations of the same term [Vcause]. The operating terms must thus be understood in such an abstract way (cf. Langacker 1987: 68).

Each of the three different causative types – the *COMPACT* type, the *AND* type, and the *PURP* type – will now be discussed by making use of these terms and their combinations in what follows.[3]

2.3   The *COMPACT* type

The first type of causative construction to be considered is called the *COMPACT* type of causative construction, which can be schematically represented as:

(3) $S_1(\ldots$ [Vcause] $\oplus$ [Veffect] $\ldots)S_1$

The term *COMPACT* is mnemonic in that it captures the contiguity or the compactness of [Vcause] and [Veffect]. At least in the prototypical case, no other elements can intervene between these two terms. Note that the terms, the actual order of which is language-particular, are bound within a single clause. The symbol '⊕' is thus used to indicate that the ordering of [Vcause] and [Veffect] depends on individual languages. For instance, the schema in (3) covers [Vcause] + [Veffect], where [Vcause] precedes [Veffect] and [Veffect] + [Vcause], where [Veffect] precedes [Vcause]. This particular type of causative construction is indeed exactly the type of causative that most attention has been paid to in numerous grammatical descriptions and in various universal characterizations of causative constructions (Nedyalkov and Silnitsky 1973, Comrie 1975, 1976b, 1981a [1989], 1985, Marantz 1984, Gibson and Raposo 1986, Baker 1988, and Davies and Rosen 1988, to name a few). The so-called 'morphological causative type' thus belongs to the *COMPACT* type, a fine example of which is the Japanese causative sentence in (2) above (i.e. *tomar-ase-*). Recall that the grammars of two-thirds of the sample do not fail to discuss the morphological causative type. The *COMPACT* type also includes the so-called 'lexical causative', where the ordering of [Vcause] and [Veffect] cannot be determined because they are fused together to the extent that they are not susceptible to a straightforward morpheme-by-morpheme analysis.

2.3.1   *[Vcause] as less than a free morpheme*

The most frequent means of forming causatives on the model in (3) is to add affixes to noncausative verbs: morphological causativization. Languages that place the element of [Vcause] before that of [Veffect] in morphological causatives, or schematically [Vcause] + [Veffect], are said to have causative prefixes.

In Bilaan, a South Mindanao language, the causative prefix *f(a)-* is used to causativize verbs (Abrams 1970: 6–15).[4] The following causative sentences all appear in what Abrams calls subject focus.

(4) BILAAN
a.   f-tam-gu   dale salò
     CP-light-I them lamp
     'I have them light the lamp.'
b.   f-bat   ale deg   ditù di   yéél
     CP-throw they by-me there into water

'They have me throw them into water.'

c. f-alob   ale ngà ku yê
   CP-wash they child by mother
   'They have the mother wash the child.'

In Abkhaz, a Caucasian language, the causative prefix is *r-*, which is attached to both intransitive and transitive verbs, whereas a different type of causative construction, the *PURP* type, is used with respect to ditransitive verbs (also see 2.5.2 and 6.4) (Hewitt 1979: 170–171).

(5) ABKHAZ
a. də-sə-r-gə̀lo-yt'
   him-I-CP-stand-FIN
   'I stand him up.'
b. yə-ç-s-àmxa-y-r-š-we-yt'
   his-self-I-unwillingly-him-CP-kill-DYN-FIN
   'I unwillingly make him kill himself.'

In Abkhaz, it is crucial in terms of pronominal prefixes where the causative prefix *r-* ends up. Some transitive verbs are used in combination with a preverb, e.g. *q'a*. If noncausative verbs appear with a preverb, the causative prefix can occur either before the verb proper or the complex of the preverb and the verb proper. If the causative prefix precedes the preverb, that is, the complex as a whole, then no other element can separate the preverb and the verb proper, even though in the corresponding noncausative verb, pronominal prefixes or even a negative element can intervene between the preverb and the verb. This fact bolsters the view that whichever of the preverb or the verb it is attached to, the causative prefix, an element of [Vcause], is a kind of barrier to other verbal prefixes, thus preserving the compactness of [Vcause] and [Veffect]. Thus, in (6.c) the personal desinence, or pronominal prefix *s-*, breaks up the contiguity of the preverb and the verb proper. On the other hand, in (6.a) and (6.b), wherein the causative prefix precedes the complex of the preverb and the verb, the personal desinences are prevented from disturbing the contiguity of the preverb and the verb.

(6) ABKHAZ
a. yə-b-sə̀-r-q'a-c'e-yt'
   it-you-I-CP-PV-do-FIN
   'I made you do it.'
b. yə-b-s-mə̀-r-q'a-c'e-yt'
   it-you-I-NEG-CP-PV-do-FIN

'I did not make you do it.'

c. yə-q'a-s-c'e-yt'
    it-PV-I-do-FIN
    'I did it.'

Further, compare (6.a) and (6.b) with (7), which shows that the causative prefix can be bonded directly to the verb, thereby pushing the preverb aside.

(7) ABKHAZ
    a-pə-r-q'a-ra
    ART-PV-CP-cut-INF
    'to make cut'

Languages that place causative affixes after noncausative verb stems, that is, [Veffect] + [Vcause], are said to make use of causative suffixes.

Basque, an isolate spoken in the northeast part of Spain bordering with France, has a causative suffix -*erazi* (Saltarelli 1988: 220–222). This suffix applies to both intransitive and transitive verbs.

(8) BASQUE
a. azken-ean kotxe-a   ibil-eraz-i
    end-LOC car-SG/ABS walk-CS-PERF
    d-u-te
    3SG/ABS(-PRES)-AUX-3PL/ERG
    'Finally, they have made the car work.'
b. maleta-k   abioi-ez   bidal-eraz-i
    case-PL/ABS plane-INST send-CS-PERF
    n-izk-io-n
    1SG/ERG(-PST-AUX)-3PL/ABS-3SG/DAT-PST
    'I had him send the cases by plane.'

As with Abkhaz, Basque relies on a different type of causative construction, the *PURP* type, to express causation with respect to ditransitive verbs (see 2.5.1 and 6.4 for further discussion).

Swahili is another language equipped with a set of causative suffixes. In this well-known member of the Central Bantu group, both intransitive and transitive verbs are subject to causative suffixation (Ashton 1947, Comrie 1976b, and Vitale 1981). The causative suffixes, -*Vsh*, -*Vz*, where *V* stands for a variable vowel, are illustrated in:

(9) SWAHILI
a. ni-me-(u)-ja-z-a   mtungu
    I-PERF-(OBJ)-fill-CS-IND pot
    'I have filled the pot.'
b. mwalimu a-li-m-fungu-zish-a   msichana mlango
    teacher SUB-PST-OBJ-open-CS-IND girl   door
    'The teacher made the girl open the door.'
c. Asha hu-m-pig-ish-a   Ahmed mke wake
    Asha HAB-him-beat-CS-IND Ahmed wife his
    'Asha causes Ahmed to beat his wife.'

There are also a small number of languages that may be seen to combine prefixing and suffixing of [Vcause]. In these languages, the element of [Veffect] is surrounded by the discontinuous element of [Vcause] or what is sometimes known as a causative circumfix.

According to Comrie (1976b: 282), in Georgian, a South Caucasian or Kartvelian language, there is a causative prefix *a-* and a causative suffix *-eb*, which must appear together in the present, but not in the aorist.

(10) GEORGIAN
a. kališvil-i çqal-s   a-duǧ-eb-s
    girl-SUB water-DO CP-boil-CS-PRES
    'The girl brings the water to the boil.'
b. mama-Ø   mdivan-s   çeril-s   a-çer-ineb-s
    father-SUB secretary-IO letter-DO CP-write-CS-PRES
    'Father makes the secretary write a letter.'

Ki-Meru, a Bantu language spoken in Eastern Kenya, is another language that has a causative circumfix, i.e. *ith ... i* (Hodges 1977: 111). Unfortunately, no actual causative sentences are available from the grammatical description.

Only three languages are found in the sample wherein the element of [Vcause] is placed inside the element of [Veffect]. This type of causative affix is known as the causative infix.

Nancowry, an Austroasiatic language spoken on the islands of Nancowry in the Nicobars, has a causative infix in use (Radhakrishnan 1981: 49, 58–60). In this language, in fact, there are two causative affixes in the form of *ha-* and *-um-*.[5] Whereas the prefix is attached to monosyllabic roots, the infix goes with disyllabic roots. As Radhakrishnan does not provide actual causative sentences containing this infix, only a couple of causative verbs are reproduced here:

(11) NANCOWRY[6]
non-causative: palo?   'lose'   pa?ɯ̃y   'bad smell'
causative: pumlo? 'cause to lose' pum?ɯ̃y 'cause to smell bad'

Lepcha (or Rong), a Tibeto-Burman language, has an uncommonly used causative infix -y- (Mainwaring 1876, Benedict 1943, and Matisoff 1976). This infix is, in fact, known to be the result of a blind phonetic process which once palatalized verb roots when they were prefixed by the Proto-Tibeto-Burman causative element *s-, which subsequently disappeared (Benedict 1943, Matisoff 1976).

Kammu (or Khmu), a Mon-Khmer language, is also a language that is known to use a causative infix (Svantesson 1983: 109; cf. Premsrirat 1987).

Incidentally, infixing seems to be the least used means of morphological causativization in the languages of the world. Further, far more languages employ causative suffixes than causative prefixes, although no statistical study of the sample has been carried out to confirm this. In a way, however, the tendency is expected when two of Greenberg's (1963b) classic universals are taken into account together with recent findings about basic word order. According to him, if a language is exclusively suffixing, it is postpositional; if it is exclusively prefixing, it is prepositional (Universal 27). In other words, there is a strong correlation between the position of affixes and the position of adpositions. Further, languages with normal SOV order are postpositional (Universal 4). Thus, it can be deduced that SOV languages tend to use suffixation. It has also been observed that the majority of the world's languages have SOV as their basic word order (Mallinson and Blake 1981, Hawkins 1983; but cf. Tomlin 1986, who does not recognize any statistical difference between SOV and SVO). Hence, the majority of the world's languages rely on suffixation, rather than prefixation, as has in fact been noted by Wachowicz (1976: 70–71) with respect to causative affixes (also see Hall 1987, 1988, Hawkins and Cutler 1988, Hawkins and Gilligan 1988, and Siewierska 1994 for possible explanations of the preference for suffixation; for the correlation between the ordering of affixes, word order types, and genetic/areal distribution, see Siewierska and Bakker in press).

There are other languages that exhibit very unusual means of causativization, quite different from the ones illustrated so far, although they all belong to the model of the *COMPACT* type in (3). For example, Nama, a Khoisan language, may reduplicate the element of [Veffect] to indicate the causative meaning (Hagman 1977). Bāgandji, an Australian Aboriginal language, replaces the final vowel of noncausative verbs with a different one in order to produce causative verbs (Hercus 1982). In some languages, the voice quality of a consonant of a noncausative verb is changed to express causation, e.g. Lahu, a Lolo-Burmese language (Matisoff 1973, [1982], 1976), Hayu, a Himalayan language (Matisoff 1976), and Pengo, a Dravidian language (Burrow and Bhattacharya 1970). Finally, a tonal change is used to indicate the causative meaning in Lushai, a Central Kukish language (Bright 1957b, Matisoff 1976), and Lahu, a Lolo-Burmese language (Matisoff 1973 [1982]).

For the sake of completeness, one more subtype of the *COMPACT* type must also be mentioned, which is classified under the lexical causative in the morphological typology.[7] There are languages that do not have any morphological means of forming causative verbs, but that rely on zero-derivation (or what are often referred to as 'labile' alternations in Caucasian linguistics). Greek seems to be such a language (Joseph and Philippaki-Warburton 1987: 170). There are some forms that are used for both noncausative and causative functions.

(12) GREEK
a. pijéno
    go-1SG
    'I go.'
b. pijéno   to peðí   s to sxolío
    go-1SG the + child-ACC to the + school-ACC
    'I take the child to school.'

According to Norman (1988: 91–129), Classical Chinese was similar to Greek in this respect, e.g. *lái* 'to come' vs *lái* 'to cause to come'. Another well-known language that behaves like Greek or Classical Chinese to a certain extent is English (e.g. *melt*, *boil*, etc.), although there are also a few causative affixes in use (e.g. *-fy*, as in *solidify*, *purify*, etc.). In terms of the schema of the *COMPACT* type of causative, these languages all exhibit the extreme case of the compactness of [Vcause] and [Veffect]. To put it differently, the degree of the formal fusion of [Vcause] and [Veffect] is maximal. Another classic example of the maximum fusion of [Vcause] and [Veffect] is demonstrated by causative members of such suppletive pairs as *umeret'* 'to die' vs *ubit'* 'to kill' in Russian, or *die* vs *kill* in English.

However, there seem to be languages that do not rely on the COMPACT type of causative construction at all. They do not resort to morphological causativization, zero-derivation, or suppletion. Djaru seems to be a language of this rare kind. According to Tsunoda (1981: 76), there are no morphological causative verbs in this Australian language. Further, in Djaru, zero-derivation of causative verbs does not seem to be in use either. Heine (1980: 22) points out that Luo and Dasenech, both non-Bantu languages of Kenya, lack morphological causativization. However, it remains to be seen whether these African languages are similar to Greek or to Djaru.

Finally, there are also languages that may have some additional (seemingly unproductive) morphemes added to the amalgamation of the basic verb and the causative affix, usually destroying their adjacency. In other words, these languages display a type of COMPACT causative that is further removed from the prototypical COMPACT type in (3) than ordinary morphological causatives, because the formal fusion (or compactness) of [Vcause] and [Veffect] is, due to some intervening material, less strong than in morphological causatives. In Straits Salish (the Songish dialect in this case), spoken in British Columbia, Canada, there is a causative suffix *-tx^w* (Raffo 1972: 151). When this suffix is used to derive causative verbs, a purposive suffix *-(ə)s* must follow the basic verb and precede the causative suffix. Thus, the compactness of the terms [Vcause] and [Veffect] is somewhat destroyed by the intruding purposive suffix. Bandjalang, an Australian language, is similar to Strait Salish in this respect. Crowley (1978: 97–101) notes that some twelve of the irregular verbs in this language have to be in purposive form in order to undergo morphological causativization. This effectively disrupts the contiguity of the terms [Vcause] and [Veffect], since the purposive morpheme is stranded in between them. Kanuri, a Saharan language spoken in northeastern Nigeria, resembles Straits Salish and Bandjalang in that the regular verbs which belong to what Hutchison (1976: 28) calls the *+ngin* class can be morphologically causativized with a proviso that the applied morpheme *-k* follows the verb root (Hutchison 1976: 43).

(13) KANURI
 a. fâ-ngìn
     'I wake up.'

    b.   yìtè-fá-gè-kìn
         'I wake up someone.'

In (13.b), the verb root is preceded by the causative prefix *yìtè-* and followed by *-gè*, the actual surface form of the applied suffix *-k*. In a sense, Kanuri is not as deviant from the other *COMPACT*-type languages as Straits Salish and Bandjalang are, because the contiguity of [Vcause] and [Veffect] is, due to the suffixing of the applied morpheme, not disturbed at all. However, it has to be explained why this applied morpheme, which Hutchison (1976: 42) relates to the dative postposition, is placed immediately after the causative verb, just as it has to be explained why in the first place the purposive element must appear in morphological causative verbs in Straits Salish and Bandjalang. In 3.4.2, a diachronic explanation will be provided as to how this kind of 'irregular' *COMPACT* causative subtype may have been brought about.

2.3.2   *[Vcause] as a free morpheme*

So far, the term of [Vcause] has been shown to represent morphemes bonded to the element of [Veffect] to varying degrees. However, bound morphemes are not the only ones that the term of [Vcause] is realized by. Independent lexical verbs can also be instantiations of [Vcause] in languages of the *COMPACT* type. By independent lexical verbs are meant free morphemes that can stand on their own. In other words, they are not morpho(phono)logically bonded to the basic verb, unlike causative affixes, which are. For this reason, this particular *COMPACT* subtype is regarded as less 'compact' than the other *COMPACT* subtype discussed in 2.3.1, namely the so-called 'lexical' and 'morphological' causative types. Nevertheless, it retains the essential property of the *COMPACT* type: the physical adjacency of the terms of [Vcause] and [Veffect].

    In Alamblak, a Papuan language spoken in the East Sepik Province of Papua New Guinea, [Vcause] and [Veffect] go together in what Bruce (1984, 1988) rather confusingly calls 'serial causatives' (cf. 2.4.3). As these two elements form a kind of grammatical unit, pronominal verbal affixes or cross-referencing affixes are attached to the unit as a whole, not to any individual member of the unit. Note that all the personal desinences appear after the unit, as if they did not wish to disturb the unity of [Vcause] and [Veffect], as in:

(14) ALAMBLAK
yimar fërpam hay-noh-më-r-a
man potion give-unconscious-RPST-3SG-1SG
'The man gave me a potion, causing me to become unconscious.'

The third person singular suffix *-r*, which stands for the causer NP
yimar, is attached to the end of the [Veffect], although it is
conceptually associated with the [Vcause], *hay*. In this context, it
must be noted that the whole verbal unit carries a single tense
marking *-më*. The tense marker has its scope over the whole
construction of [Scause] and [Seffect]. In fact, Bruce (1988) provides
three more pieces of evidence in support of the view that the
sequence of [Vcause] and [Veffect] functions as a single grammatical
unit. First, the sequence has no potential intonational break at all
(Bruce 1988: 25). Secondly, the scope of elevational suffixes and a
negative word is over the whole sequence (Bruce 1988: 26–28).
Thirdly, in Alamblak discourse as in many other languages, a new
episode is usually introduced by repeating the last predicate of the
previous episode. Indeed, when 'serial predicates' like the causative
one in (14) are used to close an episode, they are invariably
recapitulated by the same 'serial' forms to open the next episode
(Bruce 1988: 31).

In Balawaia, an Austronesian language spoken in Papua New
Guinea, the elements of [Vcause] and [Veffect] similarly form a
single grammatical unit. The unit as a whole attracts all pronominal
and pronominal-cum-tense affixes (Kolia 1975: 130).

(15) BALAWAIA
gita bae bite-kala-gabagaba-ria
we pig we:NPRES-make-shout-them
'We made the pigs squeal.'

The verbal affixes surround the unit as if they did not wish to come
into it. Incidentally, the verb *kala* also has a factitive meaning, as in:

(16) BALAWAIA
tamagu   tarigu   gena gio   kalato
father:my brother:my POSS spear he:make-COMPL
'My father made a spear for my brother.'

In this respect, Balawaia resembles English in that an ordinary
factitive verb is also exploited as the element of [Vcause].

In Bena-Bena, a Papuan language spoken in the Goroka sub-district of the Eastern Highlands District, Papua New Guinea, the burden of carrying mood marking, personal desinences, and the like is divided between the elements of [Vcause] and [Veffect]. These markings, however, do not come in between the [Vcause] and [Veffect], as is the case with Balawaia. Young (1971: 14–15) notes that all affixes including the object prefix apply to the whole unit. The last member of the unit carries various affixes, with a partial exception that the object prefix may be attached to the other member of the unit which the object is associated with. In the following causative sentence, then, the object prefix is borne by the element of [Vcause], and the other verbal suffixes such as tense and mood are borne by the element of [Veffect].

(17) BENA-BENA
ne-le'mo hoti-'ehi-be
me-take stand-PST-IND
'He caused me to stand.'

Noteworthy is that in (17) the object prefix is not allowed to be attached to the final constituent of the complex unit, unlike the other verbal suffixes. This arrangement successfully prevents the sequence of the two verbs from being destroyed. In other words, the possibility that the object marking interrupts the sequence by the nature of its status as a prefix is ruled out by the constraint on the object prefix in Bena-Bena. This phenomenon leads Young (1971: 14) to point out that the unit 'functions as a unified and coordinated verb expression ... signalling a composite meaning'.

In Jacaltec, a Mayan VSO language spoken in the Highlands of Guatemala, the elements of [Vcause] and [Veffect] can optionally be contiguous. Craig (1977) discusses the two elements of [Vcause] *iptze* 'to force, to oblige' and *a'a'* 'to make', both of which can be used in combination with intransitive or transitive verbs. Although she takes as basic the word order in which the elements of [Vcause] and [Veffect] are not contiguous due to the intervening causer NP, Craig (1977: 319) notes that there is an alternative word order wherein these two verbs are contiguous, and that the alternative word order is permitted **only** in causatives.

(18) JACALTEC
a. chiptze ya'   naj   munlahoj
    forces CL/he CL/him to work

'He forces him to work.'

b. chiptze munlahoj ya' naj

In (18.a), the two verbs in question are not contiguous, whereas in (18.b), they are next to each other, with the causer NP *ya'* and the causee NP *naj* extraposed to a position immediately after the verbal unit. A comparable situation arises when the element of [Vcause] is *a'a'*. The elements of [Vcause] and [Veffect] can be adjacent to each other, regardless of the transitivity of the latter:

(19) JACALTEC
a. cha'   xewoj ix   naj
    makes to rest CL/she CL/him
    'She makes him rest.'
b. xa' ija'   ix   ya'   tawet
    made to carry CL/she her water to you
    'She made you carry her water.'

In Kobon, an East New Guinea Highlands language, a complex verb sequence is formed to express causation, when the element of [Veffect] is intransitive (Davies 1981: 164–165).

(20) KOBON
a. dö ñig   hong g-öp
    salt water spill-PERF/3SG
    'The salt water has spilt.'
b. yad dö ñig   hong gɨ yu-bin
    1SG salt water spill   throw-PERF/1SG
    'I have spilt the salt water.'

Note that in (20.b), the single aspect marker has its scope over the whole verbal unit, supporting the view that it is indeed closely knit. In Kobon, incidentally, for intransitive verbs of effect the *AND* type to be discussed in 2.4.2 can alternatively be used, while for transitive verbs of effect, the *AND* type is the only choice available.

There are languages that because of intervening elements do not display so tight a unit of [Vcause] and [Veffect] as the foregoing languages, thereby deviating yet further from the prototypical *COMPACT* type in (3). In other words, the languages to be examined below exhibit a far lower degree of the formal fusion of [Vcause] and [Veffect].

In Alawa, the term [Vcause] is realized by either of the two lexical verbs *uřka* 'cause' or *muta* 'give', in linear sequence with the element of [Veffect]. Which verb of cause is chosen depends on the transitivity of the basic verb involved (Sharpe 1972: 99).[8]

(21) ALAWA
lilmi-ři mař a-muta-ya-nguřu da an-kiřiya
man-ERG carry he-give-PST-her PRT CL-woman
'The man made the woman carry it.'

In this Australian Aboriginal language, tense and personal desinences are borne by what Australianists call a 'catalyst'. In (21), the element of [Vcause] functions as such a catalyst, carrying both tense and person markings. Note, however, that the personal desinence *a-* for the causer NP, *lilmi*, comes in between the elements of [Vcause] and [Veffect]. So, in this *COMPACT* type of causative in Alawa, the unity of [Vcause] and [Veffect] is not as tightly knit as that in, for instance, Alamblak.

Tigak, an Austronesian language spoken in the New Ireland Province, Papua New Guinea, also employs a similar *COMPACT* type of causative construction. A mysterious element *a-* intervenes between the elements of [Vcause] and [Veffect] (Beaumont 1979: 82–83).

(22) TIGAK
rig-a   vil   a-ngan-i
they-PST make ?-eat-her
'They made her eat.'

The prefix *a-* is left unglossed (as marked by *?*) in Beaumont's grammatical description of the language. In fact, no explanation is provided for it. It is thus assumed here that it neither expresses grammatical information such as tense, nor carries any semantic content. The unit of [Vcause] and [Veffect] in Tigak is much more strongly constructed than that in the Alawa causative discussed above, in which the grammatical element disrupts the sequence of [Vcause] and [Veffect]. However, the unit in Tigak is, by the same criterion, less strongly knit than that in the Alamblak causative, which is not disturbed at all. However, the fact remains that in Tigak the two terms [Vcause] and [Veffect] function as a syntactic unit, since the object suffix *-i* in (22) is attached to the last member of the unit, as is the case with other noncausative verb compounds:

(23) TIGAK
ga   giak gavan-i
he-PST send remove-him
'He sent him away.'

In (23), the object suffix is logically or conceptually associated as
closely with the verb *giak* as with the other verb of the compound,
gavan. However, the object suffix is bonded to the last member of the
verb compound. This, in fact, is known to serve as a diagnostic test
for recognizing verb compounds in Tigak, in which there are only a
few verbs participating in verb compounds. Indeed, *giak* and *gavan*
belong to this restricted class of verbs (Beaumont 1979: 82).

Romance languages such as French, Spanish, and Italian are
similar to the languages that have so far been examined in this
subsection, although, as will be shown, the unity of [Vcause] and
[Veffect] in the former group is not so strong as that in the latter one.
For instance, in the Romance languages adverbs are able to come in
between [Vcause] and [Veffect] under certain restricted circumstances. Only French will be discussed here, since Spanish and
Italian do not seem to be significantly different from French in this
respect (Comrie 1976b: 296–303). In French causatives, the elements
of [Vcause] and [Veffect] are independent lexical verbs and they are
found to be adjacent to each other, as in:

(24) FRENCH
Je ferai   lire le livre   à Nicole
I make + FUT read the book (ACC)   Nicole (DAT)
'I'll make Nicole read the book.'

This superficial contiguity is bolstered by the fact that clitic pronouns
that are logically or semantically associated with [Veffect] are
positioned before the whole sequence of [Vcause] and [Veffect].

(25) FRENCH
a. Je le   lui   ferai   lire
    I it (ACC) her (DAT) make + FUT read
    'I'll make her read it.'
b. *Je ferai   le   lire à Jean
    I make + FUT it (ACC) read   Jean (DAT)
    'I'll make Jean read it.'

In the ungrammatical sentence of (25.b), the clitic pronoun, which is the logical object of [Veffect], cannot occur before [Veffect], whereas in the grammatical sentence of (25.a), the contiguity of [Vcause] and [Veffect] is preserved with the clitic pronouns appearing before the whole sequence of [Vcause] and [Veffect]. Other hackneyed arguments will not be rehearsed here; interested readers are referred to Kayne (1975), Aissen (1979), Rouveret and Vergnaud (1980), Quicoli (1980), Marantz (1984), Zubizarreta (1985), Gibson and Raposo (1986), Goodall (1987), Di Sciullo and Williams (1987), and Baker (1988), *inter alia*.

There is evidence, however, that this contiguity is not really watertight. As has already been noted, the unit can be disturbed by the negative element *pas* and adverbials, as shown in (26) and (27), respectively.

(26) FRENCH
a. Je ne   ferai   pas   partir Georges
    I NEG make + FUT NEG leave George
    'I won't make George leave.'
b. *Je ne ferai partir pas Georges.

(27) FRENCH
Je fais   toujours partir Jean
I make always   leave John
'I always make John leave.'

It really is significant that in French such free morphemes as adverbials can destroy the contiguity of [Vcause] and [Veffect]. Compare (26) or (27) with the Tigak causative in (22), in which the contiguity of [Vcause] and [Veffect] is disrupted by the 'meaningless' prefix *a-*, and also with the Alawa causative in (21), where a personal desinence (i.e. an inflectional morpheme bearing a grammatical meaning) intervenes between the elements of [Vcause] and [Veffect]. Due to lack of data, it is not possible directly to compare French with Tigak or Alawa in terms of the formal fusion of [Vcause] and [Veffect]. However, it is possible to compare French and Alamblak. Because no elements are permitted between [Vcause] and [Veffect] in Alamblak, it is predicted that the unit in the Alamblak causative is much strongly formed than that in the French causative. Indeed, this seems to be the case. Recall that in Alamblak discourse each new episode tends to start with a repetition of the last predicate of the previous episode. When that predicate happens to be a sequence of [Vcause] and [Veffect], the whole sequence must be repeated at the beginning of the next episode. In French, there is a comparable phenomenon that may confirm the prediction. In coordination of verb phrases involving the unit of [Vcause] and [Veffect], the second occurrence of [Vcause], *faire*, can be omitted optionally, as in (28.b) (Kayne 1975: 218–219).

(28) FRENCH
a. Marie fera   danser Jean et   fera   chanter
     Mary make + FUT dance John and make + FUT sing
     Paul
     Paul
     'Mary will make John dance and make Paul sing.'
b. Marie fera danser Jean et chanter Paul.
     'Mary will make John dance and Paul sing.'

If the unit were as strong as that in Alamblak, the second occurrence of *faire* would be indispensable, that is to say, (28.b) should not be grammatical. Unlike Alamblak, then, French still treats the members of the unit, i.e. [Vcause] and [Veffect], as separable, although it allows them to stay together in most cases.

2.4   The *AND* type

The second type of causative construction to be examined is called the *AND* type, which can be modelled on the following schema.

(29) $S_1(S_2(\dots[Vcause]\dots)S_2 + AND + S_2(\dots[Veffect]\dots)S_2)S_1$

In contrast to that of the *COMPACT* type, the schema in (29) indicates that in the *AND* type there are two clauses involved, one containing [Vcause] and the other containing [Veffect]. The clause boundary is made distinct by means of an element coordinating the two clauses, schematized here as *AND*. The most striking thing about the schema in (29) is that, unlike with the *COMPACT* type, the order of the two clauses is fixed, or cannot be reversed. [Scause] must precede [Seffect], not *vice versa*. This particular type of causative construction presses the temporal sequence of [Scause] and [Seffect] into service to express causation. The term *AND* is schematic of either overt or covert (i.e. zero) markings. In the case of covert *AND* marking, the juxtaposing of the two clauses alone iconically performs the function of registering the temporal sequence of the events denoted by the clauses (see

Haiman 1985a for the most lucid and forceful exposition of iconicity in syntax). In the case of overt *AND* marking, on the other hand, the same function of registering the temporal sequence is carried out by a coordinating device. However, it is also the physical linear sequence of the clauses that contributes to the interpretation of temporal sequence. To put it differently, what the overt *AND* marker does may be to 'facilitate' the iconic interpretation of the linearity of [Scause] and [Seffect]. Therefore, the sequence of [Scause] and [Seffect] in that order must be maintained, regardless of whether or not the term *AND* is realized overtly.

As with languages of the *COMPACT* type, most of the languages to be examined here deviate from the prototypical schema in (29) in terms of the formal fusion of [Scause] and [Seffect] (ultimately, of [Vcause] and [Veffect]). In some languages, the tense marking in one clause will have its scope over the whole construction. In others, each of the clauses may carry its own tense marking. The formal fusion is much stronger in the former case than in the latter (cf. Foley and Van Valin 1984: 208–224). Further, the term *AND* may be realized as an affix bonded to one of the clauses, instead of a free morpheme. The fusion is much stronger when the term *AND* is realized as a bound morpheme than when it is realized as a free morpheme. For one thing, the physical distance between [Scause] and [Seffect] is shorter in the first case than in the second (e.g. Bybee 1985a: 12, Haiman 1985a: 105).

2.4.1   The overt AND type

Vata, a Kru language spoken in Ivory Coast, is a language whose *AND* type of causative construction contains an independent element of *AND*. The term *AND* is thus realized by the universal coordinate conjunction *le* ('universal' in that it coordinates conjuncts of various syntactic categories, be they NPs, PPs, or S) (Koopman 1984: 24–25).

(30) VATA
ǹ gbā   le   yÒ-Ò   lī
I speak CONJ child-DEF eat
'I make the child eat.'

It is not at all unusual that in Vata a verb of speech is used to function as [Vcause], since the act of causation can be performed either verbally or nonverbally.

More frequent, however, are languages wherein the element of *AND* is bonded to the end of [Scause]. These bound morphemes are normally found on the element of [Vcause], indicating that the following clause of [Seffect] is temporally posterior to [Scause]. In Mianmin, a Mountain Ok language spoken in West Sepik Province, Papua New Guinea, there is a sequential suffix *-(t)a*, which is used to connect [Scause] and [Seffect].

(31) MIANMIN
awok-o   men-e   ki-mab-o-a   aai-e
mother-CL child-CL command-FUT-she-SEQ water-CL
fuela-n-a-mab-e   bo
bathe-PUNT-NU-FUT-he IND/EMP
'The mother will make the child bathe.'

The element of [Vcause] is *kimanin*, 'to watch over, command' (Smith and Weston 1974: 138–139). In (31), the connecting suffix *-a* clearly demarcates the boundary between the two clauses. Each verb has its full panoply of tense marking and personal desinences. Note that the whole construction in (31) is under the scope of a single mood marker *bo*, since the two clauses together refer to a single causative situation (cf. Foley and Van Valin 1984: 220–222).

Exactly the same can be said of Orokaiva, a Papuan language of the Binandere family (Healey, Isoroembo, and Chittleborough 1969: 57).

(32) OROKAIVA
embo na   ami-ta meni e-n-u   ji   neinei humbu-to
man   SUB him-of son do-PST + he-SEQ wood some take-PUNT
puvu-n-a
come-PST + he-IND
'The man made his son fetch some firewood.'

The connecting suffix *-u* is attached to the end of the element of [Vcause]. Note that, as in Mianmin, each verb has its own portmanteau suffix of subject and tense, while the mood or the illocutionary force marker *-a*, which appears once on the [Veffect], has its scope over the whole sequence of the two clauses.

Yessan-Mayo, a Sepik language of Papua New Guinea, is also reported to have a causative construction similar to those in Mianmin and Orokaiva (Foreman 1974: 141–142).

Other languages exploit what is known as the switch reference system (Jacobsen 1967 and Haiman and Munro 1983a, 1983b) for purposes of expressing the term *AND* in causatives. Waskia, a Kowan language (within the Trans-New Guinea Phylum), extends its switch reference system to causative function. One of the functions of the switch reference suffix *-se* is to indicate that two events denoted by the two clauses linked by the suffix are temporally successive (Ross and Paol 1978: 18–22). The suffix is attached to the verb of the first clause or [Scause].

(33) WASKIA
gerekma ke   sumatin nunga amapir-am-se
teacher SUB student them cause-PST + 3SG-SR
dawamala urat biter-un
hard   work do-PST + 3PL
'The teacher made the students work hard.'

Unlike the connecting suffixes in Mianmin or Orokaiva, however, the switch reference suffix in Waskia can be used only when the subject of the first clause is different from that of the second. In causatives such as in (33), the subject of [Scause] is indeed different from that of [Seffect]. Note that in (33) each verb has its own panoply of person and tense markings, suggesting that the two clauses are coordinate to each other (cf. Foley and Van Valin 1984: 244–245).

There are also languages wherein the switch reference system is pressed into service to express causation, but wherein, unlike Waskia, a single instance of tense marking has its scope over the whole construction or both [Scause] and [Seffect]. Amele, spoken just south of the town of Madang, Papua New Guinea, is such a language. In this language, closely related to Waskia, the switch reference system is put to use to carry out causative function (Roberts 1987: 222), as in:

(34) AMELE
a. ija od-ude-ce-min   na qete-i-a
    1SG do-3SG-SR-1SG tree cut-3SG-TPST
    'I made the man cut the tree.'
b. uqa ma-he-ce-b   sab man-ag-a
    3SG say-2SG-SR-3SG food roast-2SG-TPST
    'She made you cook the food.'

According to Roberts (1987: 100), the tense/mood element appearing in the second clause also applies to the first clause. Although the two clauses can be regarded as coordinate to each other in (34), it also has to be recognized that [Scause] is less independent than that in

Waskia. (34) is, in fact, a case of 'cosubordination', in the sense of Foley and Van Valin (1984: 241–244), since although one clause is not embedded in the other, the [Scause] is dependent on the [Seffect] for various kinds of grammatical information.

Gahuku, an East New Guinea Highlands language, is similar to Amele in that the switch reference system is pressed into service to express causation, and in that a single tense marker exerts its influence over the whole combination of [Scause] and [Seffect]. The switch reference suffix in question is -*go* (Deibler 1976: 97–102).[9]

(35) GAHUKU
golini z-ek-a-go   numukuq minuve
rain   hit-STA-3SG-SR house-in I-stay-PST
'Rain caused me to stay home.'

American Indian languages have also long been known to possess the switch reference system (Haiman and Munro 1983b). However, in the sample only one American Indian language has been found, wherein the switch reference system is exploited for causative function, i.e. Diegueño.[10] This may not necessarily mean that the 'functional extension' is not as prevalent in American Indian languages as in Papuan. It could well be due to lack of relevant information, since the grammatical descriptions of most of the American Indian languages in the sample are biased toward areas other than syntax.[11]

In Diegueño, there is the suffix -*m*, which indicates that the verb to which it is attached has a subject different from that of the one which it is in immediate constituency with (Langdon 1970: 153). The same suffix is also found in the context of causatives.

(36) DIEGUEÑO
ʔən^{y}a·-c ʔəwi·-m   a·sup-s
I-SUB I-make-it-SR it-falls-indeed
'I made it fall.'

Diyari, an Australian Aboriginal language spoken in South Australia, also takes advantage of the switch reference system to express causation. The element of [Vcause] in Diyari is *nganka-* (Austin 1981a: 200). Along with Amele and Gahuku, but unlike Waskia, Diyari marks only one of the verbs for tense. Diyari, however, differs from the Papuan languages in that it is the first verb, not the second, that bears tense marking, and in that it is also the second verb that carries the switch reference suffix.

(37) DIYARI

<u>n</u>ulu kana-li   nganka-yi   nawu kupa   tarka-nantu
3SG/A person-ERG cause-PRES 3SG/S child-ABS stand-SR
'The person made the child stand.'

There is reported to be a clear intonational break between the two clauses in (37). In fact, it falls between the element of [Vcause] and *nawu* (Austin 1981a: 188). Note that although the explicit marker of *AND* does not fall on the end of the first clause, the Diyari causative sentence in (37) conforms to the *AND* model in (29). The two clauses appear in the required sequence, that is, [Scause] before [Seffect]. Further, the connection between the clauses is clearly signalled by the switch reference suffix.

Examples of the *AND* type of causative also come from African languages, wherein the so-called 'sequential marker' is put to use to register the term *AND* in causatives. Lango, a Nilotic language spoken in Uganda, relies on the *AND* type of causative when the element of [Veffect] is two or more place verb (cf. 6.4 and 6.5).

(38) LANGO

lócà òdìò   àtín òkwànò   búk
man 3SG-press-PERF child 3SG-read-PERF book
'The man forced the child to read the book.'

According to Dimmendaal (1982: 294–295), the subject marking on [Veffect], *òkwànò*, is said to be in sequential mood, as in Turkana, which will be discussed in detail below.[12] The sequential mood indicates that the first clause (or the event denoted by it) is temporally precedent to the second clause (or the event denoted by it). Also note that in (38) there is no tense marking. Instead, aspect marking appears on each of the verbs. As is expected (Comrie 1976a), the perfective aspect is assigned a past interpretation (Noonan 1981: 34). There is evidence that the two clauses are more or less independent in that each clause can command its own aspect marking (Noonan 1981: 110). Thus, the two clauses do not need to agree in aspect. Furthermore, the clauses may be negated independently of each other in (38).

Nandi, a Southern Nilotic language, is more or less similar to Lango in that sequential mood is marked on the element of [Veffect] (Dimmendaal 1982: 295).

(39) NANDI
ki-a-·ka-ci   kipe·t kɔ-kɛr kâ·t
PST-I-give-to Kibet 3-shut house
'I made Kibet close the door.'

As opposed to Lango, however, Nandi makes use of tense, not aspect, for temporal reference. Furthermore, a single instance of tense marking on [Vcause] has its scope over the whole sentence.

Similar to Nandi is Turkana, an Eastern Nilotic language, although the element of [Vcause] alone bears aspect marking, not tense. In this language, widely spoken in Kenya, there is a set of personal desinences or pronominal prefixes only used in what Dimmendaal (1983a: 174–177) calls the 'subsecutive' mood. One of the functions that Dimmendaal identifies with this particular mood is to signal a subsequent action or process. The same mood marking appears as the element of *AND* in the causative, as in:

(40) TURKANA
à-sub-a-kɨn-ì   a-yɔ̀ŋ ŋési` to-lep-ò a-kàal
I-do-LK-DAT-ASP I-NOM her   3-milk-V camel
'I will have her milk the camel.'

Note that there is only one aspect marker in (40), governing both clauses involved.

So far, languages wherein the term *AND* is reflected in either [Vcause] or [Veffect] have been surveyed. In the sample, there is one language which exhibits a case of 'double' marking of *AND*, that is to say, the term *AND* is expressed twice. Hyman (1981: 96) reports that in Noni, an Eastern Beboid language, there is the independent sequential marker ɛ, which only appears after the main clause with certain past tense markings. When this sequential marker is absent, only the tonal pattern of the [Veffect] then expresses sequential mood. When the sequential marker and the [Veffect] in sequential mood cooccur, however, it is a case of double marking of *AND*.

(41) NONI
me mbéὲ ŋgè wan ɛ   bee
I   NFUT make child SEQ cry
'I made the child cry.'

In (41), the sequential marker ɛ comes in between the subject NP *wan* and [Veffect], since the sentence is in nonprogressive aspect (Hyman 1981: 95). It may thus be suggested that in (41) the clause boundary is between the NP *wan* and the [Veffect]. In progressive aspect, however, the sequential marker falls between the element of [Vcause] and the subject NP of the [Seffect].

(42) NONI
me ŋgè-é   ɛ   wan bee-lè
I   make-PROG SEQ child cry-PROG
'I am making the child cry.'

Finally, Manam provides striking data as to how differently the *AND* type of causative construction and the ordinary coordinate construction may behave, although the same structure is used for both causative and coordinate functions. This Austronesian language has an overt marker of *AND*, *-be*, in its *AND* type of causative. In fact, it is attached to the element of [Vcause].

(43) MANAM
wása ʔúsi i-emaʔ-í-be   i-moaʔúsu
wind cloth 3SG/REAL-cause-3SG/OBJ-and 3SG/REAL-move
'The wind made the loin cloth move.'

The elements of [Vcause] and [Veffect] each carry personal desinences and what Whorf (1956) calls 'status' (cf. Foley and Van Valin 1984: 213). Despite the overt presence of the term *AND*, however, there is evidence that the clausal independence of [Scause] and [Seffect] is severely reduced. When the negative element *tago* occurs before [Vcause], its scope is over the whole causative construction, not just over [Scause] alone (Lichtenberk 1983: 449). The behaviour of the negative element in causative sentences is in stark contrast with that of the same negative element in noncausative coordinate sentences, in which two clauses are linked by the same coordinating marker *-be* (Lichtenberk 1983: 519).

(44) MANAM
amári ísi tágo i-ráʔe-be   alúlu   anúa
sun   yet NEG 3SG/REAL-go + up-and messenger village
i-péreʔ-i
3SG/REAL-leave-3SG/OBJ
'The sun had not risen yet, and the messenger left the village.'

In (44), the scope of the negative marker is only over the clause in which it actually appears. In other words, the polarity of the second clause is not affected at all. Thus, the scope of the negative element *tago* in the causative in (43) is diametrically different from that in the noncausative in (44), although the same grammatical structure, i.e. two clauses connected by the clitic coordinator *-be*, is used in both cases. This difference can be explained if it is recognized that the *AND* type of causative in Manam has been reduced in terms of the clausal independence of [Scause] and [Seffect]. Also compare the Manam causative in (43) with the Lango counterpart in (38), where [Scause] and [Seffect] may be negated separately (Noonan and Bavin 1981: 49).

2.4.2 *The covert* AND *type*

In contrast to those which have overt expressions of the term *AND*, there are languages in which the term *AND* is covert: zero marking of *AND*. In this *AND* subtype, the ordering of [Scause] and [Seffect] alone performs the function of the overt marker of *AND*. It is well documented in the languages of the world that the linear ordering of clauses iconically reflects the temporal sequence of the events that these clauses denote (see Haiman 1985a). In the languages to be surveyed in this subsection, this iconic interpretation is taken full advantage of to express causation.

In Babungo, a Grassfield Bantu language, the covert *AND* type of causative construction is used when basic verbs lack corresponding morphologically derived causative verbs (cf. 6.4) (Schaub 1985: 211).

(45) BABUNGO
ví yàa yísə̀ (laa) ŋwə̀ gə̌ ntó'
they-IMPERF PST make-PERF (that) he go-PERF palace
'They made him go to the palace.'

Note that the sole function of the optional element *laa* is simply to mark the clause boundary, very much like the complementizer *that* in English. Therefore, it does not constitute an instantiation of the term *AND*.

There are also languages that employ the covert *AND* type of causative without using such a clause boundary marker. In Atchin, a Coastal Malekula language spoken in New Hebrides, two separate clauses, one expressing cause and the other expressing effect, are simply juxtaposed to each other without any overt connecting element. Capell and Layard (1980: 85) provide the following sentence.

(46) ATCHIN
mar   kete   ni-wat mu   tsöv
3PL/PST make stone 3SG/PST fall
'They made the stone fall.'

Note that the two clauses carry their own tense and person markings.
Kinyarwanda, a Bantu language spoken in Rwanda (Central East
Africa), is similar to Atchin. Kimenyi (1980a: 160–163) notes that in
this language there are two independent elements of [Vcause], i.e.
-teer- and *-tum-*. When the second verb is chosen as [Vcause], the
covert *AND* type of causative is used to express causation.

(47) KINYARWANDA
umukoôbwa y-a-tum-ye   n-á-andik-a
girl   she-PST-cause-ASP I-PST-write-ASP
amábárúwa meênshi
letters   many
'The girl caused me to write many letters.'

As in Atchin, both clauses seem to be fully independent, having their
own tense marking. Further, each verb also carries its own personal
desinence in the form of cross-referencing prefixes.

Unlike Atchin and Kinyarwanda, Kobon and Yapese do not
maintain the full clausal independence of [Scause] and [Seffect]. In
Kobon, the *AND* type of causative comes into play, when the element
of [Veffect] is either transitive or ditransitive, in which case the
COMPACT type cannot be employed (Davies 1981: 165; cf. 2.3.2).

(48) KOBON
nipe g-aj-ip   yad mab rɨb-pin
3SG do-DUR-PST/3SG 1SG tree cut-PERF/1SG
'He made me cut the tree.'

Note that in (48) only the element of [Vcause] bears tense marking,
although both verbs contain aspect marking (cf. Atchin and Kinyarwanda in this particular respect).

Similar to Kobon is Yapese, a language belonging to the Western
Malayo-Polynesian group along with Chamorro and Palauan (Jensen
1977: 287).

(49) YAPESE
kea   n'ënigiy-eeg ku   guub   u   roem
PST/3SG cause-1SG   PERF come/1SG from there
'He caused me to come from there.'

Making specific reference to the sentence in (49), Jensen (1977: 319) points out that the time of the action of the two verbs is sequential. Further, there should be a symmetry of tense, although the second verb does not carry explicit tense marking. Thus, the perfective aspect is not allowed in future tense. Inceptive aspect *nga* must instead be used. In this respect alone, the *AND* type of causative in Yapese seems to exhibit more reduced clausal independence than those in Atchin and Kinyarwanda.

In Patep, an Austronesian language of the Buang family spoken in the Morobe Province of Papua New Guinea, causation is expressed by the covert *AND* type of causative.

(50) PATEP
vimwo titev vông ngidax i tu   xôn   ên he
spirit tree do rock   it close together on they/PL
'The Titev spirit caused the rock to close around them.'

Lauck (1976: 19) notes that in (50) there should be a symmetry of aspect in the two clauses with one aspect marker on [Veffect] having its scope over the whole sentence. As in Manam, the sentence as a whole may be negated, that is, one negative particle affecting the polarity of the whole causative sentence (Lauck 1976: 19). Further, the sentence in (50) must be uttered as one phonological unit. This points to a sharp contrast with the overt *AND* type of causative in Diyari, where there is a distinct intonational break between [Scause] and [Seffect] (Austin 1981a: 188).

The reduction of the clausal independence can, in fact, be observed even in different dialects of the same language. For instance, in Twi, a language spoken on the Gold Coast, West Africa, there is a dialectal difference in terms of the clausal independence.

(51) TWI
a. wo-mã́   o-kòe
   they-made he-went
   'They made him go away.'
b. wo-mãã   no   kore
   they-made 3SG/OBJ went
   'They made him go away.'

The causative sentence in (51.a) is from the Akuapem dialect, whereas that in (51.b) is from the Akyem dialect (Christaller 1875 [1964]: 70). Note that the subject NP of [Seffect] is expressed in the form of a cross-referencing affix in [Veffect] in the Akuapem sentence. In contrast, the situation is different in the Akyem dialect, in which the causee NP is no longer expressed in the element of [Veffect]. Instead, the element of [Vcause] governs the causee NP, as evidenced by the fact that the latter now appears in object form. It therefore seems that the causative construction in the Akyem dialect is more reduced than that in the Akuapem dialect. In fact, the Akyem causative in (51.b) may be regarded as an example of the serial causative, which will be discussed below.

2.4.3   *The serial causative*

In the present subsection, languages of the *AND* type will be examined in which the clausal independence of [Scause] and [Seffect] is further reduced than has been exemplified so far. Over the last two decades, a syntactic construction called 'the serial verb construction' has drawn a lot of attention from many scholars, especially of African and South Asian languages. This construction is found widely in the languages of West Africa and South Asia including China, and also in many creoles scattered around the world (see Sebba 1987 for an overview of the serial verb construction).[13] The verbs involved are known to share the same tense, aspect, mood, and polarity, all being characteristic of a great degree of formal fusion. Quite frequently, the serial verb construction is found to carry out causative function as well.

Lord (1974) seems to be the first linguist to draw attention to the fact that the serial verb construction is pressed into service to express causation. She argues that in Yoruba what Awobuluyi (1973) calls the causative verb could be best described by assigning to it the same syntactic structure as the serial verb construction (cf. Stahlke 1970, Awobuluyi 1973, Lord 1973, 1974, Schacter 1974, Leynseele 1975 for the serial verb construction in Yoruba and other Kwa languages of West Africa; also Durie 1988 on the serial verb construction in Austronesian languages).

(52) YORUBA
Fẹ́mi̱´ t̀ i´ Akin ṣubú
Femi push Akin fall
'Femi pushed Akin to fall.'

Lord (1974) provides both syntactic and semantic evidence that the causative in (52) is very much reduced in terms of clausal independence. Semantically, the 'VPs all refer to subparts or aspects of a single overall event, unlike other genuine complex sentences'. In addition, 'the second VP is always in some sense a further development, result, goal of the first VP' (Lord 1974: 196–197). Further, there is no sign of a complementizer or the subject high tone (SHT), which appears after the subject NP of the embedded clause. As in Patep or Manam, one negative element *ko* or *ma* in the serial verb construction has its scope over the whole sentence. The last point bears further discussion. First, compare (53) and (54):

(53) YORUBA
  a. Bólá kò mú Fémi wá síbí
     Bola NEG make Femi come here
     'Bola did not bring Femi.'
  b. *Bólá mú Fémi kò (mấ / ̍kò/ ̍mấ) wá síbí

(54) YORUBA
  a. Bólá kò mú kí Fémí ́   wá síbí
     Bola NEG make COMP Femi SHT come here
     'Bola did not make Femi come here.'
  b. Bólá mú kí Fémi ́   mấ wá síbí
     Bola make COMP Femi SHT NEG come here
     'Bola made Femi not to come here.'

In the serial causative in (53.b), the negative cannot appear before the [Veffect]. It instead has to be placed before the [Vcause], having its scope over the whole sentence, as in (53.a). In (54), on the other hand, the negative can occur before either [Vcause] or [Veffect] as the causative construction is of the 'complement taking causative' construction (incidentally, it is also of the AND type); either the [Scause] or [Seffect] can be negated independently of each other. The scope of the negative is thus local not global in (54). In other words, the clausal independence of [Scause] and [Seffect] is rather well preserved in the nonserial AND type of causative in Yoruba.

Wheatley (1985: 412–413) notes that in Yi a similar serial verb construction is used for causative function, and that the order of [Vcause] and [Veffect] iconically reflects the logical or temporal priority of cause over effect.[14]

(55) YI
t'i^{33} va^{33}ts'o^{33} tsi^{33} va^{55}ło^{32} t^{33}
her husband   make pig pen build
'[She] made her husband build a pig pen.'

Wheatley (1985: 415) points out that when aspectual or modal modification is found in sentences such as (55), its scope is over the whole sentence, not just the preceding verb. Sranan, a creole spoken in Surinam, also uses a similar serial causative construction (Sebba 1987: 56, 79–81).

(56) SRANAN
Kofi meki en   go na   wowoyo
Kofi make 3SG/OBJ go LOC market
'Kofi made him/her go to the market.'

As with Yi, a single negative marker will have its scope over the whole sentence in (56). So, the same comment can be made of the tense, aspect, and mood markings, which appear only once in the sentence. Further, note that the causee NP appears in an object pronominal form, suggesting that it is under the 'government' of [Vcause]. However, Sranan has an alternative (nonserial) causative sentence in which [Seffect] is not so reduced, as in:

(57) SRANAN
Kofi meki a   go na   wowoyo
Kofi make 3SG/SUB go LOC market
'Kofi made him/her go to the market.'

This example clearly shows that the causee NP, which appears in a subject pronominal form, is not governed by [Vcause]. In fact, it is the subject NP of [Seffect]. The formal reduction observed in (56) is, therefore, not evident in (57) (cf. Twi in 2.4.2). Unfortunately, it is not known which of the two is more widely used or a more recent innovation.

According to Li and Thompson (1976), the serial verb construction was also used in Chinese from the first century AD, although it had been completely lost by the nineteenth century. In fact, it gave way to what Li and Thompson (1976: 480) call 'the compound causative', which is subsumed under the *COMPACT* type of causative in the present study.[15] Li and Thompson (1976: 483) cite from historical documents the following serial causative sentences, which are no longer grammatical in modern Mandarin Chinese, although they are still grammatical in some dialects of Wu.

(58) CHINESE
a. yoù shi   zhi sǐ
    then shoot him dead

'Then (he) shot him dead.'
b. shǐ-huáng   wúdaò   fén shū jín
Shi-Emperor no reason burn book finish
'The Shi Emperor unreasonably burned all the books.'

Compare (58) with a couple of examples of the compound causative
in (Li and Thompson 1976: 480):

(59) CHINESE
a. lā-bu-cháng
pull-not-long
'cannot lengthen'
b. lā-de-cháng
pull-can-long
'can lengthen'

2.5 The *PURP* type

In this section, the last type of causative construction, namely the
PURP type, will be examined. At the outset, it has to be emphasized
again that in the current literature this particular type of causative
construction has not yet been given proper recognition. While it is
described in an odd number of grammatical descriptions, it is always
treated as nothing more than a syntactic causative, whereby its richer
grammatical diversity is simply left ignored.

The *PURP* type of causative is modelled on the schema of:[16]

(60) $S_1(S_2(\dots$ [Veffect] $\dots)S_2$ + PURP + [Vcause] $\dots)S_1$ *or*
$S_1(\dots$ [Vcause] $\dots S_2(\dots$ [Veffect] $\dots)S_2$ + PURP)S_1

The term *PURP* represents any element that signals a sense of goal,
purpose, and the like, hence *PURP(ose)*. In its prototypical form,
thus, (60) is schematic of the type of purposive construction
consisting of two clauses, one denoting event$_x$ carried out for the
purpose of realizing event$_y$ denoted by the other. From the schema in
(60), the following can be extrapolated: the event of [Seffect] is not
factually substantiated or has not yet occurred (at least in the
prototypical form of the schema). To put it differently, the event
denoted by [Seffect] or event$_y$ is no more than a goal or purpose yet
to be realized by means of the event denoted by [Scause] or event$_x$.
As in the case of the *COMPACT* and *AND* types, languages of the
PURP type are also found to deviate from the prototypical form in

(60) in terms of the formal fusion of [Scause] and [Seffect] or, ultimately, of [Vcause] and [Veffect].

What elements are instantiations of the term *PURP*? They can be grouped in three different categories: (a) case markers mainly associated with NPs, e.g. allative, dative, benefactive, purposive, etc.; (b) verbal markings of future tense, irrealis, subjunctive mood, incompletive aspect, etc., or what Givón (1994) collectively calls 'the IRREALIS modality'; and (c) independent, separate purposive particles.

The allative case marker is indicative of spatial direction of movement. The benefactive (or dative) case marker encodes the abstract direction of benefit (or an object) to the beneficiary (or the recipient). That these case markers tend to be metaphorically extended to encode a highly abstract notion of goal or purpose is well documented, initially under the localist thesis and later in cognitive grammar (Anderson 1971, Diehl 1975, Lakoff and Johnson 1980, Givón 1982, Radden 1985, Genetti 1986, Heine and Claudi 1986, Heine, Claudi, and Hünnemeyer 1991a, and Svorou 1994). For instance, the metaphorical extension from beneficiary to purpose or goal is not improbable, since both relations can be reduced to direction of movement from one point (the benefactor or goal-achiever) to another (the beneficiary or goal). When an action is performed for the benefit of someone, the beneficiary can be (re)interpreted as the ultimate destination of the action (or the benefit). This 'destinational' aspect of the benefactive case marker is likened metaphorically to the purpose or goal of an action (Heine, Claudi, and Hünnemeyer 1991a: 150–154, Lakoff 1993: 219, 223). The general idea is, thus, that metaphorical transfers occur from more concrete (or less abstract) to less concrete (or more abstract) notions as part and parcel of the general human problem-solving strategy, whereby concepts more immediately accessible to human experience are exploited for the expression of less accessible, more abstract concepts (most strongly articulated in Heine and Claudi 1986, and Heine, Claudi, and Hünnemeyer 1991a). This kind of metaphorization is so well documented and studied that it will not be belaboured here. Ample data will instead be presented below to demonstrate how these case markers are actually used as instantiations of the term *PURP*. The case markers in question all express the meaning of goal or purpose. Further, a goal or purpose is, by definition, something that is yet to be realized, that is to say, future-projecting or nonfactual.

This sense of future-projecting or nonfactuality is also evident in verbal markings used as *PURP*, e.g. future tense, irrealis, subjunctive mood, or incompletive aspect. These markings, which Givón (1994: 266) identifies as part of the broader domain of 'IRREALIS modality', are all used to indicate that the event of effect is unrealized, future-projecting, or nonfactual. This future-projecting sense is in turn responsible for the emergence of the sense of goal or purpose (Givón 1994: 275). The clause containing the element of *PURP* or the [Seffect] plus *PURP* thus gives rise to the sense of purpose or goal in conjunction with the [Scause].

Finally, there are also languages that make use of particles or independent words that directly express the sense of goal or purpose. Such particles are attached to neither the [Scause] nor the [Seffect].

2.5.1 *Case markers as* PURP

Case marking either appears directly on the nominal that it is associated with, or it is incorporated into the verb that governs that nominal. The former is characterized as 'dependent marking' and the latter as 'head marking' in Nichols (1986). The data on hand show that both types of case marking are indeed put to use in performing the function of *PURP* in the *PURP* type of causative construction. For instance, dependent marking of *PURP* appears at the end of [Seffect], marking the whole clause as a purposive clause. Note that in verb-final languages, the element of *PURP* ends up at the end of [Veffect], but in that case it is regarded as a case marker, not as a verbal marker.

The Kunjen dialects spoken in the central Cape York Peninsular area of North Queensland use the *PURP* type of causative to an extent (Sommer 1972). In this language, the element of [Vcause] is an independent lexical item *amba-*, which has a separate clause of effect in its domain. However, in causative sentences where the element of [Veffect] is either transitive or middle, the case marker -*aɣ* is attached to the end of [Seffect], and, ultimately, of [Veffect] (Sommer 1972: 118). Note that in (61), two NPs are bracketed for ease of comprehension.

(61) KUNJEN
arŋg ugŋganiyar   [ud il] [iŋun abm]   atan-aɣ
child frighten-SUB-AG dog he   him person bite-PURP
ambar
cause-REPST

'The frightened child caused the dog to bite him.'

Sommer (1972: 118) finds the appearance of the purposive marker in causatives to be highly unexpected. However, if the case marker *-aɣ* is associated with goal or purpose, it is not at all unexpected, since it functions as the term *PURP.* The same marker is indeed found to signal allative and purposive nominals in Kunjen (Sommer 1972: 44). In (62), for instance, it expresses the purposive role of the NP *egŋ.*

(62) KUNJEN
abm   ay egŋ-aɣ   igun   ay lalaŋan
person I food-PURP go-REPRES I uncle-DAT
'I am going for food for Uncle.'

Djaru, another Australian language (spoken in the East Kimberley region), is similar to Kunjen in that the case marker of goal or purpose is used to signal the term *PURP* in causatives. As has already been discussed in 2.3.1, this language does not have any lexical or morphological means to express causation (Tsunoda 1981: 76). The element of [Veffect] is marked by a set of *PURP* suffixes that have a strong resemblance to the dative case marker. The suffixes, the distribution of which is incompletely understood, are *-waɹag, -gaɹa, -waɹa,* and *-g* (Tsunoda 1981: 119).

(63) DJARU
a.   guju-ŋgu   mawun gingi-waɹa   man-i
    meat-ERG man   satiated-PURP cause-PST
    'The meat made him satiated.'
b.   mawun-du jambagina binari-waɹa   man-i
    man-ERG child   knowing-PURP cause-PST
    'A man taught a child.'

Unfortunately, no better examples than (63) can be retrieved from Tsunoda (1981). The *PURP* marker in (63) can be compared with the dative case marker, a couple of examples of which are provided in (64). What Tsunoda (1981: 59) calls 'dative 2' encodes purpose or destination and has the form of *-gura* or *-wura.*

(64) DJARU
a.   mawun jan-an   jagu-wura
    man   go-PRES fish-DAT
    'A man goes for fish.'

b. mawun jan-an   ŋura-wura
   man   go-PRES camp-DAT
   'A man goes to the camp.'

Although the dative 2 markers and the *PURP* markers are not exactly alike in form, their very strong resemblance (i.e. similar consonant skeletons) cannot be denied, especially when in Australian languages there is a high degree of case syncretism between dative and purposive relations (Blake 1977: 35–37, 1987a: 35–40, and Dixon 1980: 321) and when case forms, i.e. ergative and locative, are usually distinguished by different vowels (Hale 1976, Dixon and Blake 1979: 11). Incidentally, Tsunoda (1981: 122) notes that some speakers omit the *PURP* marker *-waɽa* in (63.b).

In Houailou, an Oceanic language in central New Caledonia, a similar situation is found (Lichtenberk 1978: 108):

(65) HOUAILOU
a. na waa vɛ-bavara
   3SG do PURP-flat
   'He flattens it.'
b. na waa vɛ-ə
   3SG do PURP-good
   'He improves it.'

The *PURP* marker has the same shape as the purposive case marker as in (Lichtenberk 1978: 91):

(66) HOUAILOU
na bɔri tɯrɯ   yɛ dɛvā kebõ vɛ   mwã   ne-bo   kʌʔ
3SG SEQ ask+for GL a   basket PURP container leftovers pot
'Then he asked for a basket to use as a container for the leftovers.'

As in Djaru, the *PURP* marker is sometimes omitted from the causative for unknown reasons, as in (Lichtenberk 1978: 81):

(67) HOUAILOU
na bɔri waa aʔraʔ-re
3SG SEQ do eat-3PL
'Then she made them eat.'

Worth noting here is the suffix *-re*, which appears on the element of [Veffect]. It is the third person plural object pronominal suffix. This suggests that the causee NP is governed by [Vcause], not by [Veffect]. This observation, together with the fact that the *PURP* marker is omitted from (67), may further suggest that the sequence of [Vcause] and [Veffect] *waa a ʔra ʔ* may be a single syntactic unit, which in turn attracts the pronominal suffix for the causee NP, as in the *COMPACT* type of causative (cf. 2.3.2). Speculative as it may sound, Houailou seems to be in transition from the *PURP* type to the *COMPACT* type (see 3.3 for further discussion).

In Gbeya, the preposition *ha* is used to signal the presence of the term *PURP*. This Niger-Congo language, according to Samarin (1966: 64–65), uses *é* 'put, leave' as the element of [Vcause]. Note that the [Seffect] as a whole is preceded by the preposition *ha*.

(68) GBEYA
é há wĭ-ré té sé
put BEN people come first
'Let people come first.'

The *PURP* marker *ha* also functions as the benefactive preposition, as in:

(69) GBEYA
ndó ró tɛ   kofɛa há   bisa kó ró
they   come bride BEN boy their
'They would come for the bride for the sake of the boy.'

In the Lhasa dialect of Tibetan, the allative case marker is used to express the term *PURP* in causatives (Goldstein and Nornang 1970).

(70) TIBETAN
nɕɛ̀ qhō lɛɛqa che-ru   cūù-pəyĩ̄
I   him work do-ALL cause-1SG/PST
'I made him work.'

The *PURP* marker *-ru* has the same shape as the case marker that encodes direction toward an entity (Hannah 1973: 78–79).

Kolami, a Dravidian language spoken in the Maharashtra State of India, also exhibits the *PURP* type of causative with the form *-Vng* (*V* as a variable vowel), functioning as both the dative/allative case marker and the *PURP* marker (McNair and McNair 1973).

(71) KOLAMI
amd amnun   aaDav-ing   kuuTel lop-eng   iTTen
he   he-UND jungle-ALL cows   drive-ALL put
'He made him drive the cows in the jungle.'

Note that the nominal *aaDav* 'jungle' is 'flagged' by the allative case marker *-ing*, and that the same marker appears on the element of [Veffect] to express the term *PURP*.

Basque, an isolate language spoken at the borders between Spain and France, also exploits its allative case marker to signal the term *PURP* in one of its causative constructions, as in (72). In Basque, as discussed in 2.3.1, the *COMPACT* type of causative cannot be used when [Veffect] is ditransitive, or when it is transitive with animate direct object (Saltarelli 1988: 221) (also see 6.4).

(72) BASQUE
Mikel-ek   Jon   Edurne-ri   liburu-a   eros-te-ra
Mikel-ERG Jon-ABS Edurne-DAT book-SG/A buy-NML-ALL
behar-tu   z-u-en
force-PERF 3SG/E-AUX-PST
'Mikel forced Jon to buy a book for Edurne.'

The same form functions as the allative case marker, as is shown in (Saltarelli 1988: 2):

(73) BASQUE
bihar   ez   n-a-u   parke-ra
tomorrow NEG 1SG/ABS-PRES-AUX(-3SG/ERG) park-ALL
eraman-go
carry-FUT
'She will not take me to the park tomorrow.'

Sawu (otherwise known as Savu, Hawu, or Havu) is also another language of the *PURP* type where a case marker is pressed into service to function as *PURP*. Walker (1982: 59) notes that when the independent causative verb *tao* 'make' is in use, the element of [Veffect] is prefixed with *pa*, which also functions as the locative-cum-allative preposition (Walker 1982: 16).

In the languages of the *PURP* type that have so far been surveyed, the term *PURP* is expressed by a (natural) class of case markers (or dependent marking). Alternatively, the verb or predicate itself can 'carry' a case marker that registers the role of a nominal. To put it differently, case markers may be incorporated into the verb, i.e. head marking (Nichols 1986). It will, therefore, be interesting to see whether or not there are indeed languages that employ 'incorporated' case markers to express the term *PURP* in causatives.

Only one such language has, however, been found in the sample. It is Ijo, a Niger-Congo language spoken in southern Nigeria (Williamson 1965). The verbal suffix *-mo* marking nominals of directional role is used normally in association with transitive directional verbs (Williamson 1965: 35–37), as in:

(74) IJO
   a. tobou weni-mó
       child walk-DIR
       'Walk towards a child'
   b. áru-bi àki tín kaka-mo
       canoe take tree tie-DIR
       'Tie the canoe to a tree.'

In (74), the directional or allative role of the NPs *tobou* and *tín* is indicated by the verbal suffix *-mo*. The same suffix also turns up in the causative construction.

(75) IJO
   a. áràú tobóú mìe búnu-mo-mi
       she child make sleep-DIR-PST
       'She made the child sleep.'
   b. erí áru-bi mìe bile-mo-mí
       he canoe make sink-DIR-PST
       'He made the canoe sink.'

Williamson (1965: 54) does not explain why the same directional suffix is used in both the noncausative in (74) and the causative in (75). It is claimed here that the original incorporated allative case marker has been pressed into service to signal the term *PURP* in causatives (see 3.3 for discussion of the possible diachronic development of the allative case marker to the *PURP* marker in Ijo).

2.5.2   Verbal markers as PURP

Now, attention is shifted to some of the languages that fall under the second category of *PURP* marking. These languages use verbal markings such as future tense, irrealis, subjunctive mood, incompletive aspect, etc., as markers of *PURP*. These verbal markings all have one sense in common: nonfactuality, or what Foley and Van Valin (1984: 213) would call absence of actuality (cf. Palmer 1986: 17–18). Nonfactuality means that a given event has not yet been realized or that it is yet to take place. Future tense is used to express nonfactuality because of its inherent future-projecting nature. It thus encodes the epistemic modality. Further, future tense is consistently associated with the modality of stronger manipulation (Givón 1994:

317). Thus, it also encodes what Givón (1994: 266) calls the valuative(-deontic) modality. Subjunctive is also known to indicate nonfactuality as well as to express its usual illocutionary force, e.g. imperative. In fact, subjunctive is also found to span the two submodes of epistemic and valuative modalities, the former relating to lower uncertainty and the latter to weaker manipulation (Givón 1994: 277). This explains why subjunctive tends to occur in complements of nonimplicative, weak manipulation verbs, e.g. 'TELL', 'ASK', etc. (Givón 1994: 280).[17] Similarly, incompletive aspect involves nonfactuality in that it is used to depict an event that has not reached its ending point, as it were. Irrealis, sometimes treated under a more general category of status (Whorf 1956), is also known to express nonfactuality. Status can be viewed in terms of a continuum between real (i.e. realis) and unreal (i.e. irrealis). Potential mood is interpreted in terms of such a continuum in that it is used to indicate that the speaker is not committed to the factuality of an event, but rather to the possibility of that event coming into effect. Furthermore, incompletive aspect and irrealis also carry a valuative (-deontic) meaning, e.g. purpose, obligation, etc., because of the property of nonfactuality that they share with the valuative(-deontic) submodes, i.e. future, subjunctive, etc. (Givón 1994: 274–275; also see Foley and Van Valin 1984: 208–223).

In fact, Givón (1994) believes that future, subjunctive, and incompletive aspect are all subsumed under the (super-)modality of 'IRREALIS', which encompasses both the epistemic and valuative submodes. The common semantic denominator of these two sub-modes is indeed that of epistemic uncertainty or futurity because of the sense of nonfactuality that they have in common (Givón 1994: 275). This may be why the same grammatical marking is indeed shared between the epistemic and valuative submodes in so many languages, as will indeed be shown in the following data. For instance, future tense is used not only to make reference to future time, but also to signal a valuative sense of intent or purpose (cf. Traugott 1989).

Regardless of what the actual temporal reference of the whole causative sentence may be, these nonfactual verbal markings must appear on [Veffect] to signal that the [Seffect] denotes an event that is yet to be realized or that has not yet occurred. Thus, while [Scause] is marked by a grammatical element that expresses the actual temporal reference of the whole 'causative' situation, e.g. past tense, [Seffect], however, must bear the nonfactual verbal marking in question. This gives rise to pragmatic inferencing that the event denoted by [Scause] takes place for the purpose of realizing the event denoted by [Seffect]. The sense of purpose may in turn lead to the meaning of manipulation, which is part and parcel of the 'semantics' of causation. Thus, there seems to be pragmatic inferencing at work in the verbal marking type of *PURP*, as opposed to the metaphorical extension in the case marking type of *PURP* in 2.5.1.

In Agaw, a Cushitic language, subjunctive mood carries out the function of *PURP* in causatives. In this language, spoken in a very large area in the northern half of Ethiopia (Hetzron 1969: 1), the *PURP* type of causative is called for, when the element of [Vcause] is *cewŋ* 'to do'. The element of [Veffect] must appear in subjunctive mood.

(76) AGAW
ə́nt   desátíta   cewúɣà
you-SUB study-NEG/SUBJ-2SG do-3SG-PERF/DEF
'He made you not to study.'

According to Hetzron (1969: 16), 'subjunctive [mood] expresses "in order that"'. As an example of the noncausative sentence where subjunctive mood is in use, Hetzron offers: *ŋni desáta kasáwí* 'He goes to study'. The subjunctive mood thus expresses a sense of goal or purpose. Finally, Agaw seems to be in the process of reduction of [Seffect], since the causee NP, which appears in subject form in (76), can optionally turn up in object form, *kówa*:

(77) AGAW
kówa   desátíta   cewúɣà
you-OBJ study-NEG/SUBJ-2SG do-3SG-PERF-DEF
'He made you not to study.'

The example in (77) suggests that what governs the causee NP has been changed from [Veffect] to [Vcause], a typical sign of formal reduction of [Seffect].

Another African language, Swahili, is similar to Agaw in that it also exploits subjunctive mood to express the term *PURP* in its causative construction. According to Vitale (1981: 78–80, 152–168), [Veffect] is in subjunctive mood in conjunction with the independent lexical verb of cause, *-lazimisha* 'to force' or *-fanya/-fanyiza* 'to cause'.

(78) SWAHILI
a. Ahmed a-li-m-fanya mbwa a-l-e samaki
    Ahmed he-PST-him-make dog he-eat-SUBJ fish
    mkubwa
    large
    'Ahmed made the dog eat a large fish.'
b. Ali a-li-m-lazimisha mtoto a-pand-e mti
    Ali he-PST-him-force child he-climb-SUBJ tree
    'Ali forced the child to climb the tree.'

In (78), the element of [Vcause] alone carries tense marking, although person marking appears on both the [Vcause] and [Veffect]. Incidentally, Vitale (1981: 155) points out that the *PURP* type of causative is more general and less constrained than the *COMPACT* type that Swahili also uses (see 2.3.1).

Two other African languages, Maasai (Nilotic) and Obolo (Niger–Congo), described in Tucker and Mpaayei (1955) and Faraclas (1984), respectively, are similar to the two foregoing African languages in that [Veffect] must be in subjunctive mood.

The use of subjunctive mood for the expression of *PURP* is also found in Tzotzil, a Mayan language spoken in Mexico:

(79) TZOTZIL
a. l-i-y-ak' ʔak'otaj-ik-on
    COMPL-1ABS-3ERG-make dance-SUBJ-1SG/ABS
    'He made me dance.'
b. ʔa li Xun-e l-i-y-ak'-be
    TOP the Xun-CLIT COMPL-1ABS-3ERG-make-IO
    j-tuch'-Ø turasnu
    1ERG-cut-SUBJ peach
    'Xun made me cut peaches.'

Note that with intransitive verbs the subjunctive marker is *-ik/-uk*, whereas with transitive ones it is zero (Aissen 1987: 16–17). In (79), the causee NP is cross-referenced in [Vcause] as well as in [Veffect]. Aissen (1987: 214) notes that the cross-referencing of the causee NP in [Vcause], however, is optional, thus suggesting that the same kind of clausal reduction of [Seffect] as in Agaw may be in progress in Tzotzil. Finally, as expected, subjunctive normally marks subordinate clauses of purpose, as in (Aissen 1987: 16–17):

(80) TZOTZIL
tal   ?elk'aj-uk   ta Muk'ta Jok'
came steal-SUBJ at Muk'ta Jok'
'They came to steal at Muk'ta Jok'.'

As indicated earlier, it is not just subjunctive mood that is pressed
into service to express the term *PURP.* Future tense is also exploited
for the same function, as can be seen in Mezquital Otomi. In this
Otomanguean language spoken in Mexico, the element of [Veffect]
is in future tense, irrespective of the tense of [Vcause] (Hess 1968:
85):

(81) MEZQUITAL OTOMI
míxápi   da?yɛncwábǐ   ya   ?bʌhņ̃ą
he-was-causing-him he-FUT-place-it the-PL offering
káda ?nǎ ra sǎnto
each one the saint
'They were making him give offerings to each of the saints.'

Thus, [Veffect] appears in future tense in asymmetry with the past
tense of [Vcause]. Each clause in (81) retains its full clausal
independence, as is evidenced by its ability to host the cross-
referencing affixes or personal desinences of the NPs under its own
influence.

Jacaltec, which has already been shown to possess the *COMPACT*
type of causative, also relies on the *PURP* type of causative, pressing
future tense into service to carry out the function of *PURP* (Craig
1977: 239).

(82) JACALTEC
x-ø-(y)-iptze   ix   xo'   ø-s-tx'ah-a'
ASP-ABS3-ERG3-force CL/she CL/her ABS3-ERG3-wash-FUT
xil kape s-ti'   ha'
clothes ERG3-mouth water
'She forced her to wash the clothes by the river.'

One more thing about this language that bears mention is that there
seems to be variation within the speech community between the
PURP type of causative as in (82) and the *AND* type of causative,
when the element of [Vcause] is *iptze.* Craig (1977: 271) observes
that some speakers use a coordinating suffix *-n(i),* i.e. an instantiation
of the term *AND,* in lieu of future tense, as in:

(83) JACALTEC
xc-ach-w-iptze   hin   haw-echma-ni
ASP-ABS2-ERG1-force ABS1 ERG2-wait-and
'I forced you to wait for me.'

The usual function of the coordinating suffix, i.e. sequential function, is illustrated in (Craig 1977: 34–35, 65–69):

(84) JACALTEC
xichecoj ix   slah-ni   yunin   ix
started   CL/she finished-and her child CL/she
'She started (it) and [then] her child finished (it).'

It will be an interesting piece of socio-historical research to determine which of these two types of causative is an innovation and how it came into competition with the other type.

A similar situation is observed in Aboriginal languages of Australia. In Ungarinjin (or Ngarinjin), spoken in northwestern Australia, future tense is used on [Veffect] (Rumsey 1982: 157–166).

(85) UNGARINJIN
warmaḷa-yu njuminda   gudmaṟari
desert-ALL FEM-3SG-FUT-take 2PL-do-PST-DUAL
'You two made him/her/me take her to the desert.'

According to Rumsey (1982: 157–166), the future tense on [Veffect] is essential. Otherwise, e.g. with past tense, (85) cannot be interpreted as a causative, but only as reported speech (e.g. *You two said that he/she/I took her to the desert*).

Wik-Munkan is another Australian language that is similar to Ungarinjin (Sayers 1976: 85):

(86) WIK-MUNKAN
pam thawin   ngant minh   nhinthanak
man said-they-PL us-to protein pig-for
iiyan   thantang
go-we-PL-FUT them-with
'(lit.) The man said for us to go for pigs with them.' *or*
'The man made us go for pigs with them.'

Yidiny, a language spoken in North Queensland, also uses a similar *PURP* type of causative. Dixon (1977: 314) reports that he got the following sentence when he asked his informant to give a sentence in Yidiny for *X made me laugh*:

(87) YIDINY
ŋnyany   ŋunydu:ŋ budi:ny maŋga:-na
1SG/OBJ that-SUB tell-PST laugh-FUT
'That (person) told me to laugh.'

C.J. Williams (1980: 122) also met with a response similar to that
which Dixon reported, in another Australian language, Yuwaalaraay
(New South Wales):[18]

(88) YUWAALARAAY
gi:r nu: guwa:y   birali:du:lu   nama ma:da:y
3SG/SUB say-NFUT child-DIM-ERG the   dog-ABS
gigirmaligu
kick-FUT-PURP
'She told the child to kick the dog.'

Incidentally, in Yuwaalaraay the element of [Veffect] is double-
marked by the case and verbal markers of *PURP*. In (88), the future
tense marking is immediately followed by the purposive case marker,
-*gu* (cf. Noni in 2.4.1).
    It is worth noting that in the above Australian languages, the
utterance verb, e.g. 'TELL', 'SAY', etc., is used as the [Vcause].
This may be in support of Givón's (1990: 530) claim that meaning
or form tends to spread along continuous portions of what he refers
to as the scale from manipulation to cognition/utterance. The scale,
in fact, ranges from successful intended causation, attempted manipulation, preference (or aversion), epistemic anxiety, epistemic certainty (or uncertainty), to utterance. So, in the languages in question
the meaning and form of utterance have indeed extended to those of
manipulation (i.e. causation). This extension seems natural in that
human manipulation can be carried out by either nonverbal (e.g.
physical force) or verbal (e.g. social superiority) means.
    There are also languages of the *PURP* type which rely on what
Whorf (1956) calls status to express the term *PURP*. Chichimeco
Jonaz, an Otomanguean language spoken in Mexico, takes advantage
of potential mood to signal the term *PURP* in causatives (Suarez
1984: 38):

(89) CHICHIMECO JONAZ
íno? uség   síma?an nungwǽn?
he   told-me dog   I:POT-kill
'He made me kill the dog.'

Suarez (1984: 38) notes that in Chichimeco Jonaz the verb meaning 'to say, tell' is used as the element of [Vcause], as in (89) (see above for Givón's claim).

There also seem to be languages of the *PURP* type that employ incompletive aspect to register the term *PURP* in causatives. In Vai, there is incompletive aspect, which is normally interpreted as referring to customary action (Welmers 1976: 90–91, 99; also see Comrie 1976a: 24–32 and Givón 1994: 270). When the lexical verb of cause, *ma*, is used in causatives, the element of [Veffect] must appear in incompletive aspect, regardless of the aspect of [Vcause] (Welmers 1976: 102).

(90) VAI
á-'à   à mà   mù-ì   àá fóófóóe bì
he-CM it make-COMPL we-CM his loads   carry-INCOMPL
'We made us carry his loads.'

The low tone on the [Veffect] marks incompletive aspect in Vai along with what Welmers (1976: 90) calls a construction marker *i* after the subject NP. Note the asymmetry of aspect in (90). The [Scause] is in completive aspect, whereas the [Veffect] is in incompletive aspect. The pronoun *à* before the element of [Vcause] is used in anticipation of [Seffect], which is relatively common in Vai complex constructions (Welmers 1976: 101–102).

Finally, there are languages of the *PURP* type which use verbal purposive marking to register the term *PURP*. Purposive marking is 'semantically modal in that [it] express[es] an attitude by the subject of the sentence, explaining what intention [or purpose] he has in carrying out the action indicated' (Palmer 1986: 174). Shuswap, a Salish language spoken in Canada, is such a language. There is the verbal prefix *ʔs-*, whose function is to mark subordinate clauses of purpose, as in (Kuipers 1974: 43–44, 72, 86–87):

(91) SHUSWAP
ʔex   k°əx°   ɣ-yéxəs ʔs-x°úp-s
PROG-be 1PL/EXCL ART-pack PURP-go-1PL/EXCL
'We are packing to go.'

The same purposive prefix appears in the causative construction:[19]

(92) SHUSWAP
k°ú-k°lm-kn ʔs-wlím-s
make-1SG   PURP-laugh-3POSS
'I make him laugh.'

In Abkhaz, a Caucasian language spoken in the former Autonomous Soviet Socialist Abkhazian Republic, subordinate clauses of purpose are signalled by the purposive modal marking *-rt°'* (Hewitt 1979: 201).

(93) ABKHAZ
s-ca-rt°'   sə-q'o-wp'
I-go-PURP I-be (STAT)
'I am ready to go.'

The same purposive suffix is used in conjunction with the [Vcause], *a-q'a-c'a-ra* 'to make', when the element of [Veffect] is ditransitive (Hewitt 1979: 171).

(94) ABKHAZ
d-bə-l-ta-rt°'   (ø)q'a-s-c'ò-yt'
him-to-you-she-give-PURP it-PREV-I-make-FIN
'I make her give him to you.'

2.5.3 *Independent* PURP *marking*

In this subsection, languages of the *PURP* type which employ an independent marker or a particle to register the term *PURP* will be surveyed. This type of *PURP* marking is different from the other types studied in 2.5.1 and 2.5.2 in that the element of *PURP* is not bonded to any element within the construction.

Lahu is a language in which such a particle is used to an extent in its *PURP*-type causative. In this Tibeto-Burman language, there is the particle *tù*, which signals an unreal, future, hypothetical, or purposive action (Matisoff 1973 [1982]: 461–465, 1976: 438–441).

(95) LAHU
έ   hɔ̀ ğa tù   mɔʔ-qɔ qhɔ á-phὲʔ-šī   jû̂ʔ   pî
baby cry get PURP mouth   LOC hot peppers pierce give
ve yò
PRT DECL
'In order to get the baby to cry we stick hot peppers into its mouth.'

The same purposive particle occurs in the *PURP* causative of Lahu, as in:

(96) LAHU
yɔ̂ cân-pā ši̱ tù   te gâ   ve
he enemy die PURP do want PRT
'He wants to make the enemy die.'

Incidentally, in Lahu the *PURP* type of causative is obligatory when a causative sentence is produced out of a sentence that already contains a *COMPACT*-type causative (i.e. double causatives, e.g. *Mary* made *Tom* feed *the twins*).

Greek also uses a particle of *PURP*, in fact, the subjunctive particle *na* (Joseph and Philippaki-Warburton 1987: 171; also Lightfoot 1979: 282–294). Recall that Greek does not have any morphological means of causativization (cf. 2.3.1). The element of [Vcause] is either *kano* 'to make' or *vazo* 'to put'.

(97) GREEK
a. ékana   ton jáni   na   fíji
   made-1SG/ACT the + John-ACC SUBJ leave-3SG
   'I made John leave.'
b. évala   ton jáni na   tis   milísi
   put-1SG/ACT the + John SUBJ her-GEN speak-3SG
   'I got John to speak to her.'

Note that the clauses of [Scause] and [Seffect] maintain their full clausal independence, and that the clause boundary is clearly demarcated by the subjunctive particle *na*. Indeed, the same particle is seen to perform its usual function of marking subordinate clauses of purpose, as in (Joseph and Philippaki-Warburton 1987: 31):

(98) GREEK
írθa   na   se   voiθíso
came-1SG SUBJ you-ACC help-1SG
'I came (in order) to help you.'

Kanakuru is similar to Greek in that a purposive particle is used in causatives. In this Chadic language spoken in northeastern Nigeria, the subjunctive particle *bela* or *bəra* has the function of marking subordinate clauses of purpose that it precedes (Newman 1974: 111–112). The same particle is used to express the term *PURP* in causatives, as in:

(99) KANAKURU
nà wùi   áráì   bɔlà púlé-ní
I   cause-PERF soup-DEF SUBJ boil-3SG/SUBJ/VI
'I caused the soup to boil.'

Note that in (99), the element of [Veffect] has a tone associated with subjunctive (Newman 1974: 41), although it will be ignored here, since the association is not exclusive to subjunctive.

Russian is slightly deviant from the above three languages in that the element of *PURP* and the clause boundary marker are combined to form a single word; the subjunctive element *by* is bonded to the clause boundary marker *čto*. The resulting word *čtoby* is used to mark subordinate clauses of purpose (Maltzoff 1985: 174–175). But since, at least technically, the clause boundary marker itself is attached to neither [Scause] nor [Seffect], the whole word will be treated as a subjunctive particle for purposes of the present investigation. Compare (100) and (101):

(100) RUSSIAN
ja šdelal tak, čtoby Džon ušel
I did   thus SUBJ John left
'I made John leave.'

(101) RUSSIAN
ja prišel, čtoby vy rasskazali mne ob   ètom
I came   SUBJ you told   to-me about it
'I came so that you would tell me about it.'

Ewondo, a Northwest Bantu language spoken in southern Cameroon, is interesting in that it may be said to exhibit a mixture of the second and third categories of *PURP* marking: verbal and independent. The element of [Veffect] must have the tone pattern of jussive mood, which seems to be very akin to subjunctive mood in nature (Redden 1980: 113–116). In addition, a separate purposive particle *naa* is used. The sentence in (102) is thus an example of a noncausative with the double marking of *PURP* (*nə* is a variant of the particle *naa*):

(102) EWONDO
a-vɔ́   mɔ̄ máan nɔ́ mɔ́-və   wa
he-gave me present PURP I/JUSS-give you
'He gave me a present to give to you.'

In (103), a causative sentence is illustrated, in which a free lexical verb, i.e. *bo* 'make, cause', appears as the element of [Vcause]. The purposive particle is used in conjunction with the jussive mood in [Veffect], as in the case of ordinary subordinate clauses of purpose (Redden 1980: 171).

(103) EWONDO
məə́bɔ́ naa   á-digi   ndzaag
I-made PURP 3/JUSS-burn wood
'I made him burn the wood.'

2.6 Implicativity: a residual issue

Although a good deal of data have so far been provided in support of the *PURP* type of causative construction, it is not possible to tell for the majority of the languages surveyed here whether their *PURP* causatives are implicative or not (cf. Kartunnen 1971a). This is due mainly to the fact that most grammatical descriptions, unfortunately, pay virtually no attention to this particular semantic aspect of the causative construction. It is, however, suspected that in most (definitely not all) of the *PURP*-type languages in the present language sample, the *PURP* type of causative may be implicative due to semantic neutralization of the term *PURP*. By the semantic neutralization is meant that the original meaning of goal or purpose encoded in the term *PURP* is weakened or lost, whereby originally nonimplicative causatives become partially or fully implicative. In this respect, Latin serves as a good example. Latin puts subjunctive mood to use in order to signal the term *PURP* in its causative construction: the element of [Vcause], *facere*, *efficere*, or *curare*, followed by a subordinate clause in subjunctive mood, which is in turn preceded by the clause boundary marker *ut* (for detail, see Woodcock 1959 [1985]: 103, F. Palmer 1986: 174–182, and Vincent 1988a: 69).[20] With respect to the semantic neutralization of the term *PURP* in Latin, Woodcock (1959 [1985]: 100) has the following to explain (also see L. Palmer 1954 [1966]: 329–330, F. Palmer 1986: 180–182, but Hamp 1982 for a different view):

> To begin with, the subordinate subjunctive can have indicated only a possible or hypothetical result. But the use of the subjunctive having become established to **mark a connexion of cause and effect**, the reality or unreality of the action denoted by the subjunctive verb came to be considered irrelevant. Thereafter, the subjunctive was used in the

subordinate clause merely to indicate the connexion between two events, even when the event expressed in the subjunctive was a real fact.... Such subordinate clauses are called Consecutive, as showing what follows as a result. [emphasis original]

From this, it follows that the Latin subjunctive mood was first semantically neutralized in causatives. As will be further demonstrated in Chapter 4, the semantic neutralization was also triggered initially in Korean *PURP*-type causatives and is still in progress. It remains to be seen, however, whether the semantic neutralization of the term *PURP* always extends from the causative construction to noncausative constructions or both ways. This is an important area of future research, especially because crosslinguistically the purposive marker and the resultative marker, more often than not, also share the same morphology (Stassen 1985: 72).

Finally, it also has to be noted that the semantic neutralization of *PURP* may not necessarily be concomitant with the formal fusion of [Scause] and [Seffect]. As it will be taken up in 3.5, suffice it to mention one example here: Kammu (or Khmu). In the *COMPACT* type of causative in Kammu, causative verbs are produced by attaching the prefix *p-* to basic verbs. However, causative sentences built on *p*--prefixed verbs turn out to be fully nonimplicative (Svantesson 1983: 106), as in:[21]

(104) KAMMU
kə̀ə p-ŋmɔ́ɔŋ nàa, nàa pə́ə mɔ́ɔŋ
he CP-sad   she she not sad
'He tried to make her sad, but she didn't become sad.'

The sentence in (104) clearly shows that negation of the effect relation or the [Seffect] is grammatically perfect, indicating that the causative sentence is indeed nonimplicative.

Notes

1. The typological work that the present writer knows makes use of the largest language data base is Tomlin (1986). His data base contains 1063 languages. As Blake (1988: 216–217) points out, however, Tomlin uses quite a few secondary sources, which may not be concerned with basic word order at all. This is clearly indicative of the fundamental problem that typologists are confronted with: only a fraction of the world's languages provide data that are sufficient in both quantity and

quality. At the same time, it must be borne in mind that the problem is far from insurmountable, as was demonstrated in Greenberg (1963b).

2. The causer can be rewritten as [Ncause] and the causee as [Neffect]. But the terms causer and causee will be retained here, since they are well established in the literature on causatives and causation.

3. The names of the three types are selected for mnemonic purposes, as will be shown. They could simply be called Type I, Type II, and Type III.

4. The genetic classifications provided by the authors of the grammatical descriptions are generally followed in this study. If no such genetic classification is given by the author, the genetic classification of Ruhlen (1987) is adopted. This does not necessarily mean that the present writer wholeheartedly adopts his classification. Rather, it is because it is the latest overall genetic classification of the world's languages available on the market. Therefore, not all readers are expected to agree with the genetic classification of some languages or language groups presented in this work. Nevertheless, the decision to follow Ruhlen (1987) has no bearing on the main points of the present work.

5. According to Radhakrishnan, the causative infix is diachronically a prefix. Some additional prefix attached to verb roots has been reanalysed as part of roots in modern Nancowry. However, the affix -*um*- is treated here as an infix, because this diachronic information is not available to modern speakers of Nancowry.

6. Given the schema in (3), i.e. the sequences of [Vcause] + [Veffect] and [Veffect] + [Vcause], both circumfixing and infixing languages may cause some problem of representation. However, no serious problem is envisaged, as long as discontinuity of either the [Vcause] element or the [Veffect] element is recognized or captured. Therefore, circumfixing languages such as Georgian and infixing languages such as Nancowry can be represented as follows (the Georgian causative verb is *a-duǧ-eb* 'causative prefix–boil–causative suffix: to cause to boil'; the Nancowry causative verb is *p-um-loʔ* 'to lose–causative infix–lose: to cause to lose'):

a. GEORGIAN

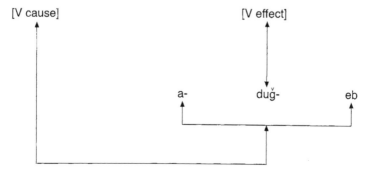

[V cause]   [V effect]

a-   duǧ-   eb

b. NANCOWRY

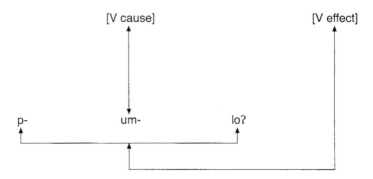

The element of [Vcause] in Georgian branches into two lines connecting the discontinuous causative morpheme, while it is the element of
[Veffect] in Nancowry that does the branching. The bondedness
between the elements of [Vcause] and [Veffect] in both languages is
equal in strength and identical to that in the languages that rely on
causative prefixes or suffixes. The schema in (3), then, captures this
characteristic common to all the morphological causative types.

7. It may be argued that the lexical causative type may not fit in with the
schema in (3), since the lexical causative verb cannot be analysed
morphologically, i.e. morpheme by morpheme. In response to this kind
of objection, the schema in (3) could be revised as:

(i)
$$S_1 (\ldots \{ [\text{Vcause}] \oplus [\text{Veffect}] \} \ldots) S_1$$

The sequence of [Vcause] and [Veffect] is surrounded by curly braces,
which by convention indicate the morphemic boundary. The sequence
is not susceptible to any morphological analysis.

8. Incidentally, the lexical verb of cause *uřka* is used when the [Veffect]
is intransitive, while *muta* is chosen when the [Veffect] is transitive
(Sharpe 1972: 99).

9. So far, languages that use general coordinating affixes or switch
reference affixes in causatives of the *AND* type have been examined. It
is then plausible to hypothesize about the existence of grammatical
elements which may be intermediate between the general coordinating
and switch reference affixes. Abelam, spoken in Sepik District, Papua
New Guinea, has a connecting suffix *-kʌ* or *-gʌ*, which indicates that
the action of the second clause is subsequent to that of the first clause

in the sentence. Although the suffix occurs when the subject of the second clause is identical to that of the first, Laycock (1965: 72) notes that it occurs more frequently when the subject of the second clause differs from that of the first. One can speculate that in Abelam, a functional change is in progress, from a general coordinating suffix to a switch reference suffix. This line of speculation is, in fact, expressed by Haiman (1983a, 1987), who argues with convincing evidence that the switch reference suffixes in Papuan languages can be diachronically traced back to a coordinating conjunction marker, the proto-Eastern New Guinea Highlands form of which is, in fact, reconstructed as *kV by Haiman (1987: 350). Note the strong physical resemblance of the Abelam suffix to the reconstructed form.

10. Oswalt (1977, 1983) suggests, contra the position taken here, that in Kashaya (or Western Pomo) the causative suffix has been extended to be used as part of the switch reference system. In Kashaya, there is a causative suffix -(h)qa, which should be used in a few special situations where a wish is expressed, or verbs of emotional or volitional attitude are involved (Oswalt 1977: 50, 1983: 285–286). Another language which is claimed to be similar to Kashaya in terms of the directionality of change between the switch reference and causative is Chechen-Ingush, a Caucasian language (Nichols 1985). Whether it is always from the switch reference to the causative that the functional change takes place or the other way around, or even both ways, is a matter that cannot be settled here. It is left as an open question.

11. Papuan languages started to be studied when syntax was the 'prima donna' of linguistics, whereas American Indian languages were described when morpho(phono)logy reigned supreme in the discipline.

12. Noonan (1981) and Noonan and Bavin (1981) do not discuss the sequential mood in Lango.

13. There has been a long-standing controversy over how to recognize the serial construction in general terms. It is evident in light of the controversy that such language-general terms are hard to come by. Witness Sebba's work (1987), in which serial verb constructions in languages known as serializing are contrasted with seemingly similar constructions in languages known as nonserializing. It is suspected that there is almost no value in recognizing the serial verb construction as such. There can be no clear-cut distinction between serial and nonserial, since as has so far been shown in this chapter, there is always a continuum between juxtaposition of two independent clauses in a single sentence, and juxtaposition of two verbs in a single clause. The so-called 'serial verb construction' is, then, somewhere in between the prototypical *AND* type and the prototypical *COMPACT* type, but closer to the former type. Most of the problems associated with the defining of the serial verb construction thus stem from the failure to recognize such a continuum. It is impossible to devise a single set of criteria to

characterize it as a discrete category.

14. Yi is not the name of a single language, but that of four or five major languages or groups of dialects that form the Loloish branch of the Tibeto-Burman family (Wheatley 1985: 401).

15. The *COMPACT* type of causative in Chinese is not watertight, since some grammatical elements can intervene between [Vcause] and [Veffect], as in (59) (Li and Thompson 1976: 480).

16. Of course, the actual position of *PURP* is language-particular, just as is the position of *AND* in the *AND* type of causative.

17. It may not be in a way surprising that future tense behaves like subjunctive mood in this respect, particularly because in many languages the common source of future tense is none other than subjunctive mood (Lyons 1977: 817, Foley and Van Valin 1984: 217, Givón 1994: 275).

18. Barry Blake (personal communication) recollects exactly the same experience while working on Kalkatungu, another Australian language.

19. It is very interesting to note that in Straits Salish, a language closely related to Shuswap, the purposive marker *-(ə)s* is used in conjunction with the causative suffix *-tx^w* (cf. 2.3.1). Notice the formal similarity of the purposive suffix in Straits Salish to that in Shuswap, as in (91) and (92). In Chapter 3, an attempt will be made to explain the appearance of the purposive suffix in Straits Salish in evolutionary terms. Straits Salish seems to be at a later or more advanced stage of diachronic change than Shuswap is, insofar as the causatives are concerned.

20. If the clause is positive, the clause boundary marker plus subjunctive mood is used for both purposive and consecutive functions (see below on what is a consecutive clause). On the other hand, the clause boundary marker *ut* changes to *ne*, if the subordinate clause is a negative purposive clause. But the marker *ut* is retained with a following *non*, when the clause is both negative and consecutive (cf. F. Palmer 1986: 180).

21. Note that the English translation given contains additional material (i.e. *tried*) compared to the original Kammu sentence, because the 'correct' translation will be ungrammatical in English: **He made her sad, but she didn't become sad.*

Chapter 3

The evolution of causative affixes

3.1 Introduction

Since the classic paper by Greenberg (1963b) on word orders and their correlations, a number of linguists have attempted to incorporate typological facts into diachronic explanations (see Greenberg 1978b for his own epitomization of the interface between diachrony, synchrony, and language universals). The most prominent type of such research has been the use of synchronic word order universals in the reconstruction of word order, as found in Lehmann (1974), Vennemann (1973, 1975), Friedrich (1975), and Hawkins (1983) (however, see Watkins 1976). Although all these studies have undoubtedly kindled much interest in relating word order typology and reconstruction of word order, what they claim to have excavated in their diachronic research is anything but conclusively established. The fundamental weakness of this kind of research is the assumption that languages are consistent in terms of word order correlations, when the majority of the world's languages are known to be inconsistent (Comrie 1981a [1989]: 205). On the other hand, some linguists (e.g. Givón 1971a, 1971b, Weir 1986, Hall 1987, 1988, and Craig and Hale 1988), under the linguistic archaeologist's manifesto – 'Today's morphology is yesterday's syntax' – have attempted either to reconstruct earlier word order on the basis of synchronic distribution of morphological affixes (cf. Comrie 1980, Mallinson and Blake 1981, and Kefer 1985 for some pitfalls of this kind of approach), or to trace origins of morphological affixes to earlier lexical sources. Although most of the word order-related works, in particular, seem to have failed because there are a large number of counterexamples, there are no inherent contradictions in the embracing of the typological methodology in diachronic linguistics (Comrie 1981a [1989]: 212).

In this chapter, a diachronic investigation of the latter type of linguistic archaeology will be undertaken. An attempt will be made to propose a diachronic model of causative affixes from a universal-typological perspective and further to trace possible sources of causative affixes in addition to those already suggested in the literature. Such an attempt is made possible on the basis of the universal typology of causative constructions that has been presented in Chapter 2. The universal typology can be of great assistance in setting limits to the potential for sources of causative affixes, since it predicts or sanctions only particular types of causative construction (cf. Croft 1990: 203–245 on diachronic typology). Conversely, the validity of the typology of causative constructions can be further strengthened if it can be shown to be indirectly involved in predicting the possible sources of causative affixes: *a fortiori* major sources of causative affixes can be discovered due to the particular perspective that has motivated the typology. Finally, on the basis of the diachronic model of causative affixes, the restrictions on the occurrence of causative affixes and purposive morphemes in some languages (cited in 2.3.1) will also be explained.

Will it be possible to propose such a diachronic model when the majority of the world's languages lack historical documentation? Indeed, Lightfoot (1979: 6–7) warns that languages without such ample historical documents as Chinese, Tamil, and those of Indo-European and Semitic families cannot form an appropriate basis for work on syntactic change. If one strictly follows Lightfoot's advice, one cannot venture into any serious diachronic research on languages that do not have earlier historical recordings. Lightfoot's pessimistic warnings will not be accepted here, because a serious diachronic investigation can be carried out under the assumption that a universal typology delimits the variation of a given construction, e.g. the causative construction. In particular, it will be shown that on the basis of the universal typology of causative constructions, causative affixes can be traced back to their origins. In other words, lack of historical documentation can be offset by argument for and justification of a given diachronic analysis. In fact, even Lightfoot (1979: 380) himself acknowledges, albeit in a slightly different context, that grammatical reanalyses require argument and justification, even where there is an abundance of (historical) data. For example, if one wants to establish that form *y* has historically derived from form *x*, an abundance of data regarding these two forms is not a sufficient condition at all for proving that form *x* is the ancestor of form *y*. This is because the data themselves do not justify the origin of form *y*. What is needed here is a conceptual frame of reference that justifies the diachronic relationship between the two forms. In fact, such a procedure is the basis for distinguishing polysemy from homonymy. Therefore, in the case of lack of historical recordings, the attitude taken by Lightfoot does not advance our general understanding of diachronic phenomena, except for noting that the formal similarity between form x and form y is accidental. However, if one makes the same assumption that has been taken here, what one can at least establish is that form x and form y cannot possibly have any diachronic relationship. What will be provided in this chapter, then, is such a general conceptual frame of reference that can show linguists where to look for origins of causative affixes in individual languages in which they specialize. It has to be made clear at the outset that, although a number of languages are presented as providing support for the diachronic model of causative affixes, no claim is laid as to the actual history of each of these languages. This is a matter for language specialists to confirm or disconfirm, as the case may be. What is presented here is the present writer's own crosslinguistic observation built on a few sporadic observations made by other linguists that in many languages causative affixes have strong formal resemblance to certain coherent groups of elements that are characterized as *PURP*. At the same time, a diachronic model will be provided that can **argue for** and **justify** the more-than-chance relationship that may exist between causative affixes and noncausative elements including *PURP*.

3.2   Other studies on origins of causative affixes

To the best of·the present writer's knowledge, the earliest explicit reference to possible relationships between causative affixes and other (noncausative) morphemes is a comparative morphological study of Tibeto-Burman languages by Wolfenden (1929). Even though it is the oldest of the studies that will be reviewed here, Wolfenden's classic work is definitely not the least insightful of them in that he appeals to metaphorical extension to account for the observed similarity between causative affixes and directive or benefactive affixes in some of the Tibeto-Burman languages.

Wolfenden (1929: 46–48) notes that the causative affix *s-* in Tibetan may have originated from the general directive element, since the latter also appears in a group of verbs in the form of *s-*; e.g. *s-pro-ba* 'to make go out' vs *s-neg(s)-pa* 'to run to or towards'. He regards this general directive element as indicating either (a) general direction into the condition or state denoted by the verb or (b) action to, towards, or for an entity. This directive element is then metaphorically extended to the causative, since like the causee in the causative construction, the object of the directive element undergoes the same kind of change in condition or state, or is subject to the same kind of movement by another entity. He (1929: 199–200) postulates for Burmese the same development from a directive element to a causative affix on the basis of the fact that the same regular aspiration of the initial consonants of verb roots recognized as being characteristic of an old directive element also occurs in causativized verbs. A more interesting case comes from Ao, which has a causative suffix -*dâk-tsa-* (Wolfenden 1929: 139, 152). What is noteworthy is the fact that in Ao the causative affix consists of two components, *dâk* and *tsa* (see section 3.4). As Wolfenden (1929: 137–139) himself notes, -*tsa*- is a dative-directive affix denoting that the action is accomplished for the benefit of some entity other than the actor. The other component, -*dâk*-, is traced back to the same root as the Tibetan verb *ajug-pa* 'to cause, to compel'. However, he (1929: 139) is not completely sure whether the second element of the causative affix is indeed the same as the directive element in Ao:

> The second element -*tsa*- . . . is perhaps comparable to the B.[urmese] causative suffix -*če*, though, on the other hand, it [the causative -*tsa*-] may be nothing but the Ao [dative-]directive element -*tsa* . . . indicating that the (causative) verbal action falls upon an external object and not on the speaker. . . . If -*tsa*- is this directive element, it is not a little interesting that here in Ao association with roots carrying a causative sense has elevated it from its originally purely directive function to an apparently 'causative' one, just as it did Tibetan -*s*-.

Wolfenden is here relying on the kind of metaphorization mechanism that is reminiscent of the so-called 'localist theory' (e.g. Anderson 1971, Diehl 1975, Radden 1985, Heine, Claudi, and Hünnemeyer 1991a and 1991b): metaphorical transfers occur from more concrete (less abstract) notions to less concrete (more abstract) notions. However, his explanation is far short of being of the kind of conceptual framework that is alluded to in 3.1. It is, therefore, not at all clear in his explanation on what grounds the directive element, rather than the causative element, is basic. One can easily argue for the opposite direction of change, i.e. from causative to directive (not to mention why the dative-directive affix is used in addition to the causative affix). What is lacking in his account is an independent parameter to determine the direction of change. The universal typology of causative constructions in Chapter 2 provides such a parameter, because it clearly indicates the direction of change regarding these two functions: from directive to causative.

It is in Givón (1971a) that the linguistic archaeologist's manifesto quoted earlier is promulgated. Givón outlines with a great deal of plausibility how independent lexical elements may change into affixes. Although he discusses causative affixes originating primarily from higher lexical verbs 'to cause' or [Vcause], his main concern is to establish the correlation between word order, on the one hand, and prefixes and suffixes, on the other. In OV languages, lexical causative verbs become suffixes, whereas in VO languages, they become prefixes (see Figure 3.1 and Figure 3.2; both are taken from Givón 1971a).[1] Thus, Givón (1971a: 412) demonstrates that one primary source for causative affixes is lexical verbs of cause, although he does not indicate what other nonprimary sources of causative affixes there may be.

Comrie (1981a [1989]: 176) cites in passing as evidence for the causative affix as an indicator of increase in valency (due to the introduction of the causer; see 6.2) the fact that in many languages the same morphology is used in both morphological causativization and ditransitivization of monotransitive verbs. In Wolof, the suffix -*al* functions as a causative suffix as in (1) and also as a ditransitivizing (applicative) suffix as in (2):

OV (syntax)   suffixation (morphology)

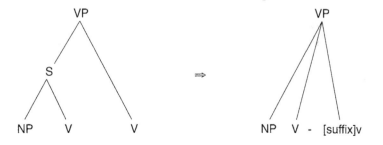

Figure 3.1

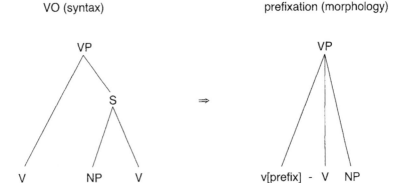

VO (syntax)   prefixation (morphology)

Figure 3.2

(1) WOLOF
Di   naa toog-al nenne bi
FUT 1SG sit-CS child the
'I will make the child sit.'

(2) WOLOF
Mungi dyàng-al eleew yi   tééré-ém
he   read-DTR pupil the-PL book-his
'He is reading his book to the pupils.'

The use of the same morphology is claimed to be purely syntactically motivated in that the only function of the morphology in both cases is to increase the valency of the basic verb, since there is no necessary connection with control or semantic causation types, e.g. direct vs indirect causation. However, a serious question remains unanswered: why is none other than the applicative marker, which is recognized in Chapter 2 as an instantiation of the term *PURP*, used to function as a causative affix? Or if a language like Wolof has more than one valency-increasing affix (e.g. comitative, instrumental, as well as applicative), why does the causative affix have the same form as whatever marker is an instantiation of the term *PURP*, and not comitative, for instance? Unless this is answered, Comrie's putative syntactic explanation is nothing more than an interesting piece of observation.

   Finally, Tuggy (1987) is an ambitious piece of work to account for a striking feature of (Uto-)Aztecan languages: the use of verbal suffixes as both causatives and applicatives (cf. Langacker 1977a: 144–147). Indeed, anyone who has studied grammatical descriptions of the Aztecan languages will have undoubtedly noticed this interesting and peculiar phenomenon. Tuggy attempts to 'demystify' this Aztecan puzzle by using Cognitive Grammar developed by Langacker (1983, 1987). However, his account fails to lend much needed insight into the cognitive nature of causation, not to mention the diachrony of causative affixes, although his work is basically synchronic. It is not clear at all in his exposition what the diachronic relation of causative and applicative affixes is (i.e. which is derived from which). Tuggy notes that in Tetelcingo Nahuatl, as in other Aztecan languages, the same suffix -*liya* functions as both causative and applicative, as shown in (3):

(3) TETELCINGO NAHUATL
a. ni-k-mewi-liya
   I-him-arise-CS
   'I raise him.'
b. ni-k-tesi-liya[2]
   I-her-grind=corn-APPL
   'I grind corn for her.'

The basic motivation that Tuggy (1987: 598) promotes for the similarity between the causative and applicative suffixes (which share the same form in (3)) is that the applicative function in (3.b) involves the causing of possession: the process of grinding corn by the causer (or the grinder) results in someone possessing a quantity of dough. In other words, the possessive relation is caused by the process of grinding itself. This causation relation in (3.b) is of the same kind of relation found in (3.a). The process of the causee's rising is caused by the causer's (unspecified) action. This similarity, then, is the basic motivation for the use of the same suffix in both causative and applicative in Tetelcingo Nahuatl. Therefore, in Tuggy's words (1987: 603), 'we have here a direct and powerful expression of the close relationship of causatives to applicatives'. This kind of analysis is not new at all, *pace* Tuggy (1987: 587), who claims that it is Cognitive Grammar that can make such an analysis possible. In fact, his analysis is very reminiscent of Generative Semantics. For instance, Seuren (1973: 37–38) proposes a similar analysis of indirect objects or datives. The sentence *He gave the patient advice* is derived via the predicate-raising rule from an underlying structure like *He caused the patient to have advice* (also see Comrie 1975: 25). Tuggy's contribution is important in that it addresses the long-overdue issue of the Aztecan phenomenon. However, it fails to produce any (new) insightful analysis of the phenomenon, not to mention of the diachronic mechanism of causative affixes.

3.3   A diachronic model of causative affixes

Where do causative affixes come from? In order to answer this question, it is first necessary to see what types of causative construction are available in the languages of the world. The universal typology of causative affixes provided in Chapter 2 does just that: the *COMPACT, AND*, and *PURP* types. The next thing to do is to determine what potential sources these causative types may contribute for causative affixes. To put it in another way, it is most important to relate these causative types to causative affixes, since (at least intuitively) they seem to be the natural providers of causative affixes.[3]

What is the typical morphological causative verb made of? The element of [Veffect] will form an essential part of the morphological causative verb. One of the two essential components of causative verbs is the basic verb denoting the action or state of the causee. The other essential component is, of course, whatever represents the element of [Vcause]. The typical morphological causative verb is, then, a verb in which the element of [Vcause] is morphologically fused with that of [Veffect]. The *COMPACT* type of causative construction must, then, be excluded from the present consideration, because it is the very type of causative construction that is schematic of the typical morphological causative, i.e. [Vcause] $\oplus$ [Veffect]. This leads to the other two causative types. The *AND* and *PURP* types must be taken into account in order to see whether they have anything to contribute to the sources of causative affixes. The schemata for the prototypical *AND* and *PURP* types of causative construction are presented below for ease of reference:

(4) *AND* Type
$S_1(S_2 (\dots [Vcause] \dots)S_2 + AND + S_2(\dots [Veffect] \dots)S_2)S_1$

(5) *PURP* Type
$S_1(S_2(\dots [Veffect] \dots)S_2 + PURP \dots [Vcause] \dots)S_1$ *or*
$S_1(\dots [Vcause] \dots S_2(\dots [Veffect] \dots)S_2 + PURP)S_1$

The most obvious source of causative affixes in both types in (4) and (5) is the element representing [Vcause]. Independent causative verbs are reduced to affixes, which are then attached to basic verbs, i.e. [Veffect]. The diachronic mechanism of causative affixes originating from independent lexical elements of [Vcause] is that of formal reduction, widely discussed and documented in the literature (e.g. Givón 1971a). So, no more will be said about this particular source. One may, however, wonder at this point what will happen to the term *AND* or *PURP* in the process of the amalgamation of the elements of [Vcause] and [Veffect]. This question will be addressed shortly.

The other prominent participants besides [Veffect] in the above schemata are the terms *AND* and *PURP*. When they are frequently used in causative constructions, they will be associated strongly with causation *per se*. This functional association is increasingly strengthened via frequent use of either the *AND* or the *PURP* type of causative construction (see Bybee 1985a: 119–123 on the role of frequency in various morphological phenomena). If it is further assumed that either the term *AND* or the term *PURP* somehow takes over the function of [Vcause], then it may also be an excellent source of causative affixes. In fact, the verb of [Vcause] tends to be highly semantically bleached in the sense that it is not specific in terms of the type of causing action. In many languages, the (independent) causative verb is semantically general with the meaning of 'do', 'make', or 'cause', etc. In functional terms, such generality in meaning is tantamount to nothing more than the signalling of causative function. If the schemata in (4) and (5) are by now identified as functioning as causatives, the presence of either *AND* or *PURP* will instead be sufficient to signal causative function by being associated strongly with the causative. To put it differently, the semantically bleached [Vcause] is now largely predictable and even redundant, thus very much subject to complete loss, as Kiparsky (1982: 67) observes:

> Morphological material which is predictable on the surface tends to be more susceptible to loss than morphological material which is not predictable on the surface.

This means that the term *AND* and the term *PURP* are now legitimate proxies for the term [Vcause]. Further, when the terms *AND* and *PURP* are institutionalized as the element of [Vcause], it seems plausible enough to suggest that they become (derivational) affixes through formal reduction, which is well known to affect independent lexical verbs of cause.[4] It is not unusual in languages that such a take-over occurs. A good example that immediately comes to mind is the nasal vowels in French. The nasal stop is understood to have dropped out after the preceding vowel took over nasality, as exemplified in:

(6) a. /bɔn/ > /bɔ̃/ : 'good'
    b. /bɔnte/ > /bɔ̃te/ : 'goodness'

A more relevant example comes from Lahu, a Lolo-Burmese language of Northern Thailand, which was discussed in 2.3.1 and 2.5.3. In this language, an original causative prefix *s-, which has now disappeared, is responsible for alternations between voiced and voiceless initials in such pairs as (Matisoff 1973 [1982]: 32–34; also Hopper and Traugott 1993: 148–149):

(7) LAHU
    a. dɔ̀ 'drink' : tɔ 'give to drink'
    b. dɛ̀ 'come to rest' : tɛ 'to put down'

The function of the original causative prefix is now taken over by the change in voicing. More interestingly, there is a tonal change from a lower to a mid or high tone, which is related to the change in voicing. However, when the initial consonant does not exhibit a distinction in voicing, e.g. /m/ or /c/ as in (8) below, the tonal difference is what performs the function of the original causative prefix.

(8) LAHU
    a. mɔ̀ 'see' : mɔ 'show'
    b. câ 'eat' : cā 'feed'

Therefore, in Lahu the change in voicing or tone effectively performs the very function that the now extinct causative prefix used to.

The following diachronic model is now proposed to adumbrate how the term *AND* or *PURP* ends up as a causative affix:

■   *Stage I:* The originally noncausative construction, i.e. the juxtaposition of two clauses (i.e. *AND* type) or the purposive construction (i.e. *PURP* type), begins to be used to express causation. At this stage, the presence of the [Vcause] element is absolutely necessary.

■   *Stage II:* The strengthened association of the *AND* or *PURP* construction with causation is such that the term [Vcause] can optionally be omitted.

■ *Stage III:* The [Vcause] element no longer appears in the *AND* or *PURP* construction. The originally noncausative construction has now become a genuine causative construction via a complete take-over of [Vcause] by *AND* or *PURP*, although there may remain some grammatical traces that indicate that *AND* or *PURP* is not originally the element of [Vcause].

■ *Stage IV:* The element of *AND* or *PURP* becomes formally or morphophonologically reduced to an affix, which is then attached to the element of [Veffect]. In other words, the element of *AND* or *PURP* now becomes a fully **derivational** causative affix. Unlike Stage III, there may not necessarily be any grammatical traces available that indicate that *AND* or *PURP* is not the original element of [Vcause]. At this particular stage, the 'new' causative affix is expected to behave just like usual derivational affixes. It now comes to lose productivity or generality or it may have limited applicability of being added to only a restricted number of stems. It further becomes prone to lexicalization, just like any other derivational affixes (on such a grammatical behaviour of derivational affixes, especially causative ones, also see Bybee 1985a: 16–19). Clearly, this 'usual derivational behaviour' will differentiate the final stage from the penultimate stage.

The diachronic model here is only an approximation of what may happen in the functional take-over of the causative function by the element of *AND* or *PURP* and its subsequent reduction into an affix. It is subject to further modification in light of more 'transitional' languages, some examples of which will be reviewed shortly. Not much theoretical importance will be imputed to each of the stages of the model, since, for one thing, there will surely be languages intermediate between any two of the stages. These four stages are to be regarded only as guideposts, marking off conspicuous points, largely by impression, on the continuum from the originally non-causative syntactic constructions to morphological causatives. Further it should be borne in mind that the model does not claim that all languages that have either *AND* or *PURP* type of causative in use **must** go through all these four stages. It only outlines how causative affixes **may** have arisen out of *AND* or *PURP*, if there are reasons to believe that there is a diachronic relation between causative affixes, on the one hand, and the term *AND* or *PURP*, on the other. Therefore, it is quite possible that languages continue to use the *PURP* type of causative without the term *PURP* ever assuming the function of [Vcause], and further being reduced to an affix.

So far, the terms *AND* and *PURP* have been depicted as having an equal chance of changing into causative affixes. It should be noted, however, that in the sample no languages of the *AND* type have been found for any of the noninitial stages, i.e. except for Stage I. It is suspected that this is not accidental, e.g. due to lack of data. Although the possibility that the term *AND* ends up as a causative affix cannot be ruled out completely, the term *AND*, in comparison with the term *PURP*, seems to be an extremely poor source of causative affixes. There seem to be two complementary reasons for this state of affairs. First, more often than not, the function of the term *AND* is carried out by the juxtaposing of two clauses alone (i.e. zero marking), rather than by means of overt *AND* markers, as has already been shown in 2.4.2. In contrast, the term *PURP* is always marked by overt linguistic elements (i.e. nonzero marking). Secondly, there is a semantic differential between *AND* and *PURP*. In other words, the term *AND* is not semantically loaded in that its presence is not a necessary condition for the interpretation of temporal sequence of [Scause] and [Seffect]; the linear order of the two clauses alone iconically promotes such an interpretation. In fact, this is why it is the term *AND*, not the term *PURP*, that can be realized as zero. Note that even overt markers of the term *AND* are almost void of any semantic content or even redundant owing to the iconic interpretation of the linear order of the two clauses involved. On the other hand, the term *PURP* is semantically loaded in that it specifically contributes the semantic content of goal or purpose to the construction in which it is contained. Without the presence of the term *PURP*, it is extremely difficult to obtain the meaning of goal or purpose.[5] Therefore, the semantic differential (and/or difference in formal realization) between *AND* and *PURP* seems to play a crucial role in the diachronic outcomes of these two terms. It has already been pointed out that overt markers of the term *AND* are also redundant and void of semantic content. This particular aspect of overt markers of the term *AND* makes them very susceptible to complete loss, even before they are given a chance to compete with the element of [Vcause] and to take over causative function from it. It is also quite possible that, being void of semantic content, these markers may be 'squeezed out' into oblivion when the originally independent lexical element of [Vcause] is transformed into a derivational affix (i.e. when the originally **biclausal** *AND*-type causative is formally reduced into a **monoclausal** *COMPACT*-type causative). Whichever scenario may turn out to be right, it is the semantic redundancy or lack of semantic content of the term *AND* that seems to facilitate or precipitate its own demise. Therefore, the functional take-over of the kind that has been depicted above may not occur at all. Rather, the original [Vcause] element will retain its causative function and, further, it will be formally reduced to an affix. In a sense, the term *AND* is no match for the lexical element of [Vcause] as a candidate for becoming a causative affix. The term *AND* thus seems to be a poor source of causative affixes.

In contrast, the term *PURP* is a very competitive source of causative affixes: (a) it is very resistant to obliteration due to its semantic loadedness; hence (b) it can stay around long enough to take over the causative function of the term [Vcause]. Further, the aspect of the term *PURP* described in (a) – resistance to obliteration – suggests a need to have another look at the diachronic path of the original [Vcause] element being reduced to a causative affix *à la* Givón (1971a, 1971b). Recall the question concerning the fate of the terms *AND* and *PURP* in the amalgamation of the [Vcause] and [Veffect] elements. Their semantic differential is believed to have a lot to do with their (different) behaviours in the amalgamation process as well. If the *PURP* element is resistant to obliteration owing to its semantic loadedness, it is quite likely that it may be trapped in between the elements of [Vcause] and [Veffect]. The term *PURP* is more likely to survive the process of amalgamation of the elements of [Vcause] and [Veffect]. On the other hand, the term *AND* is more likely to be dropped or squeezed out in the process of the amalgamation of [Vcause] and [Veffect] due to its semantic redundancy or lack of semantic content. In 3.4.2, a few languages will be documented in support of the resistance of the term *PURP* in the amalgamation process.

The best way to demonstrate that the kind of diachronic path that has been depicted so far is real is to make reference to languages that display each stage of the diachronic model. Since this is not possible at present for the *AND* type of causative for the reasons provided, the following discussion will be confined to *PURP*-type languages.

Korean seems to have just begun to exploit a noncausative purposive construction to express causation (i.e. Stage I). In Korean, subordinate clauses of purpose are marked by *-ke*, as in:

(9) KOREAN
Kim ssi-ka   ai-tɨl-i   koŋpu-ha-ke   paŋ-esə
Kim Mr-NOM child-PL-NOM study-do-PURP room-from
na=o-ass-ta
get=out-PST-IND
'Mr Kim left the room so that the children would study.'

The same purposive marker appears between the element of [Vcause] and that of [Veffect] in the so-called 'syntactic causative construction' in Korean:

(10) KOREAN
Kim ssi-ka   ai-tɨl-i   koŋpu-ha-ke   ha-əss-ta
Kim Mr-NOM child-PL-NOM study-do-PURP cause-PST-IND
'Mr Kim made the children study.'

The presence of the [Vcause] element in causatives like (10) in Korean is obligatory. Further, the causative sentence in (10) is nonimplicative. Thus, it is possible that the children did not study at all, despite their father's attempt to make them do so.[6] In other words, (10) is still very much of a purposive sentence. Note that in modern Korean the morphological causative suffix *-I-* cannot be applied to verbs like *koŋpu-ha* as in (10), in which case only the *PURP* type of causative construction is allowed. For further evidence that the Korean syntactic causative is still in the process of evolving from the purposive construction, see Chapter 4.

Thai is a language that seems to be at Stage II of the diachronic model. According to Noss (1964: 177), there is a conjunction that marks subordinate clauses of purpose, *hây* (the following examples are taken from Vichit-Vadakan 1976).

(11) THAI
khǎw khiǎn còtmǎay hây   khun tòop
he   write letter   PURP you answer
'He wrote a letter so that you would answer.'

The conjunction *hây* also appears in the causative construction, where the element of [Vcause] is *tham* 'do' or 'make'.

(12) THAI
Sǎakhǎa tham hây   nísaa tii chǎn
Saka   cause PURP Nisa hit I
'Saka made Nisa hit me.'

However, there are also causatives without *tham*, but only with the
PURP marker *hây*.

(13) THAI
Săakhăa hây   dèk   wîŋ
Saka   PURP child run
'Saka had a child run.'

In Thai, then, the *PURP* element can function optionally as the
element of [Vcause] on its own. It also appears as a genuine *PURP*
element in both causative and noncausative constructions. This
suggests that Thai seems to have grammaticalized the noncausative
construction as a causative construction to a greater extent than
Korean.

Ịọ, a Niger-Congo language, is also a language of Stage II. The
term *PURP* is used in both causative and noncausative constructions
and at the same time the element of [Vcause] is optional.[7] While
arguing that the word order in Niger-Congo can be reconstructed as
SOV, Givón (1975a: 95, 99) claims that the causative suffix -*mọ* in
Ịọ can be traced back to a full (now extinct) causative verb 'make/
cause', following the lower clause at some earlier stage of its history.
That claim will not be accepted here. Instead, it is argued that the
suffix -*mọ* is a *PURP* element, which sometimes appears with the
[Vcause] element in the *PURP* type of causative construction.
Indeed, the causative suffix -*mọ* is the same as the directional suffix
-*mọ* marking nominal arguments of directional role (cf. 2.5.1).

(14) ỊỌ
a. tọbọụ wẹnị-mọ́
   child walk-DIR
   'Walk towards the child.'
b. áru-bị   àki tịn kaka-mọ
   canoe-the take tree tie-DIR
   'Tie the canoe to a tree.'

The directional suffix -*mọ* is attached to what Williamson (1965: 35)
calls transitive directional verbs and it has a meaning of 'towards' or
'in regard to'. The causative suffix has exactly the same form as this
directional suffix, although neither Williamson nor Givón makes this
observation.

(15) IJO
a. erí áru-bị   bìle-mọ-mị
    he canoe-the sink-CS-ASP
    'He sank the canoe.'
b. wónì uru akị́-n`i   u-bọu-mọ́-mí
    we wine take-ASP him-drink-CS-ASP
    'We made him drink the wine.'

Clearly, the term *PURP* is here being used in place of the element of [Vcause] in Ijọ. It can be said with some certainty that the functional take-over of [Vcause] by the element of *PURP* has taken place. But has the take-over been completed in Ijọ? That is, is Ijọ a language of Stage III of the diachronic model? It seems that it is not yet. As both Williamson (1965: 54–57) and Givón (1975a: 95) note, in certain cases a separate lexical element of [Vcause] *mịẹ* can be used in conjunction with the so-called 'causative suffix' *-mọ*. Compare (15.a) with (16):

(16) IJO
erí áru-bị   mìẹ bile-mọ-mí
he canoe-the make sink-CS-ASP
'He made the canoe sink.'

Further compare (17.a) and (17.b):

(17) IJO
a. áràụ́ tobọụ́ mìẹ   bụ́nụ-mọ-mị
    she child make sleep-CS-ASP
    'She soothed the child to sleep.'
b. áràụ́ tobọụ́ bụ́nụ-mọ-mị
    she child sleep-CS-ASP
    'She laid the child down to sleep.'

It seems that the term *PURP* has not been completely institutionalized as a genuine element of [Vcause], since the original element of [Vcause] can appear in its company.[8] Without the diachronic model of causative affixes put forward in this chapter, it is difficult to explain why a separate lexical verb of cause or [Vcause] is used in addition to the 'causative suffix', which is already attached to the verb of effect or [Veffect]. In (16) and (17.a), the suffix *-mọ* is used to register the presence of the term *PURP* and it is not a genuine (or fully fledged) causative suffix at all, as evidenced by the presence of *mịẹ*, the element of [Vcause]. On the other hand, in (15) and (17.b) the suffix *-mo* functions in lieu of the element of [Vcause], hence the absence of *mie*. It is thus concluded that the so-called causative suffix *-mo* is neither a fully fledged causative suffix nor historically derived from an old independent lexical verb of cause. Instead, it is very much a genuine *PURP* element, since it marks directional arguments, as in (14). It is, however, in process of taking over causative function from the original element of [Vcause], since it can appear on its own without the company of the element of [Vcause], as in (15.a) and (17.b).

The penultimate stage (or Stage III) of the model in which the element of [Vcause] is left out permanently and obligatorily is exemplified by the causative construction from Yaqui, an Uto-Aztecan language (Lindenfeld 1973). In this language, the term *PURP* functions both as a fully fledged element of [Vcause] and as a purposive marker in noncausative constructions. The original element of [Vcause] has completely dropped out of use in the causative construction. Lindenfeld (1973: 103–104) notes that what she calls 'the command markers' *-sae* and *-ʔiʔa* are freely inter-changeable particles that mark subordinate clauses that express an order:

(18) YAQUI
hu-ka   ili   usi-ta   ne tehwa-k aman a   wee-sae-kai
this-DEP little child-DEP I   tell-STA there him go-PURP-DEP
'I told the little girl to go there.'

These command or *PURP* markers function as if they were genuine elements of [Vcause], since in causative sentences no element of [Vcause] can appear at all:

(19) YAQUI
in   kuuna   baci-ta   hoʔara-po nee hipu-ʔiʔa
my husband corn-DEP house-in   I   have-PURP
'My husband makes me keep corn in the house.'

Lindenfeld (1973: 104, 105) points out that the higher verb or the element of [Vcause] cannot occur in a sentence like (19) and that there is in fact no verb meaning 'to cause' in Yaqui. One may argue that these command markers may have been genuine causative suffixes all along, and that they may not have originated from the term *PURP*. However, evidence that this is not correct comes from the fact that the subject of the lower clause or the causee NP is marked for dependency, which is regarded as characteristic of subjecthood in the embedded clause (Lindenfeld 1973: 65, 104). In sum, the element of *PURP* in Yaqui, while functioning as a genuine *PURP* marker in noncausative constructions, has completely taken over the function of the [Vcause] element, which has now disappeared from the language.

As to the final stage of the model, the term *PURP* now functions as a fully fledged element of [Vcause], but in morphologically reduced form, i.e. a causative affix bonded to the element of [Veffect]. This particular stage, then, marks the 'rebirth' of the term *PURP* as a derivational causative affix.

3.4   Causative affixes: a diachronic track-down

In this section, evidence bearing on the final stage of the diachronic path will be provided: causative affixes which may be diachronically related to various instantiations of *PURP*. It must be reiterated that the evidence to be presented here is not conclusive by any means. What has been provided here is a general conceptual framework in which an attempt can be made to relate causative affixes to what have been identified as instantiations of the term *PURP* in 2.5. Such a framework will do either of the two: (a) to relate causative affixes to earlier sources in languages for which no such attempt has so far been made (the majority of the languages to be surveyed in this section fall into this category); or (b) to reexamine hitherto claimed sources of causative affixes in languages for such an attempt has already been made (e.g. Ijo̩ in 3.3). Therefore, in what follows it is not claimed that the causative affix **must** be related to the term *PURP* in a given language, but it is suggested that given the general diachronic model, the causative affix **may** be related to the term *PURP*. This important point must be borne in mind.

It is now clear from the discussion of the diachronic model in 3.3 that it is the term *PURP* (more accurately instantiations of the term *PURP*) in addition to the term [Vcause] that proves to be an excellent source of causative affixes. The other term, *AND*, does not seem to be such a good source, for the reasons already explained. Whether there are indeed any languages the causative affixes of which are historically related to the term *AND* can be determined only by further research. In what follows, therefore, only those languages will be discussed in which various instantiations of *PURP* may have become petrified as causative affixes.

3.4.1 From PURP markers to causative affixes

In 2.5, languages whose causative constructions contain the term *PURP* were examined. This term is schematic of various instantiations such as dative, locative, allative, directional, goal, benefactive, and purposive case markers. Most of these markers are found to express a sense of goal or purpose through metaphorical extension, and others, perhaps, more directly. They all thus register the presence of the term *PURP* in one way or another. On the basis of the diachronic model, a prediction can be made about varying degrees of formal resemblance between these markers and causative affixes. It is no longer a theoretical problem to account for the seemingly disparate observations made by Wolfenden and Tuggy among others (cf. 3.2). In some Tibeto-Burman languages, causative affixes have a striking resemblance to directional affixes. In Aztecan languages, the causative suffixes formally resemble the applicative suffixes, an important part of the meaning of which is benefactive. It can now be inferred that in these languages either the directional or the applicative affix has become the causative affix proper after its service as *PURP* in the causative construction, and its subsequent take-over of the function of [Vcause]. More languages like the Tibeto-Burman and Aztecan languages will be cited below, thus adding further to the observations already made by Wolfenden and Tuggy, but within the conceptual framework that makes sense of these observations. A uniform account of the formal resemblance between causative affixes and various instantiations of *PURP* has in fact been long overdue. It is hoped that the diachronic model in 3.3 and what follows will do it justice.

In Lamang, the Chadic language spoken in northeastern Nigeria and northern Cameroon, there is a causative suffix in use, -ŋà; this causative was originally restricted to motion verbs, but in Lamang it applies to at least one nonmotion verb (Wolff 1983: 123–124). Wolff (1983: 105, 124) suggests that this rather restrictive causative suffix is diachronically related to the benefactive preposition ŋgà (Wolff 1983: 243). As evidence for this relationship, Wolff (1983: 124) refers to the fact that the causative suffix -ŋà has a variant in the form of -ŋgà in the imperative. In addition, this language has a morphological process that derives causative verbs from intransitive verbs by the addition of the causative suffix -ýv' (Wolff 1983: 114). This particular suffix is also used to convey (a) the idea of reducing the object which is affected by the action of the verb; and (b) the idea of downward movement. Wolff (1983: 114) notes that there is a kind of locative-directional notion or meaning attached to the two other functions carried out by the suffix -*v́v'*. This may be indicative of one of its original meanings. Köhler (1981: 507) reports that in Kxoe there is a causative suffix in the form of *kà*. The directional preposition in this Central Khoisan language is none other than *kà*. In fact, Heine and Reh (1984: 137) think that in Kxoe the causative is derived from the directional preposition.

Pomo (Southern) is an American Hokan language in which the causative suffix -*q*- can be used in lieu of a separate lexical causative verb *ʔxe* (Moshinsky 1974: 74). There are two vertical directional morphemes which contain -*q*-: -*qla*- 'downward' and -*qlo*-, -*ql*- 'upwards, uphill, up off the ground' (Moshinsky 1974: 57, 58). It is not implausible to infer that the same form -*q*- is shared by the causative suffix and various directional morphemes. This inference is further bolstered by the fact that many forms containing -*q*- are in fact ambiguous between causatives and direction-related meanings (Moshinsky 1974: 56):

(20) POMO
a. cíqat: 'carry a lot of things away from here' *or* 'hand someone a bowl or a glass full (to cause someone to hold a bowl or a glass full)'
b. ʔtáqat: 'take two away from here' *or* 'give two to someone (to cause someone to have two)'

The morpheme -*q*- has two functions in (20): causative and direction to somewhere (away from the speaker). Again, Pomo points to a possible common denominator between causation and direction.

Southern Agaw, a Cushitic language, is reported to have a causative suffix -*s*- in addition to -*c*-, which is the more established causative suffix *par excellence* (Hetzron 1969: 61–63). According to Hetzron, the causative suffix -*s*- must have been **the** causative suffix in Southern Agaw, as is in other Cushitic languages. The dative (-instrumental) suffix in Southern Agaw is none other than -*s*- (Hetzron 1969: 21).

Khasi, a Mon-Khmer language, is also interesting in that the same prefix *pyn*- functions as both causative and benefactive (note that the benefactive prefix appears directly on the verb, i.e. head marking):[9]

(21) KHASI
a. Causative
   iap 'to die': **pyn**iap 'to kill'
   long 'to be': **pyn**long 'to create'
b. Benefactive
   kren 'to speak': **pyn**kren 'to speak for another'
   repair (loan from English): **pyn**repair 'to repair for someone'

It seems that this causative prefix is very productive to the extent that it even applies to recent loan words such as *repair* (Henderson 1976: 501), although, in an earlier description of the language (Rabel 1961: 102), it was reported to play a decidedly minor role in Khasi.

Southern Sierra Miwok, an Amerindian language spoken in central California, is another language in which a close relation between causative and benefactive functions is formally apparent (Broadbent 1964). There is a set of causative suffixes in this Miwok language, two of which concern us here: *-na* and *-nY*. The first suffix has two functions: benefactive (appearing on the verb, as in Khasi) and causative (Broadbent 1964: 74–75):

(22) SOUTHERN SIERRA MIWOK
a. Causative
   takp- 'to thirst': takyp**na**- 'to make one thirsty'
   cyt?yt-·e- 'to like it': cyte·**na**- 'to make someone like it'
b. Benefactive
   ?enh- 'to make': ?enyh**na**- 'to make for someone'
   kose·-nY 'to cook': kose**nna**- 'to cook for someone'
   myl·i- 'to sing': myl·i**na**- 'to sing for someone'

A piece of evidence for the common thread running between the causative and benefactive suffixes comes from the fact that the variants of present (im)perfect and imperative modal suffixes following either the causative suffix or the benefactive suffix are exactly the same. The present (im)perfect has *-na-* or *-nak-*, and the imperative has *-ni-*, *-n-*, or *-X-* (Broadbent 1964: 74–75). Further, the second suffix in question, *-nY*, also has a causative or benefactive meaning (Broadbent 1964: 76):

(23) SOUTHERN SIERRA MIWOK
a. Causative
   ?yw·y- 'to eat': ?ywy·**nY**- 'to feed'

b.   Benefactive
    kala··ŋ- 'to dance': kalaŋn**Y**- 'to dance for'
    liw·a- 'to talk': liwa·n**Y**- 'to talk for'

Swahili, a Bantu language, has a causative suffix *-ish-*, which applies to both intransitive and transitive verbs (Ashton 1947, Comrie 1976b, Driever 1976, Vitale 1981). The following is taken from Driever (1976: 43).[10]

(24) SWAHILI
baba a-li-m-fung-ish-a   mtoto mlango
father SUB-PST-OBJ-close-CS-IND child door
'The father made the child close the door.'

According to Driever (1976: 130), some of her informants who accepted it with slight reluctance interpreted (24) as the applicative: *The father closed the door for the child.* This can be taken as a piece of evidence that the causative suffix *-ish-* may have been an instantiation of the term *PURP*. In other words, the Swahili causative suffix may have originated from the applicative suffix which is by now almost dead, but which for some speakers may still retain its original function. Of course, this is only speculative at the present stage of the investigation. Incidentally, Swahili has a separate applicative suffix:

(25) SWAHILI
Hasani a-li-m-bomo-le-a   Ali ukuta
Hasan SUB-PST-OBJ-pull=down-APPL-IND Ali wall
'Hasan pulled down the wall for Ali.'

As has been shown in 2.5, the term *PURP* is also realized as such verbal markers as future tense, subjunctive mood, irrealis, etc. The diachronic model of causative affixes suggests that these markers also may end up as causative affixes. Thus, the model provides a uniform diachronic conceptual framework in which causative affixes can be traced back to their origins.

In Abkhaz, a Caucasian language, there is the causative prefix *r-*, which applies to both intransitive and transitive verbs (Hewitt 1979: 170–171):

(26) ABKHAZ
a. d-gàlo-yt'
    he-stand-FIN
    'He is standing up.'

b. də-sə-r-gə̀lo-yt'
him-I-CP-stand-FIN
'I stand him up.'

c. yə-q'a-s-c'è-yt'
it-PREV-I-do-FIN
'I did it.'

d. yə-b-sə̀-r-q'a-c'e-yt'
it-you-I-CP-PREV-do-FIN
'I made you do it.'

Subordinate clauses of purpose are marked by the verbal suffix *-rc*,
-razə, or *-ranə* (Hewitt 1979: 42):

(27) ABKHAZ
s-y°ə̀za də-z-bà-rc (*or* -razə̀, -ranə̀) à-kalak' (a-)ax's-co-yt'
my-friend him-I-see-PURP   ART-town it-to-I-go-FIN
'I am going to town to see my friend.'

It is noteworthy that the common part of these three purposive
markers is the same as the causative prefix. Hewitt (1979: 199–201)
also argues on the basis of its cooccurrence restrictions of cross-
referencing prefixes that the common form *r* of the purposive
markers is further related to the non-finite future tense (see 2.5.2; also
see Givón 1994: 275 for the relationship between purposive and
futurity). At any rate, it demands an explanation why the same form
appears in both causative and purposive constructions.

In Wiyot, an Amerindian language (Almosan-Keresiouan), the
causative suffix *-iy* is attached to intransitive verbs of what Teeter
(1964: 57) calls 'the i-stem' to derive causative verbs:

(28) WIYOT
lag- 'go': lag**iy** 'cause to go'

Interestingly enough, but not unexpectedly, one of the subjunctive
suffixes in Wiyot is none other than *-iy*. Evidence for the relatedness
of these two suffixes comes from the fact that the subjunctive suffix
applies to the verbs of the i-stem, as does the causative suffix (Teeter
1964: 58).

In Luiseño, an Uto-Aztecan language, there is a set of causative
suffixes (Kroeber and Grace 1960: 46–48). One of these is *-pi* (or
occasionally *-pa*) (Kroeber and Grace 1960: 140):

(29) LUISEÑO
a. qarápax 'to fall': qará**pi** 'to make to fall'

b. laqápax 'to be smooth': laqápi 'to smoothen'

The same form appears as a suffix marking the subordinate clause of purpose (Kroeber and Grace 1960: 147):

(30) LUISEÑO
huní?ax ya?a·ci po-ŋe-**pi**
'showed the man [so] that he might leave.'

It is an unmistakable fact that the same form is used for both causative and purposive functions.

Now, three large language groups will be surveyed in a summary fashion: Amerindian, Australian, and Austronesian. Since it is widespread in these three groups, suffice it simply to note that the phenomenon exists.

In 3.2, Tuggy's work in Uto-Aztecan languages was discussed briefly. In these languages, the causative suffix and the applicative suffix are known to share the same forms. However, the present investigation shows that the phenomenon is not confined to Uto-Aztecan languages. Other Amerindian languages also share the same forms for both functions. In Classical Nahuatl (Aztecan), there are two main ways of morphologically deriving causative verbs: (a) one involves vowel contrast and is restricted to intransitive verbs; (b) the other regular causativizing process involves the suffixing of either -*tia*, which applies to both intransitive and transitive verbs, or -*lia* and -*huia*, which are generally restricted to intransitive verbs (Andrews 1975: 85–101). As Tuggy (1987) also notes, Classical Nahuatl is no exception to the phenomenon characteristic of the Aztecan languages: the same forms are used for both causative and applicative functions. Indeed, in Classical Nahuatl there are three applicative suffixes: -*ia*, -*lia*, -*huia*, the last two being the more frequent (Andrews 1975: 102–103). The applicative suffixes register in the verbal complex the semantic role of dative, directional, or benefactive, *inter alia*. Again, it is an unmistakable fact that virtually the same forms are used for both functions. Other (Uto-)Aztecan languages that behave like Classical Nahuatl are Michoacán Nahuatl (Sischo 1979: 354–355), Huasteca Nahuatl (Beller and Beller 1979: 281–282), North Puebla Nahuatl (Brockway 1979: 177), Tetelcingo Nahuatl (Tuggy 1979: 105–108, 1987), and Western Tarahumara (Burgess 1984: 107). Jacaltec, a Mayan language, also displays the same phenomenon common in the Aztecan languages. According to Day (1973: 44), the forms -*ŋe*, -*tze*, and -*te* are used for both causative and applicative functions. Maidu, a Penutian language, uses the same form, -*ti*, for causative and benefactive (or applicative?) functions (Shipley 1964: 40, 44).

A similar situation is observed in the Australian family (see Dixon 1980 and Blake 1987a for a general introduction to these languages). Before the data are presented from the Australian languages, readers are urged to recall from 2.5.1 that in the *PURP* type of causative construction of Basque the [Seffect] is marked by the nominalizing suffix -*te* as well as the *PURP* marker, the allative marker -*ra*. In the process of reduction of the element of [Vcause] (originally a *PURP* element in the present case), the nominalizer may be trapped in between the elements of [Vcause] and [Veffect]. Indeed, this line of diachronic reasoning is supported by some of the Australian languages to be surveyed here. Gumbaynggir has the causative suffix -*ygura*, which derives causative verbs from intransitive verbs (Eades 1979: 304). Eades entertains two possible analyses for this causative suffix: (a) *ygu* (purposive verbal marker that can be traced back to a dative/allative suffix) plus *ra*; (b) the present tense suffix *y* and *gura*. The first analysis is preferred to the second here, because the present tense does not contribute to nonfactuality, the essential property of the second category of *PURP* elements (see 2.5.2), and because the second analysis also has to account for the form *gura*, just as much as the first one has to account for *ra*. At any rate, in Gumbaynggir the causative suffix is unmistakably related to the dative/allative suffix -*gu*. In Pitta-Pitta the causative suffix -*la* is used to form causative verbs from intransitive verbs (Blake 1979b: 204). The same suffix is used on the verb to mark the semantic role of beneficiary (Blake 1979b: 205). In Ngandi, there are two allomorphs of the causative suffix: -*guba* and -*nʔguba* (Heath 1978a: 91–92). The purposive case or dative case marker in Ngandi is -*ku*. It can be conjectured that the causative suffix contains the cognate of the dative/purposive case marker.[11] If this is the case, the question to be answered is: what, then, is -*nʔ*, part of the remainder? Heath suggests that this may be related to the now obsolete nominalizing suffix -*nʔ* (Heath 1978a: 91, 127). Ngandi thus provides an example where the nominalizing marker is trapped in the take-over and the subsequent reduction process of the term *PURP*. Nunggubuyu is another language with a similar causative suffix development to Ngandi. Part of the causative suffix -*jga/-jgi*, i.e. -*j*-, is possibly the archaic nominalizing suffix (Heath 1984: 393). Note that the remaining form of the causative suffix can be traced back to the dative -*gu/-ku*, one of the most widespread morphemes in Australian languages via vowel changes, a phenomenon which is very widely attested in these languages (Hale 1976, Dixon and Blake 1979: 11, Blake 1987a: 35, 40). Walmatjari requires the causative suffix *-kuji* to cooccur with the nominalizing suffix *-u* (Hudson 1978: 48). Again, note the formal resemblance of the causative suffix to the dative/benefactive/purposive case marker *-ku*. In Yidiny, the causative suffix *-ŋa-l* is exactly the same form used on the verb to register the dative/locative semantic roles (Dixon 1977: 305–318).[12]

The last language family that will be surveyed is Austronesian. It is an unmistakable fact about the Austronesian family that the causative affix is formally akin or similar to the verbal affix of benefactive or directional role. In Indonesian, the causative suffix *-kan* converts both intransitive and transitive verbs into causative ones. The same suffix appears on the verb to add locative/benefactive meaning (MacDonald 1976: 54–55, Tampubolon 1983: 44–51). Javanese is, not surprisingly, similar to Indonesian in that the same form *-(q)aké* is used for purposes of deriving causative verbs and registering benefactive and directional roles (Horne 1961: 207–208). The form *-(q)aké* is a Ngoko (informal style) form, the Krama (formal style) counterpart is *-(q)aken* (Horne 1961: 228). Winstedt (1914 [1957]: 89–90, 98–99) reports that Malay has the causative prefix *pə-* and the causative suffix *-kan*. Winstedt (1914 [1957]: 98) points out that the causative suffix is related to the directional preposition *akan*. Walker (1976: 30–31) reports that in Lampung the causative suffix *-ko* is used to form causative verbs and that it is also used to give the basic stems benefactive meaning. Sundanese (Hardjadibrata 1985: 18–20), Melayu Betawi (Ikranagara 1975: 175, 179), and Balinese (Barber 1977: 156–157, 159, 164) are similar to the above Austronesian languages in that the same form is used for both causative and benefactive functions. The languages to follow all clearly have reflexes of the Proto-Oceanic causative prefix **paka-* (Pawley 1972, Bradshaw 1979, Schütz 1986). Bikol has the causative prefix *pa-* (Mintz 1971: 165). The same prefix is used to indicate direction in Bikol (Mintz 1971: 180–181). Maori is another language which seems to have a reflex of **paka-* as the causative prefix, i.e. *whaka-*. According to Biggs (1969: 83), the same prefix is attached to locatives and adds the meaning of 'in the direction of'. In Tagalog, the causative prefix that De Guzman (1978: 336) claims to be the most productive of all derivational affixes in the language is none other than *pa-*. According to Blake (1925 [1967]: 264–265), the prefix is also used to derive verbs of motion from locative nouns, etc.: directional function (see 3.5). Other Austronesian languages that are akin to the above ones are Cebuano (Wolff 1966: 479, 1967: 261), Haroi (Goschnick 1977: 110–111), Hiligaynon (Motus 1971: 286–287, Wolfenden 1975: 102–142), Kaliai-Kove (Counts 1969: 68, 76–77, 111), Marshallese (Bender 1969: 111–112, Zewen 1977: 60–61) (these languages use the same forms for both causative and directional functions), and Casiguran Dumagat (Headland and Healey 1974: 32–37, 39) (this language uses the same prefix *pa-* for both causative and benefactive functions).

3.4.2 PURP *trapped in the amalgamation process*

In the sample, there are some languages in which additional affixes or elements are bonded to the morphological combination of [Vcause] and [Veffect]: the cooccurrence of causative affixes with unproductive and seemingly meaningless elements (cf. 2.3.1). In these languages, certain affixes must accompany causative affixes in the morphological derivation of causative verbs. There do not seem to be any obvious reasons why they have to cooccur with causative affixes without making any semantic contributions to the morphological derivation in question. In this subsection, such 'deviations' will be explained in light of the diachronic model of causative affixes.

In 3.3, it has been argued that the term *PURP* is resistant to obliteration (or reduction for that matter) owing to its semantic loadedness and/or to the fact that it is always realized as nonzero elements. As a consequence, there is much likelihood of its being trapped in the reduction process of the element of [Vcause] in the *PURP* type of causative construction. The sequence of the element of *PURP* and that of [Vcause] as a whole may then be reanalysed as a causative affix in the overall reduction process, as schematized in Figure 3.3. Therefore, the additional affix bonded to the morphological combination of the elements of [Vcause] and [Veffect] may well be the element of *PURP* trapped in the reduction process. It thus becomes worthwhile to examine those languages in which unproductive affixes are obligatorily required in the morphological derivation of causative verbs. It will be shown below that such additional affixes are indeed instantiations of the term *PURP* caught up in the reduction process of the elements of [Vcause] and [Veffect] *à la* Givón.[13]

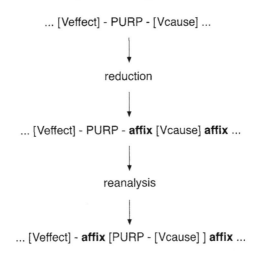

Figure 3.3

In Bashkir, a Turkic language, the contiguity of the basic verb and one of the causative suffixes is broken up by the additional suffix *-GÄ.* Poppe (1964: 70) notes that the causative suffix *-GÄr* contains one of the causative suffixes *-r*, and that the remaining form *-GÄ* is only an 'unproductive' suffix. It seems, however, that this unproductive suffix is an instantiation of the term *PURP* trapped in between the elements of [Vcause] and [Veffect]. In Bashkir, the dative suffix marking direction, goal, etc., is none other than *-GÄ* (Poppe 1964: 36).

In Songish, a dialect of Straits Salish spoken in British Columbia, Canada, a similar situation is observed. In this language, there is a causative suffix *-tx^w* (Raffo 1972: 151). The purposive element (or the element of *PURP*) *-(ə)s* is found to appear in between the basic verb and the causative suffix:

(31) STRAITS SALISH
a. kwə́n-s-tx^w   tuʔ nı́l
    see-PURP-CS DET 3SG/EMPH
    'Cause him to see.'
b. ʔéleʔ   łtə ʔuʔ xlá-s-tx^w
    to:be + here 1PL ASP feed-PURP-CS
    'We cause (someone) to feed them.'

In Kanuri, a Saharan language spoken in northern Nigeria, what

Hutchinson (1976: 43) calls the '+*ngin*' class verbs must be followed by the applied morpheme -*k* when they are morphologically causativized by *yìtè-*:

(32) KANURI
a. fâ-ngìn
    'I wake up.'
b. yìtè-fá-gè-kìn
    'I wake up someone.'

In (32.b), the allomorph *gè* of the applied morpheme follows the causative prefix. According to Hutchinson (1976: 42), this applied morpheme functions as an indicator of dative, benefactive, or directional semantic role. The applied morpheme in Kanuri is thus an instantiation of the term *PURP* or a fossilized *PURP*. Also note that the *PURP* element in Kanuri is not exactly trapped in between the elements of [Vcause] and [Veffect]. In fact, the causative prefix and the *PURP* element surround the basic verb, thereby illustrating how the causative circumfix may come into being, when the *PURP* marker and the element of [Vcause] end up on the **different** sides of the basic verb in the reduction process. Yet the Kanuri example clearly provides support for the diachronic scenario in Figure 3.3, since the *PURP* element must cooccur with the causative prefix.

Bandjalang is an Australian language that also adds support to the diachronic scenario in Figure 3.3. According to Crowley (1978: 88), this language has about fifteen irregular verbs. When the causative suffix -*ma* is added to some twelve of these irregular verbs, the roots should be in their purposive forms (italicized in the following examples) (Crowley 1978: 88):

(33) BANDJALANG
a. dung 'cry': dung-*bi:ɲ*-**ma** 'cause to cry'
b. yan 'go': yan-*bi:ɲ*-**ma** 'cause to go'
c. bala:n 'die': bala:ɲ-*bin*-**ma** 'cause to die'

In light of the tendency for irregular verbs to be remnants of the old language system (see Crowley 1978: 99–101 for arguments for the irregular verbs as part of the older Bandjalang language; e.g. English irregular verbs, which are carried over from its old verb conjugation system), the fact that only irregular verbs have to combine the purposive suffix with the elements of [Vcause] and [Veffect] suggests that: (a) in its earlier history Bandjalang had a *PURP* type of causative construction; (b) the language has now lost the construction; and (c) part of the construction, that is, the element of *PURP*, is still visible in fossilized or petrified form with respect to the twelve causativized irregular verbs. In Bandjalang, the purposive suffix is trapped in the time capsule of the *PURP* type of causative construction.

Finally, it seems appropriate to end this 'diachronic journey' by going back to the question that evidently puzzled Wolfenden almost seven decades ago. It was noted in section 3.2 that he (1929: 139, 152) was not sure whether *-tsa-* in the Ao causative suffix *-dâk-tsa* was related to the directive element. Now, it can be seen that *-tsa* is indeed the directive element that was used to serve as the *PURP* marker, which has come to be reanalysed as part of the causative suffix proper.

It is possible that the term *PURP* be caught up in the amalgamation process of the elements of [Vcause] and [Veffect]. On the basis of the model of causative affixes, the evolutionary path of the 'irregular' kind of causative verb can be reconstructed with reasonable certainty: the reanalysis of the whole sequence of *PURP* and [Vcause] as a causative affix. The existence of languages exhibiting the development in Figure 3.3 is not only important in confirming the differential characteristics of the terms *PURP* and *AND* (so far, not a single language has been found where the term *AND* is trapped between the elements of [Vcause] and [Veffect]); it also has far more important implications for any synchronic theory of causative constructions. In 2.5, the existence of the *PURP* type of causative construction has been identified, whereby the need is set forth to recognize it as a genuine causative construction. The evidence from languages such as Bashkir, Songish, etc., further strengthens the view that the *PURP* type of causative is indeed a genuine causative construction, and should be recognized as such in any synchronic theory of causative constructions. If the ordinary purposive construction had not been exploited to express causation in these languages, there would be no other way to account for the obligatory presence of the term *PURP* in their morphological causative verbs.

3.5   Implicativity and reduction

In 2.6, it has been pointed out that the term *PURP* may become semantically neutralized to the effect that implicativity is 'restored' in the originally nonimplicative *PURP* causative, as is indeed the case with Latin (see 5.4 on how implicativity is restored via pragmatic inferencing). By making reference to the existence of nonimplicative *COMPACT* (or morphological) causatives, it has also been suggested that the formal reduction of [Scause] and [Seffect] may not necessarily be concomitant with the semantic neutralization of the term *PURP*. At least three languages with such a nonimplicative *COMPACT* type of causative construction are found in the sample; interestingly enough, all from the Austric phylum. Svantesson (1983: 106) reports that in Kammu (or Khmu) the causative sentence in (34.a) with the causative prefix *p-* does not imply the validity of the effect or caused event, whereas that in (34.b) certainly does so.

(34) KAMMU
a. kə̀ə p-ŋ̀mɔ́ɔŋ nàa
   he CP-sad she
   'He did something in order to make her sad.'
b. kə̀ə tòk   mɔ́ɔŋ nàa
   he cause sad she
   'He did something which made her sad.'

Svantesson (1983: 106) proves this by showing that it is (34.a), not (34.b), that can be followed by negation of the whole sentence or of the effect part of the proposition; in fact, (35.b) consists of (34.a) and the negated version of (34.b):[14]

(35) KAMMU
a. kə̀ə p-ŋ̀mɔ́ɔŋ nàa, nàa pə́ə mɔ́ɔŋ
   he CP-sad   she she not sad
   'He tried to make her sad, but she didn't become sad.'
b. kə̀ə p-ŋ̀mɔ́ɔŋ nàa, kə̀ə pə́ə tòk   mɔ́ɔŋ nàa
   he CP-sad   she he not cause sad she
   'He tried to make her sad, but did not manage to do so.'

In Malagasy, the causative prefixes *amp(a)-* and *an(a)-* are involved in the morphological amalgamation with the element of [Veffect] (Randriamasimanana 1986: 207). However, causatives with *an(a)-* are always nonimplicative (in Randriamasimanana's words, they lack 'entailment'). Those with *amp(a)-*, on the other hand, may or may not be implicative, depending on their semantic causative types (Randriamasimanana 1986: 75–85). Thus, the following sentences are fully grammatical:[15]

(36) MALAGASY
a. N-amp-andidy ny mofo an'i Jeanne i Paoly kanefa tsy
    PST-CP-cut   the bread   Jeanne Paul but   not
    nandidy izy
    PST-cut she
    'Paul was having Jeanne cut the bread but she did not.'
b. N-an-doka   ny varvarna i Paoly fa tsy
    PST-CP-with + hole the door   Paul but not
    n-aha-loka
    PST-CP-with + hole
    'Paul was making a hole in the door, but did not succeed.'

De Guzman (1978: 337–338) notes the same phenomenon in Tagalog: sentences built on causative verbs containing the causative prefix *pa-* do not imply the validity of the effect relation. Unfortunately, De Guzman provides no actual examples.[16]

Since the *PURP* type of causative (at least in its prototypical form) is inherently nonimplicative due to the term *PURP* (whereas the *AND* type is inherently implicative), it may be conjectured that in earlier histories of these languages the nonimplicative causative constructions in question may originally have been of the *PURP* type, despite the formidable formal reduction of *PURP* and [Veffect]. Indeed, the causative prefix in Tagalog *pa-* has been related to the term *PURP* in 3.4.1. Although it is not clear whether the causative prefixes in Malagasy and Kammu can also be related ultimately to the term *PURP*, the fact that their *COMPACT* causatives are still nonimplicative leaves room for suggesting that they may also have been derived historically from the *PURP* type of causative. Thus, even if there is no formal relationship between the causative affix and the term *PURP*, the absence of implicativity in a given *COMPACT*-type causative may point to its origin, i.e. the *PURP* type of causative construction, since nonimplicativity is the defining feature of the *PURP* type, but not of the *AND* type (also see 5.2). The strength of this claim is, of course, based totally on the strength of the universal typology of causative constructions and of the diachronic model of causative affixes.

3.6 Closing remarks

Needless to say, what has been claimed so far should be verified in each of the languages cited in this chapter (and in as many languages as possible in the future) on the basis of historical evidence, where and when available. It has been said repeatedly that what has been offered here is a general conceptual framework in which possible origins of causative affixes can be identified, and hitherto claimed origins of causative affixes can be reexamined. No claim is laid as to the actual histories of the languages that have been discussed in this chapter. The kind of diachronic model as put forth here should be most welcome to diachronic linguistics, since the majority of the world's languages lack sufficient historical data along the lines demanded by Lightfoot (1979), and since verification in each language of the world is evidently impossible. The diachronic model of causative affixes proposed here at least provides a falsifiable conceptual framework of language change and certainly forms a very strong foundation on which the universal typology of causative constructions can be rigorously tested, and at worst it sets the agenda for future diachronic research in individual languages.

Finally, it should be pointed out that the diachronic model developed in this chapter deals with various instantiations of the term *PURP* (and, at least theoretically, *AND*) used in lieu of or as causative affixes, be they in full or reduced form. In other words, the model indicates the direction of change from *PURP* (or *AND*) to causative affixes. It is not concerned with any extended direction of change: from causative affixes to noncausative markers. A case in point can be drawn from Bantu languages, in which causative affixes are further exploited to express instrumental meaning. In Kinyarwanda, the causative suffix *-iish-* is also used to mark instrumental case in the verbal complex (Kimenyi 1980a: 32–33, 164–172). Evidence that these suffixes are conceptually related to each other comes from the fact that the instrumental suffix undergoes the same allomorphic changes as the causative suffix (Kimenyi 1980a: 238). In Nkore-Kiga, the causative suffix *-sa* is also used to express instrumental role (Taylor 1985: 98–99). Compare:

(37) NKORE-KIGA
a. n-aa-mu-bo-orek[yes]a   amaino
     I-TOP-him-them-show-CS teeth
     'I made him show them his teeth.'
b. y-aa-gi-hindu[z]a   enkoni
     he-TOP-it-turn-INST stick
     'He turned it round with a stick.'

The semantic extension of the causative suffix to the instrumental case marker in the Bantu languages can be accounted for if it is assumed that the instrumental argument or NP (e.g. *stick* in (37.b)) is anthropomorphized as a human intermediary, just like a human causee argument: an instrument is regarded as an intermediary agent whom the causer uses to bring about her desired effect. The same phenomenon can also be observed in some Australian languages (Blake 1987a: 69): the causative affix is also used to encode the instrumental role. This kind of extension has nothing to do with causation *per se*. The diachronic model of causative affixes itself is not concerned with such a second order or subsequent extension of causative affixes.[17] It predicts that the sources of causative affixes are: [Vcause], *PURP*, and potentially *AND*.

Notes

1. Vennemann (1973: 21–22) suggests that the prerequisite for grammaticalization of lexical causative verbs into affixes is that the higher and lower verbs should be contiguous. Mallinson and Blake (1981: 423–424) refute Vennemann's suggestion, arguing that there is no such prerequisite: noncontiguous lexical causative verbs can be grammaticalized by gravitating to the lower verb. Heine and Reh (1984) provide ample evidence in African languages for Mallinson and Blake's position. Bybee (1985a: 39–41) also shares Mallinson and Blake's position: 'Morphology is not immovable fossilized syntax.'
2. It is not known whether this sentence has an additional meaning: *I cause her to grind corn.*
3. The present writer is operating here under the hypothesis of uniformitarianism: languages of the past are not different in nature from languages of the present (Croft 1990: 204). This is a very important assumption for constructing a diachronic model of causative affixes (or any diachronic model for that matter), since the primary intention of this chapter is to trace the origins of causative affixes.
4. One may point out that the use of 'formal reduction' here is largely inappropriate, because these terms are already morphologically bonded to the [Veffect] in the majority of the cases cited in Chapter 2. However, the use is far from inappropriate, because the parameter is inherently a continuous notion: derivational affixes such as causatives are morphophonologically more bonded to their hosts than such grammatical markers as case, tense, mood, etc. The terms *AND* and *PURP* are closer to these grammatical affixes than to derivational affixes. Therefore, it is completely appropriate to speak of formal reduction when the elements of *AND* and *PURP* are changing into derivational affixes,

despite the fact that they are already bonded to the element of [Veffect].
Cf. Bybee (1985a), who explores the continuum of fusion ranging from
lexical to syntactic and finds on the basis of crosslinguistic evidence
that derivational affixes are more tightly bonded to their hosts than
inflectional or grammatical affixes are. The term formal reduction
should be interpreted precisely in this sense.

5. One may argue that the term *AND* is not semantically loaded, because
it is more often realized as zero, and the term *PURP* is semantically
loaded, because it is hardly realized as zero. This is a potential chicken-
or-egg debate, because it can be argued that, for instance, the term *AND*
is often realized as zero, because it is not semantically loaded. This is
why the two reasons are regarded here as complementary.

6. Evidence that syntactic causative sentences in Korean like (10) are
nonimplicative comes from grammatical sentences such as the following:

(i) KOREAN
Kim ssi-ka   ai-tɨl-i   koŋpu-ha-ke   ha-əss-ɨna
Kim Mr-NOM child-PL-NOM study-do-PURP cause-PST-but
ai-tɨl-i   koŋpu-ha-ci=an-əss-ta
child-PL-NOM study-do-NEG-PST-IND
'*Mr Kim made his children study, but they did not.'

The ungrammatical English translation indicates that the causative
sentence in English is implicative.

7. However, unlike Thai, Ịọ does not seem to use the term *PURP* to mark
subordinate clauses of purpose, but rather it uses the term to mark the
directional arguments (or directional NPs), as will be illustrated below.
Whether Ịọ uses the *PURP* element to mark the subordinate clause of
purpose remains to be determined by further research.

8. Both Edith Bavin and Hilary Chappell point out that the causative with
the term [Vcause] and the one without it are specialized for different
semantic causative types, i.e. indirect vs direct. This kind of semantic
specialization is indeed well documented. as has been discussed briefly
in 1.1. It must be pointed out, however, that the optional omission of the
term [Vcause] must first be accounted for before explaining the
semantic specialization. In other words, the issue of the specialization
is a totally different matter from what is the focus of the present
investigation, i.e. the **types** of causative construction and the functional
take-over of [Vcause] by *PURP*.

9. In Relational Grammar, this is known as advancement.

10. Some of Driever's glosses have been changed in accordance with the
convention that was used for the earlier Swahili example in Chapter 2.

11. Stops in Australian languages have both voiced and voiceless allo-
phones (Dixon 1980: 137); voicing in stops is not phonemic.

12. Dixon (1977: 128) notes that Yidiny is unusual in that it has ergative
     -*ŋgu* and locative -*la*, when almost all Australian languages show
     virtually exact correspondence between locative and ergative forms, the
     only difference being that locative ends in -*a* and ergative in -*u*, and
     when the frequent pattern is:

	ergative	*locative*
onto vowel-final disyllabic stems	-ŋgu	-ŋga
onto vowel-final trisyllabic stems	-lu	-la

     Dixon further notes that in Yidiny there is no surface trace at all of
     locative -*ŋga*. However, it is possible that the seemingly extinct locative
     suffix -*ŋga* may have its trace in the locative/dative verbal marker -*ŋa-l*,
     which is also a causative suffix, although it has to be admitted that the
     locative NP governed by this marker should refer to only some
     language or speech style (Dixon 1977: 306). This observation on Yidiny
     is due to Barry Blake.

13. As shown earlier in 3.4.1, nominalizers may also be trapped between
     the elements of [Vcause] and [Veffect].

14. Incidentally, Kammu militates against Haiman's (1985a) hypothesis
     that conceptual fusion is iconically reflected by linguistic fusion. In
     Kammu, the conceptually more dependent causation (implicative) is
     expressed by the less linguistically fused causative construction, while
     the conceptually less dependent causation (nonimplicative) is expressed
     by the more linguistically fused causative construction.

15. One may suspect that the use of the progressive form of the verb in the
     English translations of the following Malagasy sentences represents
     imperfective aspect inherent in the original Malagasy (basic) verbs (e.g.
     Aktionsart), thus undermining the claim that nonimplicativity is
     inherent in the Malagasy causative itself. However, this is not the case.
     Randriamasimanana (personal communication) explains that he has
     used the progressive form of the verb in his English translations in order
     to reflect the absence of entailment or of implicativity in the causatives
     in question, not the Aktionsart of the Malagasy basic verb. Otherwise,
     the translations for (36.a) and (36.b) would be ungrammatical: **Paul
     had Jeanne cut the bread, but she did not* and **Paul made a hole in the
     door, but he did not succeed*, respectively. Further, Malagasy has
     separate aspect-cum-passive affixes, and the causative in (36) cannot
     contain such affixes, be they perfective or imperfective (Randriamasi-
     manana 1986: 34, 43, 44).

16. John Taylor (personal communication) points out that a similar
     situation is also observed in Zulu. The morphological causative formed
     with -*isa*- appears to be nonimplicative:

(i) ZULU
Nga-sebenz-isa   umuntu kodwa aka-sebenz-anga/
I + PST-work-CS man   but   he + NEG-work-PST
kodwa we-hluleka
but   he + PST-be + incapable
'I made the man work, but he didn't work/but he couldn't.'
He also believes that it may well be a quite general Bantu feature.

17. Further, the diachronic model of causative affixes is not concerned with the way a change in voicing or tone has assumed causative function from the original causative prefix *s- in Lahu, as has been exemplified in (7) and (8). It would instead be concerned with the way how the causative prefix *s- came into existence in the first place.

Chapter 4

Korean: a *PURP*-type language

4.1 Introduction

In the two previous chapters, both synchronic and diachronic evidence has been provided in support of the existence of the hitherto unrecognized type of causative construction, namely the *PURP* type. It has been demonstrated that the erstwhile complex purposive construction is exploited for causative function, and that, owing to its frequent association with causative function, it is 'metamorphosed' into a fully fledged causative construction. Further, the *PURP* marker may eventually take over causative function from the element of [Vcause], and become fused with the basic verb as a causative affix *par excellence*.

The functional shift from purposive to causative is usually accompanied by formal reduction of the main clause and the subordinate clause of purpose (but cf. 3.5). For this reason alone, a theory of clause linkage is highly desirable for the explicating of the relationship between the ordinary complex purposive construction and the *PURP* type of causative construction. That theory must also be syntactico-semantically based, because it is essential not only to 'measure' different degrees of clause linkage that the two constructions exhibit, but also to relate their different degrees of clause linkage directly to purposive and causative semantic relations. The theory should, for instance, be able to answer why, in general, causative function is mapped onto a construction that is more fused than purposive function is, not *vice versa*. The Clause Linkage Theory, part of Role and Reference Grammar (hereafter RRG) (Olson 1981, Foley and Van Valin 1984, Van Valin 1993b; cf. Lehmann 1988) is one such theory. RRG offers a very sophisticated diagnostic system which can not only determine the degree of bondedness between clauses but also relate clause linkage to various interclausal semantic relations, or *vice versa* (cf. Klaiman 1986, Song 1994).

In this chapter, Korean, a *PURP*-type language, will be examined in great detail by drawing on the Clause Linkage Theory. In 3.3, this language is described as being in the first stage of the evolutionary path from purposive markers to causative affixes. That is to say, in Korean the *PURP* type of causative construction is still in the process of evolving from the complex purposive construction. The present discussion will provide a very useful and enlightening analysis of the kind of grammatical change that may occur in the process of the ordinary purposive construction being exploited for causative function. Further, certain problems which the Korean data pose for the Clause Linkage Theory will be addressed, whereby the need is set forth to incorporate diachronic aspects into any grammatical theory including RRG (cf. Bybee 1988).

4.2 *PURP* causative and purposive constructions

Korean has lexical, morphological (both of the *COMPACT* type) and syntactic (the *PURP* type) causatives (for more detail, see Song 1988d, 1993). The lexical causative type involves suppletion, as illustrated in (1).

(1) *COMPACT* Type (Lexical Causative)
   a.   kiho-ka   ka-əss-ta
          Keeho-NOM go-PST-IND
          'Keeho went.'
   b.   əməni-ka   kiho-lɨl   ponɛ-əss-ta
          mother-NOM Keeho-ACC send-PST-IND
          'The mother sent Keeho.'

There is no formal similarity between the basic verb and the causative one. There are only few such lexical causative verbs in Korean.

The morphological causative type involves a process in which causative verbs are derived from noncausative ones by adding the causative suffix *-I-*, which may be realized as *-i-*, *-hi-*, *-li-*, *-ki-*, *-ku-*, *-cu-*, or *-wu-*. This type can be exemplified by the pair of sentences in (2), in which the causative verb *wus-I-* is morphologically related to the basic verb *wus-*.

(2) *COMPACT* Type (Morphological Causative)
a. cini-ka   wus-əss-ta
    Jinee-NOM smile-PST-IND
    'Jinee laughed.'
b. kiho-ka   cini-lɨl   wus-I-əss-ta
    Keeho-NOM Jinee-ACC smile-CS-PST-IND
    'Keeho caused Jinee to smile.'

The derivational process is not very productive, being confined to a handful of verbs.[1]
The syntactic or *PURP*-type causative, which is extremely productive, involves a higher verb *ha-*, literally meaning 'do' and an 'embedded' clause clearly marked by the so-called 'complementizer' *-ke*:

(3) *PURP* Type (Syntactic Causative)
    kiho-ka   cini-eke   kwail cɨp-ɨl   masi-ke
    Keeho-NOM Jinee-DAT fruit juice-ACC drink-PURP
    ha-əss-ta
    do-PST-IND
    'Keeho caused Jinee to drink the fruit juice.'

The complementizer *-ke* also appears as a marker of the subordinate clause in the ordinary purposive construction (e.g. Sohn 1973, Patterson 1974):

(4) kiho-ka   cini-ka   pathi-e   o-ke   kɨnyə-ɨi
    Keeho-NOM Jinee-NOM party-LOC come-PURP she-GEN
    cip-e   cənhwa-lɨl   kəl-əss-ta
    home-LOC phone-ACC dial-PST-IND
    'Keeho called Jinee at home so that she could come to the party.'

This interesting fact has never received any serious attention at all (cf. Langacker's position cited in 1.4). Typically, the complementizer is regarded as 'semantically void' (e.g. Kang 1986). Note that the causee NP marked by dative *-eke* in (3) can also appear as the subject NP of the 'embedded' clause (i.e. marked by nominative *-ka*), as in (5), on the analogy of (4), although it is less preferable to (3) (see 4.5).

(5) kiho-ka cini-ka kwail cɨp-ɨl
  Keeho-NOM Jinee-NOM fruit juice-ACC
  masi-ke(-lɨl) ha-əss-ta
  drink-PURP (-ACC) do-PST-IND
  'Keeho caused Jinee to drink the fruit juice.'

In common with Aissen (1979), (5) will be called the 'complement causative' construction. The syntactic difference between (3) and (5) is that the complement clause in (5) can optionally be marked by accusative *-lɨl*. In other words, the whole complement clause is a logical argument of the higher verb *ha-* in (5). The same does not, however, apply to the purposive construction in (4), in which the subordinate clause of purpose functions as an adverbial adjunct in relation to the main verb or clause. This explains why (6), which is (3) with the 'embedded' clause (or (5) with the complement clause) omitted, is ungrammatical, and why (7), which is (4) with the subordinate clause of purpose omitted, is fully grammatical:

(6) *kiho-ka ha-əss-ta[2]
  Keeho-NOM do-PST-IND

(7) kiho-ka kɨnyə-ii cip-e cənhwa-lɨl
  Keeho-NOM she-GEN home-LOC phone-ACC
  kəl-əss-ta
  dial-PST-IND
  'Keeho called her at home.'

The causee NP in (3) can also be marked by accusative *-lɨl* as in (8):

(8) kiho-ka cini-lɨl kwail cɨp-ɨl masi-ke
  Keeho-NOM Jinee-ACC fruit juice-ACC drink-PURP
  ha-əss-ta
  do-PST-IND
  'Keeho caused Jinee to drink the fruit juice.'

On the other hand, the subject NP of the subordinate clause of purpose in (4) cannot appear in either accusative or dative. It must only be marked by nominative.

(9) *kiho-ka cini-lɨl/eke pathi-e o-ke
  Keeho-NOM Jinee-ACC/DAT party-LOC come-PURP
  kɨnyə-ii cip-e cənhwa-lɨl kəl-əss-ta
  she-GEN home-LOC phone-ACC dial-PST-IND

'Keeho called Jinee at home so that she could come to the party.'

Despite the foregoing differences between the *PURP*-type causative construction and the purposive construction, there are a few reasons to believe that there is a strong affinity between them. First, the same form, -*ke*, appears in both constructions, although it is an obvious point. In the *PURP*-type causative, it is the *PURP* marker, whereas in the purposive construction it marks the subordinate clause as purposive. As has been demonstrated in Chapter 2, the purposive marker is crosslinguistically used as an element of *PURP* in the *PURP* type of causative construction. Clearly, the form -*ke* in (3) or (5) is not a semantically void complementizer. Secondly, if a separate NP is inserted between the lower and higher verbs in the *PURP*-type causative, and if the causee NP is marked by nominative, the construction is no longer interpreted as a causative, but it must instead be understood as a noncausative sentence with a subordinate clause of purpose. Compare (10) with (5) for this change of interpretation:

(10) kiho-ka   cini-ka   kwail cip-il   masi-ke
     Keeho-NOM Jinee-NOM fruit juice-ACC drink-PURP
     kəcismal-il ha-əss-ta
     lie-ACC   do-PST-IND
     'Keeho told a lie so that Jinee would drink the fruit juice.'

Thirdly, the *PURP* causative, as in (3), can potentially be interpreted in a noncausative way, that is, with the effect that no causation on the part of the subject NP of the main clause is involved. Thus, it may be understood in such a way as mere directing, advising, etc., is performed by the subject NP of the main clause. To put it differently, the 'embedded' clause is interpreted as being that of purpose. Hence, the alternative interpretation of (3) may be: *Keeho did (something) so that Jinee could drink the fruit juice.* As evidence for this, it can be pointed out that the *PURP* causative in Korean does not necessarily imply the truth of the complement clause, that is, nonimplicative in the sense of Kartunnen (1971a) and Givón (1980) (see Patterson 1974: 17, and Haiman 1985a: 140–142). Therefore, the reason why (11) below is not regarded as anomalous is that its first conjunct is interpreted as containing a purposive clause, rather than as constituting a fully implicative causative sentence. This suggests that the *PURP* causative construction in Korean has not yet become fully implicative:

(11) kɨ-ka   na-lɨl/eke   kimchi-lɨl   mək-ke   ha-əss-ɨna
he-NOM I-ACC/DAT pickle-ACC eat-PURP do-PST-but
nɛ-ka (kimchi-lɨl)   ani   mək-əss-ta
I-NOM (pickle-ACC) NEG eat-PST-IND
'He told me to eat pickled cabbage, but I did not eat it.'

Note that the causee NP in (11) is not marked by nominative as in
(10), since in (11) no explicit NP is inserted before the main verb *ha*-
to specify the type of action that the subject NP of the main clause
performed.

4.3 The Clause Linkage Theory

As a preliminary to the RRG account of the *PURP* causative and
purposive constructions, the Clause Linkage Theory of Olson (1981),
Foley and Van Valin (1984), and Van Valin (1993b) will be briefly
outlined here.[3] In this theory, a clause is conceived of as a layered
structure of grammatical units, smaller units within larger ones. The
layers of grammatical units can be diagrammatically represented as
in Figure 4.1. The nucleus consists of the verb or predicate of the
clause, being the innermost layer of the clause. The core consists of
one or two arguments, depending on the valence of the verb. The
outermost layer, the periphery, consists of setting NPs and secondary
participants, e.g. beneficiary. In contrast to arguments/NPs, which
are constituents of the layers, there is a set of operators which have
the corresponding layer under their scopes. The operators that have
their scopes over the nucleus are generally aspect as well as
directionals that express a directional orientation of the nucleus.[4] The
operators that have their scopes over the core layer are called
modality by Foley and Van Valin (1984: 214), as modality 'character-
izes the speaker's estimate of the relationship of the actor of the event
to its accomplishment, whether he has the obligation, the intention,
or the ability to perform it'. Operators pertaining to the periphery
layer are status, tense, evidentials, and illocutionary force.

Various constructions are built up by means of what Foley and Van
Valin call junctures, the joining of elements from different clauses at
the three layers. That is, a nuclear juncture is a construction with a
complex nucleus. A core-level juncture results from the joining of
two cores, each with its own nucleus and core arguments, although
it involves sharing of core arguments. Finally, clausal junctures

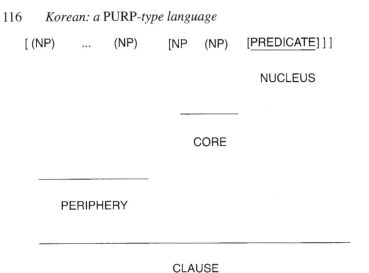

[(NP)   ...   (NP)   [NP   (NP)   [PREDICATE]]]

NUCLEUS

CORE

PERIPHERY

CLAUSE

Figure 4.1

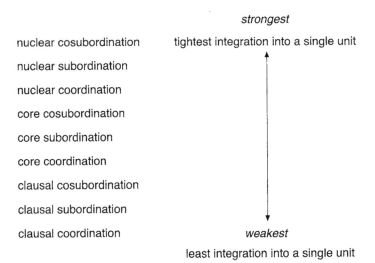

                                    strongest
nuclear cosubordination   tightest integration into a single unit

nuclear subordination

nuclear coordination

core cosubordination

core subordination

core coordination

clausal cosubordination

clausal subordination

clausal coordination   *weakest*
                            least integration into a single unit

Figure 4.2

(previously known as peripheral junctures in Foley and Van Valin 1984) arise from the joining of two clauses with independent peripheries. Any individual member of each juncture is called a junct. It is to be noted that differences within the juncts are permitted at the level of juncture and below, but everything above it must be shared by both juncts. For instance, if a given juncture is at the core level, the juncts must share the same periphery, i.e. the same peripheral arguments and the same peripheral operators, but they do have different nuclear operators as well as different nuclei.

In Foley and Van Valin's theory of clause linkage, dependence and embeddedness are not equivalent to each other.[5] Using these two parameters, three different types of syntactic linkage are

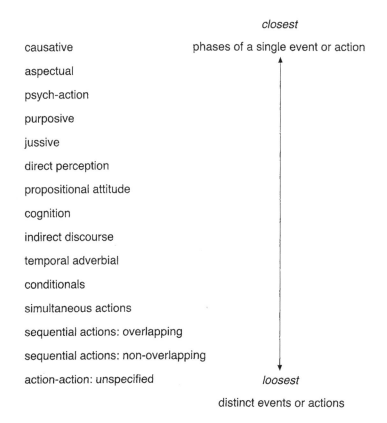

closest

| causative | phases of a single event or action |

aspectual

psych-action

purposive

jussive

direct perception

propositional attitude

cognition

indirect discourse

temporal adverbial

conditionals

simultaneous actions

sequential actions: overlapping

sequential actions: non-overlapping

action-action: unspecified   *loosest*

distinct events or actions

Figure 4.3

recognized: (a) coordination; (b) subordination; and (c) cosubordination. Coordination is characterized as [–embedded] and [–dependent], subordination as [+embedded] and [+dependent], and cosubordination as [–embedded] and [+dependent].

Based on these premises, Foley and Van Valin develop their clause linkage theory, as follows. The levels of the clause are distinguished in terms of sententiality: PERIPHERY > CORE > NUCLEUS. The nexus types are also ordered in terms of independence and scope of the pertinent operators on the three levels of the clause: COORDINATE > SUBORDINATE > COSUBORDINATE. Then, the Syntactic Bondedness Hierarchy (SBH) is proposed in the form of Figure 4.2. Corresponding to the SBH, the Interclausal Semantic Relations Hierarchy (ISRH), which expresses the degree of semantic

strongest	*closest*
nuclear cosubordination	causative
nuclear subordination	aspectual
nuclear coordination	psych-action
core cosubordination	purposive
core subordination	jussive
core coordination	direct perception
clausal cosubordination	propositional attitude
clausal subordination	cognition
clausal coordination	indirect discourse
weakest	temporal adverbial
	conditionals
	simultaneous actions
	sequential actions: overlapping
	sequential actions: non-overlapping
	action-action: unspecified
	loosest

Figure 4.4

cohesion between the propositional units linked in the complex syntactic structure, is proposed (see Figure 4.3).[6] The SBH and ISRH are then combined into the Interclausal Relations Hierarchy (IRH) in the form illustrated in Figure 4.4. Foley and Van Valin point out that there is no one-to-one correspondence between syntactic and semantic relations. For instance, they (1984: 271) claim:

> ... if a language has only core and [clausal] junctures, causative, [aspectual] and psych-action relations will be realized in the most tightly linked core junctures the language has.

Naturally, this specific claim will be tested in light of the discussion that follows.

4.4 Clause linkage in *PURP* causative and purposive constructions

First, neither the *PURP* causative construction nor the purposive construction is a nuclear juncture, since the contiguity of the lower and higher verbs is not watertight. A negative particle can intervene between the two verbs in the *PURP* causative construction.

(12) əməni-ka   ai-eke   yak-ɨl   mək-ke   ani
     mother-NOM child-DAT medicine-ACC eat-PURP NEG
     ha-əss-ta
     do-PST-IND
     'The mother did not cause the child to take the medicine.'

As for the purposive construction, elements including a negative particle can come between the lower and higher verbs, as has already been illustrated in (4). The negative particle is expected to have its scope only over the main clause in (12), not over either the lower clause alone or the lower clause and the main clause together. A similar comment applies to the purposive construction. Further, the *PURP* causative construction allows a separate aspect marker each for the verbs, thus having one of the aspect markers stranded between the two verbs, as in (13).

(13) əməni-ka   ai-eke   yak-ɨl
     mother-NOM child-DAT medicine-ACC
     mək-ko-iss-ke   ha-ko-iss-ta
     eat-COMP-DUR-PURP   do-COMP-DUR-IND

'The mother is causing the child to be taking the medicine.'

Again, the same can be said of the purposive construction. Clearly, the *PURP* causative construction and the purposive construction are not instances of a nuclear juncture, wherein two (or more in some languages) verbs form a single nucleus.

In fact, nuclear juncture constructions in Korean do not allow anything between the two composite verbs. In (14), nothing except for the phonological filler -ə-, which has no syntactic or semantic significance, can appear between *pulɨ-* and *cu-*.

(14) a. əməni-ka   atɨl-eke   cacaŋka-lɨl
       mother-NOM son-DAT lullaby-ACC
       pulɨ-ə-cu-əss-ta
       sing-PF-give-PST-IND
       'The mother sang a lullaby for the son.'
    b. *əməni-ka   atɨl-eke   cacaŋka-lɨl
       mother-NOM son-DAT lullaby-ACC
       pulɨ-ə-ani-cu-əss-ta
       sing-PF-NEG-give-PST-IND
       'The mother did not sing a lullaby for the son.'

The negative particle should thus precede the whole composite nucleus:

(15) əməni-ka   atɨl-eke   cacaŋka-lɨl ani
     mother-NOM son-DAT lullaby-ACC NEG
     pulɨ-ə-cu-əss-ta
     sing-PF-give-PST-IND
     'The mother did not sing a lullaby for the son.'

Further, the aspect marker *iss-* can appear only after the verb *cu-* and before the tense marker, thus maintaining the contiguity of the two verbs. Note that the aspect marker has its scope over the whole complex nucleus. The verb *pulɨ-* is dependent on the verb *cu-* for aspect marking, indicating that (14.a) is not a coordination. The nuclear juncture construction in (14.a) has the function of what Foley and Van Valin (1984: 197–208) call a 'valence increaser'. In Korean, the verb *pulɨ-* sanctions only two arguments. So, the secondary participant or the beneficiary argument is introduced via the nuclear juncture. The verb *pulɨ-* is not an argument of the verb *cu-* (indicating that the juncture is not a subordination). The three NPs *əməni, atɨl,* and *cacaŋka* are arguments sanctioned by the complex nucleus.

Example (14.a), then, is a case of nuclear cosubordination, i.e. [–embedded] and [+dependent].

Traditionally, both the 'embedded' clause of the *PURP* causative construction and the adjunct clause of the purposive construction are regarded as subordinate. In terms of the Clause Linkage Theory, then, they will both be instances of clausal subordination. It is claimed here, however, that while the purposive construction is indeed a case of clausal subordination, the *PURP* causative construction is a case of core coordination.

As a model *PURP* causative sentence, consider:

(16) əməni-ka   atɨl-eke/-ɨl   nol-ke   ha-əss-ta
     mother-NOM son-DAT/ACC play-PURP do-PST-IND
     'The mother caused the son to play.'

It is obvious that the causee NP *atɨl* is a logical core argument of the lower verb, that is, the actor of *nol-*. There is also evidence that the same NP is a core argument of the higher verb *ha-* as well. It can appear as the subject NP when (16) is turned into a passive.

(17) atɨl-i   əməni-eke   nol-ke   ha-yə-ci-əss-ta
     son-NOM mother-DAT play-PURP do-PF-PASS-PST-IND
     'The son was caused to play by the mother.'

This shows that the causee NP serves as the undergoer or a core argument of the higher verb. Both juncts, then, share a core argument in (16), which is therefore a core juncture.

Further, the clefting of (16) suggests strongly that the *PURP* causative does not involve an embedded clause.

(18) əməni-ka   nol-ke   ha-əss-tɨn   salam-ɨn
     mother-NOM play-PURP do-PST-REL person-TOP
     atɨl i-ta
     son is-IND
     'It is the son whom the mother caused to play.'

Note that in Korean clefting involves a general head NP like *salam* 'person' or *kəs* 'thing'. On the other hand, if the 'embedded' clause as a whole is clefted, the following ungrammatical sentence occurs.

(19) *əməni-ka   ha-əss-tɨn   kəs-ɨn   atɨl-eke/-ɨl
      mother-NOM do-PST-REL thing-TOP son-DAT/-ACC
      nol-ke   i-ta
      play-PURP is-IND

'*It is the son to play that the mother caused.'

This suggests that *atɨl-eke/-ɨl*, not *atɨl-eke/-ɨl nol-ke*, is a syntactic argument of the verb *ha-*. To put it differently, *atɨl-eke/-ɨl nol-ke* is not a single constituent (cf. Foley and Van Valin 1984: 247 for an analogous phenomenon in English). The foregoing two pieces of evidence lead to the conclusion that (16) is an instance of core-level juncture. Now, compare the *PURP* causative with the complement causative (in Aissen's sense), which also exhibits a core-level juncture (see 4.5 for justification). In Korean, object NPs can be fronted for pragmatic reasons.

(20) a. əməni-ka   atɨl-ɨl   cha-əss-ta
         mother-NOM son-ACC kick-PST-IND
         'The mother kicked the son.'
     b. atɨl-ɨl   əməni-ka   cha-əss-ta
         son-ACC mother-NOM kick-PST-IND
         'same as (20.a).'

The causee NP in (16) can also be fronted:

(21) atɨl-eke/-ɨl   əməni-ka   nol-ke   ha-əss-ta
     son-DAT/ACC mother-NOM play-PURP do-PST-IND
     'The mother caused the son to play.'

If the causee NP were marked by nominative *-ka*, that is, if (16) were a complement causative, the fronting of the causee NP would be impossible as in any other case of core-level subordination.

(22) a. *atɨl-i   əməni-ka   nol-ke   ha-əss-ta
         son-NOM mother-NOM play-PURP do-PST-IND
         'The mother caused the son to play.'
     b. !əməni-ka   apəci-ka   alɨmtap-ta-ko
         mother-NOM father-NOM pretty-IND-COMP
         sɛŋkak-ha-n-ta
         think-do-PRES-IND
         'The father thinks that the mother is pretty.'

Example (22.a) is only grammatical in the sense of *The son caused it that the mother played.* In (22.b), even this kind of possibility is ruled out because of the selectional restriction on *alɨmtap-*, which is not applicable to male humans. This difference between the *PURP* causative and complement causative constructions, both of which are core junctures, leads to the nexus type of (16). For that, the distribution of core-level operators must be examined.

Foley and Van Valin consider modality to be such an operator, and Foley and Olson (1985) list manner adverbials as core operators since they describe the manner in which an actor performs an action. In (16), each verb can be separately modified by modality auxiliary verbs. To put it in another way, an auxiliary verb that immediately follows the higher verb *ha-* does not have its scope over the whole sentence.

(23) a. əməni-ka   atɨl-eke/-ɨl   nol-ke   ha-lsuiss-ta
       mother-NOM son-DAT/-ACC play-PURP do-able-IND
       'The mother can cause the son to play.'
    b. əməni-ka   atɨl-eke/-ɨl   nol-suəp-ke
       mother-NOM son-DAT/-ACC play-unable-PURP
       ha-lsuiss-ta
       do-able-IND
       'The mother can cause the son to be unable to play.'

In Korean, the auxiliary verbs can only have deontic meaning, not epistemic, unlike English modals *can* or *must*, which may have both meanings. Example (23.a) shows that the sentence is only concerned with the mother's ability, not the son's. Example (23.b) further confirms that this is indeed the case. If the modal auxiliary verb in (23.a) has its scope over the whole sentence, (23.b) should be ungrammatical, since the lower verb has a contradictory modal auxiliary verb. This indicates that the nexus type of the *PURP* causative construction is coordination, not cosubordination. Note that in determining the juncture level of (16), the possibility of subordination is precluded, because the clefting evidence earlier showed that *atɨl-eke/-ɨl nol-ke* 'the son to play' is not embedded under the higher verb *ha-*. The example in (16) does not have a subordinate nexus contra both traditional and transformational grammarians.

The evidence for coordination in the *PURP* causative construction is further corroborated by the fact that manner adverbials like *cosimsiləpke* 'carefully' can never modify the actors and the verbs of both higher and lower clauses in (16) at the same time. For that to be possible, the same adverbial must be used for each verb:

(24) a. əməni-ka   cosimsɨləpke atɨl-eke/-ɨl   nol-ke
         mother-NOM carefully   son-DAT/-ACC play-PURP
         ha-əss-ta
         do-PST-IND
         'The mother carefully caused the son to play.'
     b. əməni-ka   cosimsɨləpke atɨl-eke/-ɨl
         mother-NOM carefully   son-DAT/-ACC
         cosimsɨləpke nol-ke   ha-əss-ta
         carefully   play-PURP do-PST-IND
         'The mother carefully caused the son to play carefully.'

In (24.a), the adverbial has its scope over either the higher clause or
the lower clause, but never over the whole sentence. Example (24.b)
clearly vindicates that this is indeed the case: a separate adverbial is
used to modify the manner of each of the actors. It is, therefore,
concluded that the *PURP* causative construction is a core-level
coordination.

Now as for the purposive construction, consider the following
model sentence:

(25) əməni-ka   atɨl-i   nol-ke   nolɛ-lɨl
     mother-NOM son-NOM play-PURP song-ACC
     ha-əss-ta
     do-PST-IND
     'The mother sang a song so that the son could play.'

The sentence in (25) clearly contains a purposive clause, since an NP
nolɛ-lɨl 'a song' occurs between the lower and higher verbs. It is
obvious that the purposive clause is subordinate as it constitutes an
outer peripheral argument (outer, since it does not appear in the
logical structure of the verb *ha-*; cf. Foley and Van Valin 1984: 81–95
for the distinction between inner and outer peripheries). Being an
outer peripheral argument subordinate to the verb *ha-*, its deletion
does not render (25) ungrammatical (cf. (7)):

(26) əməni-ka   nolɛ-lɨl   ha-əss-ta
     mother-NOM song-ACC do-PST-IND
     'The mother sang a song.'

The predicate of the purposive clause in (25) indeed chooses its own
outer peripheral arguments independently of the higher predicate:

(27) əməni-ka   atɨl-i   paŋ-esə   nol-ke
mother-NOM son-NOM room-LOC play-PURP
cəŋwən-esə nolɛ-lɨl   ha-əss-ta
garden-LOC song-ACC do-PST-IND
'The mother sang a song in the garden so that the son could play in the room.'

This indicates that (25) exhibits the nexus type of subordination, whereby the other two nexus types, i.e. coordination and cosubordination, are ruled out. And the nexus is at the clausal level. The purposive construction, then, is an instance of clausal subordination.

4.5   Problems for the Clause Linkage Theory

In terms of the ISRH in Figure 4.3, the purposive construction will rank as purposive, much lower than the causative, or the *PURP* causative construction in the present case. This difference in ranking between the two constructions is not unnatural in semantic and pragmatic terms. First, in the situation expressed by the purposive construction, there is never a logically necessary connection between the action denoted by the higher verb and that denoted by the lower verb. This is indeed syntactically reflected by the optionality of the purpose clause, as in (26). In other words, the action denoted by the lower verb is not logically dependent on the action denoted by the higher verb. Thus, in (25), the playing of the son may or may not happen independently of the singing of the mother. On the other hand, in a (successful) causative situation the playing of the son is dependent totally on the causing act of the mother: the playing of the son could not have happened but for the causing act of the mother. To put it simply, there may be a cause and effect relation in (16), unlike in (25).

Furthermore, though closely related to the above argument, it is the *PURP* causative construction, not the purposive construction, that may be interpreted as implicative. So, (16) may imply the truth of (28), whereas (25) does not:

(28) atɨl-i   nol-ass-ta
son-NOM play-PST-IND
'The son played.'

Givón (1980) explains implicativity in terms of binding, independence, and success. When these parameters are applied to the two constructions in question, it is indeed the *PURP* causative construction that comes out as a conceptually tighter relation. For instance, the causee NP in (16) has less independence than the subject NP of the subordinate clause of purpose in (25).

Further, the *PURP* causative construction is a core-level coordination, whereas the purposive construction is a clausal subordination. According to the SBH in Figure 4.2, core coordination is of a stronger linkage than clausal subordination. Thus, the correlation between form and function in these two Korean constructions is correctly accounted for by the IRH in Figure 4.4. To put it differently, the correlation in question constitutes a case of diagrammatic iconicity (Haiman 1985a: 9–18). The semantic cohesion (or conceptual distance in Haiman 1985a or relevance in Bybee 1985a, 1988) is iconically manifested by the corresponding syntactic bondedness.[7]

So far, Foley and Van Valin's Clause Linkage Theory fares well. However, there seem to be two problems in Korean causatives that militate against the IRH. First, why is causation, which is the strongest relation on the ISRH in Figure 4.3, not expressed by the strongest syntactically bonded juncture-nexus type available in Korean, or nuclear cosubordination, as in (14.a)?

> (14) a. əməni-ka   atɨl-eke cacaŋka-lɨl
>   mother-NOM son-DAT lullaby-ACC
>   puli-ə-cu-əss-ta
>   sing-PF-give-PST-IND
>   'The mother sang a lullaby for the son.'

Instead, causation is expressed by a much weaker juncture-nexus type, namely core coordination. To quote Foley and Van Valin (1984: 271–272) *in toto*:

> Thus, for example, if a language has only core and [clausal] junctures, causative, [aspectual] and psych-action relations will be realized in the **most** tightly linked core-junctures the language has.... This claim also does not preclude the possibility documented above, that a particular semantic relation may have more than one syntactic manifestation.... If, for example, causation can be expressed more than one way in a language, one of those ways must be in the **most** tightly linked construction found in the language [emphasis added].

Since the verb in a morphological causative (and that in a lexical causative for that matter) is a single nucleus, the morphological causative is not relevant to the Clause Linkage Theory (Foley and Van Valin 1984: 104). In other words, the morphological causative type cannot be one of the 'syntactic manifestations' that causative relation may have. But what if the complement causative construction, in the sense of Aissen (1974a, 1979), is the alternative way to express causation?

The fact that the whole complement can optionally be marked by accusative *-lɨl* in the complement causative construction is itself strong evidence that the complement clause is indeed a core argument of (or embedded under) the higher verb *ha-* (cf. (5)). Hence, the accusative marker can appear right after *-ke*. Compare (29.a) and (29.b):

(29) a. əməni-ka   atɨl-i   nol-ke   ha-əss-ta
        mother-NOM son-NOM play-PURP do-PST-IND
        'The mother caused her son to play.'
     b. əməni-ka   atɨl-i   nol-ke-lɨl   ha-əss-ta
        mother-NOM son-NOM play-PURP-ACC do-PST-IND
        'The mother caused her son to play.'

Further evidence that the complement is embedded under the higher verb comes from the fact that only complement causatives exemplified in (29) can be used as an answer to the following question:

(30) muəs-ɨl   əməni-ka   ha-əss-nɨnya
     what-ACC mother-NOM do-PST-Q
     'What did the mother do?'

Note that in (30) the argument questioned is a core argument of the verb *ha-*. The *PURP* causative construction cannot be used as an answer to (30). Instead, the *PURP* causative is appropriate for questions of the kind in (31).

(31) nuku-eke/-lɨl   əməni-ka   nol-ke   ha-əss-nɨnya
     who-DAT/-ACC mother-NOM play-PURP do-PST-Q
     'Whom did the mother cause to play?'

Clearly, the complement causative constitutes an instance of subordination, having an entire full clause as a core argument – in fact, a periphery embedded in a core. Indeed, the complement causative construction comprises an instance of core subordination, a far more weakly linked juncture-nexus type than the nuclear cosubordination

in (14.a). Thus, the question posed earlier remains unanswered: why
is causation not expressed by the strongest syntactically bonded
juncture-nexus type available in Korean?

The three constructions that have so far been examined are listed
below with their juncture-nexus types identified.

(32) *CONSTRUCTIONS*   *JUNCTURE-NEXUS TYPES*
    a. *PURP* causative   ⟺   core coordination
    b. complement causative   ⟺   core subordination
    c. purposive   ⟺   clausal subordination

In terms of the SBH in Figure 4.2, it is the complement causative
construction that is the most tightly linked of all the three. The *PURP*
causative is the second most tightly linked. As expected, the
purposive construction is the least tightly linked of the three. There
are, however, two things that compel one to question the status of the
complement causative construction in terms of the IRH in Figure 4.4.
First, many Korean speakers, including the present writer, tend not
to use the complement causative to express causation. Rather, they
use it to express actions with purposes. Secondly, if they ever use it
to express causation (e.g. at a linguist's urging), many report that it
does not imply the truth of the complement. An informal survey has
been carried out with sixteen Koreans to test the initial suspicion. A
total of 87.5 per cent of the subjects claimed that the *PURP* causative
construction is implicative. Only 50 per cent of the subjects indicated
that the complement causative is implicative. This leads to the second
problem for the Clause Linkage Theory: why do speakers choose the
PURP causative over the complement causative to express causative
relation, when, according to the IRH, it is the latter that exhibits the
tighter syntactic linkage of the two? Bear in mind that the result of
50 per cent obtained with the complement causative must be
evaluated in light of the fact that almost all the informants tend not
to use it to express causation. It seems that the complement causative
has begun to fall out of use in Korean. Instead, a less tightly linked
construction or the *PURP* causative is now favoured as far as the
expression of causation is concerned. Is it the case, then, that the IRH
fails to make correct predictions for Korean? The two problems
raised in this section for the Clause Linkage Theory thus boil down
to: why is causation, the strongest semantic relation, not realized
etically by the most tightly linked construction in Korean?

4.6   A diachronic solution to the problems

The problems that have just been addressed can be neutralized if it is assumed that language practises therapy, not prophylaxis (cf. Lightfoot 1979: 123–124). Language change proceeds without consideration of all the possible effects that it may inadvertently have on the language system as a whole.

The *PURP* causative is evolving from the purposive construction in Korean. And given the fact that the complement causative is intermediate between the *PURP* causative and purposive constructions, the following diachronic evolution can be suggested:

(33) purposive → complement causative → PURP causative

The way that the complement causative initially developed from the purposive construction seems to be like this: Korean started to press the purposive construction into service to express causation, presumably as a more productive way of expressing causation, since the morphological causative type became lexically restricted or nonproductive for various reasons (see Bybee 1985a, and Chapter 6). The purposive construction thus carried a dual function, causation and action with a purpose. The dual function of the purposive construction must, however, have had serious implications for language use. That is, in order to disambiguate the causative use of the purposive construction from its original purposive use, Korean seems to have tightened the syntactic linkage of the higher and lower clauses (cf. similar formal reduction in the numerous languages surveyed in Chapter 2). Hence, the favourite use of the *PURP* causative over the complement causative. Note that it is not for the purposive function, but for the causative function that the tighter syntactic linkage has taken place. Causative relation is a much stronger semantic relation than purposive relation.

Korean reflects the tighter clause linkage by turning the purposive construction into what Silverstein (1976a, 1980, 1993) calls a 'normal form', by which reduction of the full panoply of case markers is meant. The more tightly linked the dependent clause is to the adjacent clause, the more case marking possibilities in it are curtailed (also Foley and Van Valin 1984: 278, Givón 1990: 537–555). In the complement causative, which is the direct descendant of the purposive construction, there is still a full panoply of case markers permitted, since the causee NP is marked by nominative case (and other argument NPs in appropriate cases). Compared to this, the *PURP* causative cannot have the causee NP marked by the nominative marker. In fact, in the *PURP* causative, it is either the accusative or the dative case marker that appears on the causee NP: Korean has effectively reduced the case marking possibilities in the dependent clause via 'normalization'. This state of affairs plays havoc with Foley and Van Valin's Clause Linkage Theory, as has been demonstrated in the previous section.

If it is assumed, however, that the therapy with regard to the *PURP* causative has not been completed, this unfortunate situation may turn out to be only transitional. Recall that Korean has already the most tightly linked juncture-nexus type, i.e. nuclear cosubordination, as exemplified in (14.a), and that the presence of this particular type in Korean is also problematic for the Clause Linkage Theory, since it is not used for causative relation at all. It is suggested here that the 'drift' of the *PURP* causative has not arrived at its final destination. That is to say, the *PURP* causative may undergo further development to 'iron out' the unfortunate hitch that has happened in the process of the change. As Korean is an SOV language, the amalgamation of the causative verb *ha-* and the lower verb in the *PURP* causative is a very distinct possibility, as is clearly evident in nuclear cosubordination. This will be possible if the purposive morpheme *-ke* becomes semantically neutralized or bleached, as in fact has happened in the case of Latin, or as is indeed crosslinguistically quite common (see 2.6; also Stassen 1985: 72). Once that happens, the morpheme *-ke* will function as no more than the phonological filler that occurs between the two predicates or verbs in the nuclear juncture. Then, the *PURP* causative construction will effectively comprise an instance of the *COMPACT* type of causative, in which the terms [Vcause] and [Veffect] are adjacent to each other. In other words, when the neutralization of the purposive morpheme *-ke* is finalized, the therapy will have run its full course. This is, of course, all very speculative. However, the fact that the Korean *PURP* causative has already taken the first step toward the kind of ultimate change described here is not to be discounted.

One of the most important implications that can be drawn from the present discussion is that diachronic aspects of language cannot be ignored or brushed aside as 'noises' in constructing any grammatical theory. RRG is not different from many other grammatical theories in that it is indifferent to, or unable to accommodate, the diachronic side of language. It indeed proposes a very rigid correlation between semantic relations and syntactic linkage types, as reflected in the IRH in Figure 4.4. Inevitably, the kind of unfortunate hitch that has been identified here is very likely to cause problems for the IRH. Any viable grammatical theory must allow for diachronic aspects of language as an integral part. In conclusion, a grammatical theory must be responsive to both synchronic and diachronic sides of the 'coin' called language (for a similar view see Langacker 1987: 51–52).

Notes

1. For example, the syntactic causative in (3) below cannot be converted into a sentence with a morphologically derived causative verb built on the basic verb *masi-*.
2. (6) can only be used as an answer to a sentence questioning the identity of the subject NP, e.g.:

   (i) nu-ka   kɨ i:l-ɨl   ha-əss-nya?
       who-NOM the work-ACC do-PST-Q
       'Who did the work?'

3. Despite the fact that the Clause Linkage Theory of RRG is one of the most comprehensive of its kind, it is not very well known or widely practised. For this reason alone, the brief discussion of the theory seems to be warranted. In this book, Foley and Van Valin (1984) will be used as a primary source, unless indicated otherwise. Although RRG has undergone changes over the years (as in Van Valin 1993a), the basic theoretical assumptions and constructs remain intact (cf. Song 1994).
4. Klaiman (1986) identifies some difficulty in applying this diagnostic test to verbs that cannot be marked for aspect.
5. In Van Valin (1993b), these two parameters are still independent of each other, but they stand in a hierarchical relationship.
6. Van Valin (1993b) provides a more elaborate ISRH than Foley and Van Valin (1984). In this chapter, Van Valin's revised ISRH will thus be followed.
7. Haiman (1985a: 106–107) suggests that two ideas are conceptually close to the extent that they: (a) share semantic features, properties, or parts; (b) affect each other; (c) are factually inseparable; (d) are perceived as a unit, whether they are factually inseparable or not. Bybee (1985a: 13–16) defines relevance as follows: a meaning element is relevant to another meaning if the semantic content of the first directly affects or modifies the semantic content of the second. Further, the

parameter of relevance has a formal correlate degree of relatedness in a morphophonological sense: the more relevant meaning x is to meaning y, the more tightly the linguistic expression of x is fused to that of y.

Chapter 5

The functional basis of the typology

5.1   Introduction

In Chapter 2, a new typology of causative constructions has been provided on the basis of 408 languages. In that typology, three different types of causative construction have been identified: the *COMPACT* type, the *AND* type, and the *PURP* type. The *COMPACT* type is very well known and widely discussed. The *AND* type is relatively well known, although it has not been discussed from the overall perspective adopted in this book. The *PURP* type, however, has never been recognized *sui generis*. If recognized as a causative at all, it has been either classified as or relegated to the syntactic type of causative. It has received little or no treatment even in those grammatical descriptions that actually provide data on this type of causative construction. For instance; no attempt has been made to explain why the element of *PURP* appears at all in causatives. Far more frequently than not, the nature of the term *PURP* is simply left undetermined. Consequently, it has never been discussed in any general theory of causative constructions. Perhaps this is not surprising at all, since, as Langacker (1987: 81) notes with a great deal of lamentation, modern (theoretical) linguistics is notorious for ignoring low-level grammatical morphemes for purposes of grammatical analysis:

> The only way to demonstrate [the status of grammatical morphemes as symbolic units] is by analyzing a substantial and representative class of examples, **including cases generally agreed to be void of semantic content**, and showing that a coherent and revealing account of linguistic phenomena emerges just in case they are attributed specific meanings [emphasis added].

As readers may recall, the above statement by Langacker captures the spirit of the *modus operandi* of the present investigation. Indeed, the new typology of causative constructions has emerged as the semantic content of the term *PURP* has been identified correctly and dealt with in its own right.

As Mallinson and Blake (1981: 6) correctly point out, however, the mere typologizing of causative constructions will be indeed 'a rather sterile occupation unless there is some useful application of the material collected [and classified]'. Every attempt must, therefore, be made to take full advantage of the typology in the seeking of high-level explanations. Thus, in Chapter 3, the diachronic model of causative affixes has been developed on the basis of the typology. The limits within which languages are found to vary with respect to causation have been interpreted in such a way to identify the potential sources of causative affixes. It is thus made possible to trace the origins of causative affixes in languages for which little or no historical documentation exists. Further, implications can be drawn from the typology for the nature of language, and, more ambitiously, for the nature of the human mind. To that end, an attempt will be made in the present chapter to answer questions such as: Does the typology of causative constructions put forward in Chapter 2 have any extralinguistic basis? If so, what is the nature of that basis? Does it reflect in any way how the human mind cognizes causation? As will become clear, answers to these questions are bound to be speculative to an extent. But at this stage it is firmly believed to be most important to first ask these questions and try to answer them. In that way, the groundwork will be laid for questions of a higher level to be formulated.

5.2   Implicativity as the distinguishing feature

Before the kind of discussion alluded to above can be presented, the tripartite typology of causative constructions must be revised to the exclusion of the *COMPACT* type, because both *AND* and *PURP* types of causative, as has been noted repeatedly in Chapters 2 and 3, exhibit formal reduction of varying degrees. Indeed, causatives of these two types may move toward the (prototypical) *COMPACT* type, which represents the amalgamation of [Vcause] and [Veffect]. The *COMPACT* type is thus the ultimate outcome of formal reduction of the *AND* or *PURP* type. Therefore, the *COMPACT* type must be taken out of the typology for purposes of the present chapter, since it is the 'diachronic residue' of the other two types, as it were. Why such formal reduction occurs in causative constructions falls outside the purview of this book (but for possible explanations see Haiman 1985a, Bybee 1985a, 1988, Foley and Van Valin 1984, *inter alia*).

Furthermore, formal reduction evident in the *AND* and *PURP* types of causative is not unique to the causative construction *per se*, as has been shown in 1.1. So, it is also found in other constructions, as Haiman (1985a: 102–147) provides ample examples of formal reduction in diverse grammatical phenomena ranging from phonological disjuncture to clause embedding. In fact, formal reduction permeates language, as any introductory historical linguistics textbook will attest, in phonology, morphology, and syntax (cf. Zirmunskij 1966, Kiparsky 1982, Haiman 1985a, Hall 1987, 1988). This suggests that before an attempt is to be made on the basis of the typology to gain an understanding of human cognition of causation, what is not unique to the causative construction must be removed from that typology: the *COMPACT* type.

The elimination of the *COMPACT* type from the typology of causative constructions has implications for the traditional typology: the lexical, morphological, and syntactic causatives. The traditional typology is based crucially on the formal distance between [Vcause] and [Veffect]. In the lexical causative, these two terms are amalgamated into a single verb beyond recognition; there is no formal distance between [Vcause] and [Veffect]. In the morphological causative, the element of [Vcause] is realized as an affix bonded to the element of [Veffect]; there is a morphemic boundary between [Vcause] and [Veffect]. In the syntactic causative, these two elements appear as separate words in different clauses, [Vcause] in the main clause and [Veffect] in the subordinate clause; there is a clause boundary between [Vcause] and [Veffect]. The traditional typology thus takes the parameter of compactness as **the** distinguishing feature of the causative types. As has been argued in 1.1, however, the parameter of compactness does not contribute much to an understanding of how causation is cognized by the human mind, let alone what it is that makes causative constructions. This is the major weakness of all explanations based on the traditional typology. In fact, it is not surprising that the parameter of compactness fails to shed much light on causation, because formal reduction is not unique to causatives after all. It is found everywhere in language.

Now, if the *COMPACT* type is removed from the typology as the diachronic residue, the main difference between the remaining two types, *AND* and *PURP*, at least in their prototypical forms, is the presence or absence of implicativity: whether or not the truth of

[Seffect] is built into the semantics of [Vcause]. For instance, in (1.a) the verb *made* is implicative. Thus, the truth of (1.b) holds, whenever that of (1.a) holds. In (1.c), on the other hand, the verb *told* is nonimplicative. Thus, the truth of (1.d) does not necessarily hold, even if that of (1.c) holds.

(1) a. John made Mary kick the man.
     b. Mary kicked the man.
     c. John told Mary to come over
     d. Mary came over.

The *AND* type of causative construction, prototypical or not, is fully implicative. On the other hand, the *PURP* type may not always be fully implicative, although it is fully nonimplicative, at least in its prototypical case. Unlike those of the *AND* type, languages of the *PURP* type in fact exhibit a cline of implicativity. As has been shown in Chapter 4, the *PURP* type of causative in Korean is not completely implicative. Implicativity of the *PURP* type causative may thus range from nil to 100 per cent in the sense discussed in 4.5. The distribution of implicativity in the non-*COMPACT* types of causative construction is depicted as follows:

(2)	*AND Type*	*PURP Type*
implicativity	100%	0%–100%

Although in the new typology, implicativity is the distinguishing feature of the non-*COMPACT* types of causative, the parameter of compactness may still have a role to play in the discussion of the causative types. As has already been shown in Chapter 3, the term *AND* or *PURP* may be formally reduced into oblivion, although *PURP* proves to be relatively resistant. However, when and if obliteration of *AND* or *PURP* happens, it may become impossible to determine whether a given causative construction is of the *AND* or the *PURP* type in origin. Further, even if it is left intact, the term *PURP* may be neutralized to the extent that it is semantically no different from the term *AND*. In that case, unless there is a reason to believe that it is an instance of the term *PURP*, it may well be identified as an instance of *AND*. To put it differently, there is a kind of common ground where it is practically impossible to ascertain which type a given causative construction belongs to. At this point, there may arise a need to appeal to compactness: to locate causatives on a continuum of compactness (e.g. on a scale of ten). The revised typology, then, recognizes that implicativity is the variable inherent in the causative construction, while the variable of compactness is independent of the causative construction. The latter variable is superimposed on the former, as it were.

Taking these points into account, Figure 5.1 illustrates the convergence of the *AND* and *PURP* types over the parameter of compactness, whereas Figure 5.2 locates languages in terms of both implicativity and compactness. In Figure 5.1, as the lines emanating from the two prototypical types converge, it becomes increasingly difficult to determine whether the causative construction in a given language is of the *AND* or *PURP* type. In Figure 5.2 the horizontal axis represents the parameter of implicativity, whereas the vertical axis represents the parameter of compactness. For instance, point A will stand for the rare group of languages such as Kammu or Malagasy, the morphological causative of which is nonimplicative. Point B will be representative of languages with implicative lexical or morphological causatives (most of the world's languages will cluster around this point). Point C marks the position of the prototypical *PURP* type, and point D that of the prototypical *AND* type. The double parameter diagram neatly locates languages in terms of implicativity and compactness, each represented by a dot. Most languages of the world may be represented more than once in the diagram, because they may have more than one causative type. Of course, Figure 5.2 is only an approximation. At this stage, it will be very difficult to pinpoint exactly the location of specific languages. Such an exercise will call for more detailed data on every

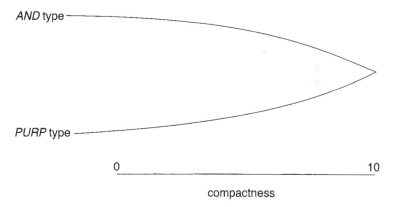

AND type

PURP type

0   10

compactness

Figure 5.1

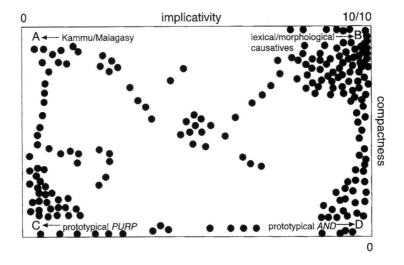

Figure 5.2

individual language in the first instance (as has been done for Korean in Chapter 4), and then for careful crosslinguistic comparison. Needless to say, that is well beyond the scope of the present investigation. Thus, Figure 5.2 is only a theoretical construction of what the distribution of the world's languages may look like in terms of the two parameters: implicativity and compactness.[1]

5.3   Cognitive basis of the typology

In this section, a cognitive model will be provided as an explanation for the typology of causative constructions. It must be emphasized at the outset that no psychological claims are made for this model. It must, however, be borne in mind that the basic thesis embodied in the model is formulated on the basis of a large number of languages from both synchronic and diachronic perspectives. At least, it offers a hypothesis about human cognition of causation that can be tested against relevant psychological evidence. Further, it seems reasonably plausible, given what is uncontroversial about human cognition: humans cognize events or stages of an event in chronological (or temporal) order (e.g. E.V. Clark 1970, 1973, Ferreiro and Sinclair 1971, Keller-Cohen 1974, Traugott 1975).[2] Despite its unavoidably tentative nature, what follows will pave the way for future research into the cognitive basis of the typology.

5.3.1 Preliminaries

All linguists agree that language is a system that connects meaning and form. For instance, in classical Transformational Grammar the representation of form is known as syntactic surface structure, while the level representing meaning is known as semantic or underlying structure. However, the notion of an abstract syntactic level such as d-structure in GB or initial stratum in RG, to name two, is by no means agreed upon in current linguistic circles, as evidenced by the fact that different syntactic theories have different numbers of (abstract) syntactic levels of representation. Further, what is taken care of at one level in one theory (or in one version of a given theory) may be done at a different level in another theory (or in another version of the same theory). Abstract syntactic structure is simply a by-product of a theoretical perspective taken (cf. Farrell 1994: 1–8).

Surface syntactic structure is, however, a structural and/or hierarchical representation of sentences uttered by the speaker. It provides information on lexical elements in the sentence, the linear sequence and/or the hierarchical organization of these elements. This syntactic representation contains only lexical elements that correspond to what the speaker actually utters. For instance, it does not have any room for abstract elements that do not correspond to the physical (speech) output by the speaker.

Semantic structure is a level representing meaning. It contains information on meaningful relations between the lexical elements of the sentence, and other semantic relations like entailment, scope relations of adverbials and quantifiers, etc. This level of representation is alternatively known as 'deep structure', 'semantic representation', or 'logical structure'. The actual form of the structure is not at issue. Suffice it to note here what kinds of information may be included in the representation.

Further, there should be rules or principles that link the syntactic surface structure and semantic structure. Again, what form they will take is of no concern here. The important thing is to acknowledge the existence of correspondence rules or principles that are designed to connect the two different structures.

There is also a nonlinguistic cognitive level of structure, which will be called 'cognitive structure'. It is nonlinguistic, because it does not belong to the domain of language, whereas both syntactic and semantic structures are part of language, since they are governed by linguistic conventions. Crudely speaking, cognitive structure may correspond to what is called thought. Thought is what humans cognize through their senses. To avoid possible confusion between thought and meaning, however, the term cognitive structure will be adopted here. Cognitive structure represents what humans cognize of emotion, experience, and the like, or what may be referred to here as cognizables (whatever is cognized by humans is a cognizable, as it is 'cognizable'). Cognitive structure must, however, be streamlined in order to be conveyed through the channel of language. It has to be (re)shaped in accordance with linguistic conventions, i.e. syntactic and semantic rules, or communicative needs (for a similar view, see Lakoff 1987 and Langacker 1987: 66–68, 99). Streamlining is in fact necessary, if language remains to be a viable communication system. As is well documented in the literature (e.g. Zipf 1935 [1965], Haiman 1985a), the language system is always caught in a balancing act between the speaker's economy in speech and the hearer's ease in comprehension. The process of streamlining is motivated ultimately by striking the balance between economy and ease. Cognitive structure is reshaped in compliance with linguistic conventions or communicative needs to enhance the speaker's economy in speech without jeopardizing the hearer's success in comprehension.

Cognizables are not holistic in nature. By that is meant that they consist of parts (in case of a static situation) or stages (in case of a dynamic situation). This can be demonstrated quite easily. The falling of a rock off the cliff may be reported or expressed as a single event: *The rock fell off the cliff.* But the cognizable itself consists of a series of stages, e.g. the initial movement of the rock from its original position on the cliff, the start of the falling, the duration of the falling, the rock hitting the ground, the resting of the rock on the ground, etc. (Langacker 1987: 143ff). Surely, all these stages are cognized by the human mind. Not all these stages, however, will necessarily be manifested by linguistic expressions. For purposes of communication, the cognitive structure (i.e. the series of stages of the event) is telescoped or reduced in accordance with the speaker's communicative needs, linguistic conventions, etc. Different stages of the event may be highlighted or suppressed. So, if a given cognizable has three constituent stages, language X may highlight Stage 1, language Y may highlight Stage 2, and so on.

This is a very plausible scenario, since a similar thing happens within the same language, among the users of the same language, or even in the single speaker's language use. The sentences in (3) represent the same cognizable.

(3) a. The starship has left the galaxy.
    b. The starship is now out of the galaxy.

In (3.a), the speaker is expressing the same cognizable by highlighting the stage of the event at which the starship has left the boundary of the galaxy. In (3.b), the speaker is expressing the same cognizable by highlighting the current position of the starship. The point is that for the starship to be in the position where it is as expressed by (3.b), it must have left the galaxy, or that if it has left the galaxy as expressed by (3.a), the starship must now be outside the boundary (cf. Langacker 1987: 39, 47–110, 116ff). If this kind of highlighting (or suppressing) takes place in the same language, it is very likely that a similar thing happens across languages. The claim is made here that this is indeed the case.

The idea of highlighting or giving expressive salience to different parts (or stages) of the same cognizable is not new at all. It is called 'imagery' by Langacker (1987: 39), who defines it as the ability to construe a situation (or cognizable) in alternative ways for purposes of communication. Similarly, Lakoff (1987: 77–79) appeals to the notion of metonymy, in which part of a cognitive model (or structure) stands for the whole cognitive model itself. Even earlier than these authors, Hjemslev (1961: 50–52, 57–58) speaks of what he calls the purport or 'thought'. The form is 'projected onto the purport, just as an open net casts its shadow on an undivided surface ... the same purport is formed or structured differently in different languages'. Perhaps what distinguishes the present investigation from these works is that it is based on crosslinguistic evidence.

5.3.2 A cognitive explanation of causation

The plan of attack in providing a cognitive explanation of causation is as follows. Languages differ in terms of highlighting or suppressing different parts of the same cognizable, e.g. causation. So, if one can first identify the different stages as formally expressed by different languages, and then put these stages together into a coherent whole, one can in fact be in a position to be able to reconstruct the whole cognitive structure of that cognizable (cf. Langacker 1987: 47). It is contended here that the typology of causative constructions as revised earlier in the present chapter provides the different stages of the cognizable of causation.

The *AND* type is a linear sequence of [Scause] and [Seffect] connected by the term *AND*. The *PURP* type is a combination of [Scause] as the main clause and [Seffect] as the subordinate clause of purpose marked by the term *PURP*. Translated into plain language, the *AND* type is the sequential ordering of the cause clause and the effect clause, the former denoting the event that the causer carries out and the latter the event that takes place as a result of the causer's action. On the other hand, the *PURP* type is the combination of the event which the (prospective) causer carries out and that which she desires to take place as a result of her action. Note that in the *AND* type both [Scause] and [Seffect] are factual; if the truth of [Scause] does not hold, neither does that of [Seffect]. In the case of the *PURP* type, however, only [Scause] is factual, in the sense that the truth of [Scause] does not entail that of [Seffect].

From the preceding discussion, three major components of causation emerge: (i) perception of some desire or wish; (ii) a deliberate attempt to realize the desire or wish; and (iii) accomplishment of the desire or wish. The component in (i) is represented by [Seffect] in the *PURP* type or [Seffect] plus *PURP*; (ii) is indicated by [Scause] in both of the *AND* and *PURP* types; and finally (iii) is manifested by [Seffect] in the *AND* type or [Seffect] plus *AND*. Ideally, the desire or wish prior to the attempt to accomplish it must be the same as that as *fait accompli*. In order to assemble these three components of causation (i.e. stages of the cognizable) into a coherent whole, a temporal dimension is appealed to, whereby (i) precedes both (ii) and (iii), and (ii) in turn precedes (iii), as in (4):

(4) (i) → (ii) → (iii)
     ['→' = progression of time]

The temporal dimension is inherent in (i), (ii), and (iii), because (ii) cannot take place prior to (i), (iii) cannot occur prior to (ii), and so on (cf. Langacker 1987: 148–149, who sees the temporal dimension as a primitive dimension of cognitive representation). The diagram in (4), then, is the tentative cognitive structure of causation, as reflected in the typology of causative constructions. In the *AND* type, (ii) and (iii) are highlighted, whereas (i) is suppressed. In the *PURP* type, on the other hand, (i) and (ii) are highlighted, and (iii) is suppressed. Note that the stage of (ii), which represents the causer's deliberate attempt to realize her desire or wish, is highlighted in both types. This is not unexpected, since without such an attempt, no causation will be possible. It is an essential or indispensable stage for causation. The structure in (4) can, of course, be elaborated on by identifying further (sub)stages in between the three stages.

The cognitive structure in (4) is strikingly similar to what DeLancey (1984b, 1985a, 1986) independently proposes for the evidential system in Lhasa Tibetan. Although he is not concerned with causation *per se*, DeLancey's analysis of the Tibetan evidential system will be reviewed here with a view to enriching further the cognitive structure in (4).

Lhasa Tibetan, a Tibeto-Burman language, obligatorily marks so-called 'evidential distinction' in non-future, non-first person sentences. DeLancey argues that a simple notion of direct versus indirect evidence cannot adequately account for the distribution of the evidential categories in perfective aspect, e.g. *-soŋ* and *-pa-red*, since they seem to code the evidential distinction with non-first person actors, on the one hand, and the volitional/nonvolitional contrast with first person actors, on the other. Consider:

(5) LHASA TIBETAN
a.   sonam-gyis thaŋ=kha bkal-soŋ
     Sonam-ERG thangka   hang-PERF/DIRECT
     'Sonam hung up a thangka.'
b.   sonam-gyis thaŋ=kha bkal-ba-red
     Sonam-ERG thangka   hang-PERF/INDIRECT
     'Sonam hung up a thangka.'

The English translation does not show the distinction between direct and indirect perception, although the glosses clearly display the distinction in Lhasa Tibetan. Hence, (5.a) can be uttered only when the speaker has obtained the information through direct sensory perception, whereas (5.b) represents the speaker's indirect knowledge that she has obtained by report from a third party or she has inferred on the basis of other knowledge (DeLancey 1985a: 65). However, these perfective-cum-evidential suffixes seem to carry the nonvolitional value with first person actors, as in (6):

(6) LHASA TIBETAN
a.   ŋa na-gi-'dug
     I   sick-IMPERF/NONVOLITIONAL
     'I am sick.'

b. ŋa-s   dkaryol bcag-soŋ
I-ERG cup   break-PERF/NONVOLITIONAL
'I broke the cup (accidentally).'

These nonvolitional suffixes for first person actors are in complementary distribution with *-pa-yin* and *-gyi-yod*, which register the volitional meaning:

(7) LHASA TIBETAN
a. ŋa-s   thaŋ=kha bkal-ba-yin
I-ERG thangka   hang-PERF/VOLITIONAL
'I hung up a thangka.'
b. ŋa-s   thaŋ=kha 'gel-gyi-yod
I-ERG thangka   hang-IMPERF/VOLITIONAL
'I am hanging thangkas.'

However, there is another perfective form, *-bźag*, which makes a further contrast with *-soŋ* and *-pa-red*.

(8) LHASA TIBETAN
sonam-gyi   thaŋ=kha bkal-bźag
Sonam-ERG thangka   hang-PERF/INFERENTIAL
'Sonam hung up a thangka.'

According to DeLancey (1985a: 66), (5.a), with *-soŋ*, reports an event which the speaker directly witnessed; (5.b), with *-pa-red*, reports an event which the speaker knows of only by report or indirect evidence; and (8), with *-bźag*, reports inference from directly perceived evidence, that is to say, the speaker did not witness the hanging of the thangka, but has seen the thangka hanging on the wall, and inferred that Sonam hung it up.

In order to account for the distribution of these suffixes and to provide an explanation of it, DeLancey (1985a, 1986) puts forward what he calls the chain of causality in the following form:

(9) VOLITION → EVENT → RESULTING STATE

The cognitive structure in (9) depicts a series of stages of a single event: an act of volition (VOLITION) causes an overt act (EVENT), which in turn causes a RESULTING STATE. Note that (9) is as temporally based as the cognitive structure of causation in (4) above. The cognitive structure in (9) first of all explains the evidential distinction made by *-soŋ* and *-bźag*. The former encodes the direct knowledge of the EVENT stage, while the latter is concerned with the direct knowledge of the RESULTING STATE. Thus the other form, *-pa-red*, involves no direct knowledge of any stage of the chain of causality. In other words, the form *-soŋ* indicates that the speaker is committed to the factuality of the actual event, but not of its ultimate cause, i.e. VOLITION; *-bźag* involves the speaker's commitment to the factuality of the resulting state, but not of any prior stage in the chain of causality; and *-pa-red* involves no such commitment to the factuality of any stage of the chain. The cognitive structure in (9) further explains why the perfective form *-soŋ* encodes the nonvolitional value as well as the evidential value. Since this form captures the actual event but not its ultimate cause, i.e. volition, it cannot encode the VOLITION stage, which constitutes the direct knowledge of the ultimate cause of the event. If any volition is involved on the part of the speaker, she must have direct knowledge of it. When no volition is involved, the ultimate cause is not subject to perception, whereas the actual event or the resulting state may be so. The cognitive structure also accounts for the distribution of the corresponding imperfective and future forms in Lhasa Tibetan (DeLancey 1985a: 69–70), although the exposition thereof is not rehearsed here. The cognitive structure proposed by DeLancey thus makes sense of the distribution of the perfective/imperfective forms in Lhasa Tibetan.

The structure in (9) has much in common with the cognitive structure of causation that has been proposed here on the basis of the crosslinguistic evidence. In fact, it seems that there is virtually no difference between these two cognitive structures, although some reservation may be expressed about their exact correspondence in terms of detail. The labels used in (9) can be easily adapted to the cognitive structure in (4). For instance, the stages of (i), (ii), and (iii) of the structure in (4) roughly correspond to DeLancey's VOLITION, EVENT, and RESULTING STATE, respectively. Instead of VOLITION, the term GOAL will, however, be adopted here, since the latter is more consonant with the term *PURP*. Volition is always required to accomplish a desire or wish. No decision on the part of the actor to perform an act, i.e. volition (DeLancey 1985a: 5), can, however, be made without the actor's initial perception of the desire or wish. Therefore, VOLITION is actually somewhere in between (i) and (ii) in the cognitive structure of causation. As noted earlier, the cognitive structure in (4) can be elaborated on by postulating further stages in between the main three stages of the causative event. Since there is no difference between the stage of (ii) and DeLancey's

EVENT, the term EVENT will be retained. As for the last stage, RESULTING STATE, it is found to be too restrictive for causation, since what the causer brings about can be either a change of state in the causee or an action performed by the causee. Therefore, the term RESULT will be accepted here.

Now, the revised cognitive structure of causation is:

(10) GOAL $\rightarrow$ EVENT $\rightarrow$ RESULT

As has already been made clear, the whole cognitive structure of causation in (10) is not utilized for linguistic or communicative purposes. Instead, different stages are highlighted or suppressed. Indeed, the following two combinations of these stages are found in the languages of the world:

(11) a. EVENT + RESULT
b. GOAL + EVENT

These combinations, then, serve as semantic structures of causation, (11.a) for the *AND* type and (11.b) for the *PURP* type. Further, the semantic structures of (11.a) and (11.b) will be mapped onto the syntactic structures in (12.a) and (12.b), respectively:

(12) a. $S_1(S_2(\ldots [Vcause] \ldots)S_2 + AND +$
$S_2(\ldots [Veffect] \ldots)S_2)S_1$
b. $S_1(S_2(\ldots [Veffect] \ldots)S_2 + PURP \ldots [Vcause] \ldots)S_1$
or
$S_1(\ldots [Vcause] \ldots S_2(\ldots [Veffect] \ldots)S_2 + PURP)S_1$

Exactly how the cognitive structure, the semantic structures, and the syntactic structures are mapped onto one another remains to be seen. It is left to psychologists, formal linguists, or neurolinguists to propose formal or neurological rules or principles of mapping. Paraphrasing Langacker (1987: 99), it is believed that the functional and/or cognitive explanation as has been put forward here is more directly relevant to linguistic analysis than formal, logical, neurolinguistic descriptions of causation that may refer to, for instance, the firing of specific neurons. Suffice it to say here that there must be certain nontranslational or nontransformational rules of mapping or correspondence (or what Langacker 1987: 76–77 calls symbolic structure), which can be represented in the crude form illustrated in Figure 5.3. The relationship between cognition and grammar, on the one hand, and those between different levels of grammar, on the other, in Figure 5.3 are strictly on a correspondence basis (as

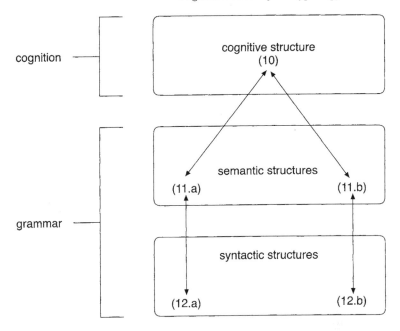

Figure 5.3

indicated by the double-headed arrows). The syntactic structures of causation mirror the semantic structures of causation on a one-to-one basis. The semantic structures, however, mirror the cognitive structure in a 'collective' manner.

Finally, the cognitive structure of causation receives further support from languages where these two different types of causative constructions, i.e. the *AND* and *PURP* types, compete with each other: variation within the same speech community. In 2.5.2, it is pointed out that in Jacaltec there is variation between the two types of causative construction. (13) is an example of the *PURP* type and (14) is an example of the *AND* type:

(13) JACALTEC
x-ø-(y)-iptze   ix xo' ø-s-tx'ah-a̱'
ASP-ABS3-ERG3-force CL/she CL/her ABS3-ERG3-wash-FUT
xil kape s-ti'   ha'
clothes ERG3-mouth water
'She forced her to wash the clothes by the river.'

(14) JACALTEC
xc-ach-w-iptze   hin   haw-echma-ni
ASP-ABS2-ERG1-force ABS1 ERG2-wait-and
'I forced you to wait for me.'

In (13), the future tense marking is recruited into service to mark the term *PURP*. As Craig (1977: 271) notes, however, some speakers use a coordinating suffix -*(n)i* in lieu of the future tense suffix, as in (14). The cognitive structure of causation in (10) can easily explain the 'concurrent' use of the two types of causative in Jacaltec. These two types are sanctioned by the cognitive structure of causation. Lango is another language in which both types of causative are in use (Noonan 1981: 124). Unlike Jacaltec, however, this language uses the *AND* type when the causer's activity is known to the speaker to have been successful, while it uses the *PURP* type when the causee's activity cannot be inferred to have actually occurred (Noonan 1981: 154; see 5.4). It will be very difficult to appreciate the variation in Jacaltec or Lango in the traditional typology of causatives, wherein these two different types of causative are lumped together as the same syntactic causative type.

5.4   Pragmatic basis of the typology

As has already been hinted at many times in this book, there seems to be a very viable 'strategy' in language to exploit existing constructions to express causation. In the *AND* type, the construction consisting of two clauses in an iconic order is pressed into service to express causation, whereas in the *PURP* type, the ordinary purposive construction is conscripted into service to carry out causative function. For the sake of convenience, this strategy will be called **the free ride policy**. The claim here is that the causative constructions are not 'exclusively motivated' in that they are made of grammatical structures the original functions of which are not causative. Causation thus takes a 'syntactic free ride' on the coordinate and purposive constructions.

The free ride policy is also evident in constructions other than causative. Stassen (1985) convincingly demonstrates on the basis of a large crosslinguistic sample that the structures that are used to express comparison are based largely on those whose original function is to express temporal chaining.[3] The view that the causative constructions are not 'exclusively motivated' also seems to have support even among generative linguists (e.g. GB, RG, etc.), albeit in a quite different context. Baker (1988: 194–196) suggests that the causative construction should be accounted for by construction-independent rules. Bordelois (1988) attempts to resolve fundamental theoretical problems in GB associated with the causative construction by reducing it to a non-exceptional status, that is to say, by arguing that it has the same d-structure as other ordinary constructions. In RG, Davies and Rosen (1988) abandon the standard RG biclausal analysis of causatives in favour of a monoclausal analysis, the major motivation behind this radical shift being that this change revokes an overarching principle unique to the causative construction and thus avoids violation of otherwise general or universal relational laws.

If, as has so far been demonstrated, the (prototypical) structures for the *AND* and *PURP* types are not exclusively motivated, what kind(s) of principle is (are) involved in guaranteeing the communicative success in expressing causation via the noncausative structures at the risk of jeopardizing the hearer's (hereafter H) correct comprehension? Apparently, the free ride policy here reduces H's success in comprehension, since the structures are potentially susceptible to both causative and noncausative interpretations, although it increases ease in production to the advantage of the speaker (hereafter S) – one form for two different functions. Thus, there has to be an underlying principle at work that ensures the balance between S's economy in production and H's success in understanding.

What will be argued for here is not new at all. In fact, it is something that has been discussed for almost three decades. However, to the best of the present writer's knowledge it has never been considered seriously with respect to the causative construction.

In their short yet provocative article, Geis and Zwicky (1971) pose a question why there is a causal reading assigned to, for instance, a pair of sentences connected by a conjunction *and*. (15) does not only express a temporal sequence of two situations, but also **invites** the inference that the first situation is a cause for the second (Geis and Zwicky 1971: 564).

(15) Martha observed the children at play and smiled with pleasure.

The causal reading associated with (15) is not semantic, that is, included in the semantic content of the sentences, but it is rather pragmatic, or, in the word of Geis and Zwicky (1971: 564), only **suggested**. That it is a pragmatic 'suggestion' is proven by the fact that (15) can indeed be expanded, as in:

(16) Martha observed the children at play and smiled with pleasure, but not in that order.

If the causal reading were indeed semantic, (16) would be anomalous. Similar comments can be made about the *AND* type of causative, which consists of two separate clauses connected by the term *AND*. A causative reading is generated pragmatically in the same way as in (15).

Geis and Zwicky (1971: 565) point out that the maxims of conversation, i.e. the maxims of quality, quantity, relevance, and manner, proposed by Grice (1967, 1975), cannot account for this particular pragmatic inference of causation (for a general exposition of the maxims, see Levinson 1983, Allan 1986). The reason why this is so is, according to Geis and Zwicky, that the inference of causation would be precluded by the maxim of quantity, according to which S must contribute as much information as required. By uttering (15), S does not say as much as the causal reading that is pragmatically inferred. In other words, what S actually says does not match what S actually means. By not saying as much as required, S should indicate that the causal reading is not intended (Levinson 1983: 146). However, it is clear that the causal inference is generated pragmatically with respect to (15) and also the *AND* type of causative. Obviously, something more than the maxims of conversation is involved here.

What about the *PURP* type of causative? The *PURP* type of causative is a construction whose original function is to encode an action performed for the purpose of bringing about another event. Here, the success of the purposive action is not determined; the event for which the purposive action was carried out is yet to come about. However, there is a pragmatic inference permitted to the effect that the success of the purposive action is assumed or taken for granted: the event for which the purposive action was performed indeed came about. In other words, wherever it comes from, the extra information is pragmatically added to the interpretation of the *PURP* type of causative. Again, this inference is precluded by the maxim of quantity for the same reason. In conclusion, there seems to be a different kind of pragmatic principle involved in generating the inferences associated with both the *AND* and *PURP* types of causative.

Atlas and Levinson (1981: 39; cf. Harnish 1976) invoke what they call the principle of informativeness in order to

> explain the data by appeal to another form of argument, one that yields interpretations that supplement 'what is said' by positing that 'what is meant' is a stronger proposition compatible both with presumptions in the context and with 'what is said'.

This principle can be paraphrased as: 'Read as much into an utterance as is consistent with what you know about the world' (Levinson 1983: 147). When S utters a sentence to H in a given context, H has a number of competing interpretations and chooses the one that best fits H's background presumptions and assumptions in the context, and the communicative intentions attributable to S in light of 'what is said', etc. (Atlas and Levinson 1981: 42). The principle of informativeness is pervasive in language interchange, as any introductory textbook in pragmatics attests. For instance, Kirsner and Thompson (1976) reach a similar conclusion when they discuss the difference between the encoded meaning and the conveyed message in what they call sensory verb complements in English.[4] On the surface, this kind of pragmatic inferencing may seem to be quite crude and not precise in human communication. However, such crudeness or impreciseness is offset by efficiency in communication. Given our limited physical energy and cognitive capacity, it is indeed quite efficient to leave unsaid what can be safely inferred, for instance by relying on what we know about human behaviour in general, as long as we are cooperative in communication.

The principle of informativeness can indeed be appealed to in order to explain the pragmatic inferencing associated with the use of the ordinary noncausative constructions for causative function. The type of sentence in (17) is what has been shown in 2.4 to be used to carry out causative function in many languages of the world.

(17) Mary kicked John and he cried.

Here, H is pragmatically inferring that there must be a certain relationship between the first clause and the second. Depending on the background knowledge of the world, H will choose the best 'fit' out of a number of competing interpretations, e.g. temporal, causal, or teleological (Atlas and Levinson 1981: 42). For instance, if H calculates on the basis of contextual information and particular presumptions that there must be a cause for a human's crying, a causal interpretation between the two clauses will be selected. Note that such a causal interpretation is initially triggered by the fact that S has juxtaposed the two clauses with the aid of a conjunction marker *and*. H takes it as indicative of a connection between the two clauses, since S would not juxtapose them in the first place, if otherwise. Therefore, the principle of informativeness or a principle akin to that seems to be at work in generating the pragmatic inference of causation from what is originally a simple juxtaposition of two clauses.

Atlas and Levinson's principle of informativeness can also be extended to explain the added information generated for the *PURP* type of causative. In the *PURP* type, the (complex) purposive construction is conscripted into service to express causation. The major 'semantic defect' of the *PURP* type, as it were, is that it is nonimplicative, i.e. the truth of [Seffect] is not entailed by [Scause]. Consider (18):

(18) I hit John so that he would cry.

In (18), it cannot be concluded that John actually cried. John's crying is nothing but a goal toward which the action of the main clause is oriented. In languages of the *PURP* type, however, sentences like (18) are interpreted precisely as implying the ultimate success of the subject NP of the main clause.

So far, how pragmatic inference may play a role in the interpretation of the *AND* and *PURP* types of causative construction has been sketched. Now, how such pragmatic inference actually works will be elaborated on by examining more closely how the principle of informativeness may operate in the *PURP* type of causative. As human beings, we generally possess a large amount of knowledge about human behaviour, which is accumulated, strengthened, or modified through ongoing experience within and without. Such knowledge is permanently stored in our brain or memory and can easily be retrieved when required. In communication, humans instantly access this kind of knowledge to process language interchange. The assumption that is relevant to the pragmatic inferencing involved in the *PURP* type of causative may be:

(19) Humans generally succeed in realizing goals for which they perform actions.

The assumption in (19) is a very general one that humans formulate through their experience within and without. So, the term 'goal' must be understood to be very broad and general. It includes all kinds of goal that humans are involved with, ranging from those that they set for their careers to mundane ones such as moving from the bedroom to the bathroom for urination. S assumes that H also appeals to this assumption to process the semantic content directly encoded in the *PURP* type of causative, the prototypical example of which is nonimplicative. The success of the causer's action is not determined or encoded at all. However, as both S and H share the same assumption or knowledge that human actions are success-bound, S safely assumes that H assumes that the causer's action is successful. Implicativity is thus restored via pragmatic inferencing. Given the prototypical *PURP*-type causative in (20) (note that an English example is used for ease of exposition), H will infer (21) on the basis of the semantic content of (20) and the assumption in (19) above:

(20) Judy moved backwards so that Tom would fall over.

(21) Tom fell over.

The semantic content of (20) does not, of course, contain any information on whether or not Judy's action was successful, that is, whether or not Tom's fall came about. The added information or the pragmatic inference in (21) is the output of the combination of (19) and (20) engineered by H's inferencing capabilities. H's inferencing abilities alone, however, are not the whole story of the pragmatic inferencing process in question. By uttering (20), S expects H to engage in the inferencing process and to generate successfully the inference in (21) by evaluating (20) on the basis of the assumption in (19). Truly, this is a fine example of cooperative interpersonal communication.

At this point, it may be asked what happens if S's intention is not what has been described in the foregoing: S means exactly what S says in (20). Since the pragmatic inferencing process builds on what S and H tacitly agree on, there is always a possibility of H's misreading S's intention: noncausative function. As in any other kind of human behaviour, humans assess, evaluate, modify, or revise what they intend to convey in (linguistic) communication on an ongoing basis (see Marslen-Wilson and Tyler 1980 and Marslen-Wilson, Levy, and Tyler 1982 for an insightful account of how similarly anaphor resolution is carried out in spoken language). Indeed, humans evaluate and adapt their behaviour, linguistic or otherwise, to often-changing immediate environments or circumstances. To give an everyday example, when there is little traffic (and we are not in a hurry), we walk across a street casually (we do not run!). But as soon as we observe a car approaching us fast (which itself is, in fact, a form of evaluation), we accelerate our pace or even start to run. Similarly, humans also evaluate and adapt in communication.[5] The kind of pragmatic inference in (21) generated by H is always safeguarded by what can potentially follow (20) in actual communication. It is improbable or unrealistic to assume that (20) will be all that takes place in communication between S and H. In other words, (20) is embedded in a much longer stretch of communication, on the basis of which H can always evaluate H's pragmatic inference in (21) or S can always strengthen what S believes H has pragmatically inferred. For instance, S may continue:

(22) ... and he broke his arm.

By the time H processes (22), the assumption in (19) on the basis of which H has derived the inference in (21) is now confirmed fully. Even if (20) stands alone, that is, not followed by any further confirming sentence, S reserves S's right to correct H's inference in (21) by uttering something like (23), if such an inference is not called for:

(23) ... but he did not fall over.

The pragmatic inference in (21) may in fact be more of a cline of factuality or a kind of 'ordered inferences' (cf. Smith and Wilson 1979: 158–171), as in:

(24) a. It is impossible that Tom fell over.
     b. It is possible that Tom fell over.
     c. It is probable that Tom fell over.
     d. It is certain that Tom fell over.
     e. It is a fact that Tom fell over.

According to the strength of H's pragmatic assumption in (19), H will assess the situation encoded in (20) and determine the relative factuality of it (especially if no subsequent safeguarding measures are taken by S). H will choose the fittest one among the ordered inferences in (24). It also seems that personal knowledge of the participants involved must not be ruled out (e.g. Judy is notorious for playing tricks on others; Tom is Judy's perpetual victim). To put it differently, there may also be specific assumptions at work in addition to general ones, such as (19).

Sperber and Wilson (1986) propose a general cognitive and psychologically oriented theory of communication (also see Kempson 1988).[6] According to what they call Relevance Theory, language *per se* very much underdetermines actual interpretation: information explicitly encoded by language is enriched via deductive inference. For instance, a new assumption is further created on the basis of an old assumption and a new assumption directly encoded in language. By linguistically encoding the basic assumption, S instigates H to fall back on the old assumption to derive further inference. This view of communication is well in accord with what has so far been discussed about the *PURP* type of causative (and the *AND* type, for that matter). The additional assumption in (21) is created on the basis of the evaluation of the new assumption in (20) on the basis of the old assumption in (19).

Sperber and Wilson (1986: 75–83) further make a very interesting claim that an assumption gains strength every time that it facilitates the processing of new information, and loses strength every time it makes the processing of new information more difficult. If Sperber and Wilson are correct, the fact that there is a set of ordered inferences in (24) can easily be accounted for. Language users may vary in terms of the strength of the assumption in (19), for example. Some users may have the assumption confirmed more often than others, as there are indeed people who are not deterred by failure but instead try over and over again finally to accomplish their goals, or others who are often deterred by failure. There may thus be variation in terms of implicativity even in the same speech community. As noted at the beginning of this chapter, implicativity ranges from 0 per cent to 100 per cent in the *PURP* type. Also recall from Chapter 4 that the Korean *PURP*-type causative may range from 50 per cent to 87.5 per cent in terms of implicativity. H may also fluctuate among the ordered inferences in (24), for instance in light of H's personal knowledge of the participants involved. Of course, when the purposive construction is institutionalized as a causative construction *par excellence* via its strong association with causative function (as described in Chapter 3), the pragmatic inference as in (21) will be semanticized or propositionalized, although this is not necessarily always the case.

One of the major conclusions that can be drawn from the foregoing discussion is the free ride policy: language seems to exploit existing syntactic structures (form) to communicate information (function) which they are not originally intended to convey, when pragmatic inferencing can help fill the gap between the targeted message and the actual semantic content. Thus, the structures, noncausative in origin, are pressed into service to perform causative function and are thus associated strongly with causative function. When they are frequently enough used for, and associated with, causative function, the constructions will then become institutionalized, or, as Hopper and Traugott (1993: 63) may put it, 'idiomatized' as fully fledged causative constructions. Therefore, what has been described as the independent causative construction in modern linguistics has humble origins in noncausative constructions. Recently, discourse-oriented grammarians have discovered that certain discourse preferences give rise to grammatical structures. For instance, Du Bois (1987) shows that natural discourse in Sacapultec is patterned in such a way that a clause, intransitive or transitive, tends to contain no more than one full NP, which happens to be the subject in intransitive clauses, or the object in transitive clauses, whereby the absolutive case has emerged. Similarly, in the present investigation the noncausative constructions that are frequently used for causative function indeed end up as fully fledged causative constructions. As for the causative construction, it thus seems that what grammars do best is to encode what language users do most frequently and frequently enough (cf. Du Bois 1985: 363).

Finally, it is worth briefly reconsidering in light of what precedes how the causative construction has been characterized in modern linguistics. Recall Shibatani's (1976c: 1–2) rigorous definition of causation (quoted in 1.2; also see Fillmore 1971, McCawley 1971, Dowty 1972, Comrie 1981a [1989]):

Two events qualify as a causative situation if
(a) the relation between the two events is such that the speaker believes that the occurrence of one event, the 'caused event', has been realized at t_2, which is after t_1, the time of the 'causing event'; and if
(b) the relation between the causing and the caused event is such that the speaker believes that the occurrence of the caused event is wholly dependent on the occurrence of the causing event; the dependency of the two events here must be to the extent that it allows the speaker to entertain a counterfactual inference that the caused event would not have taken place at that particular time if the causing event had not taken place, provided that all else had remained the same.

This kind of definition is in turn incorporated into the definition of the causative construction in current linguistics, as is aptly summarized by King (1987: 556):

An expression is regarded as causative ... only if two distinct events (a cause and its effect) are semantically **entailed** [emphasis added].

As has been argued at great length on the basis of crosslinguistic evidence, especially with respect to the *PURP* type, the above definition of the causative construction is too restrictive, if not inaccurate, since semantic entailment, as is prominently featured in King's definition, is not a necessary condition for being regarded as a causative expression. The existence of the *PURP* type of causative cannot be ignored nor can it be brushed off as a noncausative construction. There is an enormous amount of crosslinguistic evidence in support of its existence, as provided in Chapter 2, not to mention the diachronic evidence documented in Chapter 3.

Notes

1. One may call the *AND* type and the *PURP* type 'the implicative type' and 'nonimplicative type', respectively. However, the former set of terms will be retained here, because the *PURP* type ranges from 0 per cent to 100 per cent of implicativity. On the other hand, the presence of either *AND* or *PURP* is to a large extent exclusionary, that is, either *AND* or *PURP*.
2. There is clinical evidence for this. Horst (1932) and Williams and Zangwill (1950) report that the existence of a dissociation of memory for events and the times at which the events happened is a characteristic of the Korsakoff psychosis (Pöppel 1978: 722): the events themselves can still be remembered but the sequence of these events is lost. Carmon and Nachshon (1971) observe that patients with left hemispheric lesions in the brain do worse than the controls in reporting sequences of three to five visual or auditory stimuli (Pöppel 1978: 722).
3. Temporal chaining is defined as a cognitive process that determines the relation between two events as overlapping, preceding, or following each other.
4. The italicized part of the following sentence is an example of a sensory verb complement in Kirsner and Thompson's sense: I heard *Sarah recite the poem.*
5. This aspect of human behaviour is very different from what generative grammarians depict in their grammatical theories, e.g. the way sentences are generated by way of rigid syntactic rules and combinations thereof. In this kind of axiomatic system, there is no room for assessment, evaluation, revision, or modification (see Langacker 1987 for a most lucid elaboration of this point).

6.   In fact, what Sperber and Wilson attempt to do is to reduce the
      cooperative principle and its related maxims to a single pragmatic
      notion of relevance. As Ziv (1988) correctly points out, however, their
      notion of relevance cannot account for social aspects of language
      behaviour like politeness. Hence, some version of the Gricean cooper-
      ative principle must be retained even in Sperber and Wilson's theory of
      communication.

Chapter 6

Comrie's theory of causatives: an alternative interpretation

6.1 Introduction

Arguably, Bernard Comrie (1975, 1976b) is the only language typologist to have ever done any crosslinguistic research on causative constructions, apart from (former) Soviet linguists who have carried out typological research independently of the functional-typological framework of the West (i.e. the Leningrad [now St Petersburg] Typology Group, e.g. Nedyalkov and Silnitsky 1973). Unfortunately, he is only concerned with morphological causatives in his research. Thus, he does not deal with the lexical and syntactic causative types at all. This narrow scope of research is, as has already been noted in 1.1, characteristic of many other theories of causatives. Further, although Comrie's work is carried out in the spirit of the (then newly emerging) functional-typological framework, it perhaps unwittingly makes wrong use of certain theoretical assumptions that are generally associated with generative grammar (see 6.3).

Despite these shortcomings, a close examination of Comrie's work is deemed necessary. Above all, his work on the causative (and also numerous other areas) has not only played an extremely important role in the development of the functional-typological approach to language universals, the seeds of which, as is well known, were sown by Greenberg (1963b); but it has also contributed greatly to promotion and propagation of the approach as a viable coherent theoretical framework, as is evidenced by a string of subsequent works by others on topics ranging from basic word order to comparative constructions. Further, the influence of Comrie (1975, 1976b) is not confined to the functional-typological framework alone. It has in fact fuelled, if not engendered, both the general interest in causative constructions and the crosstheoretical debate on the role of grammatical relations in grammatical theory (e.g. Perlmutter and Postal 1974, Cole and Sadock 1977, Mohanan 1983, Marantz 1984, Gibson and Raposo 1986, Baker 1988, Davies and

Rosen 1988, Dziwirek, Farrell, and Mejías-Bikandi 1990, *inter alia*). More importantly, it has successfully established the causative as an object of inquiry within the functional-typological framework. For these reasons alone, Comrie's work on causatives deserves a separate treatment in a book like the present one.

Comrie (1975) seeks to find what (surface) grammatical relations causee NPs will bear in causative constructions wherein the erstwhile separate causative element and embedded verb are fused together. He claims that the hierarchy of grammatical relations, which he and Keenan (Keenan and Comrie 1972, 1977, 1979) earlier and subsequently found to be operative in relative clause formation across a wide range of languages, is very useful in characterizing the grammatico-relational fate of the causee NP. Although he (1976b) later expanded his language sample, Comrie's main thesis remains the same: the hierarchy predicts what grammatical relation the causee NP will assume after the amalgamation of the causative element and the embedded verb.[1]

The major disadvantage of Comrie's theory lies in the fact that very few languages, if any, conform to his paradigm case (i.e. the case which is consistent with the predictions of the theory), a fact that he (1976b: 264) fails to take serious note of (cf. Palmer 1994: 219). This is a most damaging theoretical position, despite his attempt to salvage the theory by pointing out that languages differ from the paradigm case in only one or two respects and that often this divergence is independently motivated. But the question still remains: what is the point of having such a theory when there is virtually no language that behaves exactly as it predicts? The positing of the paradigm case not only brands the deviations from the paradigm case as being indeed deviations; it also precludes a better understanding of the nonuniqueness of causative constructions in terms of NP density control: both causative and noncausative constructions are subject to the same requirement that limits the number of core NPs per simplex sentence. Since causative constructions are not different from noncausative ones in terms of NP density control, the hierarchy is plainly untenable. So is the paradigm case, since it is necessitated by the extension of the hierarchy. The hierarchy and the paradigm case, then, do not find a place in the alternative interpretation to be put forth in this chapter. The deviations are no longer deviations as such, but they are instead viewed as some of the ways utilized by languages so as to implement

NP density control. In other words, the alternative view provides a uniform account of various measures that are used for purposes of NP density control in a wide range of languages. Further evidence will be provided for the alternative interpretation from languages in which transitive verbs are obligatorily detransitivized before being subject to morphological causativization.

6.2   Comrie's theory of causatives

Comrie is explicit on what kinds of causative construction to consider in his universal theory: he deals only with causative constructions wherein the element indicating causation is fused with the verb, forming a new single derived verb, so that on the surface there is no longer sentence embedding. Note that Comrie posits for these causative constructions an abstract complex structure consisting of a matrix clause and an embedded clause. In languages such as Turkish, the fusion of the causative element and the (embedded) verb will be morphological, so that the causative element will be realized as a causative affix duly attached to the verb, e.g. Turkish *imzala* 'to sign' vs *imzala-t* 'to cause to sign'. On the other hand, in languages such as French the causative element somehow behaves as a single unit together with the embedded verb, although it will turn up as an independent lexical causative verb (for this reason, the French type of causative in (1) is called a 'quasi-morphological' causative):[2]

(1) FRENCH
Je ferai   lire le livre à Nicole
I make + FUT read the book IO Nicole
'I'll make Nicole read the book.'

Excluded from his study are suppletive causative verbs, which do not exhibit any sign of the fusion of the causative element and the noncausative verb (at least on the surface), e.g. English *kill*. Also left out from consideration are syntactic causative constructions, which have clear signs of embeddedness, e.g. English causative sentences such as *I brought it about that John fell over*, in which there is a clear clause boundary marker *that*. For a similar reason, the following English sentences or their equivalents in other languages are not taken into account in Comrie's theory:[3]

(2) ENGLISH
   a. I made John kick me.
   b. I had John shave me.

One may wonder at this point why Comrie needs to posit some abstract complex structures even for morphological verbs, when, clearly, he is associated with concrete surface analysis in the tradition of Greenberg (1963b) (cf. Comrie's (1981a [1989]: 12–15) own warnings against abstract analyses). There is indeed a strong motivation for this need hidden behind his extension of the hierarchy of grammatical relations. This will be taken up in 6.3.

The prime motivation for adducing the hierarchy of grammatical relations is to extend to causative constructions the utility of the A(ccessibility) H(ierarchy) that he and Keenan established in their universal theory of relative clause formation independently of causative constructions. In brief, the AH is proposed on the basis of the relative accessibility of different grammatical relations to available relative clause forming strategies. In some languages (typically Austronesian), relative clauses can be formed only on subject NPs. Other languages such as Kinyarwanda allow relative clauses to be formed only on subject and direct object NPs. Yet in other languages such as Literary Tamil, subject, direct object, and indirect object NPs can be relativized. Based on this kind of crosslinguistic observation, Keenan and Comrie (1972, 1977, 1979) set up a hierarchy of grammatical relations of the following form:

(3) Accessibility Hierarchy (AH)
subject > direct object > indirect object > oblique > genitive > object of comparison
[> = 'more accessible than']

Keenan and Comrie claim that relative clause forming strategies will apply to a continuous segment of the hierarchy. So, their theory predicts that, if a language can form relative clauses on a given position, then it can also form relative clauses on all positions higher or to the left on the hierarchy.[4] Indeed their theory is largely borne out by crosslinguistic data that they gathered from some 50 languages (but cf. Bauer 1982, Tallerman 1990, Song 1991b, *inter alia*).

Comrie constructs a streamlined version of the AH that he calls C(ase) H(ierarchy), and he applies it to the type of causative construction, mentioned above, that he chooses to consider:

(4) Case Hierarchy (CH)
subject > direct object > indirect object > oblique

He then attempts to demonstrate how his CH can predict the grammatical relation the causee NP will assume, when the causative and noncausative elements are fused together to form a new single derived verb. His theory runs as follows: a causative verb necessarily involves one additional argument in comparison with its corresponding noncausative verb, i.e. the causer NP argument, expressed in the following formula:

(5) NONCAUSATIVE: $n \rightarrow$ CAUSATIVE: $n + 1$
[n: number of arguments]

Since this causer argument should appear as the subject NP of the causative sentence (otherwise, the causer NP will be backgrounded; the sentence is no longer a causative sentence), the problem arises of assigning the causee NP (the subject NP prior to causativization) a new grammatical relation or syntactic position. The causee NP can no longer retain the subject relation that it assumed in the noncausative sentence, now that it is displaced from the subject position by the causer NP. This is where the CH comes into play and allegedly predicts the grammatico-relational fate of the causee NP argument. If the noncausative verb is intransitive, thus having only one argument, its corresponding causative verb will have two arguments: the causer NP and the original subject NP, which has now become the causee NP. Since the causer NP argument assumes the subject relation, the next available position on the CH is D(irect) O(bject). This is the position that the causee NP argument will take up. To put it differently, the causee NP argument has been demoted from subject to direct object. If the noncausative verb is transitive with two arguments, subject and direct object, the causative counterpart will have three arguments in accordance with the formula in (5), i.e. the original two arguments plus the newly added causer NP argument. When the causer NP argument takes up the subject relation, and the direct object of the noncausative verb retains its original grammatical relation, the causee NP will assume the next available position on the CH, i.e. I(ndirect) O(bject). Further down the CH, Comrie's theory predicts that after its abdication of the subject relation to the causer NP the subject NP of the noncausative ditransitive verb will turn up as an oblique NP in the corresponding causative sentence. The position which the demoted causee NP will occupy is, therefore, predicted by the universal theory on the basis of the CH.

Comrie calls a language that strictly conforms to the CH a 'paradigm case'. He cites Turkish as such a language (in fact, the only paradigm case language in his sample), as illustrated in the following pairs of noncausative and causative sentences:

(6) TURKISH
a. Hasan öl-dü
   Hasan die-PST
   'Hasan died.'
b. Ali Hasan-ı   öl-dür-dü
   Ali Hasan-DO die-CS-PST
   'Ali killed Hasan.'

(7) TURKISH
a. Müdür mektub-u imzala-dı
   director letter-DO sign-PST
   'The director signed the letter.'
b. Dişçi mektub-u müdür-e   imzala-t-tı
   dentist letter-DO director-IO sign-CS-PST
   'The dentist made the director sign the letter.'

(8) TURKISH
a. Müdür Hasan-a   mektub-u göster-di
   director Hasan-IO letter-DO show-PST
   'The director showed the letter to Hasan.'
b. Dişçi Hasan-a   mektub-u müdür   tarafından göster-t-ti
   dentist Hasan-IO letter-DO director by   show-CS-PST
   'The dentist made the director show the letter to Hasan.'

Further evidence that Turkish is **the** example of the paradigm case comes from noncausative two-place verbs like *başla* 'to start' that require their nonsubject arguments to be indirect object NPs. This means that in sentences with this kind of noncausative verb only the subject and indirect object positions will be occupied by the original arguments, thus leaving the direct object position unoccupied, and that in the corresponding causative sentences the causee NP will take up none other than direct object, i.e. the topmost vacant position on the CH. This is illustrated by the following pair:

(9) TURKISH
a. çocuk okul-a   başla-dı
   child school-IO start-PST

'The child started school.'
b. dişçi   çocuğ-u okul-a   başla-t-tı
   dentist child-DO school-IO start-CS-PST
   'The dentist made the child start school.'

The need to recognize the paradigm case spells a need to recognize the nonparadigm case. Comrie indeed discusses two subtypes of the nonparadigm case: extended demotion and (syntactic) doubling.

There are many languages in which the causee NP argument is marked as the agent phrase that may also appear in passive sentences, although the CH theory predicts that it will be marked as indirect object (Comrie 1975: 19–24, 1976b: 271–275). Comrie calls this phenomenon extended demotion. Consider:

(10) HINDI
Larke ne   mantrī   ko/se   patr likhvāyā
boy SUB secretary IO/INST letter write-CS
'The boy made the secretary write a letter.'

(11) FRENCH
Je ferai   manger une pomme à/par Claude
I make + FUT eat   DET apple   IO/by Claude
'I'll make Claude eat an apple.'[5]

(12) FINNISH
minä rakennutin talo-n   muurarei-lla
I   build-CS   house-DO bricklayers-INST
'I make the bricklayers build the house.'

In languages such as Hindi and French, the original subject NP (i.e. the causee NP) can be marked either as the grammatical relation predicted by the CH or as an oblique relation. In other languages such as Finnish, this choice is not even available. Finnish does not use the indirect object position for the causee NP, but it uses the adessive case, when the noncausative verb is transitive (Comrie 1976b: 273).[6] Another language that behaves the same way as Finnish is Hungarian (Comrie 1975: 20–21).

Comrie notes that it is possible for languages to allow doubling on certain syntactic positions or grammatical relations. That is, instead of taking up the grammatical relation predicted by the CH theory, the causee NP argument shares the position already occupied by another

(original) argument. Punjabi and French allow doubling on IO
(Comrie 1975: 277–278).

(13) PUNJABI

bAnde ne   masṭAr nal/nuṁ kàni mwṇdyaṁ nuṁ swn-vā-i
man   SUB teacher INST/IO story boys   IO   tell-CS-PST
'The man made the teacher read the story to the boys.'

(14) FRENCH
a. J'ai fait   donner une   pomme au professeur par Claude
    I   made give   DET apple   IO teacher   by Claude
b. J'ai fait   donner à   Claude une   pomme au professeur
    I   made give   IO Claude DET apple   IO teacher
    'I made Claude give an apple to the teacher.'

In both Punjabi and French, the causee NP may be marked as the
indirect object, although the position is already occupied by the
original indirect object of the noncausative verb. Both languages also
allow the causee NP to appear as an oblique NP, i.e. an agent phrase
(as in passive), as predicted by the CH theory. There are also
languages that allow doubling on the direct object position (Comrie
1975: 14–17, 1976b: 284–286). Latin, Southern Lappish, Arabic, and
Ewenki are some of the direct object doubling languages.

Finally, Comrie makes a very important observation that the
possibility of doubling declines as one moves from right to left on the
CH. In other words, doubling occurs freely on oblique positions, with
some restrictions on IO, with more restrictions on DO, and probably
never on subject at all.[7] He (1976b: 295) points out that this relative
possibility of doubling exactly parallels the CH, although he does not
further discuss why this may be the case (see below for a possible
explanation).

6.3   A critique of Comrie's theory

Comrie's universal theory of causative constructions, as has been
shown above, is based crucially on the validity of the CH: it is
claimed that the grammatico-relational fate of the causee NP is
predicted via the CH. However, the empirical validity of the CH
theory is very much in doubt, precisely because very few languages,
if any, conform to the paradigm case, i.e. the ideal case consistent
with its predictions. It is, therefore, quite reasonable to ask: what is

the advantage of the CH theory, when almost all languages seem to violate the predictions that the theory makes? This apparent lack of predictive power in Comrie's universal theory leads Marantz (1984: 263–264) to point out that

> the generalization that the causee in the causative of a transitive verb becomes the indirect object finds little crosslinguistic support ... some languages [e.g. Malayalam] never express the causee as goals [i.e. IO] are expressed. ... I know of no statistical study demonstrating that the causee with causatives built on transitive verbs is significantly more likely to be expressed as goals [are] than to be expressed as, say, instrumentals are. Second, in languages that allow a causee to be expressed as goals are, this expression is often not obligatory.

Despite the lack of such statistical studies, Marantz is here driving the point home: it is plainly difficult to justify the theoretical validity of the CH theory when for almost all languages it cannot predict the grammatico-relational fate of the causee NP.

Comrie (1976b: 264) seems to suggest a need to regard the paradigm case (hence the CH theory) as being some kind of prototypical case from which languages can be seen to deviate in one or more respects. Such a view cannot be taken to be legitimate at all. Prototypicality by definition involves some cluster of characteristic features, which each member of a given category possesses to a varying extent. So, some members are more or less typical of the category than others. On the other hand, Comrie's paradigm case here represents the ideal case of which all the predictions made by the theory are true. A language is either of the paradigm case or of the nonparadigm case. It is **not** the case that languages are more or less of the paradigm case. Hence, the paradigm case cannot be equated with prototypicality.

The postulation of such an idealized case is not even a necessary condition for the observing of the deviations from the paradigm case, although Comrie (1976b: 264) claims that 'the value of the paradigm case is justified by the fact that the **vast majority** of languages differ from the paradigm case in only one or two respects [emphasis added]'. Thus, he seems to suggest here that the paradigm case plays a facilitative role in bringing the deviations to light. However, it is not because of the paradigm case that these deviations come to be recognized and thus to be understood. The deviations are identified as such solely because Comrie is looking at them from the perspective of the paradigm case. It is of the utmost importance for any theory of causative constructions to investigate and account for how and why the causee NP behaves as it does across the world's languages. Therefore extended demotion and doubling should be used as part of the very empirical basis for any theory of causative constructions, not the idealized paradigm case that is **by no means** representative of the world's languages. It will be shown below that the 'deviations' from the paradigm case (i.e. extended demotion and doubling) can be better understood only if they are dissociated from the paradigm case. In fact, Comrie is forced to promote the paradigm case because he wishes to extend the CH to causative constructions. If this is not valid, the CH theory cannot be maintained at all.

What may have motivated Comrie to opt for abstract complex structures for morphological causatives (this can be called the complex underlying hypothesis)? For the morphological causative, there is only one verb, albeit derived from the fusion of the causative element and the noncausative verb. The question thus arises: why posit a complex underlying structure, when the causative verb in question is a **single** verb? The answer is: because it is the CH that Comrie attempts to extend from the theory of relative clause formation to his universal theory of causatives. Further, the CH (and also the paradigm case) is inherently associated with the complex underlying hypothesis. But why should this be so? According to Comrie, morphological causatives consist of one matrix clause and one embedded clause at a deep level, each having its own subject NP. At the surface level, however, these two clauses will be fused into a single clause (cf. Aissen 1974a). Since a clause can only have one surface subject NP by definition, the subject NP of the embedded clause must abdicate its subject relation to the causer NP, i.e. the subject of the matrix clause. The former subject of the embedded clause will then have to assume a grammatical relation other than the subject relation. It is predicted that it will take up the next available position on the CH. To put it in a different way, the embedded subject NP is demoted from the subject relation to the next highest available relation on the hierarchy.

However, if the causative does not have such a complex underlying structure, the notion of demotion loses its theoretical relevance, and so does the role of the CH in causative constructions.[8] If a sentence with a morphologically derived causative verb is regarded as having the same theoretical or structural status as a sentence with an ordinary noncausative verb, there will be no need to postulate the notion of demotion, hence no need for the hierarchy itself. If the causative has a single clause at the underlying level (this may be called the simplex underlying hypothesis), there will be only one subject NP anyway. In other words, under the simplex underlying hypothesis, there is no embedded subject NP in the first place that will be demoted according to the CH. In sum, the reality of the CH evaporates without the complex underlying hypothesis; the demotion scenario cannot be maintained.

Comrie (1975: 24–25) is fully aware of this problem, when he says: 'The constraints of the "paradigm case" ... are only required because we chose to set up the abstract underlying structures in the first place.' In fact, he entertains the possibility of having a simplex structure for the causative. But he rejects it, because it is not able to handle languages that allow doubling only in causative constructions (but see below) or a language that uses a distinct morphological case to mark the causee NP only in causative constructions (e.g. Gilyak). However, these cannot be taken as legitimate reasons for opting for the complex underlying hypothesis. For one thing, there is no logical relation between the complex underlying hypothesis and the unique invocation of a special causee NP marker. The fact that a special causee marker is used only in causatives does not necessarily mean that causatives **must** have abstract complex structures. Regardless of the validity of these reasons for which Comrie rejects the simplex underlying hypothesis, it is plainly true that the positing of complex underlying structures for causatives is needed to justify the extension of the CH to his theory of causatives.

So far, it has been shown that the CH is the meat of Comrie's universal theory, that the mechanism through which the CH is utilized is the notion of demotion, and that the theory is actualized in the paradigm case. In order to promote the CH, Comrie has to posit abstract complex structures for causative constructions. This effectively precludes the possibility that causative constructions may have the same simplex underlying structure as ordinary simplex (non-causative) ones, and, therefore, may be subject to the same kind of case marking system as these, for which simplex underlying structures are undoubtedly posited.

6.4   Data

In this section, data from a wide range of languages will be presented with a view to gaining a better or more realistic understanding of the phenomenon under discussion. Due to limitations of space, only a small number of languages can be cited; more data can easily be added. The data are fairly representative of the world's languages in this respect.

Nedyalkov and Silnitsky (1973), among others, have noted that languages tend to apply causative affixes to intransitive verbs more often than to transitive verbs.[9] In other words, it seems to be the case that transitive verbs are harder to causativize via affixes than are intransitive verbs. There are languages that simply do not add causative affixes to transitive verbs. In these languages, only intransitive verbs are allowed to undergo morphological causativization.[10] Lamang, a Chadic language spoken in northeastern Nigeria, applies causative affixes *- v́v'-* and *-`ŋ´-* to intransitive verbs only (Wolff 1983: 115, 118).[11]

(15) LAMANG
  a. *-v́v'-*
  tsxúrá 'sit down' : tsxúráatá 'set down, make sit down'
  ŋgrà '(be) black' : ŋgráatá 'blacken, make black'
  b. *-`ŋ´-*
  ghwàlà '(be) dry' : ghwàlə̀ntá 'dry something'

Uradhi, an Australian language spoken in Cape York Peninsula, is another language of this kind. Uradhi adds a causative suffix *-(ṇa)ŋa* only to intransitive verbs (Crowley 1983: 376).

(16) URADHI
  ama-:lu   mupa   ina-(ṇa)ŋa-n ura-ŋu
  man-ERG child-ABS sit-CS-PST here-OBL
  'The man sat the child down here.'

Urubu-Kaapor, a language belonging to the Tupí-Guaraní family and spoken in the northeast corner of Brazil, adds the prefix *mu-* only to intransitive verbs (Kakumasu 1986: 341).

(17) URUBU-KAAPOR
  a. ok   pyter a-mu-pu'am
    house centre 1SG-CP-stand
    'I put up the house centre pole.'

b. pe irapũimbor mu-nem   arapuha rukwer
and king vulture 3 + CP-rotten deer meat
'And the king vulture caused the deer meat to rot.'

Kakumasu (1986: 342) notes that he has not encountered any causativized transitive verbs.

Baker (1988: 196) cites Moroccan Berber as a language of this kind, since in this language causatives of intransitive verbs are free and productive (e.g. (18.a)), while those of transitive verbs are systematically impossible (e.g. (18.b)).

(18) MOROCCAN BERBER
a. Y-ss-jen   Mohand arba
    3SG/SUB-CP-sleep Mohand boy
    'Mohand made the boy sleep.'
b. *Y-ss-wt   wryaz aggzin i-wrba
    3SG/SUB-CP-hit man   dog   to-boy
    'The man made the boy hit the dog.'

Kayardild, an Australian language spoken in the south Wellesley Islands, Gulf of Carpentaria, also belongs to the group of languages that restrict the use of causative affixes to intransitive verbs. In this language, there are three causative affixes, all of which can be added only to intransitive verbs. In this context, Evans (1985: 294) notes that he heard no spontaneous causative examples with transitive (or middle) verbs, and attempts to elicit them met with bewilderment.

Turkana, an Eastern Nilotic language, prefers a syntactic means of causativization (i.e. the *AND* type; cf. 2.4.1) to morphological causativization when transitive verbs are involved (Dimmendaal 1983a: 200). So, (19.b) is preferred to (19.a) by all of Dimmendaal's informants.

(19) TURKANA
a. à-ìte-lep-ì   a-yɔŋ ŋèsi` a-kàal
    I-CP-milk-ASP I-NOM her   camel
    'I'll have her milk the camel.'
b. à-sub-a-kɪn-ì   a-yɔŋ ŋèsi` to-lep-ò a-kàal
    I-do-e-DAT-ASP I-NOM her   3-milk-V camel
    'I'll have her milk the camel.'

Other languages restrict their causative affixes to intransitive and transitive verbs; ditransitive verbs cannot be morphologically causa-tivized. Basque restricts its causative suffix *-erazi* only to intransitive (e.g. (20.a)) and transitive (e.g. (20.b)) verbs. When the noncausative verb is ditransitive, for example *eros* 'to buy', a biclausal *PURP*-type causative construction must be used, as in (20.c) (Saltarelli 1988: 221; cf. 2.5.1).

(20) BASQUE
- a. Mikel   ni-rekin etorr-eraz-i
      Mikel (A) I-COM come-CS-PERF
      d-u-t
      3A(-PRES)-AUX2-1 SG/E
      'I've made Mikel come with me.'
- b. maletak   abioiez   bidal-eraz-i
      case-PL/A plane-INST send-CS-PERF
      n-izk-io-n
      1SG/E(-PST-AUX2)-3A/PL-3SG/D-PST
      'I had him send the cases by plane.'
- c. Mikel-ek Jon   Edurne-ri liburu-a   eros-te-ra
      Mikel-E Jon-A Edurne-D book-SG/A buy-NOM-ALL
      behar-tu   z-u-en
      force-PERF 3SG/E(-PST-3A)-AUX2-PST
      'Mikel obliged John to buy the book for Edurne.'

Abkhaz is similar to Basque in that it does not use the otherwise productive causative prefix *r-* to causativize ditransitive verbs. Only intransitive and transitive verbs can undergo the morphological causativization (e.g. (21.a) and (21.b)). According to Hewitt (1979: 170–171), Abkhaz relies on the biclausal *PURP* causative construction when the basic verb is ditransitive (e.g. (21.c); cf. 2.5.2).

(21) ABKHAZ
- a. də-sə-r-gə̀lo-yt'
      him-I-CP-stand-FIN
      'I stand him up.'
- b. yə-b-sə̀-r-q'a-c'e-yt'
      it-you-I-CP-PREV-do-FIN
      'I made you do it.'
- c. d-bə̀-l-ta-r + t°'   (ø-)q'a-s-c'ò-yt'
      him-to=you-she-give-PURP it-PREV-I-make-FIN
      'I make her give him to you.'

As has so far been observed, the degree of productivity (or applicability) of morphological causatives may decline, as one moves from intransitive to transitive and on to ditransitive.

There also exist some languages which maintain the canonical number of NPs with respect to verbs or predicates by not encoding either the causee or some argument other than the causer, when these verbs are morphologically causativized.[12] In Afar, an Eastern Cushitic language, there are two causative suffixes, one exclusively for intransitive verbs and the other for transitive verbs (Bliese 1981: 128). According to Bliese (1981: 129), many causativized transitive verbs do not have the original subject NP of transitive verbs (i.e. the causee NP) specified.

(22) AFAR
'oson 'garca gey-siis-ee-'ni
they thief find-CS-they/PERF-PL
'They caused the thief to be found/they caused someone to find the thief.'

So normally, in Afar, the number of NPs per causative verb, regardless of the transitivity of the original verb, is no more than two.

In Babungo, a Benue-Congo language spoken in the North West Province, Cameroon, the causative suffix -s can be added to intransitive, semitransitive, or transitive verbs, but not to ditransitive verbs, just as in languages such as Abkhaz and Basque (Schaub 1985: 210). However, when transitive verbs are involved in causativization, unlike in Afar, the causee NP must be expressed. It is the object of the original transitive verb that is left out, or that is expressed as an optional adjunct (Schaub 1985: 211).

(23) BABUNGO
a. ŋwɔ́ fèe   zɔ̃
   he fear-PERF snake
   'He was afraid of a snake.'
b. mɔ̀ fèsɔ̀   ŋwɔ́ (nɔ̀ zɔ̃)
   I fear-CS-PERF him (with snake)
   'I frightened him with a snake.'

The original direct object in the noncausative sentence in (23.a), zɔ̃, can now either appear as a prepositional adjunct NP, nɔ̀ zɔ̃, or be omitted in the corresponding causative sentence in (23.b).

Songhai (or Sonrai), a Nilo-Saharan language, has a causative suffix -ndi, which can be added to intransitive and transitive verbs. When it is suffixed to ditransitive verbs, or three-place predicates, as Shopen and Konaré (1970: 215) call them, either the causee NP or the indirect object NP of the original verb has to be left out. This explains why the following sentence involving a three-place predicate *neere* 'to sell' is ambiguous in two ways (Shopen and Konaré 1970: 215; also Comrie 1975: 11).

(24) SONGHAI
garba neere-ndi bari   di musa se
Garba sell-CS   horse the Musa IO
'Garba had Musa sell the horse' *or*
'Garba had the horse sold to Musa.'

In other words, there is a strict requirement in this Nilo-Saharan language that there should be no more than three NPs per causative verb.

6.5   An alternative interpretation: NP density control

The general picture that is emerging from the preceding discussion is clear enough. There seems to be some kind of constraint on the number of core NP arguments allowed per causative sentence in each of the languages.[13] Some languages maintain the number of core NP arguments per causative sentence simply by preventing causative affixes from applying to transitive verbs. On the other hand, there are languages that apply causative affixes to transitive and/or ditransitive verbs as well as intransitive verbs. But in these languages, either the causee or some argument other than the causer is not encoded. But all the languages discussed above behave the same way with respect to intransitive verbs: causative affixes apply freely and productively to such verbs.

It seems that what these languages are doing is keeping the number of core NP arguments in the causative sentence from exceeding the maximum number of core NP arguments permitted in the ordinary noncausative sentence.[14] The maximum number of core NPs in the ordinary noncausative sentence is either two or three, probably depending on whether or not the indirect object relation represents a core NP argument in a given language.[15] So, in languages such as Lamang, Uradhi, and Urubu-Kaapor, the transitive verb cannot be morphologically causativized, because the number of core NPs in such a causative sentence would be three, a number of core NPs that cannot be tolerated in a single clause. These languages allow only two core NPs per causative sentence, the same number of core NPs permitted in ordinary transitive sentences. On the other hand, in languages such as Abkhaz, Basque, and Turkana, the number of core NPs allowed per simplex sentence is three, so that transitive verbs can be morphologically causativized. After all, noncausative ditransitive verbs allow three core NPs. When it comes to ditransitive verbs, these languages use biclausal *AND* or *PURP* causative constructions, which consist of two clauses, each with its own set of core NPs. Thus, the problem of NP overdensity never arises. In languages such as Afar and Songhai, a rather drastic measure is used to maintain the permitted number of core NP arguments. These languages simply do not encode one of the arguments (other than the causer), if the permitted number of arguments is exceeded. Causativization of transitive or ditransitive verbs would effectively raise the number of core NP arguments to three or four, well over the permitted number. Hence, one of the (original) core NP arguments is not expressed.[16]

In contrast, causativization of intransitive verbs is productively carried out across languages. Causative verbs built on intransitive verbs have only two core NPs, the number of core NPs allowed with transitive verbs. Hence, the NP overdensity problem that occurs with transitive and ditransitive verbs never arises. This also explains why omission of a core NP never occurs in causative sentences built on intransitive verbs in the languages that rely on such omission. It occurs only in causative sentences built on transitive (e.g. Afar and Babungo) or ditransitive (e.g. Songhai) verbs.

Why do languages rely on these kinds of measure to ensure that the causative sentence maintains the same number of core NPs as allowed in ordinary noncausative sentences? It is precisely because the causative sentence is no different from any other noncausative sentence in terms of the number of core NPs permitted. Every language seems to allow only a certain number of core NPs per simplex sentence, causative or not. In other words, there seems to be a language-particular NP density control to be observed in non-causative and causative sentences alike.[17] Although the exact number may differ from language to language, the maximum number of core NPs seems to range from two to three. All those ways in which the languages maintain the number of core NPs in causatives at a certain level can now be seen as means of keeping NP density control in effect.

Given this alternative interpretation, it is extremely difficult to maintain Comrie's CH theory. There is no need to recognize the case marking of causatives (i.e. via the CH) as different from that of noncausatives. The causative construction is not unique at all in terms of NP density control, contrary to the way Comrie has depicted it by appealing to the notion of demotion on the CH. The causative verb is, therefore, as much subject to the **same** language-specific NP density control as any other nonderived verbs. Under the alternative interpretation, the notion of demotion, i.e. the causer NP usurping the subject relation from the causee NP, simply loses its theoretical force. The causer NP does not displace the causee NP from the subject position. Rather, both the causer NP and the causee NP are taken care of by the same case marking system that is operative in both causative and noncausative constructions alike.

It has already been argued that the phenomena of extended demotion and doubling should be treated in their own right, not as some kinds of deviation from the idealized paradigm case. They should be taken as part of the basic material on which a better understanding of causative constructions can be built. Under the alternative interpretation, it is not surprising or unexpected to find in languages such as Hindi and French the causee NP appearing in oblique positions that agent phrases also assume in passive constructions. Such oblique-marked causee NPs can now be viewed as the result of the observing of the NP density control in these languages. In order to prevent the maximum number of core NPs per simplex sentence from being exceeded by the presence of the causer NP, these languages resort to expressing the causee as an adjunct, i.e. a noncore NP. It is well established that agent phrases, as, for example, in passives, are peripheral and/or optional, i.e. adjunct phrases.[18] In fact, the appearance of the causee NP as an agent phrase in Hindi and French is in nature identical to the case in Babungo above, in which the original direct object NP appears as an adjunct, if not completely omitted. Therefore, the extended demotion can be accounted for by the uniform interpretation put forward in this section: extended demotion is only one of the means that languages utilize in order to observe NP density control. In this connection, the special causative marker used only in causatives in Gilyak may also be interpreted as a kind of noncore argument marker that is put to use in compliance with NP density control.[19]

Comrie (1976b: 276–277) is at pains to justify the notion that doubling is not in itself a counterexample to the operation of the CH in predicting the grammatico-relational fate of the causee NP, since demotion is appealed to only if the causee NP cannot retain a position higher up in the hierarchy because of restrictions on doubling. He goes on to claim that if there are no such restrictions, then the doubling at that point is irrelevant with regard to the CH. This claim, however, runs counter to the very idea of the CH theory, if not the CH itself.[20] The CH comes into play only when doubling (or extended demotion, for that matter) is not allowed. It is understood that the CH theory is designed to predict 'the exponency of the embedded subject [i.e. the causee NP] in causative constructions' (Comrie 1976b: 276–277). However, it is reduced to predicting 'the exponency of the embedded subject' only when there is no doubling or extended demotion. If doubling and extended demotion do not fall out from it, what else is left to be accounted for by the CH theory other than the paradigm case, the only example of which seems to be Turkish in Comrie's sample?

Further, one must ask why doubling is allowed at all: what is it that motivates doubling in causative constructions? Is doubling only allowed in causative constructions or in ordinary noncausative constructions as well? In this connection, it is worth while reviewing how Comrie has changed his view over the years. He (1975: 25) rejects the simplex underlying hypothesis on the evidence of some languages that may allow doubling only in causative constructions. In a later work, he (1976b: 277) in fact acknowledges that there is a strong tendency in languages toward an exact parallel in doubling between causatives and noncausatives, but claims that it is only a tendency, not an absolute universal. Finally, he admits that indeed doubling in causatives parallels that in noncausatives, when he (1981a [1989]: 171) says: 'It turns out, however, that nearly all languages allowing this possibility [i.e. doubling] in causative constructions are languages that otherwise allow clauses to have two accusative objects – it is even conceivable that one should say "all languages" rather than "nearly all languages".' This means that there is no difference between causatives and noncausatives at all in terms of doubling on the direct object. In these languages, doubling is exploited in causative sentences in order to comply with NP density control, since doubling is permitted in ordinary noncausative sentences, anyway. Doubling on direct object, then, is one of the means that languages utilize to implement NP density control.[21]

As for the doubling on the indirect object position, Comrie (1981a [1989]: 171) notes that there is no such correlation or parallelism. He (1975: 14) points out that 'given the semantic notions that typically correspond to indirect objects, it is hard to imagine a simple verb that could take two indirect objects'. In other words, semantic or argument structures of noncausative verbs do not call for two indirect objects. Therefore, it is due to the nature of the mapping between syntactic NPs and semantic arguments of the noncausative verb that doubling on the indirect object position is rare in noncausative constructions. Further, it has to be added that the languages that Comrie cites as indirect object doubling languages do seem to disfavour indirect object doubling in causative constructions. This tendency is clearly noted by Comrie, although he thinks that it is due to stylistic, rather than grammatical, judgements (Comrie 1976b: 280). Obviously, it needs far more research in these languages to confirm that indirect object can really be doubled in causative constructions (cf. Kozinsky and Polinsky 1993 and Polinsky 1994).

Under the alternative view, languages that allow doubling in causative constructions are now regarded as exploiting the doubling permitted in ordinary noncausative constructions in order to conform to NP density control, although the same claim cannot be made with full confidence with respect to indirect object doubling languages.

Finally, Comrie's observation that doubling declines as one moves from right to left on the CH can be accounted for in the following way. Oblique NPs are by definition completely out of the scope of the NP density control operative in languages, since they are noncore NPs. Subject is the topmost position directly under the NP density control, i.e. the indispensable core NP. The next most important position is direct object, less of a core NP than subject.[22] Then comes indirect object. As has already been noted, indirect object may not be a grammatical relation in some languages. In turn, indirect object may be less of a core NP than direct object. So, the less it is governed by the NP density control, the more a syntactic position is susceptible to doubling in morphological causatives. The fact that there is no doubling on subject in causative constructions gives further support to the alternative view that causative constructions are not different from ordinary noncausative constructions in terms of NP density control.

Extended demotion and doubling are here viewed as part and parcel of the overall mechanism that is used by languages to implement NP density control in causative sentences, and this NP density control applies equally to noncausative sentences.

6.6   Further evidence for NP density control

The alternative interpretation put forward in 6.5 gains further support from those languages in which basic transitive verbs must be detransitivized prior to being subject to causativization. Detransitivization is a grammatical process that involves addition of some affixes to transitive verb roots. As a result, a core NP is changed to a noncore or adjunct NP, or is completely omitted. In English, for example, passivization is such a grammatical mechanism: the original subject NP (i.e. a core NP) is changed to some peripheral or adjunct NP by appearing in an agent phrase or it is completely absent. In some languages, the process involves incorporation of a core NP into the verb complex. By way of detransitivization, the number of core NPs is reduced from two to one. Causativization of the previously detransitivized verb will then bring the number of core NPs back to two, thus effectively maintaining the number of core NPs in compliance with NP density control.

In Blackfoot, an Algonquian language, there are two causative suffixes, *-ippi* and *-atti*, which apply to both intransitive and transitive verbs (Frantz 1971: 66). However, when these suffixes are added to them, transitive verbs must first be detransitivized via the suffix *-a:ki*. The net effect of this detransitivization is that the direct object NP of the original verb is changed to a peripheral or noncore argument status and thus left out of the core argument system of the verb concerned.[23] Note that in this language the verb internally records core arguments.[24] Conversely, nonrecorded arguments are by definition optional or peripheral arguments. After detransitivization of the two-place verb, only the subject NP is registered in the verb, not the direct object NP. Only after that is the causative suffix added to the now detransitivized verb, whereby the causer NP can also be registered in the verb as a core NP. Thus, only the causer and causee NPs are recorded in the verb. In Blackfoot, the number of core arguments per causative verb never exceeds two owing to the detransitivization. In effect, then, the number of core arguments in causatives is exactly the same as in (transitive) noncausative sentences.

In Halkomelem, a Salish language, morphological causativization is possible only if the noncausative verb is first detransitivized via the antipassive suffix *-əm* (Gerdts 1984: 194–195). Thus, (25.a) is ungrammatical, since the causative suffix *-st* is added to the transitive verb root *qʷəl*. In contrast, (25.b) is grammatical, since the transitive verb is antipassivized (i.e. detransitivized) before morphological causativization takes place.

(25) HALKOMELEM

  a. *ni   cən q'ʷəl-ət-stəxʷ kʷθə səplíl ʔə   łə   słéni?
         AUX 1S bake-TR-CS DET bread OBL DET woman
         'I had the woman bake the bread.'

  b. ni   cən q'ʷə́l-əm-stəxʷ θə   słéni? ʔə kʷθə səplíl
         AUX 1S bake-AP-CS   DET woman OBL DET bread
         'I had the woman bake the bread.'

Crowley (1978: 87–88) points out that in Bandjalang, an Australian Aboriginal language, the causative suffix *-ma* can be added to intransitive verbs. When they undergo the morphological causativization, however, transitive verbs must first be detransitivized via the antipassive suffix *-li*.

As noted earlier, detransitivization is achieved in two ways. One way is to add some affix to the transitive verb to detransitivize it, as in Blackfoot, Halkomelem, or Bandjalang. The other way is to incorporate the direct object NP into the verb complex as in Southern Tiwa. In this Kiowa-Tanoan language, the causative verb registers only two arguments, that is, the causer and the causee NPs. When the causative suffix *-'am* is added to transitive verbs, the direct object NP of the original verb is obligatorily incorporated into the verb complex (Baker 1988: 194–195).

(26) SOUTHERN TIWA

  a. I-'u'u-kur-'am-ban
      1SG/S:2SG/O-baby-hold-CS-PST

  b. *'U'ude i-kur-'am-ban
      baby   1SG/S:2SG/O-hold-CS-PST
      'I made you hold the baby.'

The sentence without incorporation of the direct object NP of the original verb as in (26.b) is ungrammatical. In Southern Tiwa, core arguments should be registered in the verb complex, while optionally they can appear in full forms as well. So, *'u'ude* 'baby' in (26.b) is intended to be a core argument. But as the causative verb has already reached its capacity of registering the core arguments (i.e. the causer and causee NPs), thereby being unable to record the full NP *'u'ude*, the sentence is ruled out as ungrammatical. On the other hand, in (26.a) the same NP is incorporated into the verb complex, thus effectively making the original verb intransitive.[25] The subject NP of the detransitivized verb and the causer NP associated with the causative suffix -'*am* can now be registered in the verb without any difficulty, that is, without violating the NP density control requirement in the language.

Without the alternative interpretation, it is difficult to explain why in such languages as Blackfoot, Bandjalang, Halkomelem, and Southern Tiwa transitive verbs have to be detransitivized prior to undergoing morphological causativization. Further, the alternative interpretation can explain why it is transitive verbs, not intransitive verbs, that must obligatorily undergo the grammatical treatment in question for successful morphological causativization. Equally importantly, these languages provide direct evidence against Comrie's universal theory, which is crucially dependent on the paradigm case. According to Comrie, it is the embedded subject, i.e. the causee NP, that should be demoted or displaced, while the other original arguments always retain their grammatical relations. Contrary to the paradigm case, however, the above languages clearly have the direct object of the original verb changed to a noncore NP through detransitivization. Further, the causee NP does not take up the next available position, i.e. indirect object, but it steals the direct object relation from the original direct object NP.[26] In sum, these languages do not only fail to conform to the predictions of the CH theory, but they also cast serious doubt on the theoretical validity of the paradigm case itself.

Notes

1. The same theory of causatives is presented in Comrie (1981a [1989]).
2. Comrie is largely concerned with morphological causatives, although he considers the 'quasi-morphological' causative such as in French (ex. (1)). Accordingly, this chapter will also be concerned only with morphological and quasi-morphological causatives. The term 'causative(s)' used in this chapter must be understood to refer only to these causatives.
3. Although there is no explicit clause boundary marker signalling embeddedness in (2), the fact that the direct object NPs of the lower (or embedded) verbs do not appear in reflexive forms can be taken as evidence that there is somehow a clause boundary between the NP *John* and the lower verbs, since English reflexivization is a clause-bound rule or since reflexives are locally bound in English.
4. This is only a brief outline of their universal theory of relative clause

formation. For more, see the relevant articles.

5. This chapter is not concerned with the semantic/pragmatic difference directly associated with the different case markings of the causee NP, i.e. *à* vs *par*, in French. For further detail, see Hyman and Zimmer (1976).

6. The adessive case expresses the instrument and some other locative roles in Finnish (Comrie 1976b: 273).

7. Due to lack of empirical counterevidence, Comrie (1975: 17–19) leaves open the possibility that there may be languages that allow doubling on subject position in noncausative sentences, e.g. Japanese and Korean. However, Comrie (1976b: 294–295) comes to the conclusion that there is no language that allows doubling on subject position in causative constructions.

8. Both Barry Blake and Anna Siewierska point out that Comrie's analysis can be (re)interpreted as relating to operations on predicate argument structure. This is possible, but, as will be shown here, this is not Comrie's intention.

9. Of course, not all intransitive verbs will undergo morphological causativization, owing to semantic (e.g. unaccusativity), morphological, and idiosyncratic lexical restrictions, which this chapter is not concerned with.

10. In these languages, of course, (biclausal) syntactic causative constructions will be used for nonintransitive verbs.

11. The affix -*v́v*'- represents a sequence of two vowels.

12. Comrie (1975: 9–11) calls this particular phenomenon a case of causative blockage.

13. Core arguments are those arguments strictly required by the valence of the verb in question. Noncore arguments include arguments such as locative, temporal, beneficiary, etc. Frequently, core and noncore arguments are treated differently in grammar. Across languages, core arguments tend to be crossreferenced on the verb and/or they are susceptible to various syntactic rules. Noncore arguments normally do not have these characteristics.

14. It must be understood that, in what follows, ordinary noncausative constructions or sentences are simplex sentences, unless indicated otherwise. That is, they have simple structure at both surface and underlying levels.

15. It is suspected that there is some correlation between the maximum number of core NPs per simplex sentence and the grammatical status of IO.

16. At the moment, it is not clear what factor(s) determine(s) the omission target: which core NP argument is not going to be expressed. Therefore the omission target must be mentioned in the grammar of each language of this type.

17. The notion of NP density control does not seem to be totally new. For

instance, Cattell (1976) speaks of the 'Overcrowding Principle', which is quite similar to NP density control, although Cattell's principle, in conjunction with the 'Ecology Constraint', is intended to account for various movement rules of Transformational Grammar, but not for the causative construction in question. More relevant to the notion of NP density control is Dik (1985), who puts forward what he (1985: 3, 14–20) calls the 'Principle of Formal Adjustment', whereby derived constructions are under pressure to adjust their formal expression to the prototypical expression model provided by nonderived constructions. This is in fact more or less of the essence of NP density control, although no adjustment of the kind that Dik has in mind is assumed in the NP density control hypothesis: both noncausatives and causatives are subject to the same requirement concerning the number of core NPs permitted per simplex sentence (the present writer is grateful to Anna Siewierska for drawing his attention to the existence of Dik 1985). In fact, the NP density control seems to be more closely related to the notion of the 'morphosyntactically licensed argument position (MAP) threshold' that Gerdts (1992, 1993a and 1993b) has recently invoked within the Mapping Theory, which is rooted in a Relational Grammar tradition. The MAP threshold represents the number of direct argument positions (i.e. core arguments) allowed in a given language. Thus, some may be two-MAP languages, others may be three-MAP languages, and so on.

18. In this connection, the controversy surrounding French-type causatives (as in (11)), in which the causee NP appears as an agent phrase of passives (e.g. Aissen 1974a, Comrie 1975, 1976b, 1981a [1989], Kayne 1975, Radford 1978, and Rosen 1983), is understandable. Now, it is clear that the prime motivation for expressing the causee NP as an agent phrase is NP density control operative across all simplex constructions. So, those who argue that there is passivization prior to causativization in the French-type causative are correct in pointing to the fact that the same agent phrase is used in both passives and causatives. Those who argue against this 'passive' analysis are also correct, since the ultimate motivation for expressing the causee NP as an agent phrase in causatives is in nature different from the ultimate motivation for expressing the original subject NP as an agent phrase in passives. The present writer tends to agree more with the opponents of the passive analysis of the French-type causative, because in passives it is always the original subject NP that can be omitted (owing to downgrading of the original subject NP concomitant with the promotion of the original direct object NP), whereas in causatives it is either the causee NP (e.g. Afar above) or the original direct object NP (e.g. Babungo above) that can appear as an adjunct NP or be eliminated. This can be taken as a clear piece of evidence that it is NP density control that motivates agent phrases in causatives. Otherwise, the omission of the causee NP and the

omission of the original direct object NP in causatives would be unrelated phenomena. However, under the alternative view, these seemingly disparate phenomena can be explained in a uniform fashion.

19. Comrie (1975: 23) also regards this causee marker in Gilyak as a kind of oblique marker, although, as shown in section 6.3, he believes that his complex underlying hypothesis is well motivated by the fact that the (oblique) causee marker is used exclusively in causatives.

20. In fact, Comrie (1976b: 264–266) cites lack of doubling as one of the defining features of the paradigm case. He also claims that doubling is irrelevant to the CH, the idealized case of which is the paradigm case. It seems to be very difficult to reconcile these two statements regarding the CH.

21. Whether doubling is only a case-marking phenomenon or it is also a syntactic one is not addressed in Comrie's work. Kozinsky and Polinsky (1993) tackle this very issue in Korean and Dutch, and claim that although coded as DOs in causatives, the causee and patient arguments may not both function syntactically as DOs. This is indeed an interesting idea, since it may further provide evidence for the alternative interpretation in that only one of the two arguments coded as DOs is really a DO syntactically, and the other a noncore NP.

22. Evidence that direct object is less of a core NP than subject comes from the fact that direct object can be incorporated into the verb in languages throughout the world (cf. Mithun 1984b, Tomlin 1986: 78–81). But subject incorporation is extremely rare. Further, the sequence of the verb and direct object can be replaced by a proverbial form, as in English: *Jane bought a science magazine and so did Tom.* However, there is no known language in which the subject and verb sequence can be replaced in a similar manner. This difference in behaviour strongly supports the view here that subject is more of a core NP than direct object.

23. Cf. the Babungo causative in (23), in which the original direct object must be completely omitted or appear as an optional adjunct. Note that, unlike that in Blackfoot, the noncausative verb in Babungo is not detransitivized before undergoing causativization.

24. Frantz (1971: 19) notes that with transitive animate verbs (i.e. with both animate actors and undergoers) some agreement suffixes are optional only if the NPs with which they agree are clearly present in the immediate clause.

25. Hopper and Thompson (1980) observe the tendency of indefinite, rather than definite, object NPs to be incorporated into the verb stem. The direct object NP in (26) is neither indefinite nor nonreferential. Hence, the incorporation in (26.a) is solely motivated by the NP density control in Southern Tiwa, not because of the NP properties to which Hopper and Thompson refer.

26. Comrie (1976b: 282–284) discusses Georgian, in which exactly the

same thing can be observed: the causee NP steals the indirect object relation from the original indirect object NP. However, he (1976b: 283) does not feel that this calls for any modification of his universal theory, because it is due to a general principle in Georgian: a newly created indirect object demotes an old indirect object. However, as Comrie (1976b: 283) himself notes, this phenomenon happens in noncausative constructions only in perfect tense. Further, it seems that in non-causative constructions in perfect tense Georgian marks the original indirect object NP as an oblique NP in order to distinguish it from the subject NP, which has to be marked in the dative–accusative (i.e. indirect object marker) in perfect tense. However, in causative construc-tions, the embedded subject (i.e. the causee NP) steals the indirect object relation from the original indirect object NP, regardless of tense, which Comrie (1976b: 283) also takes note of. Therefore, something else seems to motivate the causee NP and the original indirect object NP to appear as an indirect object NP and an oblique NP, respectively. It is argued that NP density control is operative here as well: the original indirect object NP is expressed as an oblique NP, because otherwise the NP density control requirement in Georgian would be violated due to the presence of the causer NP. It should be mentioned that relational grammarians (e.g. Gibson and Raposo 1986) have also pointed out that in languages such as Chamorro, Choctaw, and Tzotzil the embedded subject always surfaces as direct object, even when the basic verb is transitive. Since any further discussion of Relational Grammar is beyond the scope of this book, suffice it to say here that what has been discussed in this chapter will hold *vis-à-vis* Relational Grammar *mutatis mutandis* (Gerdts's MAP threshold, mentioned in note 17, can be regarded as an attempt to capture NP density control within the framework of Relational Grammar).

Chapter 7

Finale

This book has offered an alternative universal typology of causative constructions, a typology that can not only lend much needed insight into the nature of causation, but also 'generate significant questions that are clear, explicit, and likely to be productively answerable' (Sanders 1976: 15).

Thus, the temporally based cognitive structure of causation has been put forward on the basis of the typology: the temporal sequence of GOAL, EVENT, and RESULT. By identifying these three components of causation and assembling them into a coherent whole, the cognitive structure describes the way in which the human mind cognizes causation. It is hoped that it may, for all its tentativeness and speculativeness, provide a useful basis for an enhanced understanding of causation.

By recognizing the existence of the *AND* type and, especially, of the *PURP* type, the typology has also helped pose the question as to how these (originally) noncausative constructions are used to carry out causative function. This has in turn led to the 'discovery' of a rich pragmatic foundation of the causative constructions. It has thus been discussed how pragmatic assumptions, e.g. about human behaviour, can motivate the ordinary coordinate and purposive constructions to become institutionalized as fully fledged causative constructions. Further, it points to the existence of **the free ride policy** in language: existing constructions are conscripted into service to carry out functions other than those which they are originally designed for. It is anticipated that future research in universal typology will uncover more similar cases in areas other than causatives.

Since it sanctions only particular types of causative construction, a further question has arisen as to whether or not the typology can enable the identification of sources of causative affixes. Thus, the diachronic model of causative affixes has been developed on the basis of the typology, whereby the origins of causative affixes can be tracked down to various instantiations of the term *PURP* and potentially of the term *AND*, in addition to the hitherto known source, the term [Vcause]. The model is so powerful, it seems, that insofar as causatives affixes are concerned, it may offset lack of historical documentation, which is characteristic of the majority of the world's languages.

The traditional typology of causative constructions, which is based on the parameter of fusion or compactness (i.e. lexical, morphological, and syntactic types), or the semantic characterizations of causation which have been related to that typology, for that matter, would not be able to address the synchronic, diachronic, and functional issues which have been treated in the present work. The moral point that needs emphasis here is that the 'significant questions' that have been raised about causatives and causation in this book could not have been generated without such a factually adequate typology as the one presented in Chapter 2 being available in the first place.

Finally, it is hoped that although it is only a small step toward the understanding of causatives and causation, the present study will contribute to the generating of further 'significant questions' that can be formulated and answered in terms of human cognition and behaviour, thereby opening up a much wider range of avenues of exploring or understanding the nature of language and, ultimately, of the human mind.

Data base

This appendix alphabetically lists the languages of the data base set up for the present study, followed by the relevant references.

A

Abau	Bailey (1975)
Abelam (or **Ambulas**)	Laycock (1965), Wilson (1980)
Abkhaz	Hewitt (1979)
Aborlan Tagbanwa	Green (1979)
Acehnese	Durie (1985)
Acholi	Crazzolara (1955)
Acoma	Miller (1965)
Adzera (Amari dialect)	Holzknecht (1986)
Afar	Bliese (1981)
Agarabi	Goddard (1976, 1980)
Aghem	Hyman (1979)
Agta	Healey (1960)
Aguaruna (or **Jiraro**)	Larsen (1963)
Ainu	Patrie (1982), Refsing (1986)
Akra (or **Gã**)	Zimmermann (1858)
Alamblak	Bruce (1984, 1986, 1988)
Alawa	Sharpe (1972)
Albanian	Newmark (1957), Newmark, Hubbard, and Prifti (1982)
Alyawarra	Yallop (1977)
Ambrym (or **Lonwolwol**)	Paton (1971)
Amele	Roberts (1987)
Amharic	Leslau (1968), Titov (1976)
Anejom (or **Aneityumese**)	Lynch (1982b)
Anêm	Thurston (1982)
Anguthimri	Crowley (1981)
Apalai	Koehn and Koehn (1986)

Arabic	Aboul-Fetouh (1969; Egyptian Arabic), Cowell (1964; Syrian Arabic), Erwin (1963; Iraqi Arabic), Gamal-Eldin (1967; Egyptian Arabic), Harrell (1962; Moroccan Arabic), Mitchell (1956; Egyptian Arabic), Owens (1984; Eastern Libyian Arabic), Qafisheh (1977; Gulf Arabic), Saad (1982; Classical Arabic), Tsiapera (1969; Cypriot Maronite Arabic), Wright (1955)
Aranda	Strehlow (1944)
Arosi	Capell (1971)
Asmat	Voorhoeve (1965)
Assiniboine	Levin (1964)
Assyrian	Mercer (1966), Tsereteli (1978)
Atchin	Capell and Layard (1980)
Au	Scorza (1985)
Auca	Peeke (1973)
Awa	Loving (1973), Loving and Loving (1973), Loving and McKaughan (1973)
Awtuw	Feldman (1986)
Axininca Campa	Payne (1981)
Ayacucho Quechua	Parker (1969)
Azerbaijan(i)	Garbell (1965; Jewish Neo-Aramaic dialect), Householder and Lofti (1965)

B

Baba Malay	Lim (1988)
Babungo	Schaub (1985)
Bāgandji	Hercus (1982)
Balangao	Shetler (1976)
Balawaia	Kolia (1975)
Balinese	Barber (1977)
Balti (or **Baldi**)	Read (1934)
Baluchi	Barker and Mengal (1969), Elfenbein (1966)
Bandjalang	Crowley (1978)

Banoni	Lincoln (1976)
Barai	Olson (1975, 1981)
Bardi	Metcalfe (1975)
Bashkir	Poppe (1964)
Basque	Eguzkitza (1987), Saltarelli (1988), Wilbur (1976)
Baure	Baptista and Wallin (1967)
Bele	Schuh (1978)
Bella Coola	Davis and Saunders (1978)
Bemba	Givón (1972)
Bena-Bena	Young (1971)
Bengali	Bykova (1981), Dimock, Bhattacharji, and Chatterjee (1965), Ray, Hai, and Ray (1966)
Bhojpuri	Shukla (1981)
Biblical Hebrew	F.I. Andersen (1974), Blau (1976)
Bichelamar	Guy (1974b)
Big Nambas	Fox (1979)
Bikol	Mintz (1971)
Bilaan	Abrams (1970)
Biloxi	Einaudi (1976)
Binandere	Capell (1969), Wilson (1969)
Binongan Itneg	Walton (1975)
Bisu	Nishida (1973)
Blackfoot	Frantz (1971)
Boikin (Kwusaun dialect)	Laycock (1965)
Bolivian Quechua	Crapo and Aitkon (1986)
Bororo	Huestis (1963)
Brahui	Andronov (1980)
Brao	Keller (1976)
Breton	Hemon (1975), Press (1986)
Buginese	Sirk (1983)
Bulgarian	Rudin (1986)
Bunum	Starosta (1973)
Burarra	Glasgow and Garner (1980)
Buriat	Poppe (1960)
Burmese	Cornyn and Roop (1968), Okell (1969), Stewart (1955)
Burushaski	Lorimer (1935–1938)
Busa	Wedekind (1972)
Byelorussian	Mayo (1976)

C

Cakchiquel	Townsend (1960)
Cambodian	Huffman (1970), Jacob (1968)
Candoshi	Anderson and Wise (1963)
Canela-Krahô	Popjes and Popjes (1986), Shell (1952)
Carib	Hoff (1968)
Cashinawa	Cromack (1968)
Casiguran Dumagat	Headland and Healey (1974)
Catalan	Yates (1975)
Cayapa	Abrahamson (1962)
Cayuvava	Key (1967)
Cebuano	Bunye and Yap (1971a, 1971b), Wolff (1966, 1967)
Central Bontoc	Reid (1970)
Chacobo	Prost (1967)
Chagatay	Eckmann (1966)
Chaldean	Sara (1974)
Cham	Blood (1977)
Chamorro	Gibson (1980), Topping (1973)
Chatino	Pride (1965)
Chemehuevi	Press (1979)
Chepang	Caughley (1982)
Cheremis	Sebeok and Ingermann (1961)
Chi-Mwi:ni	Abasheikh (1979)
Chichewa	Watkins (1937)
Chichimeco Jonaz	Suarez (1984)
Chinese	Chao (1968), Chu (1983), Li and Thompson (1981), Norman (1988)
Choctaw	Davies (1986), Munro (1982)
Choltí Maya	Fought (1984)
Chrau	Thomas (1971)
Chuvash	Krueger (1961)
Classical Armenian	Godel (1975)
Classical Nahuatl	Andrews (1975)
Coatlán Mixe	Hoogshagen (1984)
Cocama	Faust (1971)
Cochabamba Quechua	Lastra (1968)
Cora	Casad (1984)
Cornish	Jenner (1904)

Cotabato Manobo	Johnston (1979)
Cree	Wolfart and Carroll (1981)
Czech	Bidwell (1971), Harkins (1953), Lee and Lee (1959 [1984]), Mikula (1936 [1940]), Sova (1962a, 1962b)

D

Daga	Murane (1974)
Dakota	Boas and Deloria (1941 [1976])
Dani	Bromley (1981), Stap (1966)
Dehu	Tryon (1968a)
Dhangar-Kurux	Gordon (1973)
Dharawal	Eades (1976)
Dholuo	Omondi (1982)
Dhurga	Eades (1976)
Diegueño	Langdon (1970)
Dihovo	Groen (1977)
Diola Fogny	Sapir (1965)
Diyari	Austin (1981a)
Djambarrpuyŋu	Buchanan (1978)
Djapu	Morphy (1983)
Djaru	Tsunoda (1981)
Djingili	Chadwick (1975)
Dobu	Lithgow (1975)
Dyirbal	Dixon (1972)
Dyula	Long and Diomandé (n.d.)

E

Eastern Armenian	Fairbanks and Stevick (1958)
Eastern Kadazan	Hurlbut (1988)
Eastern Ojibwa	Bloomfield (1956)
Eastern Pomo	McLendon (1975)
Ecuador Quichua	Orr (1962)
Enga	Lang (1975)
Engenni	Thomas (1978)
English	informant work
Eskimo	Hinz (1944)
Essejja	Shoemaker and Shoemaker (1967)
Estonian	Oinas (1967), Raun and Saareste

Ewe

(1965), Tauli (1973)
Warburton, Kpotufe, and Glover
(1968), Westermann (1930)

Ewondo

Redden (1980)

F

Faroese   Lockwood (1964)
Fasu (or **Namo Me**)   Loeweke and May (1980)
Fe'fe'   Hyman (1971)
Fijian   Hazlewood (1872), Schütz (1986)
Finnish   Atkinson (1977), Collinder (1960,
                         1969), Harms (1964), Karlsson
                         (1983)
Fore   Scott (1968, 1973, 1978)
French   Judge and Healey (1983), Kayne
                         (1975)
Frisian   Markey (1981), Tiersma (1985)
Fula   Arnott (1961, 1970)
Fulfulde   McIntosh (1984)
Futuna-Aniwa   Capell (1984a), Dougherty (1983)

G

Ga'dang   Walrod (1976, 1979)
Gadsup   Franz (1976)
Gaelic   Dorian (1978), MacKinnon (1971
                         [1974])
Gahuku   Deibler (1976)
Galab   Sasse (1974)
Galambu   Schuh (1978)
Garawa   Furby and Furby (1977)
Garo   Burling (1961)
Gbadi   Koopman (1984)
Gbeya   Samarin (1966)
Georgian   Aronson (1982), Harris (1981)
Gera   Schuh (1978)
German   Harbert (1977)
Gidabal   Geytenbeek and Geytenbeek (1971)
Goajiro   Holmer (1949)
Gonja   Painter (1970)

Grebo	Innes (1966)
Greek	Andreades (1974), Browning (1982), Goodwin and Gulick (1958), Householder, Kazazis, and Koutsoudas (1964), Joseph and Philippaki-Warburton (1987), Palmer (1980), Thomson (1966), Thumb (1964)
Guajajara	Bendor-Samuel (1972)
Guaraní	Gregores and Suárez (1967)
Guaymí	Alphonse (1956)
Gugu Yimidhirr	Haviland (1979), Zwaan (1969)
Guhu-Samane	Richert (1975)
Gujarati	Cardona (1965)
Gumbáiŋgar	Eades (1979), Smythe (1948)
Gunbalang	Harris (1969)
Gurkhali	Meerendonk (1949)
Gurung	Glover (1974)

H

Haitian Creole	Hall (1953)
Halbi	Woods (1973)
Halia	Allen (1972)
Halkomelem	Gerdts (1984)
Haroi	Goschnick (1977)
Hausa	Kraft and Kraft (1973), Smirnova (1982)
Hawaiian	Elbert and Pukui (1979)
Hebrew	Rosén (1977)
Hidatsa	Matthews (1965)
Hiligaynon	Motus (1971), Wolfenden (1971, 1975)
Hindi	Bender (1967b), Hook (1974), McGregor (1977), Saksena (1982a, 1982b)
Hiri Motu (or **Police Motu**)	Dutton and Voorhoeve (1974), Lister-Turner and Clark (1930), Wurm and Harris (1963)
Hixkaryana	Derbyshire (1979, 1985)
Ho	Burrows (1915 [1980])

Houailou	Lichtenberk (1978)
Hua	Haiman (1980a)
Huallaga (or **Huanuco**)	
Quechua	Weber (1983)
Huasteca Nahuatl	Beller and Beller (1979)
Huichol	Grimes (1964)
Hungarian	Károly (1972)

I

Iai	Tryon (1968b)
Iamalele	Beaumont and Beaumont (1975)
Iatmul	Laycock (1965), Staalsen (1972)
Iau	Bateman (1986)
Iduna	Huckett (1976)
Igbo	Carrell (1970), Meier, Meier, and Bendor-Samuel (1975)
Ignaciano	Ott and Ott (1967)
Ijọ	Williamson (1965)
Ilianen Manobo	Shand (1976)
Ilokano	Bernabe, Lapid, and Sibayan (1971), Constantino (1971)
Imbabura Quechua	Jake (1985)
Imonda	Seiler (1985)
Indonesian	Dardjowidjojo (1966), Heer (1975), MacDonald (1976), Tampubolon (1983)
Inga	Levinsohn (1976)
Iquito	Eastman and Eastman (1963)
Iraya (or **Mangyan**)	Tweddell (1958)
Irish	Bammesberger (1982), Dillion and Croínín (1961), Lucas (1979), McCloskey (1978), o'Huallacháin and o'Mícheál (1976), Stenson (1981)
Isirawa	Oguri (1985a, 1985b)
Isle de France	Baker and Corne (1982)
Isthmus Nahuat	Law (1966)
Italian	Burzio (1986), Lepschy and Lepschy (1977), Vincent (1988b)
Itonama	Camp and Liccardi (1967)

Ivatan	Hidalgo and Hidalgo (1971), Reid (1966)
Iwaidja	Pym (1985)
Ixil	Elliott (1960)

J

Jacaltec	Day (1973), Craig (1977)
Jahai	Schebesta (1926–1928)
Jamaican Creole	Bailey (1966)
Jamietepec Mixtec	Johnson (1988)
Jan-Hut	Diffloth (1976)
Japanese	Hinds (1986), Kuno (1973), Martin (1975)
Jaqaru	Hardman (1966)
Javanese	Horne (1961), Poedjosoedarmo (1986), Suharno (1982)
Jicaltepec Mixtec	Bradley (1970)
Jirel	Strahm (1975)
Jukun	Shimizu (1980)

K

Kaingang	Henry (1948)
Kala Lagaw Ya	Kennedy (1984)
Kalamian Tagbanwa	Ruch (1974)
Kaliai-Kove	Counts (1969)
Kalispel	Vogt (1940)
Kalkatungu	Blake (1979a)
Kammu (or **Khmu**)	Premsrirat (1987), Svantesson (1983)
Kanakuru	Newman (1974)
Kannada	Andronov (1969b)
Kanuri	Hutchison (1976), Lucas (1967)
Kapampangan	Forman (1971), Mirikitani (1972)
Kapau	Oates and Oates (1968)
Karen	Jones (1961)
Karok	Bright (1957a)
Kaugel	Blowers and Blowers (1970)
Kavalan	Starosta (1973)
Kayardild	Evans (1985)

Keley-i Kallahan	Hohulin (1971)
Kewa	Franklin (1971)
Khalaj	Doerfer (1971)
Kharia	Biligiri (1965)
Khasi	Henderson (1976), Rabel (1961)
Ki-Meru	Hodges (1977)
Kickapoo	Voorhis (1974)
Kikuyu	Perez (1986)
Kimaragang	Kroeger (1988)
Kinyarwanda	Dubnova (1984), Kimenyi (1980a)
Kiowa	Watkins (1984)
Kirfi	Schuh (1978)
Kiribatese (or **Gilbertese**)	Groves, Groves, and Jacobs (1985)
Kiruúndi	Perez (1986)
Klamath	Barker (1964)
Kobon	Davies (1981)
Koita	Dutton (1975b)
Kotia Oriya	Gustafsson (1973)
Kolami	McNair and McNair (1973)
Korafe	Farr and Farr (1975)
Korean	Kang (1986), Kim (1984), Lukoff (1982), Shin (1987), Sohn (1994), Song (1988b, 1988d, 1993)
Koya	Tyler (1968)
Kriol	Harris (1986)
Kuman	Trefry (1969)
Kunimaipa	Geary (1977)
Kuniyanti	McGregor (1984)
Kunjen	Sommer (1969, 1972)
Kupia	Christmas and Christmas (1973a, 1973b)
Kurdish	McCarus (1958), MacKenzie (1961–1962)
Kwaio	Keesing (1985)
Kwakiutl	Boas (1947)
Kxoe	Köhler (1981)

L

Labu	Siegel (1984)
Ladakhi	Koshal (1979)

Lahu	Matisoff (1969, 1973 [1982], 1976)
Lakher (or **Mara**)	Lorrain (1951)
Lamang	Wolff (1983)
Lamani	Trail (1970)
Lampung	Walker (1976)
Lango	Driberg (1923), Noonan (1981), Noonan and Bavin (1981)
Lao	Honts (1979), Morev, Moskalyov, and Plam (1979)
Laragia	Capell (1984b)
Lardil	Klokeid (1976)
Latin	Hammond (1976), Lakoff (1968), Palmer (1954 [1966]), Vincent (1988a), Woodcock (1959 [1985])
Lavongai	Stamm (1988)
Lelemi	Höftmann (1971)
Lenakel	Lynch (1978)
Lenni Lenape	Zeisberger (1827)
Lhomi	Vesalainen and Vesalainen (n.d.)
Limos Kalinga	Wiens (1979)
Lisu	Hope (1974)
Literary Macedonian	Lunt (1952)
Lithuanian	Dambriunas, Klimas, and Schmalstieg (1966 [1972])
Logbara (or **Ma'di**)	Crazzolara (1960)
Loko	Innes (1964)
Luangiua	Salmond (1974)
Luganda	Ashton (1954)
Luiseño	Hyde (1971), Kroeber and Grace (1960)
Luo	Stafford (1967)
Lushai	Bright (1957b), Lorrain and Savidge (1898)
Lusi	Thurston (1982)
Lwo	Crazzolara (1954)

M

Maa(sai)	Tucker and Mpaayei (1955)
Machiguenga	Snell and Wise (1963)
Mae (or **Emwae**)	Capell (1962)

Mae-Sot	Sarawit (1979)
Magi	Thomson (1975)
Maidu	Shipley (1963, 1964)
Maisin	Ross (1984)
Maithili	Williams (1973)
Makua	Stucky (1985)
Malagasy	Randriamasimanana (1986)
Malak Malak	Birk (1976)
Malay	Winstedt (1914 [1957])
Malayalam	Andrewskutty (1971), Panikkar (1973), Prabodhachandran Nayar (1972)
Mam	England (1983)
Mamanwa	Miller and Miller (1976)
Manam	Lichtenberk (1983)
Manx	Broderick (1984), Goodwin (1974), Stowell (n.d.)
Maori	Biggs (1969), Henare (1987), Hohepa (1967), Rere (1961, 1965)
Mara	Heath (1981)
Maranungku	Tryon (1970a)
Marathi	Lambert (1943)
Margany and **Gunya dialects**	Breen (1981b)
Margi	Hoffmann (1963)
Marshallese	Bender (1969), Zewen (1977)
Maung	Capell and Hinch (1970)
Mauritian Creole	Baker (1972)
Mayi	Breen (1981a)
Melayu Betawi	Ikranagara (1975)
Mende	Innes (1962, 1963, 1967)
Menomini	Bloomfield (1962)
Mezquital Otomi	Hess (1968), Lanier (1968), Wallis (1956, 1964)
Mianmin	Smith and Weston (1974)
Miao	Chang and Kworay (1972)
Michoacán Nahuatl	Sischo (1979)
Mixe	Haitsma and Haitsma (1976)
Mixtec	Hinton (1982)
Mojave	Munro (1976)
Mokilese	Harrison (1976)
Mon	Guillon (1976)

Mongolian	Binnick (1979), Poppe (1970), Street (1963)
Mono-Alu	Fagan (1986)
Mountain Koiali	R. Garland and S. Garland (1975), S. Garland (1980)
Movima	Judy and Judy (1967)
Muhiang	Alungum, Conrad, and Lukas (1978)
Mukah (or **Melanau**)	Blust (1988)
Mumuye	Shimizu (1979)
Mundari	Cook (1965)
Murinbata	Street (1980)

N

Nakanai	Johnston (1978a, 1978b)
Nama (**Hottentot**)	Hagman (1977)
Namabu	Laycock (1965)
Nancowry	Radhakrishnan (1976, 1981)
Nataoran-Amis	Chen (1987)
Navajo	Haile (1926 [1974]), Sapir and Hoijer (1967), Young and Morgan (1980)
Ndjébbana (or **Kunibidji**)	McKay (1984)
Nengone	Tryon (1967)
Nepali	Matthews (1984), Srivastava (1962)
Newari	Bendix (1984), Hale and Manandhar (1980)
Nez Perce	Aoki (1970)
Ngala	Laycock (1965)
Ngalakan	Merlan (1983)
Ngandi	Heath (1978a)
Ngankikurungkurr	Hoddinott and Kofod (1988)
Ngarinjin	Coate and Oates (1970), Rumsey (1982)
Ngiyambaa	Donaldson (1980)
Nguna	Schütz (1969)
Nicobarese	Braine (1970)
Nimboran	Anceaux (1965)
Nissan (or **Nehan**)	Todd (1978b)
Niuean	Seiter (1980)
Njuar	Douglas (1976)

Nkore-Kiga	Taylor (1985)
Noni	Hyman (1981)
North Puebla Nahuatl	Brockway (1979)
Northern Kankanay	Hettick (1974)
Northern Sahaptin	Jacobs (1931)
Norwegian	Haugen (1982), Haugen and Chapman (1982), Klouman (1984)
Nuer	Crazzolara (1933)
Núng	Saul and Wilson (1980)
Nunggubuyu	Heath (1984)
Nupe	Smith (1967)
Nyangumata	O'Grady (1964)
Nyawaygi	Dixon (1983)

O

Obolo	Faraclas (1984)
Ocotepec	Alexander (1988)
Ömie	Austing and Upïa (1975)
Oksapmin	Lawrence (1972)
Old Church Slavic	Lunt (1965), Schmalstieg (1976 [1982])
Old Icelandic	Valfells and Cathey (1981)
Old Irish	Lehmann and Lehmann (1975)
Old Prussian	Schmalstieg (1974)
Olo	McGregor and McGregor (1982)
Orokaiva	Healey, Isoroembo, and Chittleborough (1969)
Oromo	Owens (1985), Dubinsky, Lloret, and Newman (1988)
Oscan	Buck (1928)
Ossetic	Abaev (1964)

P

Paamese	Crowley (1982a, 1987)
Palauan	Josephs (1975)
Pangasinan	Benton (1971)
Panjabi	Tolstaya (1981)
Papiamentu	Fodale (1983)
Parengi (or **Gorum**)	Aze (1973)

Pashto	Lorimer (1915), Penzl (1955), Shafeev (1964)
Patep	Lauck (1976)
Pawaian	Trefry (1969)
Pazah	Starosta (1973)
Pengo	Burrow and Bhattacharya (1970)
Peñoles Mixtec	Daly (1973)
Persian	Boyle (1966), Lambton (1953), Mace (1962), Windfuhr (1979)
Pirahã	Everett (1986)
Piro	Matteson (1965)
Pitta-Pitta	Blake (1979b)
Piva	Lincoln (1976)
Polish	Brooks (1975), Corbridge-Patkaniowska (1948 [1952]), Schenker (1973), Stone (1980), Swan (1983), Teslar (1953)
Ponapean	Rehg (1981)
Portuguese	Câmara (1972), Thomas (1969; Brazilian)
Puget Sound Coast Salish	Tweddell (1950)
Puluwat	Elbert (1974)

R

Rao	Stanhope (1980)
Rejang	McGinn (1982)
Rengao	Gregerson (1979)
Reshe	Harris (1946)
Resígaro	Allin (1976)
Ritharngu	Heath (1980a)
Romontsch	Gregor (1982)
Róng (or **Lepcha**)	Mainwaring (1876)
Rotuman	Churchward (1940)
Roviana	Todd (1978a)
Rukai	Li (1973), Starosta (1973)
Rumanian	Deletant (1983), Mallinson (1986)
Russian	Beresford (1965 [1980]), Maltzoff (1985), Pulkina (1960), Ward (1955)

S

Sabah Murut	Prentice (1969, 1971)
Sakao	Guy (1974a)
Salt-Yui	Irwin (1974)
Sama (or **Bajau**)	Verheijen (1986)
Samoan	Marsack (1975), Neffgen (1918)
San Luis Potosí Huastec	McQuown (1984)
Sango	Samarin (1967a)
Sanio-Hiowe	R.K. Lewis (1972), S.C. Lewis (1972)
Sanskrit	Burrow (1955), Gonda (1966)
Sara-Ngambay	Thayer (1978)
Sarcee	Cook (1984)
Sawu (or **Savu, Hawu, Havu**)	Walker (1982)
Sayula Popoluca	Clark (1961, 1983)
Sedang	Smith (1979)
Sedik	Asai (1953)
Selepet	McElhanon (1972)
Senoufo	Mills (1984)
Sentani	Cowan (1965)
Serbo-Croatian	Babic (1973), Engelsfeld (1972), Partridge (1972), Zovko (1983)
Seychelles	Corne (1977)
Sherpa	Schöttelndreyer (1975)
Shona	Perez (1986)
Shuswap	Kuipers (1974)
Sie	Lynch and Capell (1983)
Sierra Nahuat	Robinson (1966)
Silacayoapan Mixtec	Shields (1988)
Sinhalese	Fairbanks, Gair, and De Silva (1968), Geiger (1938), Hundirapola (1975), Reynolds (1980)
Siraiki	Shackle (1976)
Sirionó	Priest and Priest (1967)
Siroi	Wells (1979)
Slovak	Miko (1972)
Somali	Bell (1953 [1969])
Sonrai	Shopen and Konaré (1970)
Sora	Starosta (1967)
Sorung	Lynch (1983b)

Southeastern Pomo	Moshinsky (1974)
Southern Agaw	Hetzron (1969)
Southern Sierra Miwok	Broadbent (1964)
South-west Tanna	Lynch (1982a)
Spanish	Bordelois (1988)
Squamish	Kuipers (1967, 1969)
Sranan	Sebba (1987)
Sre	Manley (1972)
Straits Salish (or **Songish**)	Raffo (1972)
Suena	Wilson (1974, 1976)
Sundanese	Hardjadibrata (1985)
Susu	Sangster and Faber (1969)
Swahili	Driever (1976), Myachina (1981), Vitale (1981)
Swedish	Björkhagen (1960)

T

Tabla	Collier and Gregerson (1985)
Tacana	Ottaviano and Ottaviano (1967)
Tagabili	Forsberg (1966)
Tagalog	Blake (1925 [1967]), De Guzman (1978, 1986), Ramos (1971, 1974), Schacter and Otanes (1972)
Tahitian	Tryon (1970b)
Tajik	Rastorgueva (1963)
Tamang	Everitt (1973)
Tamazight	Abdel-Massih (1968)
Tamil	Andronov (1969a), Pillai (1965), Pope (1979)
Tarascan	Foster (1969)
Tatar	Poppe (1963)
Tati	Yar-Shafer (1969)
Telefol	Healey (1965a, 1965b, 1966)
Telugu	Krishnamurti and Sarma (1968)
Temiar	Benjamin (1976)
Tera	Newman (1970)
Tetelcingo Nahuatl	Tuggy (1979, 1987)
Thai	Noss (1964), Panupong (1970), Vichit-Vadakan (1976)
Tibetan	Bell (1939), Goldstein and Nornang

	(1970), Hannah (1973)
Ticuna	Anderson (1962)
Tigak	Beaumont (1979)
Tiwi	Osborne (1974)
Toba Batak	Nababan (1981), Percival (1981),
	Tuuk (1971)
Tok Pisin	Woolford (1979a, 1979b), Wurm and
	Mühlhäusler (1985)
Tolai	Mosel (1984)
Tondano	Sneddon (1975)
Tongan	Tchekhoff (1981)
Totonac	Reid, Bishop, Button, and Longacre
	(1968)
Tswana	Cole (1955), Cole and Mokaila
	(1962)
Tunica	Haas (1950)
Turkana	Best (1983), Dimmendaal (1982,
	1983a, 1983b)
Turkish	Aissen (1974a, 1974b, 1979),
	Knecht (1986), Lewis (1967),
	Meskill (1970), Swift (1963),
	Underhill (1976)
Twi	Christaller (1875 [1964])
Tzeltal	Kaufman (1971)
Tzotzil	Aissen (1987), Cowan (1969),
	Delgaty (1960)
Tzutujil	Dayley (1985)

U

Uigur	Nadzhip (1971)
Ukrainian	Humesky (1980), Luckyj and
	Rudnyckyj (1949), Medushevsky
	and Zyatkovska (1963), Shevelov
	(1963; literary), Shklanka (1944)
Ulithian	Sohn and Bender (1973)
Uma Juman	Blust (1977)
Umbrian	Buck (1928)
Ura	Lynch (1983c)
Uradhi	Crowley (1983)
Urdu	Bender (1967a)

Urubu-Kaapor	Kakumasu (1986)
Usan (or **Wanuma**)	Reesink (1987)
Usarufa	Bee (1973)
Utaha	Lynch (1983d)
Uzbek	Raun (1969), Sjoberg (1963)

V

Vai	Welmers (1976)
Vata	Koopman (1984)
Vietnamese	Binh (1971), Clark (1978), Hoa (1971 [1974]), Quinn (1972), Thompson (1965 [1967])
Vogul	Kálmán (1965)
Votic	Ariste (1968)

W

Wahgi	Phillips (1976)
Wakhi	Lorimer (1958)
Walmatjari	Hudson (1978)
Wankumara (or **Galali**)	McDonald and Wurm (1979)
Wargamay	Dixon (1981)
Warlpiri	Hale (1981, 1982, 1983), Nash (1980)
Warndarang	Heath (1980b)
Waskia	Ross and Paol (1978)
Watjarri	Douglas (1981)
Wedau	King (1901)
Welsh	Jones and Thomas (1977), Rowland (1865), S.J. Williams (1980)
West Greenlandic	Fortescue (1984)
West Makian	Voorhoeve (1982)
Western Armenian	Bardakjian and Thomson (1977), Fairbanks (1958)
Western Bukidnon Manobo	Elkins (1970)
Western Desert	Bowe (1987), Glass (1983), Glass and Hackett (1970), Goddard (1983, 1988), Platt (1972)
Western Tarahumara	Burgess (1984)
Wichita	Rood (1976)

Wik-Munkan	Kilham (1977), Sayers (1976)
Wikchamni	Gamble (1978)
Witoto	Minor and Loos (1963)
Wiyot	Teeter (1964)
Wojokeso	West (1973)
Wolio	Anceaux (1952)

Y

Yagaria	Renck (1975)
Yakut	Krueger (1963)
Yanyuwa	Kirton (1978)
Yao	Mao and Chou (1972), Whiteley (1966)
Yapese	Jensen (1977)
Yaqui	Lindenfeld (1973)
Yareba	Weimer and Weimer (1975)
Yavapai	Kendall (1976)
Yay	Gedney (1965)
Yeletnye	Henderson (1975)
Yelogu	Laycock (1965)
Yessan-Mayo	Foreman (1974)
Yiddish	Katz (1987)
Yidiny	Dixon (1977)
Yir-Yoront	Alpher (1973)
Yoruba	Bamgbose (1966), Lord (1974), Ogunbowale (1970), Ward (1952 [1956])
Yukulta	Keen (1972, 1983)
Yupik	Jacobson (1977)
Yurak	Décsy (1966)
Yurok	Robins (1958)
Yuwaalaraay	C.J. Williams (1980)

Z

Zaparo	Peeke (1962)
Zulu	Doke (1927), Ziervogel and Louw (1967)
Zuni	Newman (1965)

Bibliography

Abbreviations used below:

AJL	*Australian Journal of Linguistics*
BLS	*Berkeley Linguistic Society*
CLS	*Chicago Linguistic Society*
FL	*Foundations of Language*
IJAL	*International Journal of American Linguistics*
JL	*Journal of Linguistics*
LI	*Linguistic Inquiry*
NLLT	*Natural Language and Linguistic Theory*
SiL	*Studies in Language*

ABAEV, V.I. (1964) *A grammatical sketch of Ossetic*. Mouton: The Hague.

ABASHEIKH, M.I. (1979) The grammar of Chi-Mwi:ni causatives. Unpublished Ph.D. dissertation, University of Illinois.

ABDEL-MASSIH, E.T. (1968) *Tamazight verb structure: a generative approach*. Indiana University Press: Bloomington.

ABOUL-FETOUH, H.M. (1969) *A morphological study of Egyptian colloquial Arabic*. Mouton: The Hague.

ABRAHAMSON, A. (1962) 'Cayapa: grammatical notes and texts', in B. Elson (ed.) (1962).

ABRAMS, N. (1970) 'Bilaan morphology', *Papers in Philippine Linguistics* 3: 1–62.

ADAMS, K.L. and N.F. CONKLIN (1973) 'Toward a theory of natural classification', *CLS* 9: 1–10.

AISSEN, J. (1974a) The syntax of causative constructions. Unpublished Ph.D. dissertation, Harvard University.

AISSEN, J. (1974b) 'Verb raising', *LI* 5: 325–366.

AISSEN, J. (1979) *The syntax of causative constructions*. Garland: New York.

AISSEN, J. (1987) *Tzotzil clause structure*. D. Reidel: Dordrecht.

AISSEN, J. and J. HANKAMER (1980) 'Lexical extension and grammatical transformations', *BLS* 6: 238–249.

AISSEN, J. and D.M. PERLMUTTER (1983) 'Clause reduction in

Spanish', in D.M. Perlmutter (ed.), *Studies in relational grammar I*. University of Chicago Press: Chicago.

AITCHISON, J. (1987) 'The language lifegame: prediction, explanation and linguistic change', in W. Koopman, F. van der Leek, O. Fischer, and R. Eaton (eds) (1987).

AITCHISON, J. (1988) 'Spaghetti junctions and recurrent routes', *Lingua* 77: 151–171.

ALEXANDER, R.M. (1988) 'A syntactic sketch of Ocotepec', in C.H. Bradley and B.E. Hollenbach (eds) (1988).

ALLAN, K. (1977) 'Classifiers', *Language* 53: 285–311.

ALLAN, K. (1986) *Linguistic meaning* (2 vols). Routledge and Kegan Paul: London.

ALLAN, K. (1987) 'Hierarchies and the choice of left conjuncts (with particular reference to English)', *JL* 23: 51–77.

ALLAN, K. (1988) Discourse structure in a Maa text: Ilgilat Le Maasai. Ms, Monash University.

ALLEN, A.S. (1984) 'French reduplication limits the arbitrariness of the sign', in P. Baldi (ed.) (1984).

ALLEN, J. (1972) 'Relationship between sentence and discourse', *Papers in New Guinea Linguistics* 16: 1–15.

ALLEYNE, M.C. (1980) *Comparative Afro-American*. Karoma: Ann Arbor.

ALLIN, T.R. (1976) *A grammar of Resígaro* (3 vols). SIL: High Wycombe, Buckinghamshire, U.K.

ALPHER, B. (1973) Son of ergative: the Yir Yoront language of Northeast Australia. Unpublished Ph.D. dissertation, Cornell University.

ALPHONSE, E.S. (1956) *Guaymí grammar and dictionary with some ethnological notes*. US Gov't Print. Off.: Washington, DC.

ALSINA, A. (1992) 'On the argument structure of causatives', *LI* 23: 517–555.

ALTENBERG, B. (1987) 'Causal ordering strategies in English conversation', in J. Monaghan (ed.) (1987).

ALUNGUM, J., R.J. CONRAD, and J. LUKAS (1978) 'Some Muhiang grammatical notes', *Workpapers in Papua New Guinea Languages* 25: 89–130.

ANCEAUX, J.C. (1952) *The Wolio language*. Smits: The Hague.

ANCEAUX, J.C. (1965) *The Nimboran language: phonology and morphology*. Martinus Nijhoff: 's-Gravenhage.

ANDERSEN, F.I. (1974) *The sentence in Biblical Hebrew*. Mouton: The Hague.

ANDERSEN, H. (1973) 'Abductive and deductive change', *Language* 49: 765–793.

ANDERSEN, H. (1974) 'Toward a typology of change: bifurcating changes and binary relations', in J. Anderson and C. Jones (eds), *Historical linguistics: proceedings of the 1st International conference on historical linguistics*. North-Holland: Amsterdam.

ANDERSEN, H. (1980) 'Morphological change: towards a typology', in J. Fisiak (ed.) (1980).

ANDERSON, D.G. (1962) *Conversational Ticuna*. SIL/University of Oklahoma: Norman.

ANDERSON, J. (1969) 'The case for cause: a preliminary enquiry', *JL* 6: 99–104.

ANDERSON, J. (1971) *The grammar of case: towards a localist theory*. Cambridge University Press: London.

ANDERSON, L. and M.R. WISE (1963) 'Contrastive features of Candoshi clause types', in B. Elson (ed.) (1963).

ANDERSON, L.-G. (1975) *The form and function of subordinate clauses*. University of Gothenburg: Gothenburg.

ANDERSON, S.R. (1980) 'On the development of morphology from syntax', in J. Fisiak (ed.) (1980).

ANDERSON, S.R. (1982) 'Where is morphology?', *LI* 13: 571–612.

ANDREADES, S.C. (1974) *A textbook of modern Greek*. Manchester. (Private publication).

ANDREWS, A. (1985) 'The major functions of the noun phrase', in T. Shopen (ed.) (1985a).

ANDREWS, J.R. (1975) *Introduction to Classical Nahuatl*. University of Texas Press: Austin.

ANDREWSKUTTY, A.P. (1971) *Malayalam: an intensive course*. The Dravidian Linguistic Association: Kerala, S. India.

ANDRONOV, M.S. (1969a) *A standard grammar of modern and classical Tamil*. New Century Book House: Madras.

ANDRONOV, M.S. (1969b) *The Kannada language*. Nauka: Moscow.

ANDRONOV, M.S. (1980) *The Brahui language*. Nauka: Moscow.

ANSRE, G. (1966) 'The verbid – a caveat to "serial verbs"', *Journal of West African Languages* 3.1: 29–32.

ANTTILA, R. (1972) *An introduction to historical and comparative linguistics*. Macmillan: New York.

AOKI, H. (1970) *Nez Perce grammar*. University of California Press: Berkeley.

ARISTE, P. (1968) *A grammar of the Votic language*. Indiana University: Bloomington.

ARNOTT, D.W. (1961) 'The subjunctive in Fula', *African Language Studies* 2: 125–138.

ARNOTT, D.W. (1970) *The nominal and verbal system of Fula*. Clarendon: Oxford.

ARONSON, H.I. (1982) *Georgian: a reading grammar*. Slavica: Columbus, OH.

ASAI, E.C. (1953) *The Sedik language of Formosa*. Kanazawa University: Kanazawa.

ASHTON, E.O. (1947) *Swahili grammar*. Longman: London.

ASHTON, E.O. (1954) *A Luganda grammar.* Longmans Green: London.

ATKINSON, J. (1977) *A Finnish grammar.* Finnish Literature Society: Helsinki.

ATLAS, J.D. and S.C. LEVINSON (1981) 'It-clefts, informativeness and logical form: radical pragmatics', in P. Cole (ed.), *Radical pragmatics.* Academic Press: New York.

AUSTIN, P. (1981a) *A grammar of Diyari, South Australia.* Cambridge University Press: Cambridge.

AUSTIN, P. (1981b) 'Case marking and clause binding evidence from Dhalandji', *CLS* 17: 1–7.

AUSTIN, P. (ed.) (1988) *Complex sentence constructions in Australian languages.* John Benjamins: Amsterdam.

AUSTING, J. and R. UPÏA (1975) 'Highlights of Ömie morphology', in T.E. Dutton (ed.) (1975a).

AWBERY, G.M. (1976) *The syntax of Welsh: a transformational study of the passive.* Cambridge University Press: Cambridge.

AWOBULUYI, O. (1967) Studies in the syntax of the standard Yoruba verb. Unpublished Ph.D. dissertation, Columbia University.

AWOBULUYI, O. (1973) 'The modifying serial construction: a critique', *Studies in African Linguistics* 4: 87–111.

AWOYALE, Y. (1983) 'On the development of the verb infinitive phrase in Yoruba', *Studies in African Linguistics* 14: 71–102.

AZE, F.R. (1973) 'Clause patterns in Parengi-Gorum', in R.L. Trail (ed.) (1973), Part I.

BABCOCK, S. (1972) 'Periphrastic causatives', *FL* 8: 30–43.

BABIC, S. (1973) *Serbo-Croat for beginners.* Kolarcev Narodni Univerzitet: Belgrade.

BAILARD, J. (1982) 'The interaction of semantic and syntactic functions and French clitic case marking in causative constructions', in P.J. Hopper and S.A. Thompson (eds) (1982).

BAILARD, J. (1983) 'V-(s)ase and FAIRE infinitive: the role of the lexicon in Japanese and old French causatives', *SiL* 7.3: 333–368.

BAILEY, B.L. (1966) *Jamaican Creole syntax: a transformational approach.* Cambridge University Press: Cambridge.

BAILEY, D.A. (1975) 'Abau grammar', *Workpapers in Papua New Guinea Languages* 9: 59–130.

BAKER, M.C. (1988) *Incorporation: a theory of grammatical function changing.* University of Chicago Press: Chicago.

BAKER, P. (1972) *Kreol: a description of Mauritian Creole.* C. Hurst & Co.: London.

BAKER, P. and C. CORNE (1982) *Isle-de-France Creole.* Karoma: Ann Arbor.

BALDI, P. (ed.) (1984) *Papers from the XIIth linguistic symposium on Romance languages.* John Benjamins: Amsterdam.

BALLARD, D.L., R.J. CONRAD, and R.E. LONGACRE (1971) 'The

deep and surface grammar of interclausal relations', *FL* 7.1: 70–118.

BAMGBOSE, A. (1966) *A grammar of Yoruba.* Cambridge University Press: Cambridge.

BAMGBOSE, A. (1973) 'The modifying serial construction: a reply', *Studies in African Linguistics* 4: 207–217.

BAMGBOSE, A. (1974) 'On serial verbs and verbal status', *Journal of West African Languages* 9: 17–48.

BAMMESBERGER, A. (1982) *Essentials of modern Irish.* Carl Winter-Universitätsverlag: Heidelberg.

BAPTISTA, P. and R. WALLIN (1967) 'Baure', in E. Matteson (ed.) (1967a).

BARBER, C.G. (1977) *A grammar of the Balinese language.* University of Aberdeen: Aberdeen.

BARDAKJIAN, K.B. and R.W. THOMSON (1977) *A textbook of modern Western Armenian.* Delmar: New York.

BARKER, M.A.R. (1964) *Klamath grammar.* University of California Press: Berkeley.

BARKER, M.A. and A.K. MENGAL (1969) *A course in Baluchi.* Institute of Islamic Studies, McGill University: Montreal.

BARON, N.S. (1974) 'The structure of English causatives', *Lingua* 33: 299–342.

BARON, N.S. (1977) *Language acquisition and historical change.* North-Holland: Amsterdam.

BARTSCH, R. and T. VENNEMANN (1972) *Semantic structures: a study in the relation between semantics and syntax.* Athenaum: Frankfurt (Main).

BATEMAN, J. (1986) *Iau verb morphology.* Badan Penyelenggar Seri NUSA, Universitas Katolik Indonesia Atma Jaya: Jakarta.

BATES, E. (1984) 'Bioprograms and the innateness hypothesis', *The Behavioral and Brain Sciences* 7: 188–190.

BATES, E. and B. MACWHINNEY (1982) 'Functionalist approaches to grammar', in E. Wanner and L. Gleitman (eds) (1982).

BAUER, W. (1982) 'Relativization in Maori', *SiL* 6: 305–342.

BAVIN, E. (1982) 'Morphological and syntactic divergence in Lango and Acholi', in R. Voßen and M. Bechhaus-Gerst (eds) (1982).

BAYER, J. (1986) 'The role of event expression in grammar', *SiL* 10: 1–52.

BAZELL, C.E. (1953) *Linguistic form.* Istanbul Press: Istanbul.

BEAMAN, K. (1984) 'Coordination and subordination revisited: syntactic complexity in spoken and written narrative discourse', in D. Tannen (ed.), *Coherence in spoken and written discourse.* Ablex: Norwood, NJ.

BEAUMONT, C.H. (1979) *The Tigak language of New Ireland.* Australian National University: Canberra.

BEAUMONT, J. and M. BEAUMONT (1975) 'Iamalele clause types and structure', *Workpapers in Papua New Guinea Languages* 12: 81–152.

BEE, D. (1973) 'Usarufa: a descriptive grammar', in H. McKaughan (ed.) (1973).

BELL, A. (1978) 'Language sample', in J.H. Greenberg, C.A. Ferguson, and E.A. Moravcsik (eds) (1978).

BELL, C.A. (1939) *Grammar of colloquial Tibetan*. Bengal Gov't Press: Alipore, Bengal.

BELL, C.R.V. (1953 [1969]) *The Somali language*. Longmans Green: London.

BELLER, R. and P. BELLER (1979) 'Huasteca Nahuatl', in R.W. Langacker (ed.) (1979a).

BELLETTI, A., L. BRANDI, and L. RIZZI (eds) (1981) *Theory of markedness in generative grammar: proceedings of the 1979 GLOW conference*. Scuola Normale Superiore: Pisa.

BENDER, B.W. (1969) *Spoken Marshallese*. University of Hawaii Press: Honolulu.

BENDER, E. (1967a) *Urdu grammar and reader*. University of Pennsylvania Press: Philadelphia.

BENDER, E. (1967b) *Hindi grammar and reader*. University of Pennsylvania Press: Philadelphia.

BENDIX, E.H. (1984) 'The metaterm "cause": exploring a definition in Newari and English', in L.J. Raphael, C.B. Raphael, and M.R. Valdovinos (eds), *Language and cognition: essays in honor of A.J. Bronstein*. Plenum: New York.

BENDOR-SAMUEL, D. (1972) *Hierarchical structures in Guajajara*. SIL/University of Oklahoma: Norman.

BENEDICT, P. (1943) 'Secondary infixation in Lepcha', *Studies in Linguistics* 1.19.

BENEDICT, P. (1972) *Sino-Tibetan: a conspectus*. Cambridge University Press: Cambridge.

BENJAMIN, G. (1976) 'An outline of Temiar grammar', in P.N. Jenner, L.C. Thompson, and S. Starosta (eds) (1976).

BENTON, R.A. (1971) *Pangasinan reference grammar*. University of Hawaii Press: Honolulu.

BERESFORD, M. (1965 [1980]) *Complete Russian course for beginners*. Clarendon: London.

BERNABE, E., V. LAPID, and B. SIBAYAN (1971) *Ilokano lessons*. University of Hawaii Press: Honolulu.

BEST, G. (1983) *Culture and language of the Turkana NW Kenya*. Carl Winter-Universitätsverlag: Heidelberg.

BEVER, T.G. and D.T. LANGENDOEN (1971) 'A dynamic model of the evolution of language', *LI* 2: 433–463.

BEVER, T.G. and D.T. LANGENDOEN (1972) 'The interaction of speech perception and grammatical structure in the evolution of language', in R.P. Stockwell and R.K.S. Macaulay (eds) (1972).

BICKERTON, D. (1977) 'Pidginization and creolization: language acquisition and language universals', in A. Valdman (ed.), *Pidgin and creole linguistics*. Indiana University Press: Bloomington.

BICKERTON, D. (1979) 'Beginnings', in K.C. Hill (ed.) (1979).

BICKERTON, D. (1981) *Roots of language*. Karoma: Ann Arbor.

BICKERTON, D. (1984) 'The language bioprogram hypothesis', *The Behavioral and Brain Sciences* 7: 173–188.

BICKERTON, D. (1986) 'Creoles and West African languages: a case of mistaken identity?', in P. Muysken and N. Smith (eds) (1986a).

BICKFORD, J.A. (1985) 'Spanish clitic doubling and levels of grammatical relations', *Lingua* 65: 189–211.

BIDWELL, C.E. (1971) *Outline of Czech morphology*. University of Pittsburgh: Pittsburgh.

BIERWISCH, M. and K. HEIDOLPH (eds) (1970) *Progress in linguistics*. Mouton: The Hague.

BIGGS, B. (1969) *Let's learn Maori*. A.H. & A.W. Reed: Wellington.

BILIGIRI, H.S. (1965) *Kharia phonology, grammar and vocabulary*. Deccan College Postgraduate and Research Institute: Poona.

BINH, D.T. (1971) *A tagmemic comparison of the structure of English and Vietnamese sentences*. Mouton: The Hague.

BINNICK, R.I. (1979) *Modern Mongolian: a transformational syntax*. University of Toronto Press: Toronto.

BIRD, C.S. and M.B. KENDALL (1986) 'Postpositions and auxiliaries in Northern Mande: syntactic indeterminacy and linguistic analysis', *Anthropological Linguistics* 28.4: 389–403.

BIRK, D.B.W. (1976) *The Malak Malak language, Daly River (Western Arnhem Land)*. Australian National University: Canberra.

BJÖRKHAGEN, I.M. (1960) *Modern Swedish grammar*. Svenska Bokförlaget: Norstedts.

BLAKE, B.J. (1976) 'Rapporteur's introduction and summary', in R.M.W. Dixon (ed.) (1976).

BLAKE, B.J. (1977) *Case marking in Australian languages*. AIAS: Canberra.

BLAKE, B.J. (1979a) *A Kalkatungu grammar*. Australian National University: Canberra.

BLAKE, B.J. (1979b) 'Pitta-Pitta', in R.M.W. Dixon and B.J. Blake (eds) (1979).

BLAKE, B.J. (1986) 'Unaccusatives: an alternative description', *Working Papers in Language and Linguistics* 19: 1–15.

BLAKE, B.J. (1987a) *Australian Aboriginal grammar*. Croom Helm: London.

BLAKE, B.J. (1987b) Redefining Pama-Nyungan: Towards the prehistory of Australian languages. Ms, Monash University.

BLAKE, B.J. (1988) 'Review of Russell S. Tomlin, *Basic word order: functional principles*', *JL* 24: 213–217.

BLAKE, B.J. (1990) *A guide to relational grammar*. Routledge: London.

BLAKE, B.J. (1994) *Case.* Cambridge University Press: Cambridge.

BLAKE, B.J. and G. MALLINSON (1987) 'Review of T. Shopen (ed.), *Language typology and syntactic description*', *Language* 63: 606–619.

BLAKE, F.R. (1925 [1967]) *A grammar of the Tagálog language.* American Oriental Society: New Haven.

BLANSITT, E.L. (1988) 'Datives and allatives', in M. Hammond, E.A. Moravcsik, and J.R. Wirth (eds) (1988a).

BLAU, J. (1976) *A grammar of Biblical Hebrew.* Otto Harrassowitz: Wiesbaden.

BLIESE, L.F. (1981) *A generative grammar of Afar.* SIL and University of Texas at Arlington.

BLOOD, D.W. (1977) 'A three-dimensional analysis of Cham sentences', *Papers in South East Asian Linguistics* 4: 53–76.

BLOOMFIELD, L. (1956) *Eastern Ojibwa.* University of Michigan Press: Ann Arbor.

BLOOMFIELD, L. (1962) *The Menomini language.* Yale University Press: New Haven.

BLOWERS, B.L. and R. BLOWERS (1970) 'Kaugel verb morphology', *Papers in New Guinea Linguistics* 12: 37–60.

BLUST, R.A. (1977) 'Sketches of the morphology and phonology of Bornean languages I: Uma Juman (Kayan)', *Papers in Borneo Linguistics* 2: 9–122.

BLUST, R.A. (1988) 'Sketches of the morphology and phonology of Bornean languages 2: Mukah (Melanau)', *Papers in Western Austronesian Linguistics* 3: 151–216.

BOADI, L.A. (1968) 'Some aspects of Akan deep syntax', *Journal of West African Languages* 5: 83–90.

BOAS, F. (1947) *Kwakiutl grammar.* AMS Press: New York.

BOAS, F. and E. DELORIA (1941 [1976]) *Dakota grammar.* AMS Press: New York.

BODEN, M.A. (1982) 'Implications of language studies for human nature', in T.W. Simon and R.J. Scholes (eds) (1982).

BOLKESTEIN, A.M. (1986) 'Review of Foley and Van Valin (1984)', *JL* 22.1: 216–221.

BORDELOIS, I. (1988) 'Causatives: from lexicon to syntax', *NLLT* 6: 57–93.

BORKIN, A. (1984) *Problems in form and function.* Ablex: Norwood, NJ.

BOSSUYT, A. (1987a) 'Headless relatives in the history of Dutch', in W. Koopman, F. van der Leek, O. Fischer and R. Eaton (eds) (1987).

BOSSUYT, A. (1987b) 'A brief reply to Mr. Weerman', in W. Koopman, F. van der Leek, O. Fischer and R. Eaton (eds) (1987).

BOWE, H. (1987) Categories, constituents and constituency order in Pitjantjatjara. Unpublished Ph.D. dissertation, University of Southern California.

BOWERMAN, M. (1988) 'The "no negative evidence" problem: how do children avoid constructing an overly general grammar?' in J.A. Hawkins (ed.) (1988a).

BOWERS, F. (1961) 'English complex sentence formation', *JL* 4: 83–88.

BOYLE, J.A. (1966) *Grammar of modern Persian*. Otto Harrassowitz: Wiesbaden.

BRADLEY, C.H. (1970) *A linguistic sketch of Jicaltepec Mixtec*. SIL/ University of Oklahoma: Norman.

BRADLEY, C.H. and B.E. HOLLENBACH (eds) (1988) *Studies in the syntax of Mixtecan languages vol. I*. SIL and University of Texas at Arlington.

BRADLEY, D. (1979a) *Lahu dialects*. Australian National University: Canberra.

BRADLEY, D. (1979b) *Proto-Loloish*. Curzon: London.

BRADSHAW, J. (1979) 'Serial causative constructions and word order change in Papua New Guinea', *Working Papers in Linguistics* (University of Hawaii) 11.2: 13–34.

BRADSHAW, J. (1980) 'Dempwolff's description of verb serialization in Yabem', *Working Papers in Linguistics* (University of Hawaii) 12.3: 1–26.

BRAINE, J.C. (1970) Nicobarese grammar (Car dialect). Unpublished Ph.D. dissertation, University of California, Berkeley.

BREEN, J.G. (1974) 'On bivalent suffixes', *Linguistic Communications* 14: 22–58.

BREEN, J.G. (1981a) *The Mayi languages of the Queensland gulf country*. AIAS: Canberra.

BREEN, J.G. (1981b) 'Margany and Gunya', in R.M.W. Dixon and B.J. Blake (eds) (1981).

BRENNENSTUHL, W. and K. WACHOWICZ (1976) 'On the pragmatics of control', *BLS* 2: 396–405.

BRESNAN, J. (ed.) (1982) *The mental representation of grammatical relations*. MIT Press: Cambridge, MA.

BRIGHT, W. (1957a) *The Karok language*. University of California Press: Berkeley.

BRIGHT, W. (1957b) 'Alternations in Lushai', *Indian Linguistics* 18: 101–110.

BROADBENT, S.M. (1964) *The Southern Sierra Miwok language*. University of California Press: Berkeley.

BROCKWAY, E. (1979) 'North Puebla Nahuatl', in R.W. Langacker (ed.) (1979a).

BRODERICK, G. (1984) *A handbook of late spoken Manx*. Max Niemeyer: Tübingen.

BRODY, J. (1984) 'Some problems with the concept of basic word order', *Linguistics* 22: 711–736.

BRODY, M. (1987) 'Review discussion: on Chomsky's knowledge of language', *Mind and Language* 2: 165–177.

BROMLEY, H.M. (1981) *A grammar of lower Grand Valley Dani.* Australian National University: Canberra.

BROOKS, M.Z. (1975) *Polish reference grammar.* Mouton: The Hague.

BROWN, J.M. (1965) *From ancient Thai to modern dialects.* Social Science Association Press of Thailand: Bangkok.

BROWNING, R. (1982) *Medieval and modern Greek.* Cambridge University Press: Cambridge.

BRUCE, L. (1984) *The Alamblak language of Papua New Guinea (East Sepik).* Australian National University: Canberra.

BRUCE, L. (1986) 'Serialization: the interface of syntax and lexicon', *Papers in New Guinea Linguistics* 24: 21–37.

BRUCE, L. (1988) 'Serialization: from syntax to lexicon', *SiL* 12: 19–49.

BUCHANAN, D. (1978) 'Djambarrpuyŋu clauses', *Papers in Australian Linguistics* 11: 143–177.

BUCK, C.D. (1928) *A grammar of Oscan and Umbrian.* Ginn: Boston.

BULL, W.E. (1968) *Time, tense and the verb.* University of California Press: Berkeley.

BUNYE, M.V.R. and E.P. YAP (1971a) *Cebuano for beginners.* University of Hawaii Press: Honolulu.

BUNYE, M.V.R. and E.P. YAP (1971b) *Cebuano grammar notes.* University of Hawaii Press: Honolulu.

BURGESS, D. (1984) 'Western Tarahumara', in R.W. Langacker (ed.) (1984).

BURLING, R. (1961) *A Garo grammar.* Deccan College: Poona.

BURROW, T. (1955) *The Sanskrit language.* Faber and Faber: London.

BURROW, T. and S. BHATTACHARYA (1970) *The Pengo language.* Clarendon: Oxford.

BURROWS, L. (1915 [1980]) *The grammar of the Ho language: an Eastern Himalayan dialect.* Cosmo: New Delhi.

BURZIO, L. (1986) *Italian syntax.* D. Reidel: Dordrecht.

BYBEE, J.L. (1985a) *Morphology: a study of the relation between meaning and form.* John Benjamins: Amsterdam.

BYBEE, J.L. (1985b) 'Diagrammatic iconicity in stem-inflection relations', in J. Haiman (ed.) (1985b).

BYBEE, J.L. (1988) 'The diachronic dimension in explanation', in J.A. Hawkins (ed.) (1988a).

BYBEE, J.L., W. PAGLIUCA, and R.D. PERKINS (1990) 'On the asymmetries in the affixation of grammatical material', in W. Croft, K. Denning, and S. Kemmer (eds) (1990).

BYKOVA, E.M. (1981) *The Bengali language.* Nauka: Moscow.

BYNON, T. (1977) *Historical linguistics.* Cambridge University Press: Cambridge.

CÂMARA, J.M. (1972) *The Portuguese language.* University of Chicago Press: Chicago.

CAMP, E. and M. LICCARDI (1967) 'Itonama', in E. Matteson (ed.) (1967b).

CAMPBELL, L., V. BUBENIK, and L. SAXON (1988) 'Word order universals: refinements and clarifications', *Canadian Journal of Linguistics* 33.3: 209–230.

CAPELL, A. (1943) *The linguistic position of South-Eastern Papua*. Australian Medical Publishing Co.: Sydney.

CAPELL, A. (1944) 'Peoples and languages of Timor', *Oceania* 14: 330–337, 15: 19–48.

CAPELL, A. (1962) *The Polynesian language of Mae (Emwae), New Hebrides*. Linguistic Society of New Zealand: Auckland.

CAPELL, A. (1969) 'The structure of the Binandere verb', *Papers in New Guinea Linguistics* 9: 1–32.

CAPELL, A. (1971) *Arosi grammar*. Australian National University: Canberra.

CAPELL, A. (1976) 'Rapporteur's introduction and summary to Topic E: simple and compound verbs: conjugation by auxiliaries in Australian verbal systems', in R.M.W. Dixon (ed.) (1976).

CAPELL, A. (1979) 'Classification of verbs in Australian languages', in S. Wurm (ed.), *Australian linguistic studies*. Australian National University: Canberra.

CAPELL, A. (1984a) *Futuna-Aniwa dictionary with grammatical introduction*. Australian National University: Canberra.

CAPELL, A. (1984b) 'The Laragia language', *Papers in Australian Linguistics* 16: 55–106.

CAPELL, A. and H.H. COATE (1984) *Comparative studies in North Kimberley languages*. Australian National University: Canberra.

CAPELL, A. and H.E. HINCH (1970) *Maung grammar*. Mouton: The Hague.

CAPELL, A. and J. LAYARD (1980) *Materials in Atchin, Malekula: grammar, vocabulary and texts*. Australian National University: Canberra.

CARDONA, G. (1965) *A Gujarati reference grammar*. University of Pennsylvania Press: Philadelphia.

CARMON, A. and I. NACHSHON (1971) 'Effect of unilateral brain damage on perception of temporal order', *Cortex* 7: 410–418.

CARRELL, P.L. (1970) *A transformational grammar of Igbo*. Cambridge University Press: Cambridge.

CASAD, E. (1984) 'Cora', in R.W. Langacker (ed.) (1984).

CATTELL, R. (1976) 'Constraints on movement rules', *Language* 52: 18–50.

CAUGHLEY, R. (1982) *The syntax and morphology of the verb in Chepang*. Australian National University Press: Canberra.

CHADWICK, N. (1975) *A descriptive study of the Djingili language*. AIAS: Canberra.

CHAFE, W.L. (1970) *Meaning and the structure of language*. University of Chicago Press: Chicago.

CHAFE, W.L. (1976) *The Caddoan, Iroquoian and Siouan languages*. Mouton: The Hague.

CHAFE, W.L. (1979) 'The flow of thought and the flow of language', in T. Givón (ed.) (1979c).

CHAFE, W.L. (ed.) (1980) *The pear stories: cognitive, cultural and linguistic aspects of narrative production*. Ablex: Norwood, NJ.

CHAFE, W.L. (1984) 'How people use adverbial clauses', *BLS* 10: 437–449.

CHANDLER, D.H. (1974) 'Verb stem classes in Northern Kankanay', *Papers in Philippine Linguistics* 5: 1–21.

CHANG, K. and B. SHEFTS (1964) *A manual of spoken Tibetan*. University of Washington Press: Seattle.

CHANG, Y. and C. KWORAY (1972) 'A brief description of the Miao language', in H.C. Purnell (ed.) (1972).

CHAO, Y.R. (1968) *A grammar of spoken Chinese*. University of California Press: Berkeley.

CHEN, T.M. (1987) *Verbal constructions and verbal classification in Nataoran-Amis*. Australian National University: Canberra.

CHENG, R.L. (1974) 'Causative constructions in Taiwanese', *Journal of Chinese Linguistics* 2: 279–324.

CHO, E. (1986) 'On the morphology of morphological causative verbs in Korean: an argument against Lieber's morpheme-based lexicon', *Studies in the Linguistic Sciences* 16: 27–43.

CHOMSKY, N.A. (1965) *Aspects of the theory of syntax*. MIT Press: Cambridge, MA.

CHOMSKY, N.A. (1970) *Current issues in linguistic theory*. Mouton: The Hague.

CHOMSKY, N.A. (1979) *Language and responsibility*. Pantheon: New York.

CHOMSKY, N.A. (1981a) *Lectures on government and binding*. Foris: Dordrecht.

CHOMSKY, N.A. (1981b) 'Markedness and core grammar', in A. Belletti, L. Brandi, and L. Rizzi (eds) (1981).

CHOMSKY, N.A. (1982) *Some concepts and consequences of the theory of government and binding*. MIT Press: Cambridge, MA.

CHOMSKY, N.A. (1986) *Knowledge of language: its nature, origin and use*. Praeger: New York.

CHOMSKY, N.A. (1987) 'Reply', *Mind and Language* 2: 178–197.

CHOMSKY, N.A. (1988) *Language and problems of knowledge*. MIT Press: Cambridge, MA.

CHRISTALLER, J.G. (1875 [1964]) *A grammar of the Asante and Fante language called Tshi [Chwee, Twi]*. Basel Evangelical Missionary Society/Gregg: Hants, UK.

CHRISTMAS, R.B. and J.E. CHRISTMAS (1973a) 'Sentence patterns in Kupia', in R.L. Trail (ed.) (1973).

CHRISTMAS, R.B. and J.E. CHRISTMAS (1973b) 'Clause patterns in Kupia', in R.L. Trail (ed.) (1973).

CHU, C.C. (1983) *A reference grammar of Mandarin Chinese for English speakers*. Peter Lang: New York.

CHUNG, S. (1977) 'On the gradual nature of syntactic change', in C.N. Li (ed.) (1977).

CHURCHWARD, C.M. (1940) *Rotuman grammar and dictionary*. Australian Medical Publ.: Sydney.

CINQUE, G. (1981) 'On Keenan and Comrie's primary relativization constraint', *LI* 12: 293–308.

CLARK, E.V. (1970) 'How young children describe events in time', in G.B. Flores d'Arcais and W.J.M. Levelt (eds), *Advances in psycholinguistics*. North-Holland: Amsterdam.

CLARK, E.V. (1973) 'How children describe time and order', in C.A. Ferguson and D.I. Slobin (eds), *Studies of child language development*. Holt, Rinehart and Winston: New York.

CLARK, E.V. and H.H. CLARK (1978) 'Universals, relativity and language processing', in J.H. Greenberg, C.A. Ferguson, and E.A. Moravcsik (eds) (1978).

CLARK, H.H. (1973) 'Space, time, semantics and the child', in T.E. Moore (ed.) (1973).

CLARK, L. (1961) *Sayula Popoluca texts with grammatical notes*. SIL/ University of Oklahoma: Norman.

CLARK, L. (1983) *Sayula Popoluca verb derivation*. SIL: Dallas, Texas.

CLARK, M. (1978) *Coverbs and case in Vietnamese*. Australian National University: Canberra.

CLARK, M. (1979) 'Coverbs: evidence for the derivation of preposition from verbs – new evidence from Hmong', *Working Papers in Linguistics* (University of Hawaii) 11.2: 1–11.

CLARK, R. (1973) 'Case markers and complementizers: a Maori example', *Stanford Working Papers on Language Universals* 12: 145–147.

CLARK, T.W. (1977) *Introduction to Nepali: a first-year language course*. SOAS: London.

CLOSE, E. (1974) *The development of modern Rumanian*. Cambridge University Press: Cambridge.

COATE, H.H.J. and L. OATES (1970) *A grammar of Ngarinjin, Western Australia*. AIAS: Canberra.

COLE, D.T. (1955) *An introduction to Tswana grammar*. Longmans Green: London.

COLE, D.T. and D.M. MOKAILA (1962) *A course in Tswana*. Georgetown University: Washington, DC.

COLE, P. (1975) 'The synchronic and diachronic status of conversational implicatures', in P. Cole and J.L. Morgan (eds) (1975).

COLE, P. (ed.) (1976a) *Studies in modern Hebrew syntax and semantics.* North-Holland: Amsterdam.

COLE, P. (1976b) 'A causative construction in modern Hebrew: theoretical implications', in P. Cole (ed.) (1976a).

COLE, P. (1976c) 'An apparent asymmetry in the formation of relative clauses in modern Hebrew', in P. Cole (ed.) (1976a).

COLE, P. (1983) 'The grammatical role of the causee in the universal grammar', *IJAL* 49: 115–133.

COLE, P. and J.L. MORGAN (eds) (1975) *Syntax and semantics 3: speech acts.* Academic Press: New York.

COLE, P. and J.M. SADOCK (eds) (1977) *Syntax and semantics vol. 8: grammatical relations.* Academic Press: New York.

COLE, P. and S.N. SRIDHAR (1977) 'Clause union and relational grammar: evidence from Hebrew and Kannada', *LI* 8: 700–713.

COLLIER, K. and K. GREGERSON (1985) 'Tabla verb morphology', *Papers in New Guinea Linguistics* 22: 155–172.

COLLINDER, B. (1960) *Comparative grammar of the Uralic languages.* Almqvist & Wiksell: Stockholm.

COLLINDER, B. (1969) *Survey of the Uralic languages.* Almqvist & Wiksell: Stockholm.

COMRIE, B. (1975) 'Causatives and universal grammar', *Transactions of the Philological Society* (1974): 1–32.

COMRIE, B. (1976a) *Aspect.* Cambridge University Press: Cambridge.

COMRIE, B. (1976b) 'The syntax of causative constructions: cross-language similarities and divergences', in M. Shibatani (ed.) (1976b).

COMRIE, B. (1976c) 'Review of Xolodovic (ed.), *tipologija kauzativnyx konstrukcij*', *Language* 52.2: 479–488.

COMRIE, B. (1978) 'Linguistics is about languages', in B.B. Kachru (ed.), *Linguistics in the seventies: directions and prospects.* Studies in the Linguistic Sciences, Special Issue, University of Illinois: Urbana.

COMRIE, B. (1980) 'Morphology and word order reconstruction', in J. Fisiak (ed.) (1980).

COMRIE, B. (1981a [1989]) *Language universals and linguistic typology.* Basil Blackwell: Oxford.

COMRIE, B. (1981b) *The languages of the Soviet Union.* Cambridge University Press: Cambridge.

COMRIE, B. (1983a) 'Form and function in explaining language universals', *Linguistics* 21.1: 87–103.

COMRIE, B. (1983b) 'On the validity of typological studies: a reply to Smith', *AJL* 3: 93–96.

COMRIE, B. (1984a) *Tense.* Cambridge University Press: Cambridge.

COMRIE, B. (1984b) 'Language universals and linguistic argumentation: a reply to Coopmans', *JL* 20: 155–163.

COMRIE, B. (1985) 'Causative verb formation and other verb-deriving morphology', in T. Shopen (ed.) (1985c).

COMRIE, B. (1986) 'RG, whence, where, whither?', *Linguistics* 24.4: 773–789.

COMRIE, B. (1987) 'Introduction' in B. Comrie (ed.), *The world's major languages*. Croom Helm: London.

CONRAD, R.J. (1978) 'Some Muhiang grammatical notes', *Workpapers in Papua New Guinea Languages* 25: 89–130.

CONSTANTINO, E. (1971) *Ilokano reference grammar*. University of Hawaii Press: Honolulu.

COOK, E.D. (1984) *A Sarcee grammar*. University of British Columbia Press: Vancouver.

COOK, W.A.S.J. (1965) A descriptive analysis of Mundari. Unpublished Ph.D. dissertation, Georgetown University, Washington, DC.

COOPER, R. (1974) 'Some problems for a higher CAUSE', in E. Voeltz (ed.) (1974).

COOPER, R. (1976) 'Lexical and nonlexical causatives in Bantu', in M. Shibatani (ed.) (1976b).

COOPMANS, P. (1983) 'B. Comrie, *Language universals and linguistic typology*: review article', *JL* 19: 455–473.

COOPMANS, P. (1984) 'Surface word order typology and universal grammar', *Language* 60: 55–69.

CORBRIDGE-PATKANIOWSKA, M. (1948 [1952]) *Teach yourself Polish*. English Universities Press: London.

CORNE, C. (1977) *Seychelles Creole grammar*. Gunter Narr: Tübingen.

CORNYN, W.S. and D.H. ROOP (1968) *Beginning Burmese*. Yale University Press: New Haven.

COSTAS, P. (1936 [1979]) *An outline of the history of the Greek language with particular emphasis on the Koine and the subsequent periods*. Ares: Chicago.

COUNTS, D.R. (1969) *A grammar of Kaliai-Kove*. University of Hawaii Press: Honolulu.

COWAN, H.K.J. (1965) *Grammar of the Sentani language*. Martinus Nijhoff: 's-Gravenhage.

COWAN, M.M. (1969) *Tzotzil grammar*. SIL/University of Oklahoma: Norman.

COWELL, M.W. (1964) *A short reference grammar of Syrian Arabic*. Georgetown University Press: Washington, DC.

CRABB, D.W. (1965) *Ekoid Bantu languages of Ogoja*. Cambridge University Press: Cambridge.

CRAIG, C. (1977) *The structure of Jacaltec*. University of Texas Press: Austin.

CRAIG, C. and K. HALE (1988) 'Relational preverbs in some languages of the Americas: typological and historical perspectives', *Language* 64: 312–344.

CRAPO, R.H. (1970) 'The origins of directional adverbs in Uto-Aztecan languages', *IJAL* 36.3: 181–189.

CRAPO, R.H. and A. AITKON (1986) *Bolivian Quechua reader and grammar – dictionary.* Karoma: Ann Arbor.

CRAZZOLARA, J.P. (1933) *Outline of a Nuer grammar.* Verlag der Internationalen: Vienna.

CRAZZOLARA, J.P. (1954) *The Lwoo.* Instituto Missioni Africano: Verona.

CRAZZOLARA, J.P. (1955) *A study of the Acooli language.* Oxford University Press: London.

CRAZZOLARA, J.P. (1960) *A study of the Logbara (Ma'di) language: grammar and vocabulary.* Oxford University Press: London.

CROFT, W. (1990) *Typology and universals.* Cambridge University Press: Cambridge.

CROFT, W., K. DENNING, and S. KEMMER (eds) (1990) *Studies in typology and diachrony.* John Benjamins: Amsterdam.

CROMACK, R.E. (1968) *Language systems and discourse structure in Cashinawa.* Hartford Seminary Foundation: Hartford, CT.

CROWLEY, T. (1978) *The middle Clarence dialects of Bandjalang.* AIAS: Canberra.

CROWLEY, T. (1981) 'The Mpakwithi dialect of Anguthimri', in R.M.W. Dixon and B.J. Blake (eds) (1981).

CROWLEY, T. (1982a) *The Paamese language of Vanuatu.* Australian National University: Canberra.

CROWLEY, T. (1982b) 'Development of a Paamese transitive suffix', in A. Halim, S. Carrington, and S. Wurm (eds) (1982).

CROWLEY, T. (1983) 'Uradhi', in R.M.W. Dixon and B.J. Blake (eds) (1983).

CROWLEY, T. (1987) 'Serial verbs in Paamese', *SiL* 11: 35–84.

CRYSTAL, D. (ed.) (1982a) *Linguistic controversies: essays in linguistic theory and practice in honour of F.R. Palmer.* Edward Arnold: London.

CRYSTAL, D. (1982b) 'Pseudo-controversy in linguistic theory', in D. Crystal (ed.) (1982a).

CUTLER, A., J.A. HAWKINS, and G. GILLIGAN (1985) 'The suffixing preference: a processing explanation', *Linguistics* 23: 723–758.

DALY, J.P. (1973) *A generative grammar of Peñoles Mixtec.* SIL/University of Oklahoma: Norman.

DAMBRIUNAS, L., A. KLIMAS, and W.R. SCHMALSTIEG (1966 [1972]) *Introduction to modern Lithuanian.* Franciscan Fathers: New York.

DARDJOWIDJOJO, S. (1966) Indonesian syntax. Unpublished Ph.D. dissertation, Georgetown University, Washington, DC.

DAVIES, J. (1981) *Kobon.* North-Holland: Amsterdam.

DAVIES, W.D. (1986) *Choctaw verb agreement and universal grammar.* D. Reidel: Dordrecht.

DAVIES, W.D. and C. ROSEN (1988) 'Unions as multi-predicate clauses', *Language* 64: 52–88.

DAVIS, P.W. and R. SAUNDERS (1978) 'Bella Coola syntax', in E.D. Cook and J. Kaye (eds), *Linguistic studies of Native America.* University of British Columbia Press: Vancouver.

DAY, C. (1973) *The Jacaltec language*. Indiana University Press: Bloomington.

DAYLEY, J.P. (1985) *Tzutujil grammar*. University of California Press: Berkeley.

DÉCSY, G. (1966) *Yurak Chrestomathy*. Indiana University Press: Bloomington.

DE GUZMAN, V.P. (1978) *Syntactic derivation of Tagalog verbs*. University of Hawaii Press: Honolulu.

DE GUZMAN, V.P. (1986) 'Some consequences of causative clause union in Tagalog', in P. Geraghty, L. Carrington, and S. Wurm (eds), *FOCAL I: papers from the 4th Int'l Conference on Austronesian Linguistics*. Australian National University: Canberra.

DEIBLER, E.W. (1976) *Semantic relationships of Gahuku verbs*. SIL/ University of Oklahoma: Norman.

DELANCEY, S. (1981) 'Lhasa Tibetan: a case study in ergative typology', *Journal of Linguistic Research* 2: 21–31.

DELANCEY, S. (1984a) 'Notes on agentivity and causation', *SiL* 8: 181–213.

DELANCEY, S. (1984b) 'Categories of non-volitional actor in Lhasa Tibetan', in A. Zide, D. Magier, and E. Schiller (eds), *Proceedings of the symposium on participant roles: South Asia and adjacent areas*. IULC: Bloomington.

DELANCEY, S. (1984c) 'Transitivity and ergative case in Lhasa Tibetan', *BLS* 10: 131–140.

DELANCEY, S. (1985a) 'Lhasa Tibetan evidentials and the semantics of causation', *BLS* 11: 65–72.

DELANCEY, S. (1985b) 'Agentivity and syntax', *CLS* 21, Part II: 1–12.

DELANCEY, S. (1986) 'Evidentiality and volitionality in Tibetan', in W. Chafe and J. Nichols (eds), *Evidentiality: the linguistic coding of epistemology*. Ablex: Norwood, NJ.

DELETANT, D. (1983) *Colloquial Romanian*. Routledge and Kegan Paul: London.

DELGATY, C.C. (1960) 'Tzotzil verb phrase structure', in B. Elson (ed.) (1960).

DERBYSHIRE, D.C. (1977) 'Word order universals and the existence of OVS languages', *LI* 8: 590–599.

DERBYSHIRE, D.C. (1979) *Hixkaryana*. North-Holland: Amsterdam.

DERBYSHIRE, D.C. (1985) *Hixkaryana and linguistic typology*. SIL and University of Texas at Arlington.

DERBYSHIRE, D.C. and G. PULLUM (1981) 'Object initial languages', *IJAL* 47: 192–214.

DERBYSHIRE, D.C. and G. PULLUM (eds) (1986) *Handbook of Amazonian languages*. Mouton de Gruyter: Berlin.

DIEHL, L. (1975) 'Space case: some principles and their implications concerning linear order in natural languages', *SIL Working Papers* (University of North Dakota) 19: 93–150.

DIFFLOTH, G. (1976) 'Jan-Hut, an Austroasiatic language of Malaysia', in N.D. Liem (ed.), *South-East Asian Linguistic Studies vol. 2*. Australian National University: Canberra.

DIJK, T.A. VAN (1977) *Text and context: explorations in the semantics and pragmatics of discourse*. Longman: London.

DIK, S. (1968) *Coordination*. North-Holland: Amsterdam.

DIK, S. (1985) 'Formal and semantic adjustment of derived constructions', in A.M. Bolkestein, C. de Groot, and L.J. Mackenzie (eds), *Predicates and terms in Functional Grammar*. Foris: Dordrecht.

DILLION, M. and D.Ó. CROÍNÍN (1961) *Irish*. Teach Yourself Books: London.

DIMMENDAAL, G.J. (1982) 'The two morphological verb classes in Nilotic', in R. Voßen and M. Bechhaus-Gerst (eds) (1982).

DIMMENDAAL, G.J. (1983a) *The Turkana language*. Foris: Dordrecht.

DIMMENDAAL, G.J. (1983b) 'Turkana as a verb-initial language', *Journal of African Languages and Linguistics* 5: 17–44.

DIMOCK, E.C., S. BHATTACHARJI, and S. CHATTERJEE (1965) *Introduction to Bengali*. East-West Center: Honolulu.

DINNEEN, F.P. (1967) *An introduction to general linguistics*. Holt, Rinehart and Winston: New York.

DIRVEN, R. and G. RADDEN (eds) (1982) *Issues in the theory of universal grammar*. Gunter Narr: Tübingen.

DI SCIULLO, A.M. and E. WILLIAMS (1987) *On the definition of word*. MIT Press: Cambridge, MA.

DIXON, R.M.W. (1972) *The Dyirbal language of North Queensland*. Cambridge University Press: Cambridge.

DIXON, R.M.W (ed.) (1976) *Grammatical categories in Australian languages*. Humanities Press: Atlantic Highlands, NJ.

DIXON, R.M.W. (1977) *A grammar of Yidin^y*. Cambridge University Press: Cambridge.

DIXON, R.M.W. (1980) *The languages of Australia*. Cambridge University Press: Cambridge.

DIXON, R.M.W. (1981) 'Wargamay', in R.M.W. Dixon and B.J. Blake (eds) (1981).

DIXON, R.M.W. (1983) 'Nyawaygi', in R.M.W. Dixon and B.J. Blake (eds) (1983).

DIXON, R.M.W. and B.J. BLAKE (eds) (1979) *Handbook of Australian languages vol. I*. Australian National University: Canberra.

DIXON, R.M.W. and B.J. BLAKE (eds) (1981) *Handbook of Australian languages vol. II*. Australian National University: Canberra.

DIXON, R.M.W. and B.J. BLAKE (eds) (1983) *Handbook of Australian languages vol. III*. John Benjamins: Amsterdam.

DOBSON, W.A.C.H. (1959) *Late archaic Chinese: a grammatical study*. University of Toronto Press: Toronto.

DOBSON, W.A.C.H. (1962) *Early archaic Chinese: a descriptive grammar*. University of Toronto Press: Toronto.

DOERFER, G. (1971) *Khalaj materials*. Indiana University Press: Bloomington.

DOKE, C.M. (1927) *Textbook of Zulu grammar*. Longmans Southern Africa: Johannesberg.

DONALDSON, T. (1980) *Ngiyambaa, the language of the Wangaaybuwan*. Cambridge University Press: Cambridge.

DOREL, M.A. (1980) 'The two verbs FAIRE in French expressions of causation', in F.H. Nuessel, Jr (ed.), *Contemporary studies in Romance languages*. IULC: Bloomington.

DORIAN, N.C. (1978) *East Sutherland Gaelic*. Dublin Institute for Advanced Studies: Dublin.

DOUGHERTY, J.W.D. (1983) *West Futuna-Aniwa: an introduction to a Polynesian Outlier language*. University of California: Berkeley.

DOUGLAS, W.H. (1976) *The Aboriginal languages of the South West of Australia*. AIAS: Canberra.

DOUGLAS, W.H. (1981) 'Watjarri', in R.M.W. Dixon and B.J. Blake (eds) (1981).

DOWTY, D. (1972) 'On the syntax and semantics of the atomic predicate CAUSE', *CLS* 8: 62–74.

DOWTY, D. (1979) *Word meaning and Montague grammar*. D. Reidel: Dordrecht.

DRIBERG, J.H. (1923) *The Lango: a Nilotic tribe of Uganda*. T. Fisher Unwin: London.

DRIEVER, D. (1976) *Aspects of a case grammar of Mombasa Swahili*. Helmut Buske: Hamburg.

DRYER, M.S. (1986a) 'Primary objects, secondary objects, and antidative', *Language* 62: 808–845.

DRYER, M.S. (1986b) Clause Union as mass descension. Ms. University of Alberta.

DRYER, M.S. (1988) 'Object–verb order and adjective–noun order: dispelling a myth', *Lingua* 74: 185–217.

DRYER, M.S. (1989) 'Large linguistic areas and language sampling', *SiL* 13: 257–292.

DRYER, M.S. (1992) 'The Greenbergian word order correlations', *Language* 68: 81–138.

DUBINSKY, S., M.-R. LLORET, and P. NEWMAN (1988) 'Lexical and syntactic causatives in Oromo', *Language* 64: 485–500.

DUBNOVA, Y.Z. (1984) *The Rwanda language*. Nauka: Moscow.

DU BOIS, J.W. (1980a) 'Beyond definiteness: the trace of identity in discourse', in W.L. Chafe (ed.) (1980).

DU BOIS, J.W. (1980b) 'The search for a cultural niche: showing the pear film in a Mayan community', in W.L. Chafe (ed.) (1980).

Du Bois, J.W. (1985) 'Competing motivations', in J. Haiman (ed.) (1985b).

Du Bois, J.W. (1987) 'The discourse basis for ergativity', *Language* 63: 805–855.

Duncan-Rose, C. and T. Vennemann (eds) (1988) *On language: rhetorica, phonologica, syntactica*. Routledge: London.

Durie, M. (1985) *A grammar of Achenese on the basis of a dialect of North Aceh*. Foris: Dordrecht.

Durie, M. (1988) 'Verb serialization and "verbal-prepositions" in Oceanic languages', *Oceanic Linguistics* XXVII: 1–23.

Dutton, T.E. (ed.) (1975a) *Studies in languages of central and southeast Papua*. Australian National University: Canberra.

Dutton, T.E. (1975b) 'A Koita grammar sketch and vocabulary', in T.E. Dutton (ed.) (1975a).

Dutton, T.E. and C.L. Voorhoeve (1974) *Beginning Hiri Motu*. Australian National University: Canberra.

Dziwirek, K., P. Farrell, and E. Mejías-Bikandi (eds) (1990) *Grammatical relations: a cross-theoretical perspective*. Center for the Study of Language and Information: Stanford.

Eades, D. (1976) *The Dharawal and Dhurga languages of the New South Wales south coast*. AIAS: Canberra.

Eades, D. (1979) 'Gumbaynggir', in R.M.W. Dixon and B.J. Blake (eds) (1979).

Eastman, R. and E. Eastman (1963) 'Iquito syntax', in B. Elson (ed.) (1963).

Eckmann, J. (1966) *Chagatay manual*. Indiana University Press: Bloomington.

Edmonson, M.S. (ed.) (1984) *Supplement to the handbook of middle American Indians*. University of Texas: Austin.

Eguzkitza, A. (1987) *Topics on the syntax of Basque and Romance*. IULC: Bloomington.

Einaudi, P.F. (1976) *A grammar of Biloxi*. Garland: New York.

Elbert, S.H. (1974) *Puluwat grammar*. Australian National University: Canberra.

Elbert, S.H. and M.K. Pukui (1979) *Hawaiian grammar*. University Press of Hawaii: Honolulu.

Elfenbein, J.H. (1966) *The Baluchi language: a dialectology with texts*. Royal Asiatic Society: London.

Elkins, R.E. (1970) *Major grammatical patterns of western Bukidnon Manobo*. SIL/University of Oklahoma: Norman.

Elliott, R. (1960) 'Ixil (Mayan) clause structure', in B. Elson (ed.) (1960).

Elson, B. (ed.) (1960) *Mayan studies I*. SIL/University of Oklahoma: Norman.

Elson, B. (ed.) (1962) *Ecuadorian Indian languages*. SIL/University of Oklahoma: Norman.

ELSON, B. (ed.) (1963) *Studies in Peruvian Indian languages I*. SIL/ University of Oklahoma: Norman.

EMENANJO, E.M. (1985) *Auxiliaries in Igbo syntax: a comparative study*. IULC: Bloomington.

ENGELSFELD, M. (1972) *Croatian through conversation*. Zagreb.

ENGLAND, N.C. (1983) *A grammar of Mam, a Mayan language*. University of Texas: Austin.

ERWIN, W.M. (1963) *A short reference grammar of Iraqi Arabic*. Georgetown University Press: Washington, DC.

EVANS, N. (1985) Kayardild: the language of the Bentinck Islands of north west Queensland. Unpublished Ph.D. thesis, Australian National University.

EVANS, N. (1988) 'Odd topic marking in Kayardild', in P. Austin (ed.) (1988).

EVERETT, D.L. (1986) 'Pirahã', in D.C. Derbyshire and G. Pullum (eds) (1986).

EVERITT, F. (1973) 'Sentence patterns in Tamang', in R.L. Trail (ed.) (1973).

FAARLUND, J.T. (1985) 'Pragmatics in diachronic syntax', *SiL* 9: 363–393.

FAGAN, J.L. (1986) *A grammatical analysis of Mono-Alu (Bougainville Straits, Solomon Islands)*. Australian National University: Canberra.

FAIRBANKS, G.H. (1958) *Spoken West Armenian*. American Council of Learned Societies: New York.

FAIRBANKS, G.H., J.W. GAIR, and M.W.S. DE SILVA (1968) *Colloquial Sinhalese*. Cornell University: Ithaca.

FAIRBANKS, G.H. and E.W. STEVICK (1958) *Spoken East Armenian*. American Council of Learned Societies: New York.

FARACLAS, N. (1984) *A grammar of Obolo*. IULC: Bloomington.

FARKAS, D.F. (1984) 'Subjunctive complements in Rumanian', in P. Baldi (ed.) (1984).

FARKAS, D.F. (1985) 'Obligatory controlled subjects in Romanian', *CLS* 21: 90–100.

FARR, J. and C. FARR (1975) 'Some features of Korafe morphology', in T.E. Dutton (ed.) (1975a).

FARRELL, P. (1994) *Thematic relations and Relational Grammar*. Garland: New York.

FAUCONNIER, G. (1983) 'Generalized union', *Communication and Cognition* 16: 3–37.

FAUST, N. (1971) 'Cocama clause types', in D. Bendor-Samuel (ed.), *Tupi studies I*. SIL/University of Oklahoma: Norman.

FEDSON, V.J. (1985) 'A note on periphrastic serial or compound causative constructions in Tamil', *CLS* 21, Part II: 13–20.

FELDMAN, H. (1986) *A grammar of Awtuw*. Australian National University: Canberra.

FERGUSON, C.A. (1978a) 'Historical background of universal research', in J.H. Greenberg, C.A. Ferguson, and E.A. Moravcsik (eds) (1978).

FERGUSON, C.A. (1978b) 'Talking to children: a search for universals', in J.H. Greenberg, C.A. Ferguson, and E.A. Moravcsik (eds) (1978).

FERREIRO, E. and H. SINCLAIR (1971) 'Temporal relationships in language', *International Journal of Psychology* 6: 39–47.

FILBECK, D. (1975) 'A grammar of verb serialization', in J.G. Harris and J.R. Chamberlain (eds), *Studies in Tai linguistics in honor of W.J. Gedney.* Central Institute of English Language Office of State Universities: Bangkok.

FILLMORE, C.J. (1968) 'The case for case', in E. Bach and R. Harms (eds), *Universals in linguistic theory.* Holt, Rinehart and Winston: New York.

FILLMORE, C.J. (1971) 'Some problems for case grammar', *Working Papers in Linguistics* (Ohio State University) 10: 245–265.

FILLMORE, C.J. (1977) 'The case for case reopened', in P. Cole and J.M. Sadock (eds) (1977).

FINER, D.L. (1985) 'The syntax of switch-reference', *LI* 16: 35–55.

FISIAK, J. (ed.) (1980) *Historical morphology.* Mouton: The Hague.

FISIAK, J. (ed.) (1984) *Historical syntax.* Mouton: Berlin.

FODALE, P. (1983) *A grammar of Papiamentu.* University of Michigan: Ann Arbor.

FODOR, J.A. (1970) 'Three reasons for not deriving "kill" from "cause to die"', *LI* 1: 429–438.

FODOR, J.A. (1976) *The language of thought.* Harvester: Hassocks (Sussex, UK).

FOLEY, W.A. (1976) Comparative syntax in Austronesian. Unpublished Ph.D. dissertation, University of California, Berkeley.

FOLEY, W.A. (1980a) 'Toward a universal typology of NP', *SiL* 4: 171–199.

FOLEY, W.A. (1980b) 'Functional grammar and cultural anthropology', *Canberra Anthropology* 3: 67–85.

FOLEY, W.A. (1986) *The Papuan languages of New Guinea.* Cambridge University Press: Cambridge.

FOLEY, W.A. and M.L. OLSON (1985) 'Clausehood and verb serialization', in J. Nichols and A.C. Woodbury (eds) (1985).

FOLEY, W.A. and R.D. VAN VALIN (1984) *Functional syntax and universal grammar.* Cambridge University Press: Cambridge.

FOREMAN, V.M. (1974) *Grammar of Yessan-Mayo.* SIL: Santa Ana, CA.

FORMAN, M.L. (1971) *Kapampangan grammar notes.* University Press of Hawaii: Honolulu.

FORSBERG, V. (1966) 'Phrases in Tagabili', *Papers in Philippine Linguistics* 1: 21–32.

FORTESCUE, M. (1984) *West Greenlandic.* Croom Helm: London.

FOSTER, M.L. (1969) *The Tarascan language.* University of California Press: Berkeley.

FOUGHT, J. (1984) 'Choltí Maya: a sketch', in M.S. Edmonson (ed.) (1984).

FOX, B.A. (1982) 'Review of Mallinson and Blake (1981)', *AJL* 2: 261–265.

FOX, B.A. (1987) 'The noun phrase accessibility hierarchy reinterpreted: subject primacy or the absolute hypothesis', *Language* 63: 856–870.

FOX, G.J. (1979) *Big Nambas grammar.* Australian National University: Canberra.

FRAISSE, P. (1984) 'Perception and estimation of time', *Annual Review of Psychology* 35: 1–36.

FRAJZYNGIER, Z. (1983) 'Marking syntactic relations in Proto-Chadic', in E. Wolff and H. Meyer-Bahlburg (eds), *Studies in Chadic and Afroasiatic linguistics*, H. Buske: Hamburg.

FRAJZYNGIER, Z. (1986) 'From preposition to copula', BLS 12: 371-386.

FRAJZYNGIER, Z. (1987) 'From verb to copula', *Lingua* 72: 155–168.

FRANKLIN, K.J. (1971) *A grammar of Kewa. New Guinea*, Australian National University: Canberra.

FRANKLIN, K.J. (ed.) (1981) *Syntax and semantics in Papua New Guinea languages.* SIL: Ukarumpa.

FRANTZ, D. (1971) *Toward a generative grammar of Blackfoot.* SIL/ University of Oklahoma: Norman.

FRANTZ, D. (1981) *Grammatical relations in universal grammar.* IULC: Bloomington.

FRANZ, C. (1976) 'Gadsup sentence structure', *Workpapers in Papua New Guinea Languages* 10: 73–191.

FRIEDRICH, P. (1975) *Proto-Indo-European syntax.* Montana College of Mineral Science and Technology: Butte.

FRIEDRICH, P. (1979) 'The symbol and its relative non-arbitrariness', in A.S. Dil (ed.), *Language, context and the imagination.* Stanford University Press: Stanford.

FURBY, E.S. and C.E. FURBY (1977) *A preliminary analysis of Garawa phrases and clauses.* Australian National University: Canberra.

GAMAL-ELDIN, S.M. (1967) *A syntactic study of Egyptian colloquial Arabic.* Mouton: The Hague.

GAMBLE, G. (1978) *Wikchamni grammar.* University of California Press: Berkeley.

GAMKRELIDZE, T. (1974) 'The problem of *l'arbitraire du signe'*, *Language* 50: 102–111.

GARBELL, I. (1965) *The Jewish Neo-Aramaic dialect of Persian Azerbaijan.* Mouton: The Hague.

GARLAND, R. and S. GARLAND (1975) 'A grammar sketch of Mountain Koiali', in T.E. Dutton (ed.) (1975a).

GARLAND, S. (1980) 'Mountain Koiali grammar: sentences, paragraphs and discourse', *Workpapers in Papua New Guinea Languages* 27: 107–222.

GAZDAR, G. (1980) 'Pragmatic constraints on linguistic production', in B. Butterworth (ed.), *Language production*. Academic Press: New York.

GEARY, E. (1977) 'Kunimaipa grammar', *Workpapers in Papua New Guinea Languages* 23: 1–271.

GEDNEY, W. (1965) 'Yay, a northern Tai language', *Lingua* 14: 180–193.

GEIGER, W. (1938) *A grammar of the Sinhalese language*. Royal Asiatic Society: Colombo.

GEIS, J. (1973) 'Subject complementation with causative verbs', in B.B. Kachru, H. Kahane, and R. Kahane (eds) (1973).

GEIS, M.L. and A.M. ZWICKY (1971) 'Invited inferences', *LI* 2: 561–566.

GENETTI, C. (1986) 'The development of subordinators from postpositions in Bodic languages', *BLS* 12: 387–400.

GEORGE, A. (1987) 'Review discussion: *Knowledge of language: its nature, origin and use*, by N. Chomsky', *Mind and Language* 2: 155–164.

GEORGE, I. (1971) 'The *á*-construction in Nupe: perfective, stative, causative or instrumental?', in C.W. Kim and H. Stahlke (eds) (1971).

GEORGE, I. (1976) 'Verb serialization and lexical decomposition', *Studies in African Linguistics* 6: 63–72.

GERDTS, D.B. (1984) 'A relational analysis of Halkomelem causals', in E.D. Cook and D.B. Gerdts (eds), *Syntax and semantics vol. 16: the syntax of native American languages*. Academic Press: New York.

GERDTS, D.B. (1992) 'Morphologically-mediated relational profiles', *BLS* 18: 322–337.

GERDTS, D.B. (1993a) 'Mapping Halkomelem grammatical relations', *Linguistics* 31: 591–621.

GERDTS, D.B. (1993b) 'Mapping transitive voice in Halkomelem', *BLS* 19: 22–34.

GEYTENBEEK, B. and H. GEYTENBEEK (1971) *Gidabal grammar and dictionary*. AIAS: Canberra.

GIBSON, J. (1980) Clause union in Chamorro and in universal grammar. Unpublished Ph.D. dissertation, University of California, San Diego.

GIBSON, J. and I. ÖZKARAGÖZ (1981) 'The syntactic nature of the Turkish causative construction', *CLS* 17: 83–98.

GIBSON, J. and E. RAPOSO (1986) 'Clause union, the Stratal Uniqueness Law and the *chômeur* relation', *NLLT* 4: 295–331.

GILBERT, G. (1986) 'The language bioprogram hypothesis: *déjà vu?*', in P. Muysken and N. Smith (eds) (1986a).

GILMAN, C. (1986) 'African areal characteristics: sprachbund, not substrate?', *Journal of Pidgin and Creole Languages* 1: 33–50.

GIVÓN, T. (1970) 'The resolution of gender conflicts in Bantu conjunction:

when syntax and semantics clash', *CLS* 6: 250–261.

GIVÓN, T. (1971a) 'Historical syntax and synchronic morphology: an archaeologist's field trip', *CLS* 7: 394–415.

GIVÓN, T. (1971b) 'Some historical changes in the noun-class system of Bantu, their possible causes and wider implications', in C.W. Kim and H. Stahlke (eds) (1971).

GIVÓN, T. (1971c) 'Dependent modals, performatives, factivity: Bantu subjunctive and what not', *Studies in African Linguistics* 2: 61–81.

GIVÓN, T. (1971d) 'On the verbal origin of the Bantu verb suffixes', *Studies in African Linguistics* 2: 145–163.

GIVÓN, T. (1972) 'Studies in ChiBemba and Bantu grammar', *Studies in African Linguistics: Supplement* 3: 1–247.

GIVÓN, T. (1975a) 'Serial verbs and syntactic change', in C.N. Li (ed.) (1975a).

GIVÓN, T. (1975b) 'Cause and control: on the semantics of interpersonal manipulation', in J.P. Kimball (ed.), *Syntax and semantics 4*. Academic Press: New York.

GIVÓN, T. (1976a) 'On the VS word order in Israeli Hebrew: pragmatics and typological change', in P. Cole (ed.) (1976a).

GIVÓN, T. (1976b) 'Some constraints on Bantu causativization', in M. Shibatani (ed.) (1976b).

GIVÓN, T. (1979a) *On understanding grammar*. Academic Press: New York.

GIVÓN, T. (1979b) 'Language typology in Africa: a critical review', *Journal of African Languages and Linguistics* 1: 199–224.

GIVÓN, T. (ed.) (1979c) *Syntax and semantics 12: discourse and syntax*. Academic Press: New York.

GIVÓN, T. (1980) 'The binding hierarchy and the typology of complements', *SiL* 4: 333–377.

GIVÓN, T. (1981) 'Typology and functional domains', *SiL* 5: 163–193.

GIVÓN, T. (1982) 'Logic vs. pragmatics, with human language as the referee: toward an empirically viable epistemology', *Journal of Pragmatics* 6: 81–133.

GIVÓN, T. (ed.) (1983) *Topic continuity in discourse: a quantitative cross-language study*. John Benjamins: Amsterdam.

GIVÓN, T. (1984) Syntax: a functional-typological introduction vol. I. John Benjamins: Amsterdam.

GIVÓN, T. (1985) 'Iconicity, isomorphism and non-arbitrary coding in syntax', in J. Haiman (ed.) (1985b).

GIVÓN, T. (1990) *Syntax: a functional-typological introduction vol. II*. John Benjamins: Amsterdam.

GIVÓN, T. (1994) 'Irrealis and the subjunctive', *SiL* 18: 265–337.

GIVÓN, T. (n.d.) Serial verbs and the mental reality of "proposition" and "event". Ms, University of Oregon.

GLASGOW, K. and M. GARNER (1980) 'Clause-level tagmemes of

Burarra', *Papers in Australian Linguistics* 12: 37–82.

GLASS, A. (1983) *Ngaanyatjarra sentences*. SIL-AAB: Darwin.

GLASS, A. and D. HACKETT (1970) *Pitjantjatjara grammar*. AIAS: Canberra.

GLASS, A. and D. HACKETT (1979) *Ngaanyatjarra texts*. AIAS: Canberra.

GLOVER, W.W. (1974) *Sememic and grammatical structures in Gurung (Nepal)*. SIL/University of Oklahoma: Norman.

GODDARD, C. (1983) *A semantically-oriented grammar of the Yankunytjatjara dialect of the Western Desert language*. Unpublished Ph.D. thesis, Australian National University.

GODDARD, C. (1988) 'Verb serialisation and the circumstantial construction in Yankunytjatjara', in P. Austin (ed.) (1988).

GODDARD, J. (1976) 'Higher levels of Agarabi grammar', *Workpapers in Papua New Guinea Languages* 10: 5–72.

GODDARD, J. (1980) 'Notes on Agarabi grammar', *Papers in New Guinea Linguistics* 20: 35–76.

GODEL, R. (1975) *An introduction to the study of classical Armenian*. Dr Ludwig Reichert: Wiesbaden.

GOLDSTEIN, M.C. and N. NORNANG (1970) *Modern spoken Tibetan: Lhasa dialect*. University of Washington Press: Seattle.

GOŁAB, Z. (1968) 'The grammar of Slavic causatives', in H. Kucera (ed.), *American contributions to the 6th International Congress of Slavists vol. 1: linguistics contributions*. Mouton: The Hague.

GONDA, J. (1966) *A concise elementary grammar of the Sanskrit language*. E.J. Brill: Leiden.

GOODALL, G. (1987) *Parallel structures in syntax – coordination, causatives and restructuring*. Cambridge University Press: Cambridge.

GOODWIN, E. (1974) *First lessons in Manx*. Yn Cheshaght Ghailckagh: Doolish.

GOODWIN, W. and C. GULICK (1958) *Greek grammar*. Blaisdell: Waltham, MA.

GORDON, K.H. (1973) 'Clause patterns in Dhangar-Kurux', in R.L. Trail (ed.) (1973).

GOSCHNICK, H. (1977) 'Haroi clauses', *Papers in South East Asian Linguistics* 4: 105–124.

GREEN, P. (1979) 'Co-existent aspect-marking phenomena in Aborlan Tagbanwa', *Papers in Philippine Linguistics* 9: 69–90.

GREENBERG, J.H. (1960) 'A quantitative approach to the morphological typology of language', *IJAL* 26: 178–194.

GREENBERG, J.H. (ed.) (1963a) *Universals of language*. MIT Press: Cambridge, MA.

GREENBERG, J.H. (1963b) 'Some universals of grammar with particular reference to the order of meaningful elements', in J.H. Greenberg (ed.) (1963a).

GREENBERG, J.H. (1966) *Language universals, with special reference to feature hierarchies.* Mouton: The Hague.

GREENBERG, J.H. (1974) *Language typology: a historical and analytic overview.* Mouton: The Hague.

GREENBERG, J.H. (1978a) 'Typology and cross-linguistic generalizations', in J.H. Greenberg, C.A. Ferguson, and E.A. Moravcsik (eds) (1978).

GREENBERG, J.H. (1978b) 'Diachrony, synchrony and language universals', in J.H. Greenberg, C.A. Ferguson, and E.A. Moravcsik (eds) (1978).

GREENBERG, J.H. (1985) 'Some iconic relationships among place, time and discourse dexis', in J. Haiman (ed.) (1985b).

GREENBERG, J.H. (1987) *Language in the Americas.* Stanford University Press: Stanford.

GREENBERG, J.H., C.A. FERGUSON, and E.A. MORAVCSIK (eds) (1978) *Universals of human language vol. 1.* Stanford University Press: Stanford.

GREGERSEN, E.A. (1977) *Language in Africa: an introductory survey.* Gordon and Breach: New York.

GREGERSON, K. (1979) *Predicate and argument in Rengao grammar.* SIL and University of Texas at Arlington.

GREGOR, D.B. (1982) *Romontsch: language and literature – the Sursilvan Raeto – Romance of Switzerland.* Oleander Press: Stoughton, Wis.

GREGORES, E. and J.A. SUÁREZ (1967) *A description of colloquial Guaraní.* Mouton: The Hague.

GRICE, P.H. (1967) Logic and conversation. Ms, Harvard University.

GRICE, P.H. (1975) 'Logic and conversation', in P. Cole and J.L. Morgan (eds) (1975).

GRIMES, J. (1964) *Huichol syntax.* Mouton: The Hague.

GRIMES, J. (1975) *The thread of discourse.* Mouton: The Hague.

GROEN, B.M. (1977) *A structural description of the Macedonian dialect of Dihovo.* Peter de Ridder: Lisse.

GROVES, J.R., G.W. GROVES, and R. JACOBS (1985) *Kiribatese: an outline description.* Australian National University: Canberra.

GUILLON, E. (1976) 'Some aspects of Mon syntax', in P.N. Jenner, C. Thompson, and S. Starosta (eds) (1976).

GUSTAFSSON, U. (1973) 'Clause patterns in Kotia Oriya', in R.L. Trail (ed.) (1973).

GUY, J.B.M. (1974a) *A grammar of the northern dialect of Sakao.* Australian National University: Canberra.

GUY, J.B.M. (1974b) *Handbook of Bichelamar.* Australian National University: Canberra.

HAAS, M. (1950) *Tunica texts.* University of California: Berkeley.

HAGMAN, R.S. (1977) *Nama Hottentot grammar.* Indiana University Press: Bloomington.

HAILE, B. (1926 [1974]) *A manual of Navaho grammar*. St Michael's Press: Saint Michaels, AZ/AMS Press: New York.

HAIMAN, J. (1974) *Targets and syntactic change*. Mouton: The Hague.

HAIMAN, J. (1980a) *Hua: a Papuan language of the Eastern Highlands of New Guinea*. John Benjamins: Amsterdam.

HAIMAN, J. (1980b) 'The iconicity of grammar: isomorphism and motivation', *Language* 56: 515–540.

HAIMAN, J. (1982) 'High transitivity in Hua', in P.J. Hopper and S.A. Thompson (eds) (1982).

HAIMAN, J. (1983a) 'On some origins of switch-reference marking', in J. Haiman and P. Munro (eds) (1983a).

HAIMAN, J. (1983b) 'Iconic and economic motivation', *Language* 59: 781–819.

HAIMAN, J. (1983c) 'Paratactic if-clauses', *Journal of Pragmatics* 7: 263–281.

HAIMAN, J. (1985a) *Natural syntax*. Cambridge University Press: Cambridge.

HAIMAN, J. (ed.) (1985b) *Iconicity in syntax*. John Benjamins: Amsterdam.

HAIMAN, J. (1985c) 'Symmetry', in J. Haiman (ed.) (1985b).

HAIMAN, J. (1987) 'On some origins of medial verb morphology in Papuan languages', *SiL* 11: 347–364.

HAIMAN, J. (1988) 'Inconsequential clauses in Hua and the typology of clauses', in J. Haiman and S.A. Thompson (eds) (1988).

HAIMAN, J. and P. MUNRO (eds) (1983a) *Switch reference and universal grammar*. John Benjamins: Amsterdam.

HAIMAN, J. and P. MUNRO (1983b) 'Introduction', in J. Haiman and P. Munro (eds) (1983a).

HAIMAN, J. and S.A. THOMPSON (eds) (1988) *Clause combining in grammar and discourse*. John Benjamins: Amsterdam.

HAITSMA, J.D. VAN and W. VAN HAITSMA (1976) *A hierarchical sketch of Mixe as spoken in San José El Paraíso*. SIL/University of Oklahoma: Norman.

HALE, A. (ed.) (1975) *Nepal studies in linguistics II: collected papers on Sherpa, Jirel*. University Press: Kathmandu.

HALE, A. (1982) *Research on Tibeto-Burman languages*. Mouton: Berlin.

HALE, A. and T. MANANDHAR (1980) 'Case and role in Newari', *Papers in South East Asian Linguistics* 7: 79–93.

HALE, K. (1975) *Gaps in grammar and culture*. Peter de Ridder: Lisse.

HALE, K. (1976) 'The adjoined relative clause in Australia', in R.M.W. Dixon (ed.) (1976).

HALE, K. (1981) *On the position of Walbiri in a typology of the base*. IULC: Bloomington.

HALE, K. (1982) 'Some essential features of Warlpiri verbal clauses',

Work Papers (SIL/AAB) 6: 217–315.

HALE, K. (1983) 'Walpiri and the grammar of non-configurational languages', *NLLT* 1: 5–47.

HALIM, A., L. CARRINGTON, and S. WURM (eds) (1982) *Papers from the third Int'l conference on Austronesian linguistics vol. 4: thematic variation.* Australian National University: Canberra.

HALL, C.J. (1987) Language structure and explanation: a case from morphology. Unpublished Ph.D. dissertation, University of Southern California.

HALL, C.J. (1988) 'Integrating diachronic and processing principles in explaining the suffixing preference', in J.A. Hawkins (ed.) (1988a).

HALL, C.J. (1992) *Morphology and mind.* Routledge: London.

HALL, R.A. (1953) *Haitian Creole.* American Anthropological Association Memoir 74: Washington, DC.

HALLIDAY, M.A.K. (1985) *An introduction to functional grammar.* Edward Arnold: London.

HAMMOND, M. (1976) *Latin: a historical and linguistic handbook.* Harvard University Press: Cambridge, MA.

HAMMOND, M., E.A. MORAVCSIK, and J.R. WIRTH (eds) (1988a) *Studies in syntactic typology.* John Benjamins: Amsterdam.

HAMMOND, M., E.A. MORAVCSIK, and J.R. WIRTH (1988b) 'Language typology and linguistic explanation', in M. Hammond, E.A. Moravcsik, and J.R. Wirth (eds) (1988a).

HAMP, E. (1982) 'Latin *ut/ne* and *ut* (... *non*)', *Glotta* 60: 115–120.

HANKAMER, J. (1977) 'Multiple analyses', in C.N. Li (ed.) (1977).

HANNAH, H.B. (1973) *Grammar of the Tibetan language.* Literary and Colloquial Books: India.

HANSSON, I.-L. (1985) 'Verb concatenation in Akha', in G. Thurgood, J.A. Matisoff, and D. Bradley (eds) (1985).

HARBERT, W. (1977) 'Clause union and German accusative plus infinitive constructions', in P. Cole and J.M. Sadock (eds) (1977).

HARDJADIBRATA, R.R. (1985) *Sundanese: a syntactical analysis.* Australian National University: Canberra.

HARDMAN, M.J. (1966) *Jaqaru: outline of phonological and morphological structure.* Mouton: The Hague.

HARKINS, W.E. (1953) *A modern Czech grammar.* King's Crown Press: New York.

HARMS, R. (1964) *Finnish structural sketch.* Indiana University Press: Bloomington/Mouton: The Hague.

HARNISH, R.M. (1976) 'Logical form and implicature', in T. Bever, J. Katz, and T. Langendoen (eds), *An integrated theory of linguistic ability.* Crowell: New York.

HARRELL, R.S. (1962) *A short reference grammar of Moroccan Arabic.* Georgetown University Press: Washington, DC.

HARRIS, A.C. (1981) *Georgian syntax: a study in relational grammar.*

Cambridge University Press: Cambridge.

HARRIS, J.K. (1969) 'Preliminary grammar of Gunbalang', *Papers in Australian Linguistics* 4: 1–49.

HARRIS, J.W. (1986) *Northern Territory pidgins and the origin of Kriol.* Australian National University: Canberra.

HARRIS, M. (1978) *The evolution of French syntax: a comparative approach.* Longman: London.

HARRIS, M. (1984a) 'On the strengths and weaknesses of a typological approach to historical syntax', in J. Fisiak (ed.) (1984).

HARRIS, M. (1984b) 'On the causes of word order change', *Lingua 63:* 175–204.

HARRIS, M. and N. VINCENT (eds) (1988) *The Romance languages.* Croom Helm: London.

HARRIS, P.G. (1946) 'Notes on the Reshe language', *African Studies* 5: 221–242.

HARRISON, S.P. (1976) *Mokilese reference grammar.* University Press of Hawaii: Honolulu.

HARRISON, S.P. (1982) 'Proto-Oceanic *aki(ni)* and the Proto-Oceanic periphrastic causative', in A. Halim, L. Carrington, and S. Wurm (eds) (1982).

HAUGEN, E. (1982) *Scandinavian language structures: a comparative historical survey.* Max Niemeyer: Tübingen/University of Minnesota Press: Minneapolis.

HAUGEN, E. and K.G. CHAPMAN (1982) *Spoken Norwegian.* Holt, Rinehart and Winston: New York.

HAVILAND, J. (1979) 'Guugu Yimidhirr', in R.M.W. Dixon and B.J. Blake (eds) (1979).

HAWKINS, J.A. (1980) 'On implicational and distributional universals of word order', *JL* 16: 193–235.

HAWKINS, J.A. (1983) *Word order universals.* Academic Press: New York.

HAWKINS, J.A. (1985) 'Complementary methods in universal grammar: a reply to Coopmans', *Language* 61: 569–587.

HAWKINS, J.A. (ed.) (1988a) *Explaining language universals.* Basil Blackwell: Oxford.

HAWKINS, J.A. (1988b) 'Explaining language universals', in J.A. Hawkins (ed.) (1988a).

HAWKINS, J.A. (1988c) 'On generative and typological approaches to universal grammar', *Lingua* 74: 85–100.

HAWKINS, J.A. and A. CUTLER (1988) 'Psycholinguistic factors in morphological asymmetry', in J.A. Hawkins (ed.) (1988a).

HAWKINS, J.A. and G. GILLIGAN (1988) 'Prefixing and suffixing universals in relation to basic word order', *Lingua* 74: 219–259.

HAZLEWOOD, D. (1872) *A Fijian and English and an English and Fijian dictionary and a grammar of the language.* Sampson Low, Marston and Co.: London.

HEADLAND, T.N. and A. HEALEY (1974) 'Grammatical sketch of Casiguran Dumagat', *Papers in Philippine Linguistics* 6: 1–54.

HEALEY, A., A. ISOROEMBO, and M. CHITTLEBOROUGH (1969) 'Preliminary notes on Orokaiva grammar', *Papers in New Guinea Linguistics* 9: 33–64.

HEALEY, P.M. (1960) *An Agta grammar.* Bureau of Printing: Manila.

HEALEY, P.M. (1965a) 'Telefol clause structure', *Papers in New Guinea Linguistics* 3: 1–26.

HEALEY, P.M. (1965b) 'Telefol verb phrases', *Papers in New Guinea Linguistics* 3: 27–53.

HEALEY, P.M. (1966) *Levels and chaining in Telefol sentences.* Australian National University: Canberra.

HEATH, J. (1975) 'Some functional relationships in grammar', *Language* 51: 89–104.

HEATH, J. (1978a) *Ngandi grammar, texts and dictionary.* AIAS: Canberra.

HEATH, J. (1978b) 'Functional universals', *BLS* 4: 86–95.

HEATH, J. (1980a) *Basic materials in Ritharngu: grammar, texts and dictionary.* Australian National University: Canberra.

HEATH, J. (1980b) *Basic materials in Warndarang: grammar, texts and dictionary.* Australian National University: Canberra.

HEATH, J. (1981) *Basic materials in Mara: grammar, texts and dictionary.* Australian National University: Canberra.

HEATH, J. (1984) *Functional grammar of Nunggubuyu.* AIAS: Canberra.

HEATH, J. (1985) 'Clause structure in Ngandi', in J. Nichols and A.C. Woodbury (eds) (1985).

HEER, G.K. DE (1975) Indonesian syntax. Unpublished Ph.D. dissertation, Cornell University.

HEINE, B. (1975) 'Language typology and convergence areas in Africa', *Linguistics* 144: 27–47.

HEINE, B. (1980) *The non-Bantu language of Kenya.* Dietrich Reimer: Berlin.

HEINE, B. (1982) *Boni dialects.* Dietrich Reimer: Berlin.

HEINE, B. (1991) 'The dative in Ik and Kanuri', in W. Croft, K. Denning, and S. Kemmer (eds) (1990).

HEINE, B. and U. CLAUDI (1986) *On the rise of grammatical categories: some examples from Maa.* Dietrich Reimer: Berlin.

HEINE, B., U. CLAUDI, and F. HÜNNEMEYER (1991a) *Grammaticalization: a conceptual framework.* Chicago University Press: Chicago.

HEINE, B., U. CLAUDI, and F. HÜNNEMEYER (1991b) 'From cognition to grammar – evidence from African languages', in E.C. Traugott and B. Heine (eds) (1991), *Approaches to grammaticalization vol. 1.* John Benjamins: Amsterdam.

HEINE, B. and M. REH (1984) *Grammaticalization and reanalysis in African languages.* Helmut Buske: Hamburg.

HEMON, R. (1975) *A historical morphology and syntax of Breton.* Dublin Institute for Advanced Studies: Dublin.

HENARE, T.W. (1987) *Conversational Maori.* Longman Paul: Auckland.

HENDERSON, E.J.A. (1976) 'Vestiges of morphology in modern standard Khasi', in P.N. Jenner, L.C. Thompson, and S. Starotsa (eds) (1976).

HENDERSON, J.E. (1975) 'Yeletnye, the language of Rossel Island', in T.E. Dutton (ed.) (1975a).

HENRY, J. (1948) 'The Kaingang language', *IJAL* 14: 194–204.

HERCUS, L.A. (1982) *The Bāgandji language.* Australian National University: Canberra.

HERINGER, J.T. (1976) 'Idioms and lexicalization in English', in M. Shibatani (ed.) (1976b).

HERSKOVITS, A. (1986) *Language and spatial cognition.* Cambridge University Press: Cambridge.

HESS, H.H. (1968) *The syntactic structure of Mezquital Otomi.* Mouton: The Hague.

HETTICK, D. (1974) 'Verb stem classes in Northern Kankanay', *Papers in Philippine Linguistics* 5: 1–21.

HETZRON, R. (1969) *The verbal system of Southern Agaw.* University of California Press: Los Angeles.

HETZRON, R. (1976) 'On the Hungarian causative verb and its syntax', in M. Shibatani (ed.) (1976b).

HEWER, P. (1976) 'A lexical approach to clause series in Kasem', *Linguistics* 171: 19–34.

HEWITT, B.G. (1979) *Abkhaz.* North-Holland: Amsterdam.

HEWITT, B.G. (1981) 'The causative: Daghestanian variations on a theme', in B. Comrie (ed.), *Studies in the languages of the USSR.* Linguistic Research Inc.: Carbondale.

HEWITT, B.G. (1984) 'Parataxis revisited (via the Caucasus)', *General Linguistics* 24: 2–20.

HIDALGO, C.A. and A.C. HIDALGO (1971) *A tagmemic grammar of Ivatan.* Linguistic Society of the Philippines: Manila.

HILL, C.A. (1978) 'Linguistic representation of spatial and temporal orientation', *BLS* 4: 524–538.

HILL, K.C. (ed.) (1979) *The genesis of language.* Karoma: Ann Arbor.

HINDS, J. (1986) *Japanese.* Croom Helm: London.

HINTON, L. (1982) 'How to cause in Mixtec', *BLS* 8: 354–363.

HINZ, J. (1944) *Grammar and vocabulary of the Eskimo language.* Society for Propagating the Gospel: Bethlehem, PA.

HJELMSLEV, L. (1961) *Prolegomena to a theory of language.* University of Wisconsin Press: Madison.

HOA, N.D. (1971 [1974]) *Colloquial Vietnamese.* Southern Illinois University Press: Carbondale.

HOCHSTER, A. (1978) 'Order and degree of fusion in causative structures', *Glossa* 12: 39–57.

HOCK, H.H. (1986) *Principles of historical linguistics*. Mouton de Gruyter: Berlin.

HOCKETT, C.F. (1963) 'The problem of universals in language', in J.H. Greenberg (ed.) (1963a).

HODDINOTT, W.G. and F.M. KOFOD (1988) *The Ngankikurungkurr language*. Australian National University: Canberra.

HODGES, K.S. (1977) 'Object relations in Ki-Meru causatives', *Studies in the Linguistic Sciences* 6: 108–141.

HOEKSTRA, T. and J.G. KOOIJ (1988) 'The innateness hypothesis', in J.A. Hawkins (ed.) (1988a).

HOFF, B.J. (1968) *The Carib language*. Mouton: The Hague.

HOFFMANN, C. (1963) *A grammar of the Margi language*. Oxford University Press: London.

HÖFTMANN, H. (1971) *The structure of Lelemi language*. Enzyklopädie: Leipzig.

HOHEPA, P. (1967) 'A profile generative grammar of Maori', *Supplement to IJAL* 33.2.

HOHULIN, R.M. (1971) 'Complex predicates in Keley-i Kallahan', *Papers in Philippine Linguistics* 4: 19–32.

HOLM, J. (1988) *Pidgins and creoles vol. I: theory and structure*. Cambridge University Press: Cambridge.

HOLMER, N.M. (1949) 'Goajiro (Arawak) III: verbs and associated morphemes', *IJAL* 15: 145–157.

HOLZKNECHT, S. (1986) 'A morphology and grammar of Adzera (Amari dialect), Morobe Province, Papua New Guinea', *Papers in New Guinea Linguistics* 24: 77–166.

HONTS, M.E. (1979) 'Cases and clauses in Lao', in N.D. Liem (ed.), *South-East Asian Linguistic Studies vol. 4*. Australian National University: Canberra.

HOOGSHAGEN, S. (1984) 'Coatlán Mixe', in M.S. Edmonson (ed.) (1984).

HOOK, P.E. (1974) *The compound verb in Hindi*. Center for South and Southeast Asian Studies, University of Michigan: Ann Arbor.

HOPE, E.R. (1974) *The deep syntax of Lisu sentences: a transformational case grammar*. Australian National University: Canberra.

HOPPER, P.J. (1985) 'Causes and affects', *CLS* 21, Part II: 67–88.

HOPPER, P.J. and S.A. THOMPSON (1980) 'Transitivity in grammar and discourse', *Language* 56: 251–299.

HOPPER, P.J. and S.A. THOMPSON (eds) (1982) *Studies in transitivity*. Academic Press: New York.

HOPPER, P.J. and S.A. THOMPSON (1984) 'The discourse basis for lexical categories in universal grammar', *Language* 60: 703–752.

HOPPER, P.J. and S.A. THOMPSON (1985) 'The iconicity of the universal categories "noun" and "verb"', in J. Haiman (ed.) (1985b).

HOPPER, P.J. and E.C. TRAUGOTT (1993) *Grammaticalization*. Cambridge University Press: Cambridge.

HORN, L.R. (1985) 'Towards a new taxonomy for pragmatic inference: Q-based and R-based implicature', in D. Schiffrin (ed.), *Meaning, form and use in context.* Georgetown University Press: Washington, DC.

HORNE, E.C. (1961) *Beginning Javanese.* Yale University Press: New Haven.

HORNE, K.M. (1966) *Language typology: 19th and 20th century views.* Georgetown University Press: Washington, DC.

HORROCKS, G. (1987) *Generative grammar.* Longman: London.

HORST, L. VAN DER (1932) 'Über die psychologie des Korsakowsyndroms', *Monatsschrift für Psychiatrie und Neurologie* 83: 65–84.

HOUSEHOLDER, F., K. KAZAZIS, and A. KOUTSOUDAS (1964) *Reference grammar of literary Dhimotiki.* Mouton: The Hague.

HOUSEHOLDER, F. and M. LOFTI (1965) *Basic course in Azerbaijani.* Indiana University Press: Bloomington.

HOWARD, I. (1971) 'On several concepts of universals', *Working Papers in Linguistics* (University of Hawaii) 3: 243–248.

HUBBARD, P.L. (1985) *The syntax of the Albanian verb complex.* Garland: New York.

HUCKETT, J. (1976) 'Iduna sentence structure', *Workpapers in Papua New Guinea Languages* 15: 127–262.

HUDSON, J. (1978) *The core of Walmatjari grammar.* AIAS: Canberra.

HUESTIS, G. (1963) 'Bororo clause structure', *IJAL* 29: 230–238.

HUFFMAN, F.E. (1970) *Modern spoken Cambodian.* Yale University Press: New Haven.

HUMESKY, A. (1980) *Modern Ukrainian.* Canadian Institute of Ukrainian Studies: Edmonton.

HUNDIRAPOLA, R. (1975) The syntactic structure of Sinhalese and its relation to that of the other Indo-Aryan dialects. Unpublished Ph.D. dissertation, University of Texas at Austin.

HURFORD, J. (1977) 'The significance of linguistic generalizations', *Language* 53: 574–620.

HURLBUT, H.M. (1988) *Verb morphology in Eastern Kadazan.* Australian National University: Canberra.

HUTCHISON, J.P. (1976) Aspects of Kanuri syntax. Unpublished Ph.D. dissertation, Indiana University.

HUTTER, G.L. (1981) 'Some Kwa-like features of Djuka syntax', *Studies in African Linguistics* 12: 291–323.

HYAMS, N.M. (1986) *Language acquisition and the theory of parameters.* D. Reidel: Dordrecht.

HYDE, V. (1971) *An introduction to the Luiseño language.* Malki Museum Press: Banning.

HYMAN, L. (1971) 'Consecutivization in Fe'fe'', *Journal of African Languages* 10.2: 29–43.

HYMAN, L. (1975) 'On the change from SOV to SVO: evidence from

Niger-Congo', in C.N. Li (ed.) (1975a).

HYMAN, L. (ed.) (1979) *Aghem grammatical structure with special reference to noun classes, tense-aspect and focus marking*. University of Southern California: Los Angeles.

HYMAN, L. (1981) *Noni grammatical structure*. University of Southern California: Los Angeles.

HYMAN, L. (1983) 'Form and substance in language universals', *Linguistics* 21: 67–85.

HYMAN, L. and K.E. ZIMMER (1976) 'Embedded topic in French', in C.N. Li (ed.), *Subject and Topic*. Academic Press: New York.

IKEGAMI, Y. (1988) 'Transitivity: intransitivization vs. causativization: some typological considerations concerning verbs of Action', in C. Duncan-Rose and T. Vennemann (eds) (1988).

IKRANAGARA, K. (1975) Melayu Betawi grammar. Unpublished Ph.D. dissertation, University of Hawaii.

INNES, G. (1962) *A Mende grammar*. Macmillan: London.

INNES, G. (1963) *The structure of sentences in Mende*. SOAS: London.

INNES, G. (1964) 'An outline grammar of Loko with texts', *African Language Studies* 5: 115–173.

INNES, G. (1966) *An introduction to Grebo*. SOAS: London.

INNES, G. (1967) *A practical introduction to Mende*. SOAS: London.

IRWIN, B. (1974) *Salt-Yui grammar*. Australian National University: Canberra.

JACKENDOFF, R. (1972) *Semantic interpretation in generative grammar*. MIT Press: Cambridge, MA.

JACKENDOFF, R. (1975) 'Morphological and semantic regularities in lexicon', *Language* 51: 639–671.

JACKENDOFF, R. (1983) *Semantics and cognition*. MIT Press: Cambridge, MA.

JACOB, J.M. (1968) *Introduction to Cambodian*. Oxford University Press: Oxford.

JACOBS, M. (1931) *A sketch of northern Sahaptin grammar*. University of Washington Press: Seattle.

JACOBSEN, B. (1986) *Modern transformational grammar*. North-Holland: Amsterdam.

JACOBSEN, W.H. (1967) 'Switch reference in Hokan-Coahuiltecan', in D. Hymes and W. Bittle (eds), *Studies in Southwestern ethnolinguistics: meaning and history in the languages of the American Southwest*. Mouton: The Hague.

JACOBSON, S.A. (1977) *A grammatical sketch of Siberian Yupik Eskimo*. Alaska Native Language Center: Fairbanks.

JAKE, J.L. (1985) *Grammatical relations in Imbabura Quechua*. Garland: New York.

JAKOBSON, R. (1957 [1971]) 'Shifters, verbal categories and the Russian verb', in *Roman Jakobson selected writings vol. 2*. Mouton: The Hague.

JAMES, D. (1983) 'Verb serialization in Siane', *Language and Linguistics in Melanesia* 14: 24–73.

JANZEN, H. (1976) 'Structure and function of clauses and phrases in Pale', in P.N. Jenner, L.C. Thompson, and S. Starosta (eds) (1976).

JÄSCHKE, H.A. (1954) *Tibetan grammar*. Ungar: New York.

JEFFERS, R. (1976) 'Syntactic change and syntactic reconstruction', in W. Christie (ed.), *Current progress in historical linguistics*. North-Holland: Amsterdam.

JEFFERS, R. and I. LEHISTE (1979) *Principles and methods for historical linguistics*. MIT Press: Cambridge, MA.

JENNER, H. (1904) *A handbook of the Cornish language*. David Nutt: London.

JENNER, P.N., L.C. THOMPSON, and S. STAROSTA (eds) (1976) *Austroasiatic studies*. University of Hawaii Press: Honolulu.

JENSEN, J.T. (1977) *Yapese reference grammar*. University Press of Hawaii: Honolulu.

JENSEN, J.T. and M. STONG-JENSEN (1984) 'Morphology is in the lexicon!', *LI* 15: 474–498.

JOHNSON, A.F. (1988) 'A syntactic sketch of Jamietepec Mixtec', in C.H. Bradley and B.E. Hollenbach (eds) (1988).

JOHNSON-LAIRD, P.N. (1969) '&', *JL* 6: 111–114.

JOHNSON-LAIRD, P.N. (1983) *Mental models*. Cambridge University Press: Cambridge.

JOHNSTON, E.C. (1979) 'Cotabato Manobo first person narrative: major features of discourse and paragraph', *Papers in Philippine Linguistics* 9: 1–17.

JOHNSTON, R.L. (1978a) Nakanai syntax. Unpublished Ph.D. dissertation, Australian National University: Canberra.

JOHNSTON, R.L. (1978b) *Serial verbs and the expression of concepts of location and motion in Nakanai*. Australian National University: Canberra.

JOHNSTONE, B. (1987) 'Parataxis in Arabic: modification as a model for persuasion', *SiL* 11: 85–98.

JONES, M. and A.R. THOMAS (1977) *The Welsh language: studies in its syntax and semantics*. University of Wales Press: Cardiff.

JONES, R.B. (1961) *Karen linguistic studies*. University of California Press: Berkeley.

JOSEPH, B. (1978) *Morphology and universals in syntactic change: evidence from medieval and modern Greek*. IULC: Bloomington.

JOSEPH, B. (1980) 'Linguistic universals and syntactic change', *Language* 56: 345–370.

JOSEPH, B. (1983) 'Relativization in modern Greek: another look at the Accessibility Hierarchy constraints', *Lingua* 60: 1–24.

JOSEPH, B. and I. PHILIPPAKI-WARBURTON (1987) *Modern Greek*. Croom Helm: London.

JOSEPH, L.S. (1972) Selected problems in the analysis of embedded sentences in Japanese. Unpublished Ph.D. dissertation, Harvard University.

JOSEPHS, L.S. (1975) *Palauan reference grammar*. University Press of Hawaii: Honolulu.

JUDGE, A. and F.G. HEALEY (1983) *A reference grammar of modern French*. Edward Arnold: London.

JUDY, R.A. and J.E. JUDY (1967) 'Movima', in E. Matteson (ed.) (1967b).

KACHRU, B.B., H. KAHANE, and R. KAHANE (eds) (1973) *Issues in linguistics: papers in honor of Henry and Renée Kahane*. University of Illinois Press: Urbana.

KACHRU, Y. (1973) 'Causative sentences in Hindi revisited', in B.B. Kachru, H. Kahane, and R. Kahane (eds) (1973).

KACHRU, Y. (1976) 'On the semantics of the causative constructions in Hindi-Urdu', in M. Shibatani (ed.) (1976b).

KAHR, J.C. (1976) 'The renewal of case morphology: sources and constraints', *Stanford Working Papers on Language Universals* 20: 107–151.

KAKUMASU, J. (1986) 'Urubu-Kaapor', in D.C. Derbyshire and G. Pullum (eds) (1986).

KÁLMÁN, B. (1965) *Vogul Chrestomathy*. Indiana University Press: Bloomington.

KAMHI, D.J. (1982) *Modern Hebrew: an introductory course*. Oxford University Press: Oxford.

KANG, Y.-S. (1986) *Korean syntax and universal grammar*. Ph.D. dissertation, Harvard University, published by Hanshin: Seoul.

KARLSSON, F. (1983) *Finnish grammar*. Werner Söderström: Juva.

KÁROLY, S. (1972) 'The grammatical system of Hungarian', in L. Benkö and S. Imre (eds), *The Hungarian language*. Mouton: The Hague.

KARTUNNEN, L. (1970) 'On the semantics of complement verbs', *CLS* 6: 328–339.

KARTUNNEN, L. (1971a) 'Implicative verbs', *Language* 47: 340–358.

KARTUNNEN, L. (1971b) *The logic of the predicate complement construction in English*. IULC: Bloomington.

KASTOVSKY, D. (1973) 'Causatives', *FL* 10: 255–315.

KATZ, D. (1987) *Grammar of the Yiddish language*. Duckworth: London.

KAUFMAN, T. (1971) *Tzeltal phonology and morphology*. University of California Press: Berkeley.

KAY, D. and C.K. MCDANIEL (1978) 'The linguistic significance of the meanings of basic color terms', *Language* 54: 610–646.

KAY, P. (1977) 'Language evolution and speech style', in B.G. Blount and M. Sanches (eds), *Sociocultural dimensions of language change*. Academic Press: New York.

KAY, P. and G. SANKOFF (1974) 'A language-universals approach to pidgins and creoles', in D. DeCamp and I.F. Hancock (eds), *Pidgins and creoles: current trends and prospects*. Georgetown University Press: Washington, DC.

KAYE, A.S. and F. MÜLLER-GOTAMA (1988) 'Review of Stassen (1985)', *SiL* 12: 186–193.

KAYNE, R.S. (1975) *French syntax: the transformational cycle*. MIT Press: Cambridge, MA.

KEEN, S. (1972) A description of the Yukulta language. Unpublished MA thesis, Monash University.

KEEN, S. (1983) 'Yukulta', in R.M.W. Dixon and B.J. Blake (eds) (1983).

KEENAN, E. (1973) 'Logical expressive power and syntactic variation in natural language', in E. Keenan (ed.), *Formal semantics of natural language*. Cambridge University Press: Cambridge.

KEENAN, E. (1976) 'The logical diversity of natural language', *The Annals of the New York Academy of Sciences* 280: 73–92.

KEENAN, E. (1978) 'Language variation and the logical structure of universal grammar', in H. Seiler (ed.), *Language universals*. Gunter Narr: Tübingen.

KEENAN, E. (1982) 'Parametric variation in universal grammar', in R. Dirven and G. Radden (eds) (1982).

KEENAN, E. (1987) *Universal grammar: 15 essays*. Croom Helm: London.

KEENAN, E. and B. COMRIE (1972) Noun accessibility and universal grammar. Paper delivered at LSA Annual Meeting, Atlanta.

KEENAN, E. and B. COMRIE (1977) 'Noun accessibility and universal grammar', *LI* 8: 63–99.

KEENAN, E. and B. COMRIE (1979) 'Data on the Noun Phrase Accessibility Hierarchy', *Language* 55: 333–351.

KEESING, R.M. (1985) *Kwaio grammar*. Australian National University: Canberra.

KEFER, M. (1985) 'What syntax can we reconstruct from morphology?', *Lingua* 66: 151–175.

KELLER, C.E. (1976) *A grammatical sketch of Brao, a Mon-Khmer language*. SIL/University of North Dakota.

KELLER, R. (1988) 'Invisible hand theory and language evolution', *Lingua* 77: 113–127.

KELLER-COHEN, D. (1974) The expression of time in language acquisition. Paper presented at the Annual Meeting of the Linguistic Society of America, New York.

KEMPSON, R. (1988) 'Logical form: the grammar cognition interface', *JL* 24: 393–431.

KENDALL, M.B. (1976) *Selected problems in Yavapai syntax*. Garland: New York.

KENNEDY, R. (1984) 'Semantic roles – the language speaker's categories (in Kala Lagaw Ya)', *Papers in Australian Linguistics* 16: 153–169.

KEY, H. (1967) *Morphology of Cayuvava.* Mouton: The Hague.

KIEFER, F. (1970) 'On the problem of word order', in M. Bierwisch and K. Heidolph (eds) (1970).

KILBY, D. (1987) 'Typology and universals in Chomsky's theory of grammar', in S. Modgil and C. Modgil (eds) (1987).

KILHAM, C.A. (1977) *Thematic organization of Wik-Munkan discourse.* Australian National University: Canberra.

KIM, C.W. and H. STAHLKE (eds) (1971) *Papers in African linguistics.* Linguistic Research: Edmonton.

KIM, N.K. (1984) *The grammar of Korean complementation.* University of Hawaii: Honolulu.

KIMBALL, J.P. (ed.) (1971) *Syntax and semantics 1.* Seminar Press: New York.

KIMENYI, A. (1980a) *A relational grammar of Kinyarwanda.* University of California Press: Berkeley.

KIMENYI, A. (1980b) 'A semiotic analysis of causative constructions', *Linguistics* 18: 223–244.

KING, C. (1901) *A grammar and dictionary of the Wedau language (British New Guinea).* Pepperdar: Sydney.

KING, R.T. (1987) 'Spatial metaphor in German causative constructions', in B. Rudzka-Ostyn (ed.) (1987).

KIPARSKY, P. (1971) 'Historical linguistics', in W.O. Dingwall (ed.), *A survey of linguistic science.* University of Maryland: College Park.

KIPARSKY, P. (1982) *Explanation in phonology.* Foris: Dordrecht.

KIRSNER, R.S. (1985) 'Iconicity and grammatical meaning', in J. Haiman (ed.) (1985b).

KIRSNER, R.S. and S.A. THOMPSON (1976) 'The role of pragmatic inference in semantics: a study of sensory verb complements in English', *Glossa* 10: 200–240.

KIRTON, J.F. (1978) 'Yanyuwa verbs', *Papers in Australian Linguistics* 11: 1–52.

KLAIMAN, M.H. (1986) 'Clause linkage in Bengali', *AJL* 6: 1–36.

KLAIMAN, M.H. (1991) *Grammatical voice.* Cambridge University Press: Cambridge.

KLOKEID, T. (1976) Topics in Lardil grammar. Unpublished Ph.D. dissertation, MIT.

KLOUMAN, S. (1984) *Learn Norwegian.* Tanum-Norli: Oslo.

KNECHT, L. (1986) 'Lexical causatives in Turkish', in D.I. Slobin and K. Zimmer (eds), *Studies in Turkish linguistics.* John Benjamins: Amsterdam.

KOEFOED, G. and J. VAN MARLE (1987) 'Requisites for reinterpretation', in W. Koopman, F. van der Leek, O. Fischer, and R. Eaton (eds) (1987).

KOEHN, E. and S. KOEHN (1986) 'Apalai', in D.C. Derbyshire and G. Pullum (eds) (1986).

KÖHLER, O. (1981) 'La langue Kxoe', in J. Perrot (ed.), *Les langues dans le monde ancien et moderne – première partie: les langues de l'Afrique SubSaharienne; et deuxième partie: pidgins et créoles.* Centre National de la Recherche Scientifique: Paris.

KOLIA, J.A. (1975) 'A Balawaia grammar sketch and vocabulary', in T.E. Dutton (ed.) (1975a).

KOOPMAN, H. (1984) *The syntax of verbs – from verb movement rules in the Kru languages to universal grammar.* Foris: Dordrecht.

KOOPMAN, W., F. VAN DER LEEK, O. FISCHER, and R. EATON (eds) (1987) *Explanation and linguistic change.* John Benjamins: Amsterdam.

KOSHAL, S. (1979) *Ladakhi grammar.* Motilal Banarsidass: Delhi.

KOZINSKY, I. and M. POLINSKY (1993) 'Causee and patient in the causative of transitive: coding conflict or doubling of grammatical relations?', in B. Comrie and M. Polinsky (eds), *Causatives and transitivity.* John Benjamins: Amsterdam.

KRAFT, C.H. and M.G. KRAFT (1973) *Introductory Hausa.* University of California Press: Berkeley.

KRISHNAMURTI, B. (1971) 'Causative constructions in Indian languages', *Indian Linguistics* 32: 18–35.

KRISHNAMURTI, B. and P.S. SARMA (1968) *A basic course in modern Telugu.* Hyderabad.

KROEBER, A.L. and G.W. GRACE (1960) *The Sparkman grammar of Luiseño.* University of California Press: Berkeley.

KROEGER, P.R. (1988) 'Case marking in Kimaragang causative constructions', *Papers in Western Austronesian Linguistics* 3: 241–276.

KRUEGER, J.R. (1961) *Chuvash manual: introduction, grammar, reader and vocabulary.* Indiana University Press: Bloomington.

KRUEGER, J.R. (1963) *Yakut manual.* Indiana University Press: Bloomington.

KRUPA, V. (1968) *The Maori language.* Nauka: Moscow.

KUIPERS, A.H. (1967) *The Squamish language.* Mouton: The Hague.

KUIPERS, A.H. (1969) *The Squamish language 2.* Mouton: The Hague.

KUIPERS, A.H. (1974) *The Shuswap language.* Mouton: The Hague.

KUNO, S. (1973) *The structure of the Japanese language.* MIT Press: Cambridge, MA.

KUNO, S. (1987a) *Functional syntax.* University of Chicago Press: Chicago.

KUNO, S. (1987b) 'Honorific marking in Japanese and the word formation hypothesis of causatives and passives', *SiL* 11: 99–128.

KURODA, S.-Y. (1965) 'Causative forms in Japanese', *FL* 1: 30–50.

KURYŁOWICZ, J. (1964) *The inflectional categories of Indo-European.* C. Winter: Heidelberg.

LAKOFF, G. (1982) 'Experiential factors in linguistics', in T.W. Simon and R.J. Scholes (eds) (1982).

LAKOFF, G. (1987) *Women, fire and dangerous things.* University of Chicago Press: Chicago.

LAKOFF, G. (1993) 'The metaphor system and its role in grammar', *CLS* 29: 217–241.

LAKOFF, G. and M. JOHNSON (1980) *Metaphors we live by.* University of Chicago Press: Chicago.

LAKOFF, G. and J.R. ROSS (1972) 'A note on anaphoric islands and causatives', *LI* 3: 121–125.

LAKOFF, G. and H. THOMPSON (1975) 'Cognitive grammar', *BLS* 1: 295–309.

LAKOFF, R. (1968) *Abstract syntax and Latin complementation.* MIT Press: Cambridge, MA.

LAKOFF, R. (1972) 'Another look at drift', in R.P. Stockwell and R.K.S. Macaulay (eds) (1972).

LAKOFF, R. (1984) 'The pragmatics of subordination', *BLS* 10: 481–492.

LAMBERT, H.M. (1943) *Marathi language course.* Oxford University Press: Humphrey, Milford.

LAMBERT, H.M. (1971) *Gujarati language course.* Cambridge University Press: Cambridge.

LAMBRECHT, K. (1984) 'Frame semantics and German binominal expressions', *Language* 60: 753–796.

LAMBTON, A.K.S. (1953) *Persian grammar.* Cambridge University Press: Cambridge.

LANG, A. (1975) *The semantics of classificatory verbs in Enga (and other Papua New Guinea languages).* Australian National University: Canberra.

LANGACKER, R.W. (1974) 'Movement rules in functional perspective', *Language* 50: 630–664.

LANGACKER, R.W. (1977a) *Studies in Uto-Aztecan grammar vol. I: an overview of Uto-Aztecan grammar.* SIL and University of Texas at Arlington.

LANGACKER, R.W. (1977b) 'Syntactic reanalysis', in C.N. Li (ed.) (1977).

LANGACKER, R.W. (ed.) (1979a) *Studies in Uto-Aztecan grammar vol. II: modern Aztec grammatical sketches.* SIL and University of Texas at Arlington.

LANGACKER, R.W. (1979b) 'Grammar as image', *Linguistic Notes from La Jolla* 6: 88–126.

LANGACKER, R.W. (1983) *Foundations of cognitive grammar.* IULC: Bloomington.

LANGACKER, R.W. (ed.) (1984) *Studies in Uto-Aztecan grammar vol. IV: southern Uto-Aztecan grammatical sketches.* SIL and University of Texas at Arlington.

LANGACKER, R.W. (1987) *Foundations of cognitive grammar vol. I.* Stanford University Press: Stanford.

LANGDON, M. (1970) *A grammar of Diegueño.* University of California Press: Berkeley.

LANIER, N. (1968) 'Three structural layers in Mezquital Otomi clauses', *Linguistics* 43: 32–85.

LARSEN, M.L. (1963) 'Emic clauses which manifest the obligatory tag-memes in major independent clause types of Aguenuna (Jiraro)', in B. Elson (ed.) (1963).

LASNIK, H. and R. FREIDIN (1981) 'Core grammar, case theory and markedness', in A. Belletti, L. Brandi, and L. Rizzi (eds) (1981).

LASS, R. (1980) *On explaining language change*. Cambridge University Press: Cambridge.

LASS, R. (1987) 'Language, speakers, history and drift', in W. Koopman, F. van der Leek, O. Fischer, and R. Eaton (eds) (1987).

LASTRA, Y. (1968) *Cochabamba Quechua syntax*. Mouton: The Hague.

LAUCK, L. (1976) 'Patep sentences', *Workpapers in Papua New Guinea Languages* 17: 5–122.

LAW, H. (1966) *Obligatory constructions of Isthmus Nahuat grammar*. Mouton: The Hague.

LAWRENCE, M. (1972) 'Oksapmin sentence structure', *Papers in New Guinea Linguistics* 16: 17–46.

LAYCOCK, D.C. (1965) *The Ndu language family (Sepik district, New Guinea)*. Australian National University: Canberra.

LAYCOCK, D.C. (1970) *Materials in New Guinea Pidgin*. Australian National University: Canberra.

LEE, H.S. (1985) 'Causatives in Korean and the binding hierarchy', *CLS* 21: Part 2: 138–153.

LEE, K.M. (1961 [1988]) *kukəsa kɛsəl*. Thap Publisher: Seoul.

LEE, M. (1988) 'Language, perception and the world', in J.A. Hawkins (ed.) (1988a).

LEE, W.R. and Z. LEE (1959 [1984]) *Teach yourself Czech*. English Universities Press: London.

LEHMANN, C. (1982) 'On some current views of the language universals', in R. Dirven and G. Radden (eds) (1982).

LEHMANN, C. (1984) 'Progress in general comparative linguistics: review article of Comrie (1981), Mallinson and Blake (1981)', *SiL* 8: 259–286.

LEHMANN, C. (1988) 'Towards a typology of clause linkage', in J. Haiman and S.A. Thompson (eds) (1988).

LEHMANN, R.P.M. and W.P. LEHMANN (1975) *An introduction to Old Irish*. Modern Language Association of America: New York.

LEHMANN, W.P. (1974) *Proto-Indo-European syntax*. University of Texas Press: Austin.

LEPSCHY, A.L. and G. LEPSCHY (1977) *The Italian language today*. Hutchinson: London.

LESLAU, W. (1968) *Amharic textbook*. University of California Press: Berkeley.

LEVIN, J.F. (1982) 'Iconicity in Lithuanian', *Folia Slavica* 5: 230–245.

LEVIN, N.B. (1964) *The Assiniboine language.* Indiana University Press: Bloomington.

LEVINSOHN, S.H. (1976) *The Inga language.* Mouton: The Hague.

LEVINSON, S.C. (1983) *Pragmatics.* Cambridge University Press: Cambridge.

LEVINSON, S.C. (1987) 'Pragmatics and the grammar of anaphora: a partial pragmatic reduction of binding and control phenomena', *JL* 23: 379–434.

LEWIS, D. (1973) 'Causation', *The Journal of Philosophy* 70: 556–567.

LEWIS, G. (1967) *Turkish grammar.* Oxford University Press: Oxford.

LEWIS, R.K. (1972) 'Sanio-Hiowe paragraph structure', *Papers in New Guinea Linguistics* 15: 1–9.

LEWIS, S.C. (1972) 'Sanio-Hiowe verb phrases', *Papers in New Guinea Linguistics* 15: 11–22.

LEYNSEELE, H. VAN (1975) 'Restrictions on serial verbs in Anyi', *Journal of West African Languages* 10: 189–218.

LI, C.N. (ed.) (1975a) *Word order and word order change.* University of Texas Press: Austin.

LI, C.N. (1975b) 'Synchrony vs. diachrony in language structure', *Language* 51: 873–886.

LI, C.N. (ed.) (1977) *Mechanisms of syntactic change.* University of Texas Press: Austin.

LI, C.N. and S.A. THOMPSON (1973) 'Serial verb constructions in Mandarin Chinese: subordination or coordination', in C. Corum, T.C. Smith-Stark, and P. Weiser (eds), *You take the high node and I'll take the low node – papers from the comparative syntax festival: the difference between main and subordinate clauses.* CLS: Chicago.

LI, C.N. and S.A. THOMPSON (1975) 'The semantic function of word order: a case study in Mandarin', in C.N. Li (ed.) (1975a).

LI, CN. and S.A. THOMPSON (1976) 'Development of the causative in Mandarin Chinese: interaction of diachronic processes in syntax', in M. Shibatani (ed.) (1976b).

LI, C.N. and S.A. THOMPSON (1981) *Mandarin Chinese: a functional reference grammar.* University of California Press: Berkeley.

LI, P.J.-K. (1973) Rukai structure. Unpublished Ph.D. dissertation, University of Hawaii.

LICHTENBERK, F. (1978) 'A sketch of Houailou grammar', *Working Papers in Linguistics* (University of Hawaii) 10: 76–116.

LICHTENBERK, F. (1979) 'Syntactic iconism, coordination, subordination and language evolution', *Working Papers in Linguistics* (University of Hawaii) 11: 79–88.

LICHTENBERK, F. (1983) *A grammar of Manam.* University of Hawaii Press: Honolulu.

LIEB, H.-H. (1978) 'Universals and linguistic explanation', in J.H. Greenberg, C.A. Ferguson, and E.A. Moravcsik (eds) (1978).

LIEBER, R. (1980) *On the organization of the lexicon.* IULC: Bloomington.

LIGHTFOOT, D.W. (1979) *Principles of diachronic syntax.* Cambridge University Press: Cambridge.

LIGHTFOOT, D.W. (1982) *The language lottery: toward a biology of grammars.* MIT Press: Cambridge, MA.

LIGHTFOOT, D.W. (1988) 'Creoles, triggers, and universal grammar', in C. Duncan-Rose and T. Vennemann (eds) (1988).

LIM, S.C. (1988) 'Baba Malay: the language of the Straits-born Chinese', *Papers in Western Austronesian Linguistics* 3: 1–61.

LIMBER, J. (1973) 'The genesis of complex sentences', in T.E. Moore (ed.) (1973).

LINCOLN, P.C. (1976) 'Banoni, Piva, and Papuanization', *Papers in New Guinea Linguistics* 19: 77–105.

LINDENFELD, J. (1973) *Yaqui syntax.* University of California Press: Berkeley.

LISTER-TURNER, R. and J.B. CLARK (1930) *Revisited Motu grammar and vocabulary.* Government Printer: Port Moresby.

LITHGOW, D. (1975) 'A grammatical analysis of a Dobu text', *Workpapers in Papua New Guinea Languages* 12: 25–56.

LOCKWOOD, W.B. (1964) *An introduction to modern Faroese.* Munksgard: Copenhagen.

LOEWEKE, E. and J. MAY (1980) 'General grammar of Fasu (Namo Me)', *Workpapers in Papua New Guinea Languages* 27: 5–106.

LONG, R.W. and R.S. DIOMANDÉ (n.d.) *Basic Dyula.* Indiana University: Bloomington.

LONGACRE, R.E. (1966) 'Trique clauses and sentences: a study in contrast, variation and distribution', *IJAL* 32: 242–254.

LONGACRE, R.E. (1968) *Philippine languages: discourse, paragraph and sentence structure.* SIL: Santa Ana, CA.

LONGACRE, R.E. (1970) 'Sentence structure as a statement calculus', *Language* 46: 783–815.

LONGACRE, R.E. (1972) *Hierarchy and constituency in New Guinea languages.* Georgetown University Press: Washington, DC.

LONGACRE, R.E. (1976) *An anatomy of speech notions.* Peter de Ridder: Lisse.

LONGACRE, R.E. (1979) 'The paragraph as a grammatical unit', in T. Givón (ed.) (1979c).

LONGACRE, R.E. (1983) *The grammar of discourse.* Plenum: New York.

LONGACRE, R.E. (1985) 'Sentences as combinations of clauses', in T. Shopen (ed.) (1985b).

LONGACRE, R.E. and F. WOODS (eds) (1976–1977) *Discourse grammar: studies in languages of Columbia, Panama and Ecuador.* SIL: Dallas.

LORD, C. (1973) 'Serial verbs in transition', *Studies in African Linguistics* 4: 269–296.

LORD, C. (1974) 'Causative constructions in Yoruba', *Studies in African Linguistics (Supplement)* 5: 195–204.

LORD, C. (1975) 'Igbo verb compound and the lexicon', *Studies in African Linguistics* 6: 23–48.

LORD, C. (1977) 'How Igbo got from SOV serializing to SVO compounding', in M. Mould and T.J. Hinnebusch (eds), *Papers from the 8th Conference on African linguistics, Studies in African Linguistics (Supplement)*.

LORD, C. (1982) 'The development of object markers in serial verb languages', in P.J. Hopper and S.A. Thompson (eds) (1982).

LORIMER, D.L.R. (1915) *Pashtu (Part I): syntax of colloquial Pashtu with chapters on the Persian and Indian elements in the modern language.* Clarendon: London.

LORIMER, D.L.R. (1935–1938) *The Burushaski language.* H. Aschehoug & Co.: Oslo.

LORIMER, D.L.R. (1958) *The Wakhi language: introduction, phonetics, grammar and texts.* SOAS: London.

LORIMER, E.O. (1939) *Language hunting in the Karakoram.* George Allen and Unwin: London.

LORRAIN, J.H. and F.W. SAVIDGE (1898) *A grammar and dictionary of the Lushai language.* Firma KLM Private Ltd: Mizoram.

LORRAIN, R.A. (1951) *Grammar and dictionary of the Lakher or Mara language.* Gov't of Assam: Assam.

LOVING, A. and H. MCKAUGHAN (1973) 'Awa verbs I: the internal structure of dependent verbs', in H. McKaughan (ed.) (1973).

LOVING, R. (1973) 'An outline of Awa grammatical structures', in H. McKaughan (ed.) (1973).

LOVING, R. and A. LOVING (1973) 'A preliminary survey of Awa noun suffixes', in H. McKaughan (ed.) (1973).

LOVING, R. and H. MCKAUGHAN (1973) 'Awa verbs II: the internal structure of independent verbs', in H. McKaughan (ed.) (1973).

LOWE, I. (1987) 'Two ways of looking at causes and reasons', in J. Monaghan (ed.) (1987).

LUCAS, J. (1967) *A study of the Kanuri language.* Dawsons of Pall Mall: London.

LUCAS, L.W. (1979) *Grammar of Ros Goill Irish Co. Donegal.* Institute of Irish Studies, Queen's University of Belfast: Belfast.

LUCKYJ, G. and J.B. RUDNYCKYJ (1949) *A modern Ukrainian grammar.* University of Minnesota Press: Minneapolis.

LUKOFF, F. (1982) *An introductory course in Korean.* Yonsei University Press: Seoul, Korea.

LUNT, H.G. (1952) *Grammar of the Macedonian literary language.* Skopje.

LUNT, H.G. (1965) *Old Church Slavonic grammar*. Mouton: 's-Gravenhage.

LYNCH, J. (1978) *A grammar of Lenakel*. Australian National University: Canberra.

LYNCH, J. (1982a) 'South-west Tanna grammar', *Papers in Linguistics of Melanesia* 4: 1–91.

LYNCH, J. (1982b) 'Anejom grammar sketch', *Papers in Linguistics of Melanesia* 4: 93–154.

LYNCH, J. (ed.) (1983a) *Studies in the languages of Erromango*. Australian National University: Canberra.

LYNCH, J. (1983b) 'Sorung', in J. Lynch (ed.) (1983a).

LYNCH, J. (1983c) 'Ura grammar sketch and vocabulary', in J. Lynch (ed.) (1983a).

LYNCH, J. (1983d) 'Utaha', in J. Lynch (ed.) (1983a).

LYNCH, J. and A. CAPELL (1983) 'Sie grammar outline', in J. Lynch (ed.) (1983a).

LYONS, J. (1971) *Introduction to theoretical linguistics*. Cambridge University Press: Cambridge.

LYONS, J. (1977) *Semantics* (2 vols). Cambridge University Press: Cambridge.

McCARUS, E.N. (1958) *A Kurdish grammar*. American Council of Learned Societies: New York.

McCAWLEY, J.D. (1968) 'Lexical insertion in a transformational grammar without deep structure', *CLS* 4: 71–80.

McCAWLEY, J.D. (1971) 'Prelexical syntax', in R.J. O'Brien (ed.), *Monograph series on languages and linguistics: 22nd Annual Round Table*. Georgetown University Press: Washington, DC.

McCAWLEY, J.D. (1976) 'Remarks on what can cause what', in M. Shibatani (ed.) (1976b).

McCAWLEY, J.D. (1981) *Everything that linguists have always wanted to know about logic*. University of Chicago Press: Chicago.

McCAWLEY, J.D. (1982) 'How far can you trust a linguist?' in T.W. Simon and R.J. Scholes (eds) (1982).

McCLOSKEY, M.J. (1978) *Transformational syntax and model theoretic semantics*. D. Reidel: Dordrecht.

MACDONALD, L. (1983) 'Tauya medial verbs', *Language and Linguistics in Melanesia* 14: 111–135.

McDONALD, M. and S.A. WURM (1979) *Basic materials in Wankumara (Galali): grammar, sentences and vocabulary*. Australian National University: Canberra.

MACDONALD, R.R. (1976) *Indonesian reference grammar*. Georgetown University Press: Washington, DC.

MACE, J. (1962) *Teach yourself modern Persian*. English Universities Press: London.

McELHANON, K.A. (1972) *Selepet grammar part I: from root to phrase*. Australian National University: Canberra.

McGINN, R. (1982) *Outline of Rejang syntax*. Badan Penyelenggara Seri NUSA, Universitas Atma Jaya: Jakarta.

McGREGOR, D.E. and A.R.F. McGREGOR (1982) *Olo language materials*. Australian National University: Canberra.

McGREGOR, R.S. (1977) *Outline of Hindi grammar*. Oxford University Press: Delhi.

McGREGOR, W.B. (1984) A grammar of Kuniyanti: an Australian Aboriginal language of the southern Kimberley, Western Australia. Unpublished Ph.D. thesis, University of Sydney.

McGREGOR, W.B. (1988) 'Mood and subordination in Kuniyanti', in P. Austin (ed.) (1988).

McINTOSH, M. (1984) *Fulfulde syntax and verbal morphology*. Kegan Paul International: London.

McKAUGHAN, H. (ed.) (1973) *The languages of the Eastern family of the East New Guinea Highland stock*. University of Washington Press: Seattle.

McKAY, G.R. (1984) 'Ndjébbana (Kunibidji) grammar: miscellaneous morphological and syntactic notes', *Papers in Australian Linguistics* 16: 119–151.

McKAY, K.L. (1974) *Greek grammar for students: a concise grammar of classical Attic with special reference to aspects of the verb*. Australian National University: Canberra.

MacKENZIE, D.N. (1961–1962) *Kurdish dialect studies*. London.

MacKINNON, R. (1971 [1974]) *Gaelic*. Teach Yourself Books: London.

McLENDON, S. (1975) *A grammar of Eastern Pomo*. University of California Press: Berkeley.

McNAIR, N. and H. McNAIR (1973) 'Clause patterns in Kolami', in R.L. Trail (ed.) (1973).

McQUOWN, N.A. (1984) 'A sketch of San Luis Potosí Huastec', in M.S. Edmonson (ed.) (1984).

MADUGU, I.S.G. (1985) 'Complex verbs in Nupe and Yoruba', *Studies in African Linguistics* 16: 295–321

MAINWARING, G.B. (1876) *A grammar of the Róng (Lepcha) language*. Baptist Mission Press: Calcutta.

MALKIEL, Y. (1981) 'Drift, slope, and slant: background of, and variations upon, a Sapirian theme', *Language* 57: 535–570.

MALLINSON, G. (1986) *Rumanian*. Croom Helm: London.

MALLINSON, G. and B.J. BLAKE (1981) *Language typology: cross-linguistic studies in syntax*. North-Holland: Amsterdam.

MALTZOFF, N. (1985) *Essentials of Russian grammar*. Passport Books: Lincolnwood.

MANLEY, T.M. (1972) *Outline of Sre structure*. University of Hawaii Press: Honolulu.

MANN, S.E. (1977) *An Albanian historical grammar*. Helmut Buske: Hamburg.

MANZINI, M.R. (1983) 'On control and control theory', *LI* 14: 421–446.

MAO, T.-W. and T.-Y. CHOU (1972) 'A brief description of the Yao language', in H.C. Purnell (ed.) (1972).

MARANTZ, A. (1984) *On the nature of grammatical relations*. MIT Press: Cambridge, MA.

MARANTZ, A. (1985) 'Lexical decomposition vs. affixes as syntactic constituents', *CLS* 21, Part II: 154–171.

MARKEY, T.L. (1981) *Frisian*. Mouton: The Hague.

MARSACK, C.C. (1975) *Teach yourself Samoan*. English Universities Press: London.

MARSLEN-WILSON, W. and L.K. TYLER (1980) 'Towards a psychological basis for a theory of anaphora', in J. Kreiman and A.E. Ojeda (eds), *Papers from the parasession on pronouns and anaphora*. CLS: Chicago.

MARSLEN-WILSON, W., E. LEVY, and L.K. TYLER (1982) 'Producing interpretable discourse: the establishment and maintenance of reference', in R.J. Jarvella and W. Klein (eds), *Speech, place, and action*. Wiley: New York.

MARTIN, S. (1961) *Dagur Mongolian: texts and lexicon*. Indiana University: Bloomington.

MARTIN, S. (1975) *A reference grammar of Japanese*. Yale University Press: New Haven.

MASICA, C.P. (1976) *Defining a linguistic area*. University of Chicago Press: Chicago.

MASTER, A. (1964) *A grammar of old Marathi*. Clarendon: Oxford.

MATISOFF, J.A. (1969) 'Verb concatenation in Lahu: the syntax and semantics of "simple" juxtaposition', *Acta Linguistica Hafniensia* 12: 69–120.

MATISOFF, J.A. (1973 [1982]) *The grammar of Lahu*. University of California Press: Berkeley.

MATISOFF, J.A. (1974) 'Verb concatenation in Kachin', *Linguistics of the Tibeto-Burman Area* 1: 186–207.

MATISOFF, J.A. (1976) 'Lahu causative constructions: case hierarchies and the morphology/syntax cycle in a Tibeto-Burman perspective', in M. Shibatani (ed.) (1976b).

MATTESON, E. (1965) *The Piro (Arawakan) language*. University of California Press: Berkeley.

MATTESON, E. (ed.) (1967a) *Bolivian Indian grammars: I*. SIL/University of Oklahoma: Norman.

MATTESON, E. (ed.) (1967b) *Bolivian Indian grammars: II*. SIL/University of Oklahoma: Norman.

MATTHEWS, D. (1984) *A course in Nepali*. SOAS: London.

MATTHEWS, G.H. (1965) *Hidatsa syntax*. Mouton: The Hague.

MATTHEWS, P.H. (1982) 'Formalization', in D. Crystal (ed.) (1982a).

MATTHIESSEN, C. and S.A. THOMPSON (1988) 'The structure of discourse and "subordination"', in J. Haiman and S.A. Thompson (eds) (1988).

MAYO, P. (1976) *A grammar of Byelorussian.* Anglo-Byelorussian Society and Dept of Russian and Slavonic Studies, University of Sheffield: Sheffield.

MEDUSHEVSKY, A. and R. ZYATKOVSKA (1963) *Ukrainian grammar.* Textbook Publishing House: Kiev.

MEERENDONK, M. (1949) *Basic Gurkhali grammar.* Sen Wah Press: Singapore.

MEIER, P., I. MEIER, and J. BENDOR-SAMUEL (1975) *A grammar of Izi, an Igbo language.* SIL/University of Oklahoma: Norman.

MEL'CUK, I.A. (1970) 'Towards a functioning model of language', in M. Bierwisch and K. Heidolph (eds) (1970).

MERCER, S.A.B. (1966) *Assyrian grammar with chrestomathy and glossary.* AMS Press: New York.

MERLAN, F. (1979) 'On the prehistory of some Australian verbs', *Oceanic Linguistics* 18: 33–112.

MERLAN, F. (1981) 'Some functional relations among subordination, mood, aspect and focus in Australian languages', *AJL* 1: 175–210.

MERLAN, F. (1983) *Ngalakan grammar, texts and vocabulary.* Australian National University: Canberra.

MESKILL, R.H. (1970) *A transformational analysis of Turkish syntax.* Mouton: The Hague.

METCALFE, C.D. (1975) *Bardi verb morphology (Northwestern Australia).* Australian National University: Canberra.

MIAO LANGUAGE TEAM, CHINESE ACADEMY OF SCIENCES (1972) 'A brief description of the Miao language', in H.C. Purnell (ed.) (1972).

MIKO, F. (1972) *The generative structure of the Slovak sentence.* Mouton: The Hague.

MIKULA, B.E. (1936 [1940]) *Progressive Czech.* Czechoslovak National Council of America: Chicago.

MILLER, G.A. and P.N. JOHNSON-LAIRD (1976) *Language and perception.* Belknap: Cambridge, MA.

MILLER, J. and H. MILLER (1976) *Mamanwa grammar.* SIL: Huntington Beach, CA.

MILLER, R.A. (1955) 'The independent status of the Lhasa dialect within central Tibetan', *Orbis* 4: 49–55.

MILLER, W.R. (1965) *Acoma grammar and texts.* University of California Press: Berkeley.

MILLS, E. (1984) *Senoufo phonology, discourse to syllable (a prosodic approach).* SIL: Dallas, Texas.

MINOR, E.E. and E.E. LOOS (1963) 'The structure and contexts of Witoto predicates in narrative speech', in B. Elson (ed.) (1963).

MINTZ, M.W. (1971) *Bikol grammar notes*. University of Hawaii Press: Honolulu.

MIRACLE, A.W., JR and J. DE DIOS YAPITA MOYA (1981) 'Time and space in Aymara', in M.J. Hardman (ed.), *The Aymara language in its social and cultural context*. University Press of Florida: Gainesville.

MIRIKITANI, L.T. (1972) *Kapampangan syntax*. University Press of Hawaii: Honolulu.

MITCHELL, T.F. (1956) *An introduction to Egyptian colloquial Arabic*. Clarendon: London.

MITHUN, M. (1984a) 'How to avoid subordination', *BLS* 10: 493–509.

MITHUN, M. (1984b) 'The evolution of noun incorporation', *Language* 60: 847–894.

MITHUN, M. (1987) 'Is basic word order universal?', in R. Tomlin (ed.) (1987a).

MITHUN, M. (1988) 'The grammaticization of coordination', in J. Haiman and S.A. Thompson (eds) (1988).

MIYAGAWA, S. (1984) 'Blocking and Japanese causatives', *Lingua* 64: 177–207.

MODGIL, S. and C. MODGIL (eds) (1987) *Noam Chomsky: consensus and controversy*. Falmer: New York.

MOHANAN, K.P. (1983) 'Move NP or lexical rules?: evidence from Malayalam causativization', in L.M. Levin, M. Rappaport, and A. Zaenen (eds), *Papers in Lexical-Functional Grammar*. IULC: Bloomington.

MONAGHAN, J. (ed.) (1987) *Grammar in the construction of texts*. Frances Pinter: London.

MOORE, T. and C. CARLING (1987) 'Chomsky: consensus and controversy: introduction', in S. Modgil and C. Modgil (eds.) (1987).

MOORE, T.E. (ed.) (1973) *Cognitive development and the acquisition of language*. Academic Press: New York.

MORAVCSIK, E.A. (1978) 'Universals of language contact', in J.H. Greenberg, C.A. Ferguson, and E.A. Moravcsik (eds) (1978).

MORENO, J.C. (1985) 'Anticausatives: a typological sketch', *CLS* 21, Part II: 172–181.

MOREV, L.N., A.A. MOSKALYOV, and Y.Y. PLAM (1979) *The Lao language*. Nauka: Moscow.

MORPHY, F. (1983) 'Djapu, a Yolngu dialect', in R.M.W. Dixon and B.J. Blake (eds) (1983).

MOSEL, U. (1984) *Tolai syntax and its historical development*. Australian National University: Canberra.

MOSHINSKY, J. (1974) *A grammar of Southeastern Pomo*. University of California Press: Berkeley.

MOTUS, C.L. (1971) *Hiligaynon lessons*. University of Hawaii Press: Honolulu.

MUFWENE, S.S. (1986) 'The universalist and substrate hypotheses complement one another', in P. Muysken and N. Smith (eds) (1986a).

Mühlhäusler, P. (1980a) 'Structural expansion and the process of creolization', in A. Valdman and A. Highfield (eds), *Theoretical orientations in creole studies*. Academic Press: New York.

Mühlhäusler, P. (1980b) 'Phases in the development of Tok Pisin', in W. Hüllen (ed.), *Understanding bilingualism*. Lang: Frankfurt.

Mühlhäusler, P. (1986) 'Bonnet blanc et blanc bonnet: adjective–noun order, substratum and language universals', in P. Muysken and N. Smith (eds) (1986a).

Munro, P. (1976) *Mojave syntax*. Garland: New York.

Munro, P. (1982) 'Comitatives (and causatives) in Chickasaw and Choctaw', *Occasional Papers on Linguistics* 11: 32–41.

Murane, E.C. (1974) *Daga grammar*. SIL/University of Oklahoma: Norman.

Muysken, P. (1981) 'Quechua causatives and logical form: a case study in markedness', in A. Belletti, L. Brandi, and L. Rizzi (eds) (1981).

Muysken, P. and N. Smith (eds) (1986a) *Substrata vs. universals in creole genesis*. John Benjamins: Amsterdam.

Muysken, P. and N. Smith (1986b) 'Introduction: problems in the identification of substratum features in the creole languages', in P. Muysken and N. Smith (eds) (1986a).

Myachina, E.N. (1981) *The Swahili language: a descriptive grammar*. Routledge and Kegan Paul: London.

Nababan, P.W.J. (1981) *A grammar of Toba-Batak*. Australian National University: Canberra.

Nadzhip, E.N. (1971) *Modern Uigur*. Nauka: Moscow.

Nagai, N. (1985) 'Japanese causatives: an analysis without grammatical relations', *CLS*, Part II: 182–192.

Nakau, M. (1973) *Sentential complementation in Japanese*. Kaitakusha: Tokyo.

Nash, D.G. (1980) Topics in Warlpiri grammar. Unpublished Ph.D. dissertation, MIT.

Nedyalkov, V.P. and G.G. Silnitsky (1973) 'The typology of morphological and lexical causatives', in F. Kiefer (ed.), *Trends in Soviet theoretical linguistics*. D. Reidel: Dordrecht.

Neffgen, H. (1918) *Grammar and vocabulary of the Samoan language*. Kegan Paul, Trench, Trubner & Co.: London.

Newman, P. (1970) *A grammar of Tera*. University of California Press: Berkeley.

Newman, P. (1974) *The Kanakuru language*. University of Leeds: Leeds

Newman, S. (1965) *Zuni grammar*. University of Mexico Press: Albuquerque.

Newmark, L. (1957) *Structural grammar of Albanian*. Indiana University Press: Bloomington.

NEWMARK, L., P. HUBBARD, and P. PRIFTI (1982) *Standard Albanian: a reference grammar for students*. Stanford University Press: Stanford.

NEWMEYER, F.J. (1980 [1986]) *Linguistic theory in America*. Academic Press: New York.

NEWMEYER, F.J. (1983) *Grammatical theory: its limits and its possibilities*. University of Chicago Press: Chicago.

NICHOLS, J. (1984) 'Functional theories of grammar', *Annual Review of Anthropology* 13: 97–117.

NICHOLS, J. (1985) 'Switch-reference causatives', *CLS* 21, Part II: 192–203.

NICHOLS, J. (1986) 'Head-marking and dependent-marking grammar', *Language* 62: 56–119.

NICHOLS, J. (1992) *Linguistic diversity in space and time*. University of Chicago Press: Chicago.

NICHOLS, J. and A.C. WOODBURY (eds) (1985) *Grammar inside and outside the clause*. Cambridge University Press: Cambridge.

NISHIDA, T. (1973) 'A preliminary study of the Bisu language – a language of Northern Thailand, recently discovered by us', *Papers in South East Asian Linguistics* 3: 55–82.

NOONAN, M. (1981) Lango syntax. Unpublished Ph.D. dissertation, University of California, Los Angeles.

NOONAN, M. (1985) 'Complementation', in T. Shopen (ed.) (1985b).

NOONAN, M. and E. BAVIN (1981) 'Parataxis in Lango', *Studies in African Languages* 12: 45–69.

NORMAN, J. (1988) *Chinese*. Cambridge University Press: Cambridge.

NOSS, R.B. (1964) *Thai reference grammar*. Foreign Service Institute: Washington, D.C.

NYLANDER, D.K. (1985) 'Serial verbs and the empty category principle in Krio', *Canadian Journal of Linguistics* 30: 15–32.

OATES, W. and L. OATES (1968) *Kapau pedagogical grammar*. Australian National University: Canberra

OCHS, E. (1979) 'Planned and unplanned discourse', in T. Givón (ed.) (1979c).

O'GRADY, G.N. (1964) *Nyangumata grammar*. University of Sydney: Sydney.

OGUNBOWALE, P.O. (1970) *The essentials of the Yoruba language*. University of London Press: London.

OGURI, H. (1985a) 'Main verb forms in Isirawa narratives', *Papers in New Guinea Linguistics* 22: 131–138.

OGURI, H. (1985b) 'Isirawa clauses', *Papers in New Guinea Linguistics* 22: 139–154.

ÓHUALLACHÁIN, C. and M. O'MÍCHEÁL (1976) *Irish grammar*. New University of Ulster: Coleraine.

OINAS, F. (1967) *Basic course in Estonian*. Indiana University Press: Bloomington.

OKELL, J. (1969) *A reference grammar of colloquial Burmese.* Oxford University Press: London.

OLSON, M. (1975) 'Barai grammar highlights', in T.E. Dutton (ed.) (1975a).

OLSON, M. (1981) Barai clause junctures: toward a functional theory of interclausal relations. Unpublished Ph.D. thesis, Australian National University.

OMONDI, L.N. (1982) *The major syntactic structures of Dholuo.* Dietrich Reimer: Berlin.

ONO, K. (1982) 'Causative constructions in Japanese', *Linguistics* 20: 97–121.

ONO, K. (1984) *A generative grammatical analysis of Japanese complement constructions.* Chunichi: Nagoya.

ORR, C. (1962) 'Ecuador Quichua clause structure', in B. Elson (ed.) (1962).

OSBORNE, C.R. (1974) *The Tiwi language.* Australian National University: Canberra.

OSWALT, R.L. (1976) 'Comparative verb morphology of Pomo', in M. Langdon and S. Silver (eds), *Hokan studies.* Mouton: The Hague.

OSWALT, R.L. (1977) 'The causative as a reference-switching mechanism in Western Pomo', *BLS* 3: 46–54.

OSWALT, R.L. (1983) 'Interclausal reference in Kashaya', in J. Haiman and P. Munro (eds) (1983a).

OTT, W.G. and R.H. OTT (1967) 'Ignaciano', in E. Matteson (ed.) (1967a).

OTTAVIANO, J.C. and I. OTTAVIANO (1967) 'Tacana', in E. Matteson (ed.) (1967a).

OWENS, J. (1984) *A short reference grammar of Eastern Libyan Arabic.* Otto Harrassowitz: Wiesbaden.

OWENS, J. (1985) *The Oromo causative: lexical grammar without lexical rules.* IULC: Bloomington.

PAINTER, C. (1970) *Gonja: a phonological and grammatical study.* Indiana University Press: Bloomington.

PALMER, F.R. (1977) 'Modals and actuality', *JL* 13: 1–23.

PALMER, F.R. (1986) *Mood and modality.* Cambridge University Press: Cambridge.

PALMER, F.R. (1994) *Grammatical roles and relations.* Cambridge University Press: Cambridge.

PALMER, L.R. (1954 [1966]) *The Latin language.* Faber and Faber: London.

PALMER, L.R. (1980) *The Greek language.* Humanities Press: Atlantic Heights, NJ.

PANIKKAR, G.K. (1973) *Description of the Ernad dialect of Malayalam.* Dravidian Linguistic Association: Kerala.

PANUPONG, V. (1970) *Inter-sentence relations in modern conversational Thai.* Siam Society: Bangkok.

PARAMASIVAM, K. (1979) 'Effectivity and causativity in Tamil', *International Journal of Dravidian Linguistics* 8: 71–151.

PARK, K. (1986) *The lexical representations of Korean causatives and passives*. IULC: Bloomington.

PARKER, F. (1982) 'OS languages: exceptions or counterexamples?', *Linguistics* 20: 163–173.

PARKER, F. and MACARI, N. (1978) 'On syntactic change', *Linguistics* 209: 5–41.

PARKER, G.J. (1969) *Ayacucho Quechua grammar and dictionary*. Mouton: The Hague.

PARTRIDGE, M. (1972) *Serbo-Croat: Practical grammar and reader*. Izdavacki Zavod: Belgrade.

PATON, W.F. (1971) *Ambrym (Lonwolwol) grammar*. Australian National University: Canberra.

PATRIE, J. (1982) *The genetic relationship of the Ainu language*. University of Hawaii Press: Honolulu.

PATTERSON, B.S.J. (1974) A study of Korean causatives. MA dissertation, University of Hawaii, also in *Working Papers in Linguistics* (University of Hawaii) 6: 1–51.

PAWLEY, A.K. (1972) 'On the internal relationships of Eastern Oceanic languages', in R.C. Green and M. Kelly (eds), *Studies in Oceanic Culture History*. Bernice P. Bishop Museum: Honolulu.

PAWLEY, A.K. (1987) 'Encoding events in Kalam and English: different logics for reporting experience', in R. Tomlin (ed.) (1987a).

PAWLEY, A.K. and F.H. SYDER (1983a) 'Two puzzles for linguistic theory: native like selection and native like fluency', in J. Richards and R. Schmidt (eds), *Language and communication*. Longman: London.

PAWLEY, A.K. (1983b) 'Natural selection in syntax: notes on adaptive variation and change in vernacular and literary grammar', *Journal of Pragmatics* 7: 551–579.

PAYNE, D.L. (1981) *The phonology and morphology of Axininca Campa*. SIL and University of Texas at Arlington.

PAYNE, J.R. (1985) 'Complex phrases and complex sentences', in T. Shopen (ed.) (1985b).

PEARCE, E. (1984) 'Variation in case marking with infinitival and clausal complements in old French', *Studies in the Linguistic Sciences* 14: 149–166.

PEEKE, C. (1962) 'Structural summary of Zaparo', in B. Elson (ed.) (1962).

PEEKE, M.C. (1973) *Preliminary grammar of Auca*. SIL/University of Oklahoma: Norman.

PENZL, H. (1955) *A grammar of Pashto: a descriptive study of the dialect of Kandahar, Afghanistan*. American Council of Learned Societies: New York.

PERCIVAL, W.K. (1981) *A grammar of the urbanised Toba-Batak of*

Medan. Australian National University: Canberra.

PEREZ, C.H. (1986) *Aspects of complementation in three Bantu languages*. IULC: Bloomington.

PERKINS, R.D. (1980) The evolution of culture and grammar. Unpublished Ph.D. dissertation, SUNY, Buffalo.

PERKINS, R.D. (1988) 'The covariation of culture and grammar', in M. Hammond, E.A. Moravcsik, and J.R. Wirth (eds) (1988a).

PERKINS, R.D. (1992) *Dexis, grammar and culture*. John Benjamins: Amsterdam.

PERLMUTTER, D.M. (1980) 'Relational grammar', in E.A. Moravcsik and J.R. Wirth (eds), *Syntax and semantics vol. 13: current approaches to syntax*. Academic Press: New York.

PERLMUTTER, D.M. and P.M. POSTAL (1974) *Lectures on relational grammar*. Summer Institute of the Linguistic Society of America: Amherst, MA.

PHILLIPS, D.J. (1976) *Wahgi: phonology and morphology*. Australian National University: Canberra.

PIKE, K. (1970) *Tagmemic and matrix linguistics applied to selected African languages*. SIL/University of Oklahoma: Norman.

PIKE, K. and E.G. PIKE (1977) *Grammatical analysis*. SIL/University of Texas at Arlington.

PILLAI, M.S. (1965) *Spoken Tamil*. Annamalai University: Annamalainagar.

PLATT, J.T. (1972) *An outline grammar of the Gugada dialect*. AIAS: Canberra.

POEDJOSOEDARMO, G.R. (1986) *Role structure in Javanese*. Badan Penyelenggara Seri NUSA, Universitas Katolik Indonesia Atma Jaya: Jakarta.

POLINSKAJA, M.S. (1989) 'Object initiality: OSV', *Linguistics* 27: 257–303.

POLINSKY, M. (1994) 'Double objects in causatives: towards a study of coding conflict', *SiL* 19: 129–221.

POPE, G.U. (1979) *A handbook of the Tamil language*. Asian Educational Services: New Delhi.

POPJES, J. and J. POPJES (1986) 'Canela-Krahô', in D.C. Derbyshire and G. Pullum (eds) (1986).

POPPE, N. (1960) *Buriat grammar*. Indiana University Press: Bloomington.

POPPE, N. (1963) *Tatar manual*. Indiana University Press: Bloomington.

POPPE, N. (1964) *Bashkir manual*. Indiana University Press: Bloomington.

POPPE, N. (1970) *Mongolian: language handbook*. Center for Applied Linguistics: Washington, DC.

PÖPPEL, E. (1978) 'Time perception', in R. Held, H.W. Liebowitz, and H.-L. Teuber (eds), *Perception*. Springer: Berlin.

PRABODHACHANDRAN NAYAR, V.R. (1972) *Malayalam verbal forms.* Dravidian Linguistic Association: Trivandrum.

PREMSRIRAT, S. (1987) 'A Khmu grammar', *Papers in South East Asian Linguistics* 10: 1–143.

PRENTICE, D.J. (1969) 'Verbal inflection in Sabah Murut', *Papers in Borneo Linguistics* 1: 9–21.

PRENTICE, D.J. (1971) *The Murut languages of Sabah.* Australian National University: Canberra.

PRESS, I. (1986) *A grammar of modern Breton.* Mouton de Gruyter: Berlin.

PRESS, M.L. (1979) *Chemehuevi: a grammar and lexicon.* University of California: Berkeley.

PRIDE, K. (1965) *Chatino syntax.* SIL/University of Oklahoma: Norman.

PRIEST, P.N. and A.M. PRIEST (1967) 'Sirionó', in E. Matteson (ed.) (1967b).

PROST, G.R. (1967) 'Chacobo', in E. Matteson (ed.) (1967a).

PULKINA, I.M. (1960) *A short Russian reference grammar.* Foreign Languages Publishing House: Moscow.

PULLUM, G. (1974) 'Review of Greenberg, Ferguson and Moravcsik (eds), *Universals of human language*', *Linguistics* 17: 925–944.

PULLUM, G. (1988) 'Citation etiquette beyond Thunderdome', *NLLT* 6: 579–588.

PURNELL, H.C. (ed.) (1972) *Miao linguistic studies.* Cornell University: Ithaca.

PYM, N. (1985) 'Iwaidja verbal clauses', *Workpapers* (SIL/AAB) Series A 9: 39–51.

QAFISHEH, H.A. (1977) *A short reference grammar of Gulf Arabic.* University of Arizona Press.

QUICOLI, C. (1980) 'Clitic movement in French causatives', *Linguistic Analysis* 6: 131–185.

QUINN, R.M. (1972) *Introductory - Vietnamese.* Cornell University: Ithaca.

RABEL, L. (1961) *Khasi: a language of Assam.* Louisiana State University Press: Baton Rouge.

RADDEN, G.C. (1985) 'Spatial metaphors underlying prepositions of causality', in W. Paprotté and R. Dirven (eds), *The ubiquity of metaphor.* John Benjamins: Amsterdam.

RADFORD, A. (1978) 'Agentitive causatives in Romance: accessibility versus passivization', *JL* 14: 35–58.

RADFORD, A. (1988) *Transformational grammar.* Cambridge University Press: Cambridge.

RADHAKRISHNAN, R. (1976) 'A note on the morphology of the causative in Nancowry', in P.N. Jenner, L.C. Thompson, and S. Starosta (eds) (1976).

RADHAKRISHNAN, R. (1981) *The Nancowry word, phonology, affixal morphology and roots of a Nicobarese language.* Linguistic Research Inc.: Carbondale.

RAFFO, Y. (1972) A phonology and morphology of Songish, a dialect of Straits Salish. Unpublished Ph.D. dissertation, University of Kansas.

RAMOS, T.V. (1971) *Tagalog structures.* University of Hawaii Press: Honolulu.

RAMOS, T.V. (1974) *The case system of Tagalog verbs.* Australian National University: Canberra.

RANDRIAMASIMANANA, C. (1986) *The causatives of Malagasy.* University of Hawaii Press: Honolulu.

RASTORGUEVA, V.S. (1963) 'A short sketch of Tajik grammar', *IJAL* 29.4, Part II and also Indiana University: Bloomington.

RAUN, A. (1969) *Basic course in Uzbek.* Indiana University Press: Bloomington.

RAUN, A. and S. SAARESTE (1965) *Introduction to Estonian linguistics.* Harrassowitz: Wiesbaden.

RAY, P.S., M.A. HAI, and L. RAY (1966) *Bengali language handbook.* Center for Applied Linguistics: Washington, DC.

READ, A.F.C. (1934) *Balti grammar.* Royal Asiatic Society: London.

REDDEN, J.E. (1980) *A descriptive grammar of Ewondo.* Southern Illinois University: Carbondale.

REESINK, G.P. (1981) 'Review article: the Whorfian hypothesis and Siroi grammar – a review of M.A. Wells' *Siroi grammar'*, *Language and Linguistics of Melanesia* 13: 81–105.

REESINK, G.P. (1987) *Structures and their functions in Usan, a Papuan language of Papua New Guinea.* John Benjamins: Amsterdam.

REFSING, K. (1986) *The Ainu language: the morphology and syntax of the Shizunai dialect.* Aarhus University Press: Copenhagen.

REHG, K.L. (1981) *Ponapean reference grammar.* University of Hawaii: Honolulu.

REID, A., R.G. BISHOP, E.M. BUTTON, and R.E. LONGACRE (1968) *Totonac: from clause to discourse.* SIL/University of Oklahoma: Norman.

REID, L.A. (1966) *An Ivatan syntax.* University of Hawaii: Honolulu.

REID, L.A. (1970) *Central Bontoc.* SIL/University of Oklahoma: Norman.

REINHART, T. (1984) 'Principles of gestalt perception in the temporal organization of narrative texts', *Linguistics* 22: 779–809.

RENCK, G.L. (1975) *A grammar of Yagaria.* Australian National University: Canberra.

RERE, T. (1961) *Conversational Maori: Rarotongan language.* Cook Islands Gov't Printers: Rarotonga.

RERE, T. (1965) *Maori lessons for the Cook Islands.* Dept. of Education: Wellington.

REULAND, E.J. (1980) 'V-raising in Dutch: anomalies explained', *CLS* 16: 269–281.

REYNOLDS, C.H.B. (1980) *Sinhalese: an introductory course.* SOAS: London.

RHODES, R. (1977) 'Semantics in relational grammar', *CLS* 13: 503–514.

RICHERT, E.L. (1975) 'Sentence structure of Guhu-Samane', in T.E. Dutton (ed.) (1975a).

RIEMSDIJK, H. VAN and E. WILLIAMS (1986) *Introduction to theory of grammar.* MIT Press: Cambridge, MA.

RIJKHOFF, J., D. BAKKER, K. HENGEVELD, and P. KAHREL (1993) 'A method of language sampling', *SiL* 17: 169–203.

RIZZI, L. (1978) 'Violations of the Wh-island constraint in Italian and the subjacency condition', *Journal of Italian Linguistics* 5: 157–195.

ROBERTS, J.R. (1987) *Amele.* Croom Helm: London.

ROBINS, R.H. (1958) *The Yurok language: grammar, texts, lexicon.* University of California Press: Berkeley.

ROBINSON, D.F. (1966) *Aztec Studies II: Sierra Nahuat word structure.* SIL/University of Oklahoma: Norman.

ROMAINE, S. (1985a) 'Review of Anna Siewierska: *The passive: a comparative linguistic analysis*', *Linguistics* 23: 505–506.

ROMAINE, S. (1985b) 'Review of Leon Stassen: *Comparison and universal grammar*', *Linguistics* 23: 507–510.

ROMAINE, S. (1988) *Pidgin and creole languages.* Longman: London.

ROOD, D.S. (1976) *Wichita grammar.* Garland: New York.

ROSBOTTOM, H. (1967) 'Guarani', in E. Matteson (ed.) (1967b).

ROSEN, C. (1983) 'Universals of clause union: a co-proposal to Gibson–Raposo typology', *CLS* 19: 338–352.

ROSEN, C. (1984) 'The interface between semantic roles and initial grammatical relations', in D.M. Perlmutter and C. Rosen (eds) (1984), *Studies in relational grammar II.* University of Chicago Press: Chicago.

ROSEN, C. (1987) 'Review of *On the nature of grammatical relations* by A. Marantz', *JL* 23: 435–445.

ROSÉN, H.B. (1977) *Contemporary Hebrew.* Mouton: The Hague.

ROSS, J.R. (1967) Constraints on variables in syntax. Ph.D. dissertation, MIT, also distributed by IULC.

ROSS, M. (1984) 'Maisin: a preliminary sketch', *Papers in New Guinea Linguistics* 23: 1–82.

ROSS, M. and J.N. PAOL (1978) *A Waskia grammar sketch and vocabulary.* Australian National University: Canberra.

ROUVERET, A. and J.-R. VERGNAUD (1980) 'Specifying reference to the subject: French causatives and conditions on representations', *LI* 11: 97–202.

ROWLAND, T. (1865) *A grammar of the Welsh language.* R. Saunderson: Bala.

RUCH, E. (1974) 'Role combinations and verb stem classes in Kalamian Tagbanwa', *Papers in Philippine Linguistics* 5: 23–60.

RUDIN, C. (1986) *Aspects of Bulgarian syntax: complementizers and WH constructions*. Slavica: Columbus, OH.

RUDZKA-OSTYN, B. (ed.) (1987) *Topics in cognitive linguistics*. John Benjamins: Philadelphia.

RUHLEN, M. (1987) *A guide to the world's languages vol. 1: classification*. Stanford University Press: Stanford.

RUMSEY, A. (1982) *An intra-sentence grammar of Ungarinjin, Northwestern Australia*. Australian National University: Canberra.

SAAD, G.N. (1982) *Transitivity, causation and passivization*. Kegan Paul International: London.

SADIQI, F. (1986) 'Raising in Berber', *Studies in African Linguistics* 17: 219–248.

SADLER, L. (1988) *Welsh syntax: a Government and Binding approach*. Croom Helm: London.

SAKSENA, A. (1982a) *Topics in the analysis of causatives with an account of Hindi paradigms*. University of California Press: Berkeley.

SAKSENA, A. (1982b) 'Contact in causation', *Language* 58: 820–831.

SALMOND, A. (1974) *A generative syntax of Luangiua: a Polynesian language*. Mouton: The Hague.

SALTARELLI, M. (1988) *Basque*. Croom Helm: London.

SAMARIN, W.J. (1966) *The Gbeya language: grammar, texts and vocabularies*. University of California Press: Berkeley.

SAMARIN, W.J. (1967a) *A grammar of Sango*. Mouton: The Hague.

SAMARIN, W.J. (1967b) *Field linguistics: a guide to linguistic field work*. Holt, Rinehart and Winston: New York.

SANDERS, G.A. (1976) *A functional typology of elliptical coordinations*. IULC: Bloomington.

SANGSTER, L.W. and E. FABER (1969) *Susu intermediate course*. Indiana University: Bloomington.

SANKOFF, G. (1979) 'The genesis of language', in K.C. Hill (ed.) (1979).

SANKOFF, G. and P. BROWN (1976) 'The origins of syntax in discourse: a case study of Tok Pisin relatives', *Language* 52: 631–666.

SAPIR, E. (1921) *Language: an introduction to the study of speech*. Harcourt, Brace and World: New York.

SAPIR, E. and H. HOIJER (1967) *The phonology and morphology of the Navaho language*. University of California Press: Berkeley.

SAPIR, J.D. (1965) *A grammar of Diola Fogny*. Cambridge University Press: London.

SARA, S.I. (1974) *A description of modern Chaldean*. Mouton: The Hague.

SARAWIT, M. (1979) 'A sketch of a dialect of Mae Sot', *Papers in South East Asian Studies* 6: 75–83.

SASSE, A.J. (1974) 'Notes on the structure of Galab', *Bulletin of the SOAS* 37.2: 407–438.

SAUL, J.E. and N.F. WILSON (1980) *Núng grammar*. SIL and University of Texas at Arlington.

SAYERS, B.J. (1976) *The sentence in Wik-Munkan: a description of propositional relationships*. Australian National University: Canberra.

SCHACTER, P. (1974) 'A non-transformational account of serial verbs', *Studies in African Linguistics* 5: 253–270.

SCHACTER, P. (1977) 'Constraints on coordination', *Language* 53: 86–113.

SCHACTER, P. (1986) 'Review of William A. Foley and Robert D. Van Valin, Jr., *Functional syntax and universal grammar*', *Lingua* 69: 172–186.

SCHACTER, P. and F.T. OTANES (1972) *Tagalog reference grammar*. University of California Press: Berkeley.

SCHANKS, R.C. and R.P. ABELSON (1977) *Scripts, plans, goals and understanding*. Lawrence Erlbaum: Hillsdale, NJ.

SCHAUB, W. (1985) *Babungo*. Croom Helm: London.

SCHEBESTA, P.P. (1926–1928) 'Grammatical sketch of the Jahai dialect', *Bulletin of the London University School of Oriental and African Studies* 4: 803–826.

SCHENKER, A.M. (1973) *Beginning Polish*. Yale University Press: New Haven.

SCHIFFRIN, D. (1987) *Discourse markers*. Cambridge University Press: Cambridge.

SCHILLER, E. (1987) 'Causativity in Southeast Asia: historical/comparative morphosyntax', in E. Bashir, M.M. Deshpande, and P.E. Hook (eds), *Select papers from SALA – 7: South Asian Languages Analysis Roundtable Conference*. IULC: Bloomington.

SCHMALSTIEG, W.R. (1974) *An old Prussian grammar*. Pennsylvania State University Press: University Park, PA.

SCHMALSTIEG, W.R. (1976 [1982]) *An introduction to old Church Slavic*. Slavica: Columbus, OH.

SCHMALSTIEG, W.R. (1980) *Indo-European linguistics: a new synthesis*. Pennsylvania State University: University Park, PA.

SCHOEN, S.C. (1981) 'Syntactic typology: methods and problems', *Working Papers in Linguistics* (University of Hawaii) 13: 39–56.

SCHÖTTELNDREYER, B. (1975) 'Clause patterns in Sherpa', in A. Hale (ed.) (1975).

SCHUH, R.G. (1978) *Bole-Tangale languages of the Bauchi Area (northern Nigeria)*. Dietrich Reimer: Berlin.

SCHÜTZ, A.J. (1969) *Nguna grammar*. University of Hawaii Press: Honolulu.

SCHÜTZ, A.J. (1986) *The Fijian language*. University Press of Hawaii: Honolulu.

SCORZA, D. (1985) 'A sketch of Au morphology and syntax', *Papers in New Guinea Linguistics* 22: 215–273.

SCOTT, G. (1968) 'Fore final verbs', *Papers in New Guinea Linguistics* 8: 45–62.

SCOTT, G. (1973) *Higher levels of Fore grammar.* Australian National University: Canberra.

SCOTT, G. (1978) *The Fore language of Papua New Guinea.* Australian National University: Canberra.

SCOTTON, C.M.M. (1967) 'Semantic and syntactic subcategorization in Swahili causative verb shapes', *Journal of African Languages* 6: 249–267.

SEARLE, J.R. (1971) 'Intentionality and the use of language', in A. Margalit (ed.), *Meaning and use.* D. Reidel: Dordrecht.

SEARLE, J.R. (1978) 'What is an intentional state?', *Mind* 88: 74–92.

SEARLE, J.R. (1980) 'The intentionality of intention and action', *Cognitive Science* 4: 47–70.

SEBBA, M. (1987) *The syntax of serial verbs.* John Benjamins: Amsterdam.

SEBEOK, T.A. and F.J. INGERMANN (1961) *An eastern Cheremis manual.* Indiana University Press: Bloomington.

SEILER, W. (1985) *Imonda, a Papuan language.* Australian National University: Canberra.

SEILER, W. (1986) 'From verb serialization to noun classification', *Papers in New Guinea Linguistics* 24: 11–19.

SEITER, W. (1980) *Studies in Niuean syntax.* Garland: New York.

SELLS, P. (1985) *Lectures on contemporary syntactic theories.* Center for the Study of Language and Information: Stanford.

SEUREN, P.A.M. (1973) Predicate raising and dative in French and sundry languages. Ms, distributed by Linguistic Agency, University at Trier.

SHACKLE, C. (1976) *The Siraiki language of central Pakistan.* SOAS: London.

SHAFEEV, D.A. (1964) 'A short grammatical outline of Pashto', *IJAL* 30, Part III.

SHAND, J. (1976) 'Ilianen Manobo sentence structure', *Papers in Philippine Linguistics* 8: 45–89.

SHARPE, M.C. (1972) *Alawa phonology and grammar.* AIAS: Canberra.

SHELL, O. (1952) 'Grammatical outline of Kraho (Ge family)', *IJAL* 18: 115–129.

SHETLER, J. (1976) *Notes on Balangao grammar.* SIL: Huntington Beach, CA.

SHEVELOV, G.Y. (1963) *The syntax of modern literary Ukranian.* Mouton: The Hague.

SHIBATANI, M. (1973a) 'Semantics of Japanese causativization', *FL* 9: 327–373.

SHIBATANI, M. (1973b) 'Lexical versus periphrastic causativization in Korean', *JL* 9: 209–383.

SHIBATANI, M. (1975) *A linguistic study of causative constructions.* IULC: Bloomington.

SHIBATANI, M. (ed.) (1976a) *Syntax and semantics 5: Japanese generative grammar*. Academic Press: New York.

SHIBATANI, M. (ed.) (1976b) *Syntax and semantics 6: the grammar of causative constructions*. Academic Press: New York.

SHIBATANI, M. (1976c) 'The grammar of causative constructions: a conspectus', in M. Shibatani (ed.) (1976b).

SHIBATANI, M. (1990) *The languages of Japan*. Cambridge University Press: Cambridge.

SHIBATANI, M. and KAGEYAMA, T. (1988) 'Word formation in modular theory of grammar: postsyntactic compounds in Japanese', *Language* 64: 451–484.

SHIELDS, J.K. (1988) 'A syntactic sketch of Silacayoapan Mixtec', in C.H. Bradley and B.E. Hollenbach (eds) (1988).

SHIMIZU, K. (1979) *A comparative study of the Mumuye dialects*. Dietrich Reimer: Berlin.

SHIMIZU, K. (1980) *A Jukun grammar*. Beiträge zur Afrikanistik: Vienna.

SHIN, S.-C. (1987) *A unifying theory of topic, conditional and relative constructions in Korean: a case for archimorpheme across syntactic categories*. Ph.D. dissertation, University of Michigan, published by Hanshin: Seoul.

SHIPLEY, W.F. (1963) *Maidu grammar*. University of California Press: Berkeley.

SHIPLEY, W.F. (1964) *Maidu texts and dictionary*. University of California Press: Berkeley.

SHKLANKA, E. (1944) *Ukranian grammar*. Midwest Litho: Saskatoon.

SHOEMAKER, J.S. and N.K. SHOEMAKER (1967) 'Essejja', in E. Matteson (ed.) (1967a).

SHOPEN, T. (ed.) (1979a) *Languages and their speakers*. Winthrop: Cambridge, MA.

SHOPEN, T. (ed.) (1979b) *Languages and their status*. Winthrop: Cambridge, MA.

SHOPEN, T. (ed.) (1985a) *Language typology and syntactic description vol. 1*. Cambridge University Press: Cambridge.

SHOPEN, T. (ed.) (1985b) *Language typology and syntactic description vol. 2*. Cambridge University Press: Cambridge.

SHOPEN, T. (ed.) (1985c) *Language typology and syntactic description vol. 3*. Cambridge University Press: Cambridge.

SHOPEN, T. and M. KONARÉ (1970) 'Sonrai causatives and passives: transformational versus lexical derivations for propositional heads', *Studies in African Linguistics* 1: 211–254.

SHUKLA, S. (1981) *Bhojpuri grammar*. Georgetown University Press: Washington, DC.

SIEGEL, J. (1984) 'Introduction to the Labu language', *Papers in New Guinea Linguistics* 23: 83–157.

SIEWIERSKA, A. (1984) *The passive: a comparative linguistic analysis.* Croom Helm: London.

SIEWIERSKA, A. (1988) *Word order rules.* Croom Helm: London.

SIEWIERSKA, A. (1994) 'The relationship between affix and main clause constituent order', in B. Haftka (ed.), *Was determiniert Wortstellungsvariation?* Westdeutscher: Opladen.

SIEWIERSKA, A. and D. BAKKER (in press) 'The distribution of subject and object agreement and word order type', *SiL.*

SILVERSTEIN, M. (1976a) 'Hierarchy of features and ergativity', in R.M.W. Dixon (ed.) (1976).

SILVERSTEIN, M. (1976b) 'Shifters, linguistic categories and cultural description', in K. Basso and H. Selby (eds), *Meaning in anthropology.* University of New Mexico Press: Albuquerque.

SILVERSTEIN, M. (1980) Of nominatives and datives: universal grammar from the bottom up. Ms, University of Chicago.

SILVERSTEIN, M. (1981) 'Case marking and the nature of language', *AJL* 1: 227–246.

SILVERSTEIN, M. (1993) 'Of nominatives and datives: universal grammar from the bottom up', in R.D. Van Valin (ed.) (1993a).

SIMON, T.W. and R.J. SCHOLES (eds) (1982) *Language, mind and brain.* Lawrence Erlbaum: Hillsdale, NJ.

SIMPSON, J. (1988) 'Case and complementiser suffixes in Warlpiri', in P. Austin (ed.) (1988).

SINGLER, J.V. (1988) 'The homogeneity of the substrate as a factor in pidgin and creole genesis', *Language* 64: 27–51.

SIRK, V. (1983) *The Buginese language.* Nauka: Moscow.

SISCHO, W.R. (1979) 'Michoacán Nahuatl', in R.W. Langacker (ed.) (1979a).

SJOBERG, A.F. (1963) *Uzbek structural grammar.* Indiana University Press: Bloomington.

SLOBIN, D.I. (1977) 'Language change in childhood and history', in J. MacNamara (ed.), *Language learning and thought.* Academic Press: New York.

SLOBIN, D.I. (1982) 'Universal and particular in the acquisition of language', in E. Wanner and L. Gleitman (eds) (1982).

SLOBIN, D.I. (1985) 'The child as a linguistic icon maker', in J. Haiman (ed.) (1985b).

SMABY, R.M. (1974) 'Subordinate clauses and asymmetry in English', *JL* 10: 235–269.

SMIRNOVA, M.A. (1982) *Hausa language.* London.

SMITH, J. and P. WESTON (1974) 'Notes on Mianmin grammar', *Workpapers in Papua New Guinea Languages* 7: 35–142.

SMITH, K.D. (1979) *Sedang grammar.* Australian National University: Canberra.

SMITH, N. (1987) 'Universals and typology', in S. Modgil and C. Modgil (eds) (1987).

SMITH, N. and D. WILSON (1979) *Modern linguistics: the results of Chomsky's revolution*. Penguin: Harmondsworth.

SMITH, N.V. (1967) *An outline grammar of Nupe*. SOAS: London.

SMITH, N.V. (1982) 'Review of Comrie 1981', *AJL* 2: 255–261.

SMITH, N.V. (1983) 'A rejoinder to Comrie', *AJL* 3: 97–98.

SMYTHE, W.E. (1948) *Elementary grammar of the Gumbáiŋgar language (North Coast, NSW)*. Australian National Research Council: Sydney.

SNEDDON, J.N. (1975) *Tondano phonology and grammar*. Australian National University: Canberra.

SNELL, B.A. and M.R. WISE (1963) 'Noncontingent declarative clauses in Machiguenga (Arawak)', in B. Elson (ed.) (1963).

SOHN, H.-M. (1973) 'A re-examination of "auxiliary" verb constructions in Korean', *Working Papers in Linguistics* (University of Hawaii) 5: 63–88.

SOHN, H.-M. (1994) *Korean*. Routledge: London.

SOHN, H.-M. and B.W. BENDER (1973) *A Ulithian grammar*. Australian National University: Canberra.

SOMMER, B.A. (1969) *Kunjen phonology: synchronic and diachronic*. Australian National University: Canberra.

SOMMER, B.A. (1972) *Kunjen syntax: a generative view*. AIAS: Canberra.

SONG, J.J. (1988a) '"Newsworthiness" and the use of active and passive in Korean', *Studia Linguistica* 42: 49–59.

SONG, J.J. (1988b) 'Clause linkage in Korean periphrastic causative and purposive constructions', *Language Research* 24: 583–606.

SONG, J.J. (1988c) 'Review of C. Randriamasimanana, *The causatives of Malagasy*', *AJL* 8: 340–343.

SONG, J.J. (1988d) 'Korean causative types and conceptualisation', *Working Papers in Language and Linguistics* (University of Tasmania) 24: 59–74.

SONG, J.J. (1990) 'On the rise of causative affixes: a universal-typological perspective', *Lingua* 82: 151–200.

SONG, J.J. (1991a) 'Causatives and universal grammar: an alternative interpretation', *Transactions of the Philological Society* 89: 65–94.

SONG, J.J. (1991b) 'Korean relative clause constructions: conspiracy and pragmatics', *AJL* 11: 195–220.

SONG, J.J. (1992) 'A note on iconicity in causatives', *Folia Linguistica* XXVI: 333–338.

SONG, J.J. (1993) 'Control and cooperation: adverbial scope in Korean morphological causatives', *Acta Linguistica Hafniensia* 26: 161–174.

SONG, J.J. (1994) 'Review of R.D. Van Valin (ed.) *Advances in Role and Reference Grammar*, John Benjamins: Amsterdam', *Languages of the World* 8: 61–66.

SONG, J.J. (1995) 'Review of B. Comrie and M. Polinsky (ed.) *Causatives and transitivity*, John Benjamins: Amsterdam', *Lingua* 97: 211–224.

Sova, M. (1962a) *A practical Czech course*. Státní Pedagogické Nakladatelství: Prague.

Sova, M. (1962b) *Czech course for English speaking students*. Státní Pedagogické Nakladatelství: Prague.

Spenst, H., I.J. Spenst, B.H. Wrisley, and G.E. Sherman (1967) 'Quechua', in E. Matteson (ed.) (1967b).

Sperber, D. and D. Wilson (1986) *Relevance: communication and cognition*. Basil Blackwell: Oxford.

Srivastava, D. (1962) *Nepali language: its history and development*. Calcutta University: Calcutta.

Staal, J.F. (1968) 'And', *JL* 4: 79–81.

Staalsen, P. (1972) 'Clause relationships in Iatmul', *Papers in New Guinea Linguistics* 15: 45–69.

Stafford, R.L. (1967) *An elementary Luo grammar with vocabularies*. Oxford University Press: Nairobi.

Stahlke, H.F.W. (1970) 'Serial verbs', *Studies in African Languages* 1: 60–99.

Stamm, J. (1988) 'A grammar of the Lavongai language', in C.H. Beaumont (ed.), *Lavongai materials*. Australian National University: Canberra.

Stanhope, J.M. (1980) *The language of the Rao people, Grengabu, Madang Province, PNG*. Australian National University: Canberra.

Stap, P.A.M. van der (1966) *Outline of Dani morphology*. Martinus Nijhoff: 's-Gravenhage.

Starosta, S. (1967) Sora syntax: a generative approach to a Munda language. Unpublished Ph.D. dissertation, University of Wisconsin.

Starosta, S. (1973) 'Causative verbs in Formosan languages', *Working Papers in Linguistics* (University of Hawaii) 5.9: 89–154.

Stassen, L. (1985) *Comparison and universal grammar*. Basil Blackwell: Oxford.

Steele, S. (1987) 'Review of *Comparison and universal grammar* by Leon Stassen', *Language* 63: 629–632.

Stenson, N. (1981) *Studies in Irish syntax*. Gunter Narr: Tübingen.

Stewart, J.A. (1955) *Manual of colloquial Burmese*. Luzac: London.

Stockwell, R.P. and R.K.S. Macaulay (eds) (1972) *Linguistic change and generative theory*. Indiana University Press: Bloomington.

Stone, G. (1980) *An introduction to Polish*. Clarendon: London.

Stowell, B. (n.d.) *A course in spoken Manx*. Manx Gaelic Society: Douglas.

Strahm, E. (1975) 'Clause patterns in Jirel', in A. Hale (ed.) (1975).

Street, C.S. (1980) 'The relationship of verb affixation and clause structure in Murinbata', *Papers in Australian Linguistics* 12: 83–113.

Street, J.C. (1963) *Khalka structure*. Indiana University Press: Bloomington.

STREHLOW, T.G.H. (1944) *Aranda phonetics and grammar*. Australian National Research Council: Sydney.

STRONG, D.R. (1980) 'Relational grammar and the diachrony of periphrastic construction in Latin and Romance', *CLS* 16: 298–310.

STUCKY, S.V. (1985) *Order in Makua syntax*. Garland: New York.

SUAREZ, Y.L. DE (1984) 'Chichimeco Jonaz', in M.S. Edmonson (ed.) (1984).

SUHARNO, I. (1982) *A descriptive study of Javanese*. Australian National University: Canberra.

SUMMER INSTITUTE OF LINGUISTICS (1964) *Verb studies in five New Guinea languages*. University of Oklahoma: Norman.

SVANE, G. (1981) 'Derivational types of causatives in Serbo-Croat', in P. Jacobsen, H.L. Krag, N. Bjerrig, L.D̆.K. Heltberg, and J. Skov-Larsen (eds), *The Slavic verb*. Rosenkilde and Bagger: Copenhagen.

SVANTESSON, J.O. (1983) *Kammu phonology and morphology*. CWK Gleerup: Malmö.

SVOROU, S. (1994) *The grammar of space*. John Benjamins: Amsterdam.

SWAN, O.E. (1983) *A concise grammar of Polish*. University Press of America: Washington, DC.

SWIFT, L.B. (1963) *A reference grammar of modern Turkish*. Indiana University Press: Bloomington.

SYEED, S.M. (1985) *Morphological causatives and the problems of the transformational grammar*. IULC: Bloomington.

TAI, J.H.-Y. (1985) 'Temporal sequence and Chinese word order', in J. Haiman (ed.) (1985b).

TALLERMAN, M. (1990) 'Relativization strategies: NP accessibility in Welsh', *JL* 26: 291–314.

TALMY, L. (1976) 'Semantic causative types', in M. Shibatani (ed.) (1976b).

TALMY, L. (1987) 'The relation of grammar to cognition', in B. Rudzka-Ostyn (ed.) (1987).

TAMPUBOLON, D.P. (1983) *Verbal affixation in Indonesian: a semantic explanation*. Australian National University: Canberra.

TARALDSEN, K.T. (1976) 'On the cyclicity of verb raising', *CLS* 12: 617–627.

TAULI, V. (1973) *Standard Estonian grammar*. Stockholm.

TAYLOR, C. (1985) *Nkore-Kiga*. Croom Helm: London.

TAYLOR, F.W. (1921) *A first grammar of the Adamawa dialect of the Fulani language (Fulfulde)*. Oxford University Press: Oxford.

TCHEKHOFF, C. (1981) *Simple sentences in Tongan*. Australian National University: Canberra.

TEETER, K.V. (1964) *The Wiyot language*. University of California Press: Berkeley.

TESLAR, J.A. (1953) *A new Polish grammar*. Oliver and Boyd: Edinburgh.

THAYER, J.E. (1978) *The deep structure of the sentence in Sara-*

Ngambay dialogues. SIL and University of Texas at Arlington.

THOMAS, D.D. (1971) *Chráu grammar*. University of Hawaii Press: Honolulu.

THOMAS, E. (1978) *A grammatical description of the Engenni language*. SIL and University of Texas at Arlington.

THOMAS, E.W. (1969) *The syntax of spoken Brazilian Portuguese*. Vanderbilt University Press: Nashville.

THOMAS, L.V. (1967) *Elementary Turkish*. Harvard University Press: Cambridge, MA.

THOMASON, S.G. and T. KAUFMAN (1988) *Language contact, creolization, and genetic linguistics*. University of California Press: Berkeley.

THOMPSON, L.C. (1965 [1967]) *A Vietnamese grammar*. University of Washington Press: Seattle.

THOMPSON, S.A. (1973) 'Resultative verb compounds in Mandarin Chinese: a case for lexical rules', *Language* 49: 361–379.

THOMPSON, S.A. (1987) '"Subordination" and narrative event structure', in R. Tomlin (ed.) (1987a).

THOMPSON, S.A. (n.d.) Information flow and 'dative shift' in English discourse. Ms, University of California, Santa Barbara.

THOMPSON, S.A. and KOIDE, Y. (1987) 'Iconicity and "indirect objects" in English', *Journal of Pragmatics* 11: 399–406.

THOMPSON, S.A. and R.E. LONGACRE (1985) 'Adverbial clauses', in T. Shopen (ed.) (1985b).

THOMSON, G. (1966) *The Greek language*. Heffer: Cambridge.

THOMSON, N.P. (1975) 'The dialects of Magi', *Papers in New Guinea Linguistics* 18: 37–90.

THUMB, A. (1964) *A handbook of the modern Greek language: grammar, texts, glossary*. Argonaut Inc.: Chicago.

THURGOOD, G., J.A. MATISOFF, and D. BRADLEY (eds) (1985) *Linguistics of the Sino-Tibetan areas: the state of the art*. Australian National University: Canberra.

THURSTON, W.R. (1982) *A comparative study in Anêm and Lusi*. Australian National University: Canberra.

TIERSMA, P.M. (1982) 'Local and general markedness', *Language* 58: 832–849.

TIERSMA, P.M. (1985) *Frisian reference grammar*. Foris: Dordrecht.

TITOV, E.G. (1976) *The Amharic language*. Nauka: Moscow.

TODD, E. (1978a) 'Roviana syntax', in S. Wurm and L. Carrington (eds) (1978).

TODD, E. (1978b) 'A sketch of Nissan (Nehan) grammar', in S. Wurm and L. Carrington (eds) (1978).

TODD, T.L. (1975) 'Clause versus sentence in Choctaw', *Linguistics* 161: 39–68.

TOLSTAYA, N.I. (1981) *The Panjabi language*. Routledge and Kegan Paul: London.

TOMLIN, R. (1986) *Basic word order: functional principles.* Croom Helm: London.

TOMLIN, R. (ed.) (1987a) *Coherence and grounding in discourse.* John Benjamins: Amsterdam.

TOMLIN, R. (1987b) 'Linguistic reflections of cognitive events', in R. Tomlin (ed.) (1987a).

TOPPING, D.M. (1973) *Chamorro reference grammar.* University Press of Hawaii: Honolulu.

TOWNSEND, W.C. (1960) 'Cakchiquel grammar', in B. Elson (ed.) (1960).

TRAIL, R.L. (1970) *The grammar of Lamani.* SIL/University of Oklahoma: Norman.

TRAIL, R.L. (ed.) (1973) *Patterns in clause, sentence and discourse in selected languages of India and Nepal.* SIL/University of Oklahoma: Norman.

TRAUGOTT, E.C. (1969) 'Toward a grammar of syntactic change', *Lingua* 23: 1–27.

TRAUGOTT, E.C. (1972) *A history of English syntax.* Holt, Rinehart and Winston: New York.

TRAUGOTT, E.C. (1975) 'Spatial expressions of tense and temporal sequencing', *Semiotica* 15: 207–230.

TRAUGOTT, E.C. (1985) 'Conditional markers', in J. Haiman (ed.) (1985b).

TRAUGOTT, E.C. (1986) 'On the origin of "and" and "but" connectives in English', *SiL* 10: 137–150.

TRAUGOTT, E.C. (1988) 'Is internal semantic–pragmatic reconstruction possible?', in C. Duncan-Rose and T. Vennemann (eds) (1988).

TRAUGOTT, E.C. (1989) 'On the rise of epistemic meanings in English: an example of subjectification in semantic change', *Language* 65: 31–55.

TRAUGOTT, E.C. and B. HEINE (eds) (1991) *Approaches to grammaticalization vol. 1.* John Benjamins: Amsterdam.

TREFRY, D. (1969) *A comparative study of Kuman and Pawaian.* Australian National University, Canberra.

TRITHART, L. (1977) 'Causatives and instrumentals', in E.R. Byarushengo, A. Duranti, and L.M. Hyman (eds), *Haya grammatical structures.* University of Southern California: Los Angeles, California.

TRYON, D.T. (1967) *Nengone grammar.* Australian National University: Canberra.

TRYON, D.T. (1968a) *Dehu grammar.* Australian National University: Canberra.

TRYON, D.T. (1968b) *Iai grammar.* Australian National University: Canberra.

TRYON, D.T. (1970a) *An introduction to Maranungku (northern Australia).* Australian National University: Canberra.

TRYON, D.T. (1970b) *Conversational Tahitian*. Australian National University: Canberra.

TSERETELI, K.G. (1978) *The modern Assyrian language*. Nauka: Moscow.

TSIAPERA, M.C. (1969) *A descriptive analysis of Cypriot Maronite Arabic*. Mouton: The Hague.

TSUNODA, T. (1981) *The Djaru language of Kimberley, Western Australia*. Australian National University: Canberra.

TUCKER, A.N. and J.T. OLE MPAAYEI (1955) *A Maasai grammar with vocabulary*. Longmans Green: London.

TUGGY, D.H. (1979) 'Tetelcingo Nahuatl', in R.W. Langacker (ed.) (1979a).

TUGGY, D.H. (1987) 'Náhuatl causative/applicatives in cognitive grammar', in B. Rudzka-Ostyn (ed.) (1987).

TUUK, H.N. VAN DER (1971) *A grammar of Toba Batak*. Martinus Nijhoff: The Hague.

TWEDDELL, C.E. (1950) *The Snoqualmie-Duwamish dialects of Puget Sound Coast Salish*. University of Washington Press: Seattle.

TWEDDELL, C.E. (1958) The Iraya (Mangyan) language of Mindore, Philippines: phonology and morphology. Unpublished Ph.D. dissertation, University of Washington.

TYLER, S.A. (1968) *Koya: an outline grammar*. University of California Press: Berkeley.

UNDERHILL, R. (1976) *Turkish grammar*. MIT Press: Cambridge, MA.

USPENSKY, B.A. and V.M. ZHIVOV (1977) 'Center–periphery opposition and language universals', *Linguistics* 196: 5–24.

VALFELLS, S. and J.E. CATHEY (1981) *Old Icelandic – an introductory course*. Oxford University Press: Oxford.

VAN VALIN, R.D. (1980a) 'On the distribution of passive and antipassive constructions in universal grammar', *Lingua* 50: 303–327.

VAN VALIN, R.D. (1980b) 'Meaning and interpretation', *Journal of Pragmatics* 4: 213–231.

VAN VALIN, R.D. (1981) 'Toward understanding grammar: form, function, evolution', *Lingua* 54: 47–85.

VAN VALIN, R.D. (1984) 'A typology of syntactic relations in clause linkage', *BLS* 10: 542–558.

VAN VALIN, R.D. (1985) 'Case marking and the structure of the Lakhota clause', in J. Nichols and A.C. Woodbury (eds) (1985).

VAN VALIN, R.D. (1987) 'The role of government in the grammar of head-marking languages', *IJAL* 53: 371–397.

VAN VALIN, R.D. (ed.) (1993a) *Advances in Role and Reference Grammar*. John Benjamins: Amsterdam.

VAN VALIN, R.D. (1993b) 'A synopsis of Role and Reference Grammar', in R.D. Van Valin (ed.) (1993a).

VENNEMANN, T. (1973) 'Explanation in syntax', in J.P. Kimball (ed.), *Syntax and semantics 2*. Seminar Press: New York.

VENNEMANN, T. (1975) 'An explanation of drift', in C.N. Li (ed.) (1975a).

VENNEMANN, T. (1984) 'Typology, universals and change of language', in J. Fisiak (ed.) (1984).

VERHAAR, J.W.M. (1985) 'On iconicity and hierarchy', *SiL* 9: 21–76.

VERHEIJEN, J.A.J. (1986) *The Sama/Bajau language in the lesser Sunda Islands.* Australian National University: Canberra.

VESALAINEN, O. and M. VESALAINEN (n.d.) *Clause patterns in Lhomi.* Australian National University: Canberra.

VICHIT-VADAKAN, R. (1976) 'The concept of inadvertence in Thai periphrastic causative constructions', in M. Shibatani (ed.) (1976b).

VILBORG, E. (1960) *A tentative grammar of Mycenaean Greek.* Institute of Classical Studies: Gothenburg.

VINCENT, N. (1988a) 'Latin', in M. Harris and N. Vincent (eds) (1988).

VINCENT, N. (1988b) 'Italian', in M. Harris and N. Vincent (eds) (1988).

VISSER, F.T. (1966) *An historical syntax of the English language.* E.J. Brill: Leiden.

VITALE, A.J. (1981) *Swahili syntax.* Foris: Dordrecht.

VOEGELIN, C.F. and F.M. VOEGELIN (1970) 'Hopi names and no names', in E.H. Swanson (ed.), *Languages and cultures of Western North America: essays in honor of Sven S. Liljeblad.* Idaho State University: Pocatello

VOEGELIN, C.F. and F.M. VOEGELIN (1976) 'Some recent (and not so recent) attempts to interpret semantics of native languages in North America', in W. Chafe (ed.), *American Indian languages and American linguistics.* Peter de Ridder: Lisse.

VOEGELIN, C.F. and F.M. VOEGELIN (1977) *Classification and index of the world's languages.* Elsevier: New York.

VOELTZ, E. (ed.) (1974) *The third annual conference on African linguistics.* Indiana University Press: Bloomington.

VOGT, H. (1940) *The Kalispel language: an outline of the grammar with texts, translations and dictionary.* Det Norske Vitenskaps-Akademi: Oslo.

VOORHIS, P.H. (1974) *The Kickapoo language.* Indiana University Press: Bloomington.

VOORHOEVE, C.L. (1965) *The Flamingo Bay dialect of the Asmat language.* Martinus Nijhoff: 's-Gravenhage.

VOORHOEVE, C.L. (1982) 'The West Makian language, North Moluccas, Indonesia: a field work report', in C.L. Voorhoeve (ed.), *The Makian languages and their neighbours.* Australian National University: Canberra.

VOẞEN, R. and M. BECHHAUS-GERST (eds) (1982) *Nilotic studies: proceedings of the Int'l symposium on languages and history of the Nilotic peoples.* Dietrich Reimer: Berlin.

WACHOWICZ, K. (1976) 'On the typology of causatives', *Working Papers on Language Universals* 20: 59–106.

WALD, B. (1987) 'Cross-clause relations and temporal sequence in narrative and beyond', in R. Tomlin (ed.) (1987a).

WALES, M.L. (1981) 'Parataxis: a penthouse next door?', *Glossa* 15: 53–82.

WALI, K. (1980) 'Oblique causee and the passive explanation', *LI* 11: 258–260.

WALI, K. (1981) 'Cause, causer and causee: a semantic perspective', *JL* 17: 289–308.

WALKER, A.T. (1982) *Grammar of Sawu.* Badan Penyelenggar Seri NUSA, Universitas Atma Jaya: Jakarta.

WALKER, D.F. (1976) *A grammar of the Lampung language: the Pesisir dialect of Way Lima.* Badan Penyelenggar Seri NUSA, Universitas Atma Jaya: Jakarta.

WALLIS, E.E. (1956) 'Simulfixation of aspect markers of Mezquital Otomi', *Language* 32: 453–459.

WALLIS, E.E. (1964) 'Mezquital Otomi verb fusion', *Language* 40: 75–82.

WALROD, M. (1976) 'Case in Ga'dang verbal clauses', *Papers in Philippine Linguistics* 8: 21–44.

WALROD, M. (1979) *Discourse grammar in Ga'dang.* SIL and University of Texas at Arlington.

WALTON, J. (1975) *Binongan Itneg sentences.* Australian National University: Canberra.

WANNER, E. and L. GLEITMAN (eds) (1982) *Language acquisition: the state of the art.* Cambridge University Press: Cambridge.

WARBURTON, I., P. KPOTUFE, and R. GLOVER (1968) *Ewe basic course.* Indiana University: Bloomington.

WARD, D. (1955) *The Russian language today.* Hutchinson University: London.

WARD, I.C. (1952 [1956]) *An introduction to the Yoruba language.* W. Heffer & Sons: Cambridge.

WARNER, R.G. (1985) *Discourse connectives in English.* Garland: New York.

WARUTAMASINTOP, W. (1973) 'Evidence for the structure of verbs in series in Thai', *Proceedings from the 6th Int'l Conference on Sino-Tibetan Language and Linguistics.*

WASHABAUGH, W. (1979) 'On the sociality of creole languages', in K.C. Hill (ed.) (1979).

WATERHOUSE, V. (1963) 'Independent and dependent sentences', *IJAL* 26: 45–54.

WATKINS, C. (1976) 'Toward Proto-Indo-European syntax: problems and pseudo-problems', in S.B. Steever, C.A. Walker, and S.S. Mufwene (eds), *Parasession on diachronic syntax.* CLS: Chicago.

WATKINS, L.J. (1984) *A grammar of Kiowa*. University of Nebraska: Lincoln.

WATKINS, M. (1937) *A grammar of Chichewa*. Linguistic Society of America: Philadelphia.

WATSON, K. (1974) 'Identity deletion phenomena in Lango', in E. Voeltz (ed.) (1974).

WEBER, D.J. (1983) *Relativization and nominalized clauses in Huallaga (Huanuco) Quechua*. University of California Press: Berkeley.

WEDEKIND, K. (1972) An outline of the grammar of Busa (Nigeria). Unpublished Ph.D. dissertation, Christian-Albrechts-Universität.

WEERMAN, F. (1987) 'Modern Dutch could be middle Dutcher than you think (and vice versa)', in W. Koopman, F. van der Leek, O. Fischer, and R. Eaton (eds) (1987).

WEIMER, H. and N. WEIMER (1975) 'A short sketch of Yareba grammar', in T.E. Dutton (ed.) (1975a).

WEIR, E.M.H. (1986) 'Footprints of yesterday's syntax: diachronic development of certain verb prefixes in an OSV language (Nadëb)', *Lingua* 68: 291–316.

WELLS, M.A. (1979) *Siroi grammar*. Australian National University: Canberra.

WELMERS, W. (1976) *A grammar of Vai*. University of California Press: Berkeley.

WEST, D. (1973) *Wojokeso sentence, paragraph and discourse analysis*. Australian National University: Canberra.

WESTERMANN, D. (1930) *A study of the Ewe language*. Oxford University Press: London.

WHEATLEY, J.K. (1985) 'The decline of verb-final syntax in the Yi (Lolo) languages of Southwestern China', in G. Thurgood, J.A. Matisoff, and D. Bradley (eds) (1985).

WHEELER, A. (1962) 'A Siona text morphologically analyzed', in B. Elson (ed.) (1962).

WHITELEY, W.H. (1966) *A study of Yao sentences*. Clarendon: Oxford.

WHORF, B.L. (1956) 'Some verbal categories in Hopi', in J. Carroll (ed.), *Language, Thought, and Reality*. MIT Press: Cambridge, MA.

WIENS, H. (1979) 'The semantic functions of focus affixes in Limos Kalinga', *Papers in Philippine Linguistics* 9: 19–47.

WIERZBICKA, A. (1979) 'Ethno-syntax and the philosophy of grammar', *SiL* 3: 313–383.

WIERZBICKA, A. (1980a) *Lingua Mentalis*. Academic Press: Sydney.

WIERZBICKA, A. (1980b) *The case for surface case*. Karoma: Ann Arbor.

WIERZBICKA, A. (1981) 'Case marking and human nature', *AJL* 1: 43–80.

WIERZBICKA, A. (1985) 'Oats and wheat: the fallacy of arbitrariness', in J. Haiman (ed.) (1985b).

WILBUR, T.H. (1976) 'Causative sentences in Basque', *Third LACUS Forum*: 537–544.

WILLIAMS, C.J. (1980) *A grammar of Yuwaalaraay*. Australian National University: Canberra.

WILLIAMS, E. (1987) 'Implicit arguments, the binding theory, and control', *NLLT* 5: 181–196.

WILLIAMS, J. (1973) 'Clause patterns in Maithili', in R.L. Trail (ed.) (1973).

WILLIAMS, M. and O.L. ZANGWILL (1950) 'Disorders of temporal judgement associated with amnesic states', *Journal of Mental Science* 96: 484–493.

WILLIAMS, S.J. (1980) *A Welsh grammar*. University of Wales Press: Cardiff.

WILLIAMSON, K. (1965) *A grammar of the Kolokuma dialect of Ịjọ.* Cambridge University Press: London.

WILSON, D. (1969) 'The Binandere language family', *Papers in New Guinea Linguistics* 9: 65–86.

WILSON, D. (1974) 'Suena grammar', *Workpapers in Papua New Guinea Languages* 8: 1–169.

WILSON, D. (1976) 'Paragraph and discourse structure in Suena', *Workpapers in Papua New Guinea Languages* 15: 5–125.

WILSON, D. and D. SPERBER (1986) 'Inference and implicature', in C. Travis (ed.), *Meaning and interpretation*. Basil Blackwell: Oxford.

WILSON, P.R. (1980) 'Ambulas grammar', *Workpapers in Papua New Guinea Languages* 26: 1–477.

WILSON, W.A.A. (1961) 'Outline of the Balanta language', *African Language Studies* 2: 139–168.

WINDFUHR, G.L. (1979) *Persian grammar: history and state of its study*. Mouton: The Hague.

WINSTEDT, R.O. (1914 [1957]) *Malay grammar*. Clarendon: Oxford.

WIRTH, J. (ed.) (1985) *Beyond the sentence: discourse and sentence form*. Karoma: Ann Arbor.

WOJCIK, R.H. (1976) 'Where do instrumental NPs come from?', in M. Shibatani (ed.) (1976b).

WOLFART, H.C. and J.F. CARROLL (1981) *Meet Cree: a guide to the Cree language*. University of Nebraska: Lincoln.

WOLFENDEN, E. (1971) *Hiligaynon reference grammar*. University of Hawaii Press: Honolulu.

WOLFENDEN, E. (1975) *A description of Hiligaynon syntax*. SIL/University of Oklahoma: Norman.

WOLFENDEN, S.N. (1929) *Outlines of Tibeto-Burman linguistic morphology*. Royal Asiatic Society: London.

WOLFF, E. (1983) *A grammar of the Lamang (Gwàd Làmàh) language*. J.J. Augustin: Glückstadt.

WOLFF, J.V. (1966) *Beginning Cebuano vol. 1*. Yale University Press: New Haven.

WOLFF, J.V. (1967) *Beginning Cebuano vol. 2*. Yale University Press: New Haven.

WOODCOCK, E.C. (1959 [1985]) *A new Latin syntax*. Methuen: London.

WOODS, F. (1973) 'Sentence patterns in Halbi', in R.L. Trail (ed.) (1973).

WOOLFORD, E.B. (1979a) *Aspects of Tok Pisin*. Australian National University: Canberra.

WOOLFORD, E.B. (1979b) 'The developing complementizer system of Tok Pisin: syntactic change in progress', in K.C. Hill (ed.) (1979).

WRIGHT, W. (1955) *A grammar of the Arabic language*. Cambridge University Press: Cambridge.

WURM, S. (1951) *Studies in the Kiwai languages, Fly Delta, PNG*. Institut für Völkerkunde der Universität: Vienna.

WURM, S. and L. CARRINGTON (eds) (1978) *Second International Conference on Austronesian Linguistics*. Australian National University: Canberra.

WURM, S. and J.B. HARRIS (1963) *Police Motu*. Linguistic Circle of Canberra: Canberra.

WURM, S. and P. MÜHLHÄUSLER (eds) (1985) *Handbook of Tok Pisin: New Guinea Pidgin*. Australian National University: Canberra.

YALLOP, C. (1977) *Alyawarra: an Aboriginal language of central Australia*. AIAS: Canberra.

YAR-SHAFER, E. (1969) *A grammar of Southern Tati dialects*. Mouton: The Hague.

YATES, A. (1975) *Catalan*. Hodder and Stoughton: London.

YOUNG, R.A. (1971) *The verb in Bena-Bena: its form and function*. Australian National University: Canberra.

YOUNG, R.W. and W. MORGAN (1980) *The Navajo language: a grammar and a colloquial dictionary*. University of New Mexico Press: Albuquerque.

ZEISBERGER, D. (1827) *Grammar of the language of the Lenni Lenape or Delaware Indians*. James King, Jr.: Philadelphia.

ZEPEDA, O. (1987) 'Desiderative-causatives in Tohonno O'odham', *IJAL* 53: 348–361.

ZEWEN, F.-X.N. (1977) *The Marshallese language: a study of its phonology, morphology and syntax*. Dietrich Reimer: Berlin.

ZIDE, A.R.K. (1972) 'Transitive and causative in Gorum', *JL* 8: 201–215.

ZIERVOGEL, D. and J.A. LOUW (1967) *A handbook of the Zulu language*. J.L. van Schaik: Pretoria.

ZIMMERMANN, J. (1858) *A grammatical sketch and vocabulary of the Akan – or Gã – language*. Basel Missionary Society: Stuttgart/Gregg International: Westmead.

ZIPF, G.K. (1935 [1965]) *The psycho-biology of language: an introduction to dynamic philology*. MIT Press: Cambridge, MA.

ZIRMUNSKIJ, V.M. (1966) 'The word and its boundaries', *Linguistics* 27: 65–91.

ZIV, Y. (1988) 'On the rationality of "relevance" and the relevance of "rationality"', *Journal of Pragmatics* 12: 535–545.

ZOVKO, C.I. (1983) *The handbook of the Croatian language.* ZIRAL: Norval, Ont.

ZUBIZARRETA, M.L. (1985) 'The relation between morphophonology and morphosyntax: the case of Romance causatives', *LI* 16: 247–289.

ZURIF, E.B. and G. CARSON (1970) 'Dyslexia in relation to cerebral dominance and temporal analysis', *Neuropsychologia* 8: 351–361.

ZWAAN, J.D. DE (1969) *A preliminary analysis of Gogo-Yimidjir.* AIAS: Canberra.

Author index

Language index

Subject index

Printed in Great Britain
by Amazon

15912976R00179